Latin America and the First World War

Using a broad variety of textual and visual sources, *Latin America and the First World War* goes beyond traditional diplomatic history and analyzes the global dimension of the history of the Great War. Filling a significant gap in transnational histories of the war, Stefan Rinke addresses political, social, and economic aspects as well as the cultural impact of the war on Latin America and vice versa. Rinke's meticulous research is based on sources from the nineteen independent states of the entire subcontinent and promises to be the most comprehensive examination to date of Latin America before, during, and immediately after the war.

Stefan Rinke is Professor of Latin American History at the Institute of Latin American Studies at Freie Universität Berlin and a former Einstein Research Fellow. He is speaker of the German-Mexican Graduate School "Between Spaces" – a cooperative doctoral program with leading Mexican universities. He is the author of twelve books, many of which have been translated into Spanish and Portuguese. Rinke is a member of the board of the journals *Geschichte und Gesellschaft* and *Iberoamericana*, and co-editor of the *Enzyklopädie der Neuzeit*.

Global and International History

Series Editors

Erez Manela, *Harvard University*
John McNeill, *Georgetown University*
Aviel Roshwald, *Georgetown University*

The Global and International History series seeks to highlight and explore the convergences between the new International History and the new World History. Its editors are interested in approaches that mix traditional units of analysis such as civilizations, nations, and states with other concepts such as transnationalism, diasporas, and international institutions.

Titles in the Series

Nathan Citino, *Envisioning the Arab Future: Modernization in U.S.–Arab Relations, 1945–1967*

Timothy Nunan, *Humanitarian Invasion: Global Development in Cold War Afghanistan*

Michael Goebel, *Anti-imperial Metropolis: Interwar Paris and the Seeds of Third World Nationalism*

Stephen J. Macekura, *Of Limits and Growth: International Environmentalism and the Rise of "Sustainable Development" in the Twentieth Century*

The Attitude of Latin American States toward the War

Latin America and the First World War

STEFAN RINKE

Freie Universität Berlin

Translated by CHRISTOPHER W. REID PhD

CAMBRIDGE
UNIVERSITY PRESS

One Liberty Plaza, 20th Floor, New York, NY 10006, USA

Cambridge University Press is part of the University of Cambridge.

It furthers the University's mission by disseminating knowledge in the pursuit of education, learning, and research at the highest international levels of excellence.

www.cambridge.org
Information on this title: www.cambridge.org/9781107566064

10.1017/9781316411735

© Stefan Rinke 2017

First published 2017. First published in German: *Im Sog der Katastrophe: Lateinamerika und der Erste Weltkrieg*, Frankfurt a.M.: Campus, 2015.

Printed in the United States of America by Sheridan Books, Inc.

A catalogue record for this publication is available from the British Library.

Library of Congress Cataloging-in-Publication Data
Names: Rinke, Stefan, author.
Title: Latin America and the First World War / Stefan Rinke, Freie Universität Berlin.
Description: Cambridge: Cambridge University Press, 2017. |
Series: Global and international history |
Includes bibliographical references and index.
Identifiers: LCCN 2016052791| ISBN 9781107127203 (hardback) |
ISBN 9781107566064 (paperback)
Subjects: LCSH: World War, 1914–1918–Latin America. |
BISAC: HISTORY / Latin America / General.
Classification: LCC D520.S8 R57 2017 | DDC 940.3/8–dc23
LC record available at https://lccn.loc.gov/2016052791

ISBN 978-1-107-12720-3 Hardback
ISBN 978-1-107-56606-4 Paperback

Contents

Figures

Preface

This book has been long in the making, and its history reflects the historiographical developments of the past two decades. When in the early 1990s I wrote my doctoral thesis on Weimar Germany and Latin America, transnational history was still a very new approach. In the meantime, the transnational perspective has arrived at the mainstream of the profession. I have profited from the rising production along the years, and my concept for a book on Latin America during the First World War that originated back then has changed quite radically. The result of this process is this book, which has benefited from discussions with many colleagues and students around the world.

The concept of global consciousness plays an important part in this study. In using it, I follow an approach developed in our Berlin research group "Actors of Cultural Globalization." A further stimulating context was Freie Universität's project *1914–1918-online: The International Encyclopedia of the First World War*. In order to finish this book, I was honored with a research fellowship by the Einstein Foundation. Both the Foundation and the Ibero-American Institute in Berlin that hosted me deserve gratitude for their generosity.

My thanks also go to those who have directly supported me in finishing this book, especially my former research assistant and now PhD student Karina Kriegesmann. I appreciate the advice of my teacher and friend Hans-Joachim König, who years ago prevented me from writing a chapter on the war into what had become a much-too-long doctoral dissertation. I am also very grateful to the many people in the libraries and archives in Latin America and elsewhere who helped me, and to my family, who missed me when I was there and supported me when I was back.

Abbreviations

AA	*Auswärtiges Amt*
AFL	American Federation of Labor
AHI	Arquivo Histórico do Itamaraty
AMRREE	Archivo del Ministerio de Relaciones Exteriores
B. A.	Buenos Aires
BD	British Documents on Foreign Affairs
CROM	Confederación Regional Obrera Mexicana
FRUS	Papers Relating to the Foreign Relations of the United States
MRE	Ministério das Relações Exteriores
MRREE	Ministerio de Relaciones Exteriores
NA	National Archives of the United States
ONI	U.S. Office of Naval Intelligence
PAFL	Pan-American Federation of Labor
R.d.J.	Rio de Janeiro
RG	Record Group

Introduction

It is strangely still on the harbor and in the markets. And for several days already, the theater and cinemas have been empty. The noise levels, however, have increased in front of the offices of the major newspapers, where masses of people have come together already at the crack of dawn to hear the latest news. When sirens sound to announce important news off the wire, orators spontaneously stand up to either condemn the war or take sides with one of the two parties. Streetcars are no longer able to pass through the streets. The air pulsates with rumors, as word spreads that the Austrian Emperor has fallen prey to an assassination attempt. Huddling together before the closed gates of banks, frustrated customers curse loudly. How was one to pay the exploding prices if you couldn't get to your money, or if your job was all of a sudden at risk like never before? All over, unemployed from the lower classes flock together, with more coming each day from the countryside. There, large foreign mining and plantation companies dismissed thousands overnight.

Meanwhile, uniformed marines and reservists from various countries march through the streets in formation. They intend to report to their consulates for military service. A few streets away, demonstrators singing the Marseillaise and "God save the Queen" tramp toward the diplomatic embassies of the Allies to proclaim their sympathy. At about the same time, vocal socialists demonstrate in favor of restoring peace. The faithful follow suit in their own way by joining pilgrimages for peace. Politicians, business owners, and bankers gather in the ministries to consult with each other about what to do next, without however finding an answer. A sense of unrest prevails far and wide, as the police institute measures to maintain public order. It is as if people are simply waiting for the storm, whose rumbling thunder is heard in the distance, to unleash a bolt of lightning and inflict unimaginable devastation.[1]

According to the press of the time, similar scenes played out with greater or lesser intensity throughout the cities of Latin America in August 1914. When news broke of the war in Europe, there was talk of a catastrophe that, because of the close-knit global entanglements, would embroil the world in an unprecedented crisis. On August 2, 1914, a commentator from *La Nación* in Buenos Aires, one of Latin America's leading newspapers, concisely summed up the view of many like-minded interpretations:

We are witnessing one of the most momentous events, and one of the greatest catastrophes, of human history. The European war, which has been inevitable for some time, plunged the world into a crisis unlike anything it has ever seen before. Indeed, our civilization, which unquestionably controls distances and time for the benefit of our species' productivity, is paying brutally with nerve and emotion for the material advantages that this mastery has borne. Just as the flash of inspiration of a discovery, an invention, or genius illuminates every layer of thought almost instantaneously from the place where it is sparked, a lightning strike at some point on the planet affects and devastates the totality of space where human beings live, work, and suffer with even greater speed and potency. This time, the lightning hits the center – the great stage of life, which shivers with apprehension and horror, as if the interminable night has already descended.... A problem arises from the explosion in Europe – from the convulsions moving social organisms today – which has never been posed until now, and whose premise is the following: There are no spectators in this drama; all of humanity is more or less directly implicated.[2]

The world dimensions of the events were in evidence to contemporary Latin American observers early on. At the same time, they consciously or unconsciously subscribed to ideas that Europeans had already cultivated before the outbreak of hostilities. For example, when German author August Niemann entertained the possibility of a "world war" in 1904, he meant nothing less than a European world or a world that would be drawn into the great European conflicts without protest.[3] The Eurocentric view that "if Europe fights, it is as though the entire world fights" had defined historiography for centuries.[4] Certainly, the war began in Europe and the majority of the front lines were located there. Beyond the continent

---

[1] This is based on the analysis of a representative selection of news items from the Latin American press in August 1914 and an essay from María Inés Tato on Buenos Aires: "La contienda europea," pp. 34–7.

[2] "Ecos del día: La catástrofe," in: *La Nación* (Buenos Aires, August 2, 1914), p. 8.

[3] Niemann, *Der Weltkrieg*. See also Langewiesche, "Das Jahrhundert Europas," p. 38.

[4] "In 1914 conflict spread from the European centre to the periphery, and it did so because the states of Europe were imperial powers. War for Europe meant war for the world."

itself, the Europeans initially dragged their colonies into the war, along with other, originally neutral states later on. Yet when historians today "refer to the war which acquired global significance due to its geographic dimension extending over numerous continents and the unfettered use of every available strategic resource," those very regions come into view that were considered peripheral from the classical Eurocentric perspective and can be recognized as actors in their own right.[5] To understand the world war as a global war, without falling prey to the epistemological trap of Eurocentrism, historiography must endeavor to look beyond the trenches. Indeed, it was not possible to be a "spectator" in the "drama" of this world war.

The First World War was undoubtedly a "global moment" that intensively involved a supposedly peripheral Latin America.[6] From the beginning, Latin Americans sensed that this war had worldwide scope. As a matter of fact, above and beyond the commentary from *La Nación*, the outbreak of war in Europe in 1914 represented for many Latin American observers a profound turning point in the unfolding of history. Because of the breakdown of the European civilizational and development model and the unreserved belief in human progress in the years from 1914 to 1918, a world where Latin America had occupied a fixed position was effectively gone. Many contemporary witnesses agreed that an era had come to an end in the days of August 1914, and a new, still uncertain age had begun.

By focusing on the First World War, it is possible to show how strong the global mindset had already been at that time in Latin America, and how much it changed over the course of four years of genocide. "Global mindset" in this context does not refer to a cosmopolitan form of thinking, but much more an awareness of the importance of worldwide interdependencies and processes of integration. Despite the considerable distances to the battlefields, the First World War was felt more than any other previous event in Latin America, and it was clear that its repercussions would impact the lives of average citizens. Of course, people in the region were by no means affected by this state of interconnectedness to the same degree. Nonetheless, the relative isolation with which they had witnessed other conflicts in Europe prior to 1914 came to an end.[7]

Strachan, *The First World War: A New Illustrated History*, London 2003, p. 68. Strachan, *The First World War as a Global War*.

[5] "Weltkrieg," in: http://de.wikipedia.org/wiki/Weltkrieg (accessed on: May 27, 2014).

[6] Conrad/Sachsenmaier, "Introduction," pp. 13–6.

[7] Conrad/Sachsenmaier, "Introduction," pp. 1–25.

Latin Americans took an active interest in the horrors, hopes, and fears that the war had triggered. They participated in the debates about the end of Western hegemony and the downfall of Europe, which took place around the world and would become emblematic of the twentieth century. The perception of the war followed a global yardstick, as Latin America was caught up in the events more than ever because of the new type of propaganda war and innovative communication technologies. In fact, it was because the media reported on the war the world over that it could become a world event. Latin America was no exception, where the media landscape had grown leaps and bounds since the turn of the century and where circulations and advertising revenue, especially in the dailies, had exploded in the 1910s.[8] From the public's viewpoint, the war was an event of significance for the entire world, which went beyond the familiar regional framework of previous conflicts. For Latin Americans, the First World War made the world's interdependency, and one's own place within it, tangible.[9]

Historians have only recently returned their focus to the role of the media in the First World War and, by the same token, to the role of the war in the development of the media.[10] In Latin America, as elsewhere, the war stimulated the massive utilization of new forms of media like photography and cinema. Press photography proved an important instrument of propaganda, which contributed to the worldwide circulation of war pictures that seemed to depict objective reality. The understanding of reality expanded, for what was real no longer simply pertained to one's own life, but also to events mediated through imagery. It was precisely in places like Latin America where there was a geographical separation from the front lines that people experienced the war, both privately and publicly, through media-produced images.[11] What is more, the First World War took place there especially as a propaganda war, which also caused a largely unprecedented form of radical hatemongering among rivals to spread in the subcontinent.

The primary concern of this book is with the perspective of Latin America. Its central question relates to the contemporary interpretive models of the world war used by Latin Americans. From the Latin

---

[8] These media-historical developments in Latin America have been largely overlooked in the research. For Rio de Janeiro, see Garambone, *A primeira Guerra Mundial*, p. 46.

[9] These observations draw on Stichweh's theory of the world event. See: "Zur Soziologie des Weltereignisses," pp. 28–9.

[10] König/Neitzel, "Propaganda, Zensur und Medien," p. 125.

[11] Paul, *Bilder des Krieges*, pp. 105–6.

American standpoint, it is necessary to consider the context of the eruptions of violence, which began in the subcontinent as early as 1910 with the Mexican Revolution. That is not to say that there was a causal connection between the civil war in Mexico and the world war. Just the same, from the perspective of many Latin Americans, both events were an example of the crisis-ridden state of a world shaken by a wave of global violence and thus at the end of its self-certainty. For Latin America, the First World War is embedded in a decade of social revolutionary upheaval and political unrest, which reached its peak between 1917 and 1919.[12] This book aims to reveal the specific Latin American associations and connotations of the First World War, which, as in the case of the Mexican Revolution, are not always apparent at first sight.

As this study deals with a region of continental proportions with nineteen nation-states – from Mexico in the north to Argentina and Chile in the south – questions immediately come to mind about the heterogeneity of experiences, along with doubts about the validity of generalizations. This book, however, does not claim to undertake a detailed investigation of each of the individual nineteen national cases. It examines much more how specific, local, social developments and perceptions become embedded in world contexts, and how certain local and regional discourses can be comprehended only in terms of the larger global discursive framework. To cite one example: the general anti-imperialistic discourse of the Global South in response to the world war evolved in Latin America in a thoroughly eclectic and contradictory manner and was distinct from its equivalent in the colonies in Africa and Asia. Unlike the latter, the spirit of supremacy persisted, not least because of internal racism. The participants in these discourses operated in transnational spaces and shared their experiences with a larger global context. This book centers on Latin America's shared history during the First World War – shared both in terms of the national entities that make up the region, but also other continents.

The goal is not to establish direct causal connections, as if the First World War first brought about and determined the changes in Latin America during this time. Of course, causes can be singled out, as in the case of the radicalization of the workers' movement from 1917. Nonetheless, it is necessary to ask about the extent to which the war

---

[12] The demand for a broader periodization of the war, which has been recently expressed in relation to Europe-centered research, hence also applies to the subcontinent. Janz, *14: Der große Krieg*, pp. 13–4. Strachan, "The First World War as a Global War," p. 11.

may have either strengthened or weakened specific tendencies. It is certainly possible to identify the concentration and acceleration of specific processes during the war years. When, for instance, Argentinian Carlos Ibarguren in 1917 compared the events in Europe to the decline of the Roman Empire, or his countryman Ricardo Rojas stated, looking back a few years later, that the war had destroyed all the known institutions of Western civilization, contemporary Latin Americans (like others elsewhere) suffered a loss of confidence in the promise of modernization.[13]

The traditional bias toward European models proved obsolete and the future had to be conceived anew.[14] Due to this attitude, the call for a reorientation of identities on a national and regional level, which had already gained momentum before the war, grew even louder. As in other regions of the world, the emphasis on nationalism and regionalism in Latin America was also a reaction to a global constellation created during the era of imperialism, which experienced both its culmination and its demise during the First World War. Latin America was not unique in this regard. The region's particular difference rather lay in the fact that the governing oligarchies understood themselves as an integral part of the European civilization that collapsed in the First World War. Consequently, after 1914, the question of redefining one's identity was much more urgent here than in other world regions. This is not the only level, however, where the influence of the global on the local becomes evident.

For decades, an awareness of the interrelationship between local development and global entanglements during the First World War was hardly expressed in the historiography of Latin America. In general, historiography tends to separate the developmental phase of the Latin American states in the "long nineteenth century" from their evolution into modern mass societies in the twentieth century. Classic overviews frequently do not suggest a turning point in their periodization until around 1930.[15] The world economic crisis, accordingly, represents the moment in which Latin American history assumed a new direction. In this view, not only is the First World War not a watershed in the region's historical evolution, but the related interpretations either do not mention the war or only do so in passing.

---

[13] Ibarguren, *La historia que he vivido*, p. 301. Rojas, *La guerra de las naciones*, p. 310.
[14] On the experience of rupture, see recently Hölscher, "The First World War as a 'Rupture,'" p. 75.
[15] See, e.g., Bakewell, *A History of Latin America*. Halperin, *Geschichte Lateinamerikas*. Chevalier, *América Latina*. Ayala Mora et al., *Historia General*, Vol. 7, *Los proyectos nacionales*.

All the same, a comprehensive historiography of the events in fact emerged early on. The first contributions that appeared at the end of the war were still trying to make sense of its impact and arguments were made as a kind of score settling. These texts uniformly concentrated on the diplomatic level and clearly distinguished in their assessments between "good" (those who supported the Allies) and "evil" (those who stayed neutral).[16] U.S. historian Percy Martin's study from 1925 was the first to take a less partisan look at the subject, though its evaluation of Mexican politics remained wholly under the sway of antirevolutionary sentiments.[17] Afterward, the First World War was not treated as a subject for some time, as it was displaced by the experience of the global economic crisis and the Second World War. It was not until the advent of dependence theory that interest was rekindled in the significance of the First World War of the twentieth century for Latin America. The theory, however, that independent industrialization and development in Latin America was only possible due to its break with external ties was put forward, not by a historian, but rather sociologist André Gunder Frank. Frank identified the period of the First World War as definitive proof. As historians examined the theories of the dependence theorists more closely, however, they proved largely untenable. Bill Albert, for example, demonstrated in his economic and social-historical work from 1988 – which today is still considered a standard work on the subject – that external dependencies rather increased as a result of the economic war and that the export sector actually grew.[18]

Frank's and Albert's concern with the First World War remained an exception until the end of the twentieth century. A different picture emerges, though, with regard to national historiography. There are thus studies on countries like Argentina, Brazil, Chile, and Mexico on diplomacy during the First World War, which nevertheless do not take account of transnational relationships.[19] What is more, in many national historiographies, the 1910s are highlighted as a transformational period. In the case of Mexico, for example, the year 1910 was undoubtedly a seminal moment because of the start of the revolution. For Bolivia, Chile,

---

[16] See, e.g., Gaillard, *Amérique latine*. Kirkpatrick, *South America and the War*. Barrett, *Latin America and the War*. Barrett, the general manager of the Pan American Union, nevertheless clarified that by no means could the maintenance of neutrality be viewed as an unfriendly act toward the Allies.

[17] Martin, *Latin America and the War*.

[18] Frank, *Latin America*, pp. 9–10. Albert, *South America and the First World War*, p. 3.

[19] Vinhosa, *O Brasil e a Primeira Guerra mundial*. Couyoumdjian, *Chile y Gran Bretaña*. Katz, *The Secret War in Mexico*. See also Rinke, "Ein Drama der gesamten Menschheit."

Guatemala, and Peru, the year 1919/1920 is acknowledged as an important turning point as a result of the incipient political and social upheavals. Clear ruptures, however, can also be identified for smaller countries of the region like Nicaragua, Haiti, or the Dominican Republic, where U.S. military intervention began in 1912, 1915, 1916, respectively, or in Panama, where the transoceanic canal was opened in 1914 just before the war broke out and the United States likewise massively reinforced its presence. The war years, however, are only rarely dealt with in particular.

Argentina is an exception. Rojas had already remarked in hindsight: "Over the last two decades, two events have fundamentally altered the Argentinians' consciousness: The democratic reform and the world war."[20] In fact, Argentinian historians consider the year 1916 momentous because it was the year that radical party candidate Hipólito Yrigoyen assumed power. At least four monographs and a collection of source material focus on the significance of the war for Yrigoyen's presidency.[21] Philip Dehne analyzes the English economic war in Argentina.[22] Especially noteworthy are the essays by María Inés Tato, which examine the mobilization of the urban masses and the public controversies during the war years.[23] In his recently published study, Olivier Compagnon undertakes a comparison between Argentina and Brazil.[24] Meanwhile, there persists an absence of studies taking a transnational approach. It is precisely by examining the region as a whole from the outside – an approach that will inform the present study – that it is possible to recognize the cross-border dynamics and thus to expand a Latin American historiography that has generally been preoccupied with individual nations.

While the First World War may have long been a marginal concern of Latin American historiography, it was even more common to find histories of the First World War concentrating almost exclusively on the

---

[20] Rojas, *La guerra de las naciones*, p. 7.

[21] Solveira, *Argentina y la Primera Guerra Mundial*. Díaz Araujo, *Yrigoyen y la guerra*. Siepe, *Yrigoyen*. Goñi/Scala/Berraondo, *Yrigoyen y la Gran Guerra*. An excellent overview of the state of research before 1994 is provided by Weinmann, *Argentina en la Primera Guerra Mundial*, pp. 21–30. See also: Tato, "La Gran Guerra en la historiografía argentina," pp. 91–102.

[22] Dehne, *On the Far Western Front*. Dehne relies exclusively on English sources.

[23] Tato, "La disputa por la argentinidad." Idem, "La contienda europea." Idem, "El llamado de la patria." Idem, "Contra la corriente."

[24] Compagnon (*L'adieu à l'Europe*) calls for respecting national differences and devalues other approaches as Eurocentric. At the same time, he falls into a trap, for he does not recognize that one methodologically reproduces Eurocentrism by giving preference to the nation as a unit of analysis.

perspectives of Europe and the United States. Here, the political and economic consequences were the main focus. On the other hand, a range of studies has emerged over the past few years, in parallel to the emergence of global-historical approaches in historiography, which deliberately embed the war in its global context. In accordance with Jürgen Kocka's demand in 2004, historians have adopted a broader understanding of the term "world war" over the past ten years and more closely studied its global dimension.[25] Not surprising, attention has been largely limited in most cases to the colonies in Africa and Asia, or to only those regions where there was combat on land or at sea, a limitation that effectively mirrors the predominant focus on the military in historiography on the First World War. Latin America is only rarely mentioned in this context; when it is, the focus is usually on providing complete depictions of the sea battles of Coronel and the Falkland Islands in 1914.[26] This can be said of Lawrence Sondhaus, for example, who aptly speaks of a "global revolution" in connection with the war, yet fails to meaningfully explore this idea in his observations.[27] Only recently has the global dimension of the war, including the mobilization of economic, social, militaristic, and cultural resources, come into focus.[28]

In world war historiography, the Latin American states that were completely neutral until 1917, and largely remained so afterward, have been perceived (like all neutral countries, with the exception of the late entrant into the war, the United States) as passive and uninteresting. Be that as it may, in the total wars of the twentieth century, neutrality could no longer be maintained passively – the neutral countries were caught up in the events in manifold ways, whether they liked it or not. As a result of their natural resources or strategic position, they possessed varying degrees of negotiating power. If the thesis of a total and global war is to be taken seriously, this deserves to be explored more meticulously.[29]

The subject of Germany's global war and revolutionizing plans has recently regained attention in connection with the remembrance of the "Fischer Controversy" fifty years ago.[30] The provocation and

[25] Kocka, "Der Große Europäische Krieg," pp. 183–4.
[26] Strachan, *To Arms*. Storey, *The First World War*, pp. 67–72. Sondhaus, *World War One*, pp. 103–9. Neiberg, *Fighting the Great War*, pp. 123–50. Segesser, *Der Erste Weltkrieg*. Liebau, *The World in World Wars*.
[27] Janz, *14: Der große Krieg*, pp. 133–40. Sondhaus, *World War One*, pp. 1–2.
[28] Janz, *14: Der große Krieg*, p. 10.
[29] Hertog/Kruizinga, "Introduction," pp. 1–2. Frey, "The Neutrals," p. 4.
[30] This has been recently noted in Jenkins, "Fritz Fischer's 'Programme for Revolution.'" See also Strachan, *World War I*, Ch. 9.

encouragement of uprisings in the colonial world also concerned Latin America, even though it was colonized only informally. Such activity was especially evident in the secret war in Mexico, and, not just Germany, but the other major powers were also actively involved with their own spies and citizens residing there. All of the belligerent nations aimed to support social revolutions or nationalistic liberation movements in their enemies' dominions.[31] These observations once again shift the imperialistic rivalry outside of Europe – one of the reasons for the First World War – to the forefront of historiographical interest, and, as a consequence, the region of Latin America.[32]

This is where this book finds its point of departure. Benefiting from the turn in historiography toward global themes and global history, this study will analyze the global dimension of the history of the First World War from the perspective of a continent, which may have existed at the margins from the European standpoint, but nonetheless experienced lasting changes due to the conflagration in Europe. The innovative potential of this study reflects three levels: the concentration on Latin America, a region that for all intents and purposes has been ignored in this context; second, the commitment to coming to terms with the changing perception and understanding of the world of the Latin American region of the Global South; and, third, the concern with the issue of the periodization of Latin American history, in which the role of the First World War has so far been ignored.

The central questions are the following: What factors caused Latin Americans from 1914 to 1918 to view the First World War as a critical turning point in their own life world? To what extent did Latin America participate in the war, directly or indirectly? How did Latin Americans perceive the war and how did they interpret it? How did people of different social classes reposition themselves in the context of the world at war given the collapse of the traditional Eurocentric world view? What kind of global mindset did they develop against this backdrop? What visions of the future did they derive as a consequence for their own development?

As the aim of this book is to cover the range of Latin American experiences at least *pars pro toto*, a comprehensive collection of sources was essential. The study is based on sources from the nineteen independent states of the entire subcontinent, whereby archival material from twelve countries is included in the evaluation. As might be expected, it was

---

[31] This observation appears in Katz, *The Secret War*, p. X.
[32] Bayly, *The Birth of the Modern World*, p. 472.

not possible from a quantitative standpoint to avoid accentuating lead-ing regional powers like Argentina, Brazil, Chile, Colombia, Peru, and Mexico, for these countries were also certainly involved in the events of the war to a greater extent. That being said, sources were consulted from countries like Bolivia, Costa Rica, Ecuador, Guatemala, Paraguay, and Uruguay, because important ideas and stimuli frequently came from these less affected countries that conveyed changing trends in the predominant world view.

The sources for this study comprise both texts and images. Images have special significance in this context, for they reached, at least in part, broad sections of the population in Latin America, which at the begin-ning of the twentieth century were mostly illiterate. This type of source is moreover important, because the First World War was also a war of images. It is thus possible to gauge, for example, the impact of the pro-paganda war, which was carried out directly in Latin America. The war found its way into the most diverse levels of imagery, making everyday images like advertising and posters also of special concern. Text sources pertain to the archival material and official publications of foreign min-istries. In addition, contemporary publications of different provenance proved especially instructive. Along with autobiographical materials, the focus was placed on analyses of the international situation, discourses on international law, short satirical texts, pulp magazines, and propaganda writings. In this context, numerous independent publications were evalu-ated, but above all periodicals, which were critical for the dissemination of images of war with their photos and other illustrations. There is a comprehensive collection of sources at the Ibero-American Institute in Berlin, although the majority of these materials are found in the respec-tive national libraries and archives.

This book is structured according to its leading questions. Beginning with a summary of the initial situation, the first chapter then depicts Latin American history from the perspective of its global entanglements since its independence. To begin with, it discusses questions concerning the integration of the new states under international law and their reac-tions to neocolonial and imperialistic efforts from Europe and the United States. Further attention is paid to the region's problematic integration into the world market and the cultural dimensions. As to the latter, mass immigration and the integration into the global communication network are especially relevant in this context.

The following focus is on Latin Americans integration into the war, and it follows a chronological scheme. The second chapter analyzes the erosion of neutrality as a result of the naval war in Latin American waters and the fight for telecommunication connections. The economic war, which the Allies carried out with particular efficacy, was critically important, for though it at times severely undermined the Latin American national economies, it also created new markets and opportunities. The workers and peasants suffered the most from these problems, but so did the newly developed middle class. The conflagration impacted the everyday lives of Latin Americans especially due to the propaganda war. Now, the general population experienced increasingly intense controversies, which were occasionally played out violently in public spaces.

The following chapter shows how Latin American governments experienced pressure from German U-boat warfare, but also from the United States to break off its relations and to enter the war. The governments, however, tended to follow their own logic. The decisions, which were turning points from the Latin American perspective, meant that the respective states were active for the first time in an originally European conflict. At the same time, the problem of foreign minorities in some countries such as Brazil and Guatemala acquired a new dimension. While these minorities had primarily fought against each other between 1914 and 1917, now the Germans were considered the enemy and were persecuted by various means. Despite the strong ripple effect, other states maintained their neutrality, although even here controversies overwhelmed public debates concerning the stance toward the war. As discussed in Chapter 4, the Latin Americans welcomed the end of the war, the peace agreement, and the establishment of the League of Nations with open arms. This gave way, however, to disillusionment about the postwar period, which began under inauspicious conditions with the collapse of the wartime economy, the revolutionary movements, and the reactions against them from 1917/1918.

The focus of the subsequent two chapters is on the change of world views. Chapter 5 shows how the war became part of everyday life through the constant production of sensationalized stories in a way that affected all social classes and different generations. The model of European civilization, which had been admired for many decades, increasingly came to symbolize barbarism. While Latin Americans felt connected to the "drama of greater humanity" at the outbreak of the war and deplored the imminent bloodbath, their attitude changed when the atrocities and war crimes were reported on in the course of 1914 at the latest. The greater the distance to Europe grew, the more clearly the "hour of America" loomed, and the more closely connected Latin Americans felt to the world.

One reaction to this direct involvement in the global conflict was a reversion to America and the project of an independent nation, which would now be provided with new plans. Chapter 6 first analyzes the rise of new nationalistic movements. Despite their at times bloody infighting, the actors who were active here – students and women's organizations, parties, anarchic, socialistic, and nationalistic groups – shared a desire for participation in public life, which traditional oligarchies however vehemently resisted. While these actors involved mostly Latin Americans with European roots, they also often made an appeal to the region's indigenous heritage. The concept of "Indo-America" emerged during this period as a new proposal for integration. Afro-Americans were not included here, yet there were already voices that spoke out against racism and embraced anticolonial arguments in the process. Just as with the social movements, the discussions did not remain limited to individual countries, but represented transnational phenomena. The binding element was the anti-imperialism now directed against the United States, which also influenced the efforts to achieve a new standing for the continent on the world stage of the postwar period. Indeed, the "drama of greater humanity" was also the drama of Latin America, for between 1914 and 1918 the entanglement of the subcontinent in the global context fundamentally changed, as did the conceptions of the world along with it.

I

The Global Context before 1914

With only a few exceptions, the former Spanish and Portuguese colonies in America reached their independence in the first third of the nineteenth century.[1] The Latin American wars of independence marked the end of the series of the Atlantic revolutions that had begun with the revolt of the colonists in New England. They were closely tied to these events, as well as to those initiated by the French Revolution and the developments that came on the heels of the Napoleonic expansion in Europe. The independent republics remained intimately involved with this Atlantic context, which contained new opportunities, but also new risks and dependencies. In Latin America's long nineteenth century, it remained the most important reference point for the integration of the region into the global context.

During this period, the now formally independent successor states of the Iberian colonial empire faced numerous challenges. Throughout the entire region, the absence of functioning state institutions, the continuation of internal power struggles, the militarization of public life, and the rise of caudillos were among the most difficult obstacles that had to be overcome on the path toward stability. The difficulties of state formation were due not least to the skepticism about a political system that had failed to adequately explain who the new sovereign was. Officially, the concern was with the formation of democracies, and yet it remained unclear as to who belonged to the *demos*, the "constitutive people." Not wanting to run the risk of inciting social upheaval, the new elites defined this more broadly or narrowly according to their

[1] See Rinke, *Las revoluciones an América Latina*.

14

own interests.[2] While the rhetoric espoused universal values, day-to-day practice nonetheless remained socially discriminatory. In the ethnically heterogeneous societies of Latin America, where the non-white populations presented a clear majority, the gap between the language of liberty and equality and the social reality was significant. The challenging state of affairs the early republics faced was also related to developments that took shape outside of the region.

FROM COLONIES TO INDEPENDENT STATES

The Americas belonged, at least in theory, to the monopoly the Spanish and Portuguese crowns had held since 1494.[3] While the advances of European rivals had contested this claim since the fifteenth century, the claim remained, despite the fact that the British, French, and Dutch settlements established in the Caribbean and elsewhere caused reality to look quite different. Just the same, the immigration ban on foreigners and other faiths remained in place in territories on the continent controlled by the Spanish and Portuguese – slaves from Africa were, of course, the exception – as did the Spanish trade monopoly.[4] In order to secure their power and wealth in the New World, the Spaniards and Portuguese had an interest in perpetuating the myth of a hermetically controlled sphere.

Colonial America was not as isolated from the rest of the world as it might have at first seemed, however. In the sixteenth century, as the Spanish Empire had consolidated its reach in America, the Portuguese and Spaniards had already further extended their spheres of influence to the east and the west. They conquered the Cape of Good Hope as well as Cape Horn, and established a sea route across the Indian and the Pacific Oceans. This gave rise to networks of trade and cultural exchange that spanned the globe for the first time.[5] Indeed, recent research suggests that the institution of regular voyages in 1571 between New Spain, now Mexico, and Manila in the Philippines – the so-called Manila Galleon – actually marks the beginning of modern globalization. Some historians argue that this development represents the origin of the cross-linking

[2] Rinke, *Historia de Latinoamérica*, p. 104.
[3] Pivotal here was the Treaty of Tordesillas from the same year. Rumeu de Armas, *El tratado de Tordesillas*, passim.
[4] Burkholder/Johnson, *Colonial Latin America*, pp. 112–4.
[5] On the impact of these new trade relations, see Gruzinski, *Les quatre parties du monde*. Matsuda, *Pacific Worlds*, pp. 64–73. Meagher, *The Coolie Trade*, pp. 193–200.

between the heavily populated continents, which would accelerate and solidify in later centuries.[6]

During the colonial reforms in the eighteenth century, the Iberian mother countries also officially allowed for a tentative opening, which reached its peak at the end of the century. It was in this context that the Spaniards loosened their 200-year-old trade monopoly in 1765. Though the imperial centers managed to again tighten their control over the colonies by introducing reform policies that increased revenue and curbed smuggling, their success was only partial. An unintended consequence was that the descendants of Europeans born in the Americas who benefited from these actions and everywhere constituted the upper social strata were not satisfied with the scope of the reforms and demanded greater liberalization. Inspired by the numerous scientific expeditions the crown had sent to the Americas to explore the potential of its colonies, the descendants wanted to secure a better use of their resources for the benefit of their respective regions. For them, the abolition of colonial restrictions was a key means toward this end. The reverence the colonial elites held for a foreign scientist like Alexander von Humboldt – who explored the Americas from 1799 to 1804 and received the honorific title "the second discoverer of America" – underscores the desire at the time to embrace the spirit of Enlightenment and break free from the increasingly intolerable colonial status. The appeal Juan Pablo Viscardo y Guzman made in 1791 for a new discovery of the Americas could thus become a call for including the entire hemisphere as an equal participant in the course of world events.[7]

Certainly, the events that unfolded in the Iberian colonial realms from 1808 and grew into independence revolutions with very different aims can also be read as an attempt to overcome the isolation imposed by Spain and – albeit to a lesser extent – Portugal. This went hand in hand with a cultural shift away from the former colonial powers: Spain and Portugal were now viewed as backward, whereas the future seemed to lie with the prestigious, apparently enlightened, and progressive Western European powers, France and England.[8] With the independence of twelve successor republics and a monarchical empire, the basis for the separation appeared to be in place by the mid-1820s. Nonetheless: Were these

---

[6] Following Adam Smith's famous dictum from *The Wealth of Nations:* Flynn/Giráldez, "Globalization began in 1571," pp. 210–1. See also ibid., "Born Again: Globalization's Sixteenth Century Origins."

[7] Stolley, "Writing Back to Empire."

[8] Rama, *Historia de las relaciones culturales,* p. 25.

formally independent states now able to freely enter into the global exchange? And, what were the relations like between Latin America and the rest of the world in the first century of independence – before, that is, there was a significant turning point internationally with the First World War?

Politically, the situation was highly complex.[9] During the wars of independence, the direct interference of third-party countries occurred only in Haiti. In Hispano-America and Brazil, the conflict was between the colonies and the mother country. However, England remained especially vital as a source of weapons, mercenaries, and also later diplomatic support. It was not the republican sister state to the north – the United States – that was the most important foreign partner of the insurgent colonies, but rather England. Despite British support, however, the problem of the lack of international recognition remained for Haiti and Hispano-America for some time due to the intransigence of France and Spain. Haiti had to pay dearly for its recognition in 1825. Spain only recognized its former colonies gradually from 1836 after the death of Ferdinand VII (1833).[10] The recognition of Brazil was carried out more smoothly, yet it, too, was associated with high costs.

Still, even after the former colonies were officially accepted into the international community, Spain, France, and England had as much of a presence in the region due to their colonial possessions as the United States, whose southwestern expansion repeatedly led to border conflicts, for instance, in Mexico and Central America. The interventions of the Europeans had a negative effect from the start and also overshadowed the newly won independence. In Hispano-America, the well-founded fear of Spain's potential reconquest or support of monarchist movements continued to fester for many decades. Of more immediate concern were the direct intrusions of other European powers, which often resulted from outstanding debt payments or claims by Europeans residing in Latin America. In other instances, strategic interests were involved, such as the desire to secure free trade on the Río de la Plata. An area of particular concern was the matter of enforcing the prohibition on the slave trade in Brazil. In each case, the sovereignty of the Latin American countries hardly played a role from the point of view of the Europeans.

[9] Vázquez, "Una difícil inserción en el concierto de las naciones."
[10] Pereira Castañares, "Las relaciones diplomáticas entre España e Hispano-américa en el siglo XIX."

After many long years of intense fighting, the young states started out their independence shouldering a severe economic burden. Free trade had been a central demand of colonialism's detractors and finally seemed within reach following independence. In many places, therefore, the elites looked to the future optimistically. These initial hopes proved premature, however, as the most contested regions suffered from looting, forced contributions, and ruin. Agriculture, mining, and proto-industries were destroyed. The silver mines that had been chiefly responsible for producing America's legendary wealth over the centuries were particularly hard hit by the conflicts. The reconstruction proved difficult because of an absence of skilled labor and especially capital. Indeed, the early failures of British interests in Mexico, Peru, and Bolivia scared potential investors away from the region.

Subsistence agriculture remained by far the most important sector of the Latin American economies. The hinterland areas, which were far removed from economic centers, were barely involved in free trade because of the prohibitively high transport costs to the interior.[11] In contrast, the export-oriented agricultural sectors benefited from the liberalization of trade that followed independence. This was true, for instance, for livestock, which expanded in regions such as the Río de la Plata area, Venezuela, and Brazil. The export of salt meat for slaves' diet proved lucrative. The marketing of plantation products such as cocoa and coffee also developed promisingly. Sugar, the traditional export product, boomed, especially in the Spanish colony of Cuba. The island gradually became more valuable to the mother country and witnessed an enormous increase in slave imports in the 1820s and 1830s. Latin America's first railway line was built in Cuba in 1834. Nonetheless, as in Brazil, the strict adherence here to slavery led to problems over the long term, for the one-sided focus on this sector permitted only slow overall economic development.[12] In the first half of the nineteenth century, agricultural exports grew only slightly overall in most of Latin America, despite relatively favorable terms of trade.

Economic life in general was especially challenging during this period due to the scarcity of funds, which was chiefly due to the flight of capital.[13] In light of this predicament, foreign trade duties emerged as the most important source of state income. Foreign trade thus became an

---

[11] Bulmer-Thomas, *Economic History*, pp. 39–40.
[12] Haber/Klein, "The Economic Consequences of Brazilian Independence."
[13] Rizo Patrón Boylan, "Las emigraciones," pp. 407–28.

increasingly important factor in Latin America's economic development. Following independence, the former colonial powers with their anachronistic monopoly claims ultimately lost their status as intermediaries of trade between America and Europe. England now gradually gained direct access to all Latin American markets where it had failed to do so before independence, such as in the Río de la Plata. From 1817, this also included the Spanish colonies of Cuba and Puerto Rico. The free trade inspired a great deal of euphoria in England and the other interested overseas trading countries such as the Hanseatic cities. There was tremendous optimism about the previously closed markets, whose potential had been widely known since Alexander von Humboldt at the latest. For this reason, the British dispatched consuls to Latin America even before they granted countries official diplomatic recognition.[14]

Latin American foreign trade rested on the friendship, commerce, and navigation treaties the young states had settled with European powers and the United States on the basis of the most-favored-nation principle. In reality, it was the Europeans who mainly benefited from the agreements. The Latin American partners had to grapple with high costs, for all the open ports and free trade in many respects significantly restricted their ability to promote their national economies in a targeted way. The most-favored-nation principle further hindered integration within Latin America. Thus, while the treaties, on one hand, formed the basis of the recognition of Latin American independence, they also created new economic dependencies on the other. In fact, with their unrivaled low-cost products, the British were soon able to supplant the locals in the market – despite the presence of U.S. and European competition since the 1820s.[15] In Latin America, free trade undoubtedly helped to prevent industrialization, for it usually spelled the end for producers who had to compete with import products.

The situation was less problematic in cases where imported items did not turn up due to transport costs that were still notoriously high in the nineteenth century. Free trade was thus far from extensive, as huge areas inland, such as the indigenous highlands with their subsistence economies, remained unaffected. Unquestionably, fiscal dependence increased everywhere as a result of the trade tariffs. There were notable differences, however, tied to geographic location. In Hispano-America, the vision

[14] Marichal: *A Century of Debt Crises*, pp. 14–6.
[15] In the case of Mexico, see above all Bernecker, *Handelskonquistadoren*. For Chile: Cavieres, *Comercio chileno*. On the economic relations to individual European countries at this stage, see the essays in Liehr, *América Latina*, pp. 363–508.

of a liberal trade zone was undermined even further by the fact that the independence of numerous new states gave rise to separate duties, which thus caused the de facto free trade zone of the colonial empire to collapse.[16] Free trade actually brought growth only to regions such as Buenos Aires that were already intimately involved with transatlantic economic cycles.[17]

Latin America's international economic integration was accompanied by a debt burden whose dimensions the governments did not initially appreciate. In the first years of independence, the region found itself already headed for its first debt crisis. As early as 1822, British investors started to put their money into Latin America, beginning with Gran Colombia; and by 1825, almost all Latin American states accepted public bonds in London.[18] This seemed to address an urgent fiscal need, for the abolition of the tax revenue had led to shortfalls and the ongoing conflicts continued to devour additional large sums. In England, there was considerable willingness to lend because the bond capital was expected to open the doors to British trade.[19] Direct investments also flowed from Great Britain into the region, as the mining industry was considered especially attractive.[20]

The investment boom would come to an end very quickly, however. Fraud, bad management resulting from ignorance of local conditions, political instability, and impatience, coupled with high expectations in an overvalued region, all provided the foundation for an inauspicious start. The Latin American economy crashed when a European banking crisis broke out in 1825. European demand for Latin American products fell sharply, and customs revenues collapsed as a result. The ensuing debt crisis showed that the borrowed capital had mostly been invested unproductively to cover the running costs and lingering war debts.[21] This resulted directly in a suspension of payments, a measure which all Latin American countries, with the exception of Brazil, had to undertake until 1828.[22] The long-term impact of this decision was grave, as it hindered access to international credit for about twenty-five years. In fact, the restructuring

---

[16] Bulmer-Thomas, *Economic History*, p. 29.
[17] Prados, *Lost Decades?* pp. 287–90 and 297.
[18] Marichal, *A Century of Debt Crises*, pp. 27–36.
[19] Dawson, *First Latin-American Debt Crisis*, pp. 22–46.
[20] Bulmer-Thomas, *Economic History*, p. 34.
[21] Of the 25 million pounds borrowed between 1824 and 1827, no less than 17 million pounds flowed into government bonds. Dawson, *First Latin-American Debt Crisis*, pp. 119–28.
[22] Marichal, *A Century of Debt Crises*, pp. 43–55.

of the debt even continued for five more years after that.[23] Investment capital was therefore missing at a crucial time in Latin America, such as when it could have been used to modernize the export sector. Dependence on foreign trade tariffs intensified markedly as a consequence. The young states were confronted with tremendous foreign debt, and instead of the expected growth, the macroeconomic indicators in many countries of the region in 1850 were still worse than in 1800.

EUROPEANIZATION OF LATIN AMERICA?

From a cultural standpoint, the search for identity and the attempt to throw off the yolk of the Spanish colonial legacy had a decisive influence on the mid-nineteenth century. In this search for self, Europe became in many respects both a reference and a model. Here, prestigious and progressive modern Western Europe was turned to, specifically, France and England. Improved communications were an important prerequisite for the gradual intensification of contacts between Europe and Latin America. The abolition of colonial restrictions on travel and trade and the density and acceleration of maritime routes, as well as the postal system, contributed greatly in this regard.

During this period, the old continent held tremendous appeal for young Latin Americans from the upper strata of society. Though there was a range of motives, the symbolic capital that could be gained by making a trip to Europe was of primary importance. From the vantage point of Latin America, Europe was the original source of knowledge, luxury, and fashion. For the wealthy, visiting the continent was more or less *de rigueur*. Political or military luminaries also traveled to Europe in order to gain experience and specific skills or to continue their education. After their return, they became important mediators of new liberal ideas and trends.[24]

Paris was the destination of choice. France and its capital city were the cultural center par excellence – a conviction deeply rooted in the imagination of the Latin American elites. French was the most widely spoken and read foreign language. Beyond this, the French government undertook cultural-political efforts to attract young members of the social elites.[25] Back home, the so-called Afrancesados spread the word about the glory

[23] Dawson, *First Latin-American Debt Crisis*, pp. 193–212.
[24] Veliz, *Centralist Tradition*, p. 171.
[25] Gazmuri, *El "48" chileno*, p. 26.

of France and attempted to recreate their own environments based on the French model. The more a Latin American capital resembled Paris, the more advanced the country was considered.[26]

The idea that Paris was the center of the world influenced the global consciousness of the Europeanized Latin American elites. As Chilean historian Benjamín Vicuña Mackenna wrote in his diary in 1853, after his first trip to Paris:

I was in Paris.... I was in the capital of the world, the heart of humanity which beats with a giant pulse and pulls the spirit of all peoples around the globe to this center of life and intelligence. A version of the universe in miniature, everything that was ever created can be found here: intelligence, virtue, the depths of human misery, the loftiest epics of history; nature, genius, heroism, joy; frenetic passion, vice, and sophistication.[27]

By the end of the nineteenth century, the assessment of the French capital was little changed. Brazilian journalist Eduardo Prado thus observed around 1890: "No doubt Paris is the world."[28]

Enthusiasm was also sparked in many places in Latin America in response to the European revolutions of 1848. However, it was one thing to celebrate the events in distant Europe and another to infer concrete policy changes from them at home. The European revolutionary crisis impacted the political culture nonetheless, especially in the southern countries of Latin America. Here, new social forms took root and formed the basis in some countries for a broadening of the bourgeois public sphere. In the second half of the nineteenth century, they would reflect wholly European developments, even if only on a small scale.[29]

From the perspective of Latin America, other European countries and cities simply could not hold a candle to France. London, on the other hand, certainly had some standing that was closely tied to Great Britain's economic influence. This fact is well demonstrated by Venezuelan Andrés Bello, the most important intellectual figure in Latin America in the first half of the nineteenth century. Bello lived in London from 1810 to 1829, where he became acquainted with the social and political reform processes in England and the teachings of Jeremy Bentham. After he returned to Latin America, he settled in Chile, where he then reformed, among other things, the education system. His influence on the reform efforts

---

[26] Burns, *The Poverty of Progress*, p. 20.
[27] Vicuña Mackenna, *Páginas de mi diario*, Vol. 1, pp. 281–2.
[28] Barreto, "Eduardo Prado," pp. 187–8.
[29] Thomson, *The European Revolutions of 1848*, pp. 100–239.

throughout the hemisphere was enormous due to his many relations with neighboring countries. It is partly because of Bello that the English model came to have a decisive impact on socioeconomic thinking in Latin America. The English model was likewise reflected in the numerous, mostly short-lived Latin American constitutions during those years, whose noble principles could nonetheless rarely withstand the reality of despotism and cronyism.

Influences from Europe, however, were not felt only because of Latin American travelers. Europeans, along with European books and periodicals, had also made their way to Latin America. Writings were of diverse provenance, and in addition to the classics of European literature, there was a preponderance of booklets with trivial content. Works by Latin American authors even often arrived in their home countries after having taken a detour through Paris, the city that was these authors' publishing center after Madrid. Every upper-class household interested in keeping up its reputation had a collection of classic texts. On the other hand, there was little left over but contempt for domestic works.[30]

For the young states eager to conceive of themselves as nations, a central idea throughout nineteenth-century Latin American history was that of progress, a notion that encompassed the entire spectrum of human existence. For the evangelists of progress, who argued that it had spread best throughout Latin America in the cities, while lagging behind in the hinterland, France and England epitomized progress most of all. In 1852, young Argentine thinker Juan Bautista Alberdi thus emphatically remarked: "In America, everything that is not European is barbaric."[31] For Alberdi and many of his Latin American contemporaries, Europeanization consequently represented the salvation of their nation. By means of European immigration, the indigenous and black population elements could be pushed aside so that the way, it was thought, might be cleared for civilization. The opposition between civilization and barbarism became a central aspect of the Latin American developmental discourse. It was suggested that immigrants preferably from northwestern Europe should populate the supposedly "empty continent" and in this manner transplant European virtues to Latin America. These ideas culminated in the racist concept of "whitening" the nation through the displacement of the non- or only partly descendant European population.[32]

---

[30] As, for example, in the case of Costa Rica; see Molina, "Mercancias culturales," p. 275.
[31] Quoted in König, "Europa in der Sicht Lateinamerikas," p. 357.
[32] Graham, *The Idea of Race*. Appelbaum, "Racial Nations."

In the eyes of the elites, the formative processes of nation and "race" went hand in hand. They followed Europe's lead, while adapting its specifications to the conditions in Latin America.

Given the attitude of certain Latin American elites who were eager to modernize, it is no surprise that European influences were able to shape the region's self-understanding, including its very nomenclature. *Latin America* is a term that stems from pan-Latinist French thinking and was freely adopted in the Americas in the 1860s. This designation made it possible to set the region apart from both its Spanish heritage and the United States, which, since the mid-nineteenth century, appeared more and more threatening due to its westward expansion and the Mexican War (1846–8). With of the use of the term *Latin America*, famous thinkers such as Chilean Francisco Bilbao or Colombian José María Torres Caicedo could make a claim regarding cultural and political autonomy in contrast to what they perceived as excessive Anglo-Saxon influence.

Despite the great willingness to imitate, in the nineteenth century there were already counter-proposals and resistance to the modernization claims of liberal elites. Even within the progressive elites there were those who opposed the whitening of the population because they correctly recognized that indigenous and African elements constituted an integral part of Latin American culture. In their view, the existence of the population with non-European roots made full Europeanization impossible. They also resented the dominance of Europeans in their own country, which was reflected by their superficial imitation. Instead, they demanded an examination of their own reality that rejected the prevailing ideology of Europeanization. Against the backdrop of romantic historicism, in Mexico, for example, the status of the indigenous element was reevaluated, even idealized.[33] Nonetheless, the Mexicans did not raise any political demands as a consequence, let alone make an effort to redefine Europeanization in the name of progress.

In reality, the mass of the population of indigenous, Afro-Americans, and Mestizos continued to be excluded from the projects of the Europeanizers, as well as from those of their critics. But this did not mean that these lower classes, above all in rural areas, but also in the growing cities, had nothing to offer in opposition to Europeanization. Their adherence to tradition and a value system that was oriented more toward the community than the individual gave them a basis for resisting

---

[33] Earle, *The Return of the Native*, pp. 100–32.

the pressure to change stemming from the Europeanized upper strata of the cities.[34]

At the turn of the twentieth century, the discourse of the elites also became more differentiated. From 1898, Panhispanism took hold, since after the loss of Cuba the immediate threat of the old colonial power no longer played a role. Here, the reference to cultural ties with the old mother country, as well as the contrast to the alleged utilitarianism of the United States, as propagated by the then perhaps most famous Latin American intellectual, Uruguayan José Enrique Rodó, were crucial. Due to the emphasis placed on traditional values, this type of thought was particularly attractive to conservative circles in Latin America. On the other hand, it was also a breeding ground for racist prejudices against the ethnic diversity of Latin America, which further gave rise to pessimistic, self-critical forecasts about the viability of the region.[35]

At the same time, another guidepost eventually came into view: the discovery of one's own America and the diversity of local ethnic groups as a potential source of strength and self-confidence. Cuban poet and freedom fighter José Marti was a pioneer of this original Latin American movement of Pan-Americanism, which found its slogan in the concept of "Our America," in contradistinction to the America of the north.[36] Between 1898 and 1914, the search for the roots of one's individual identity in the indigenous cultures and the mass of the marginalized populations, and the call for a united front to ward off the North American threat, developed into critical transformational elements in Latin American intellectual history.

INTEGRATION INTO THE WORLD MARKET

From the mid-nineteenth century, power was assumed in most Latin American states by progressive businessmen and members of the educated classes. They realized the mistakes from the first decades of independence and saw that, despite superficial changes, the economy and society tended to stagnate. Their goal was to achieve national progress, which meant overcoming regional backwardness through the gradual adoption of European models. For this purpose, they sought to integrate their countries into the world economic system by exploiting available

---

[34] Burns, *The Poverty of Progress*, pp. 81–131.
[35] Pike, *Hispanismo*, pp. 31–50. Devés Valdés, *El pensamiento latinoamericano*, Vol. 1, pp. 347 and 375.
[36] Rinke/Fischer/Schulze, *Geschichte Lateinamerikas: Quellenband*, pp. 124–6.

resources. The basic principles of liberalism predominated. In the economic domain, this meant the individual's performance and responsibility in the field of political ethics, free trade, and laissez-faire economics, as well as an international division of labor based on the export of raw materials and imported manufactured goods. The constitutions codified the liberal rights of individual freedom, equality, and personal development, and the protection of private property. In economic policy, the state was accorded the role of guarantor for a functioning export economy. The overriding conviction was that the free play of market forces and the laws of the "invisible hand" would bring the individual interests into alignment with those of society. Government interventions such as the regulation of undesirable socioeconomic developments were scorned.[37]

Economic policy thus mainly meant policies that promoted exports, especially through free trade regulations, creating free access to land, and natural resources, as well as freeing up human labor. At the same time, the governments did not recognize the consequences this policy could have on those industries not involved in export. In 1850, these sectors continued to make up a considerable part of the economy in all countries. The general view was sanguine, however: Export growth, it was presumed, would entail an increase in productivity and structural changes that were more oriented toward the modern market economy. Thus, for Latin American elites in the nineteenth century set on modernization, "progress" became a talismanic word and, in their view, could be "quantitatively measured based on the volume of exports, the number of steam engines, kilometers of railroad, or street lights."[38]

Developments in the world economy contributed to the ascent of liberalism in Latin America. In 1846, for instance, the British government drastically lowered import tariffs on agricultural products, a measure generally regarded as the beginning of the free trade era. Then, in 1860, the two admired European nations, France and England, pushed through an expansion of free trade on the international stage with the Cobden-Chevalier Treaty. Along with this, because of the enormous population growth and increasing industrialization in Europe in the second half of the century, there was a growing demand for food, raw materials, and tropical goods, especially tobacco, cocoa, coffee, and sugar. The expansion of overseas steamship connections and transportation routes to parts of the hinterland created the necessary infrastructural conditions

[37] Jaksic/Posada Carbó, *Liberalismo y poder.*
[38] Burns, *The Poverty of Progress*, p. 20.

for a successful export orientation. Moreover, due to the insufficient development of the industrial sector in Latin America, it was not possible to satisfy the demand for manufactured goods. The Latin American goods manufactured in the local factories and workshops could not compete with higher-quality and cheaper European mass consumer products. Imports therefore seemed critical. Moreover, in order to offset the trade imbalance, emphasis was placed on increasing exports.[39]

In the approximately three decades before the First World War, Latin American countries experienced strong export growth. This was particularly true for Argentina and, with some time lag, Ecuador, Brazil, Mexico, and Colombia. Despite the considerable gaps – exports thus did not really take off in Peru until after 1896 and the Colombian coffee boom did not actually begin until around 1910 – it is nevertheless important to recognize that the structures of Latin American exports in the second half of the nineteenth century underwent a substantial transformation. This was a reflection of the changes in European demand during the second industrial revolution. The dominance of precious metal exports accordingly came to an end, and customers instead benefited from the advent of new products in the mining industry like copper from Peru, tin from Bolivia, and saltpeter from Chile. In the rest of Latin America, new exports mainly consisted in agrarian products. Factories in Europe and the United States demanded rubber, mostly from Brazil, which triggered a boom there. The flourishing U.S. agro-industry spurred an explosion in sisal cultivation in Mexico's Yucatán Peninsula, with devastating consequences for the enslaved indigenous population. Europe and North America needed grain and meat to supply their growing populations. The rising incomes in the industrial countries allowed for the import of tropical luxury goods such as coffee and cocoa. Even products from tropical forests like quinine from the Andes, quebracho extract, and many others were now in great demand. In some states, however, old export structures also remained in place. This was particularly true for Cuba, which became the number one provider of sugar on the world market.

Nonetheless, the introduction of new export goods did not lead to the diversification of exports. The new commodities simply replaced the old ones, whereby the degree of concentration tended to increase. This gave rise to problematic monocultures, and the dependency on one or several markets in Europe and the United States solidified. The development of the export sectors of most countries, with the exception of Argentina and

[39] Bulmer-Thomas, *Economic History*, pp. 39–40.

Chile, remained unsatisfactory and fell far below expectations. Among other reasons, this was because the uniquely favorable conditions for exporters of primary products before the First World War, stemming from the strong demand of industrial countries, was not permanent. Indeed, growth was already repeatedly affected before 1914 by external crises in Europe and internal problems such as civil wars and natural disasters.[40]

Foreign trade was usually managed by foreign ships and merchants. In the first few decades after independence, the latter had established themselves in the harbors and capital cities of Latin America as a small, elite group. These businessmen acquired important positions by working closely with the parent companies in the home country. Relations here were founded on good contacts with the local upper class – in fact, sometimes merchants even decided to marry on the spot – and politicians, as well as knowledge of the region and its people. At first, mostly British firms predominated, and to a lesser degree French and U.S. trading houses. Later on, German firms had also established a presence in countries like Venezuela, the Dominican Republic, and Guatemala. In general, the trade and financial transactions of these merchants were already transnational in character. German merchants, for example, sold French goods, while taking advantage of English credit.

Beyond this, in many countries, trading companies invested directly in export production. Foreigners were successful in producing Chilean saltpeter, Cuban and Peruvian sugar, Mexican sisal, Central American bananas, and later Guatemalan coffee. To some degree, veritable enclaves of foreign economic activity emerged with separate transportation networks, laws, and even police forces. There was massive growth in this area from 1900 onward.

The earned capital often flowed to the mother country. It was thus only partially accumulated for the needs of future industrialization, as, for instance, when immigrants like the Germans in southern Brazil remained in their new home over the long term. In Colombia, Brazil, and Argentina, production remained largely in local hands. But even here, foreigners were critically important as lenders, transporters, insurers, and marketing organizers for the financially weak Latin American exporters.[41]

Just as Europe and the United States were the most important purchasers of Latin American exports, they were equally central as originators of

---

[40] Ibid., p. 156.
[41] Albert, *South America and the World Economy*, pp. 33–45.

imports. Britain had played a leading role since independence, but with the spread of industrialization in the course of the nineteenth century, France, Germany, the United States, and other European countries also came to assert themselves as competitors. Certainly, the four major nations controlled the markets, but they also stood in competition to one another. Latin American consumers could benefit from this as prices occasionally developed in their favor. However, cartels exerted their influence everywhere, especially in the last two decades before the First World War. The composition of the imports also changed in this period: Whereas British textiles predominated at first, efforts toward modernization aroused a demand for new products. In order to instill their sumptuous villas with the aura of modern and cultivated in Europe, the Latin American profiteers of the export bonanza enjoyed spending their proceeds on dignified English furniture and clothes, French wines and porcelain, Italian glassware and textiles, Flemish lace, and other luxury items. At the same time, they tried to hire European architects and construction firms to mimic the radiance of the Belle Époque. The slowly growing urban middle and working classes also had an interest in maintaining duty-free imports to keep the cost of living low.[42]

As a result of the increasing integration into the world economy, access to communication networks was essential. Beginning in the 1860s, the first overseas telegraph connections were established between Florida and the Caribbean islands of Cuba, Hispaniola, and Puerto Rico, and from there to northern South America. U.S. and European companies cooperated with each other in this endeavor. In the early 1870s, there was a virtual sprint to link South America to the telegraph network, which culminated in the creation of the first telegraph line between Buenos Aires and Europe in 1874. Starting out from Buenos Aires, the west coast cities of Valparaíso and Lima were connected, while, for the time being, the planned connection with the United States did not materialize.[43]

Another area in which the increasing integration into the world market on the ground in Latin America was especially noticeable was foreign investments, which took off simultaneously with the boom in trade. Particularly momentous was the construction of the railway, into which nearly one-third of the total foreign direct investment in Latin America flowed before 1914. As a symbol of progress, railways were unlike any

---

[42] Orlove, "Giving Importance to Imports," pp. 1–30.
[43] Winseck/Pike, *Communication and Empire*, pp. 61–77.

other technical achievement of the nineteenth century. As Peruvian president Manuel Pardo (1872–6) wrote:

Who would deny that the railway today is the missionary of civilization? Who would deny that Peru urgently needs such missionaries? Without railways, there can be no material progress … and no moral progress, for material progress provides for the masses' welfare and eliminates their misery and ignorance.[44]

The railway construction, which was primarily financed with British capital, flourished toward the end of the nineteenth century, especially in Argentina, Brazil, and Mexico. This led, as a consequence, to the tremendous accumulation of national debt. In many areas, the monopolistic position of the railway companies and their pricing policy incited criticism. Latin American governments faced a dilemma in their relations with the powerful European railway companies: On one hand, they had to create incentives for the Europeans to further extend the route network, for the state's developmental objective was to open up the entire country. On the other hand, due to pressure from the population, they had to ensure that the companies offered good service for as little money as possible. Aligning the two goals was no easy task. The same was true for the public utilities, which claimed the second largest share of total direct investment in Latin America. Overall, these investments contributed greatly to strengthening the focus on exports and deepening the foreign debt.[45]

The liberalization of passenger transport occurred in parallel to that of economic life. Already in the first half of the nineteenth century, Latin American countries had adopted pro-immigration laws, though until the 1860s there were still denominational barriers in many places. At times, in the second half of the century, liberal governments, in particular those of Argentina, Brazil, and Chile, actively recruited immigrants. For this purpose, they took advantage of the world exhibitions to present themselves as a modern and rich country (as in the case of Argentina), as a country of undiscovered treasures (as in the case of Bolivia and Mexico), or as a country of tropical promise (as in the case of Brazil). Consistent with the racist notions of the time, the politicians in charge wanted to primarily attract immigrants from northwestern Europe. Southern and Eastern Europeans, on the other hand, were less welcome.[46]

---

[44] Quoted in Marichal, *A Century of Debt Crises*, p. 88.
[45] Albert, *South America and the World Economy*, p. 65.
[46] Halperin, "¿Para qué la inmigración?" For the most recent discussions, see Foote/Goebel, *Immigration and National Identities in Latin America*.

In the second half of the century, there was in fact a mass migration movement from Europe. In absolute terms, Argentina was the main destination for emigrants, accepting about 5.5 million immigrants. Approximately 4.5 million went to Brazil, and as many as half a million to Uruguay. The other million or so were spread among the remaining Latin American countries. The peak of the emigration wave came in the decades before the outbreak of the First World War. Contrary to the initial hopes, the countries of origin of the mass emigration were above all Italy, Spain, and Portugal. In Argentina, more than half of the immigrants came from Italy. In Brazil, the rate of Italians averaged 39 percent. That said, of the approximately 50 million Europeans seeking a better life in the Americas from 1830 to 1930, only about one-fifth traveled to the lower hemisphere. In quantitative terms, they were mainly distributed among only a few countries like Argentina, Brazil, and, to a lesser extent, Chile and Uruguay. In qualitative terms, however, their impact was considerable wherever they went.[47]

The concentration of European emigrants in just a few Latin American countries was attributable to the favorable climatic conditions and their geographical location as neighboring states on the Atlantic coast. But even smaller countries such as Chile and Cuba took on significant numbers of immigrants. In the case of Cuba, it was mainly Spaniards, and in the case of Chile, even Germans figured prominently. There was no mass immigration, however, in Central America and the North Andean countries. The immigrants who arrived in these countries were usually wealthy planters, merchants, or experts. In this capacity, they exerted sizeable influence on the development of the respective countries. Yet mass emigration involved primarily peasant classes and workers who came to the Americas in pursuit of landownership. Toward the end of the century, however, emigrants increasingly settled in cities or were forced to move there from the countryside because acquiring land became more and more difficult. Indeed, a lack of landownership, along with many other disappointments and uncertainties, was also the reason for the comparatively high number of returning emigrants.[48]

People not only came to Latin America during this period from Europe, however. The African slave trade had been a characteristic feature of the Atlantic area since the early colonial period. Despite the prohibitions instituted by the British naval power from 1807, it came to thrive once

[47] Rinke, "Nach Norden oder Süden?" pp. 25–56.
[48] Mörner/Sims, *Adventurers and Proletarians*, pp. 13–22.

again. The Spanish colony of Cuba and the independent empire of Brazil became the main buyers, in place of the independent Hispano-American countries that had gradually abolished slavery. From 1826 to 1867, around 1.5 million slaves were brought to Latin America, before slavery was finally abolished in Cuba in 1886 and in Brazil in 1888. Even before the abolition of slavery, Latin American countries (including the latter two) had a high proportion of the free black population due to manumissions and freedom that was purchased. The share of the Afro-descendant population – which had brought its own cultural elements to the already diverse mix of Latin America – would continue to grow, especially in the Caribbean and Brazil.[49]

The same was true to an increasing extent with regard to immigration from Asia. While this wave of immigrants never achieved the same numbers as the migrations from Europe and Africa, it nonetheless gained importance in individual countries and regions. Originally intended as a substitute for slaves, the immigration of cheap labor from China – the so-called coolies – India, and other Asian countries began to take place on a large scale beginning in the 1830s. The English colonies in the Caribbean affected by the abolition of the slave trade in 1807 and the end of slavery in 1834 made use of Chinese and Indian indentured laborers early on. After the abolition of slavery in 1848, the French shipped cheap labor from their possessions in the South Asian colonies to Guadeloupe, Martinique, and Guyana. Cuba and Brazil preferred to take on Chinese contract workers, as their living conditions usually differed little from those of the slaves.[50] Around the turn of the century, Japanese laborers joined them and provided an important contingent of immigrants, especially in Peru, Brazil, and Mexico.[51]

THE IMPERIALIST RACE

The integration of Latin America into the world market was fraught with problems as mass immigration created new social challenges. It also was the cause of areas of tension in foreign relations. Often the assumed debts that were based on a rosy view of the future could not be repaid on time. The numerous civil wars that ravaged large parts of Latin America as

[49] Meißner/Mücke/Weber, *Schwarzes Amerika*, esp. chaps. 4–7.
[50] Meagher, *The Coolie Trade*, pp. 201–73. Romero, *The Chinese in Mexico*, pp. 1–11. Lai, "The Chinese Indenture System." Roopnarine, *Indo-Caribbean Indenture*, pp. 13–35. Gosine, "Sojourner to Settler: An Introduction."
[51] *Centenário da imigração japonesa*. Thorndike, *Los imperios del sol*.

an element of the nation-building processes often impacted foreigners, who then claimed rights to compensation. This led to clashes with the powerful Europeans, who revealed the limits of the desired partner-like cooperation.[52]

Added to this was the onset of the imperialist race to partition the globe. Although Britain had reached an informal hegemony in Latin America, especially in economic terms, this hardly meant the end of classical colonialism. As self-appointed guardians of the "Latin race," Spain and particularly France developed colonial aspirations from 1860 onward that went well beyond the interventions of the first half of the century. The European invaders benefited here from the temporary breakdown of the United States due to the American Civil War. Following the declaration of President James Monroe from 1823, the so-called Monroe Doctrine, they already claimed for themselves a special role in the Americas. For instance, the Dominican Republic once again came under Spanish rule from 1861 to 1865, albeit at the request of the Dominican-American caudillo Pedro Santana. From 1862, the conflict between Spain and Peru had become so intense that a war broke out three years later, with Chile, Bolivia, and Ecuador joining the Peruvian side. The warring parties did not officially declare an end to hostilities until 1879.[53]

Colonial efforts culminated in the Second Mexican Empire, established with France's support under the Habsburg Maximilian (1864–7). Just as in Peru, pending payments in Mexico also gave the Spaniards, French, and British occasion in 1861 to intervene in a country bled dry by a long civil war. Before long, France's broader objectives were revealed: True to the policy of Panlatinism that Napoleon III had already advanced in Europe, the French wanted to establish a presence in Mexico at the expense of the Anglo-Americans. Once the Spanish and the British recognized France's broader intention, they again quickly withdrew their troops from Mexico. In an alliance with the Mexican conservatives, Napoleon introduced a monarchy in Mexico that was a dependent of France under Archduke Maximilian of Austria. In addition to commercial interests, the prestige factor played a critical role. The idea of restoring a European monarchy in Latin America ultimately was not disavowed until the downfall of Maximilian's Empire due to the resistance of the Mexicans under Benito Juárez.[54] Nonetheless, the notion of

[52] Using the example of Mexico, see Bernecker, *Handelskonquistadoren*. See also Brown, *Informal Empire*.
[53] Davis, *The Last Conquistadores*.
[54] Cunningham, *Mexico*. Lida, *España y el Imperio*.

"Latinity" – of the unity of the "Latin races" due to common linguistic, religious, and historical origins – persisted.

European interventionism had thus not come to an end. Toward the end of the nineteenth century, it rather shifted toward Central America, the northern Andean countries, and the Caribbean in particular. In general, the catalyst was the political and economic instability of the governments. Above all, the civil war–like conflicts between liberals and conservatives ensured an atmosphere of continual unrest. European powers carried out numerous interventions in the three decades from 1870 to 1900. Nicaragua and Haiti were the most affected. In addition to the United Kingdom, France, and Germany, the Netherlands, Spain, Italy, Denmark, and Russia also got involved. The interventions mostly followed the same pattern: Whenever the Latin Americans failed to meet demands for payment on outstanding debts or provide compensation for alleged abuses against the interests of European citizens, the European powers delivered gunboats to lend emphasis to their diplomatic efforts. By and large, the Latin Americans saw they had no other choice but to relent. It was also not unusual for them to pledge their customs revenues from foreign trade, their most important fiscal revenue stream, for many years into the future. In the southern countries of South America, by contrast, direct military interventions hardly played a role. Still, around the turn of the century in Brazil, the notion of a "German danger" gained currency. More precisely, the suspicion emerged that Germany had imperialist ambitions in the south of the country, where many German-born immigrants lived. Even if the Europeans did not take countries like Argentina, Brazil, and Chile especially seriously, they nonetheless tended to respect them more than the smaller republics of Central America, for instance, which were often referred to around the turn of the century by the contemptuous term "banana republic."[55]

The Latin American countries, however, were by no means merely passive observers of the imperialistic division of the world, which came to a climax with the Berlin Conference of 1884–5. After emerging victorious from the War of the Pacific against its neighbors Bolivia and Peru in 1883, Chile underscored its regional hegemony with the annexation of Easter Island in 1888. This decision proved quite opportune for British trading interests, who wanted to limit French expansion in Polynesia. The Chilean desire to retain the Port of Valparaíso as an international hub between the Atlantic and Pacific played an important role, as the already foreseeable

[55] The term originated in the United States. See Rinke, *América Latina y Estados Unidos*, p. 103.

future construction of a canal through Central America threatened its privileged position on the Americas' western coast. Nonetheless, Chile's status as a colonial power in the Pacific region remained an exception.[56]

Toward the end of the nineteenth century, the international state of affairs took a dramatic turn. In 1868, the uprising against Spanish rule began in Cuba. The War of Independence lasted for several decades. In 1898, the United States exploited Spain's weakness in order to intervene militarily. The Treaty of Paris in December 1898 also officially ended Spanish colonial rule in the Americas. Henceforth, the United States would claim control rights for itself, at least in northern Latin America, and repeatedly intervene in the Caribbean. This was based on an imperialist ideology: the belief that the United States had a "Manifest Destiny" to rule over the so-called Western Hemisphere. This notion was combined with a civilizing mission in Latin America, which, in this alterity discourse, was considered the weak, inferior, and wild other. This self-awareness of one's own superiority came to bear against the backdrop of the inferiority of the "other American."[57]

The United States' interventionism was supplemented by the new Pan-Americanism ushered in by a conference in Washington in 1889/90. On balance, it concerned an active U.S. foreign economic policy toward Latin America. Ultimately, they tried to establish a customs union within the Americas under their own direction and thus form a counterweight to the dynamically expanding Europeans. As the architect of this policy, Secretary of State James G. Blaine, realized, the aim was to establish the Americas as an independent region within the global context. In 1902/3, the United States reasserted its claims to power in connection with the separation of Panama from Colombia when it secured the isthmus for the construction of an inter-oceanic canal. At the same time, it stood up to the European powers, which had taken punitive actions by blocking the Venezuelan ports. This would turn out to be the last European intervention of this kind in Latin America.[58]

The Latin American elites, however, were by no means prepared to uncritically accept the leadership of the United States. Simultaneous to the cultural movements of "Arielismo" and "Nuestra América," there was resistance from the intellectuals, in this case, international law experts. The right of intervention that the European powers and the United States

---

[56] Fischer, *Island*, pp. 136–47.
[57] Rinke, *Amércia Latina y Estados Unidos*, p. 97.
[58] Ibid., pp. 103–6.

in the nineteenth century often arrogated to themselves was based on their supposed right to protect their respective citizens and property anywhere in the world. The first to seriously question this claim was Argentinian diplomat and jurist Carlos Calvo. In his groundbreaking six-volume work on international law from 1868, he presented two principles for international cohabitation: first, the absolute right to freedom from intervention and, second, the absolute equality of foreigners and nationals.

Because this far-reaching claim could not be enforced as a general principle of law, Latin American countries strove to embed it in intergovernmental agreements as the so-called Calvo clause. As European interventionism came to a head in the Venezuela crisis of 1902, it was another Argentine, Foreign Minister Luis Drago, who attempted to give teeth to the Calvo clause with a diplomatic memorandum directed at the United States. Drago reiterated the principle of equality of all states before the law and repudiated any right to violent intervention for the recovery of debts. With the so-called Roosevelt Corollary to the Monroe Doctrine, U.S. President Theodore Roosevelt modified the meaning of Drago's message, for while he rejected the European right to intervene, he also saw the opportunity to bestow the United States with the role of a police officer in Latin America – which was hardly what Drago had in mind. Nevertheless, the Latin Americans were able to chalk up a success regarding their ideas about international law when the Peace Conference at The Hague in 1907 limited the right to intervene to cases where the borrower voluntarily accepted arbitration. In fact, this conference represented the first time there was a Latin American diplomatic presence on the world political stage.[59] In the nineteenth century, the multiethnic, multilingual continent shaped by diverse regional and national identities was integrated into the processes of global change. As a link between East and West, Latin America remained a geographic focal point for the growing exchange of goods, people, money, and information. The groundwork had been laid for Latin America's standing as the intersection between the Pacific and the Atlantic region – between the global north and south – which would come to define the region's characteristic and unique development over course of the twentieth century. The Latin American elites pursued this path deliberately to the extent that they could influence it. They thereby adhered to the liberal progressive paradigm that had originated in Europe and guided the actions of much of the world.

---

[59] Bra, *La doctrina Drago*. Fischer, *Souveränität der Schwachen*, pp. 64–5.

Just the same, toward the end of the nineteenth century some observers already repeatedly questioned the reliance on progress, and from a number of different angles. Whether it was because Latin Americans had witnessed the limits of sovereignty in the halls of diplomacy or continually found themselves in conflict with their increasingly powerful neighbor to the north; whether it was due to their interest in working out contemporary race theories or their sober recognition that unfulfilled promises of progress meant that globalization for Latin America would not be a seamless process: Latin America experienced its "postcolonial" moment long before the term was applied in the cultural and social sciences. The various forms of confusion and criticism these disappointments elicited were quite similar, and it is no wonder that they surfaced against a backdrop of increasing global interconnectedness. It was not until these entanglements became riven apart at their core that the moment seemed to have arrived for a new way into the future.

2

Neutrality under Pressure, 1914–1917

The grave events that unsettled the world in the years preceding the Great War were also felt in Latin America. One of the violent eruptions played out in the region in the form of the Mexican Revolution, which shook the confidence of Latin America's Europeanized upper strata. After the war broke out in Europe in early August 1914, the cycle of violence took on a new global dimension. The governments of Latin America wanted to stay neutral, putting their hopes in the quick end to the war that the strategists on both sides of the conflict had boastfully promised. The war, however, soon took on unprecedented dimensions: It neither passed by quickly, nor could the Latin Americans remain on the sidelines. Much to the contrary, the economic war and wartime propaganda that reached unprecedented scope made the consequences of the conflagration felt throughout the region from the beginning.

A HARBINGER OF VIOLENCE: THE REVOLUTION IN MEXICO

With a circulation of around 90,000, the publication *Caras y Caretas* in Buenos Aires was the largest and most professional Latin American magazine of the time. For its first issue after the outbreak of war in Europe on August 8, 1914, it printed a pictorial narrative with the title "The War: Children's Fairy Tales with Fatal Consequences for the Grown Ups." Within its pages, the reader could see how the god of war, Mars, was bored with the peace conference at The Hague and therefore invented new weaponry (see Figure 2.1). After testing the arms and achieving the desired effect in Turkey, the Balkans, and Mexico, Mars embarked on even

FIGURE 2.1 The god of war sows violence around the world.
Source: Manuel Redondo, "La guerra," in: *Caras y Caretas* (August 8, 1914).

greater challenges, inciting panic across Europe. Apart from the fact that the series of images was a sample of the comic's immediate antecedents from the pen of Manuel Redondo, the publication is notable because the illustrator here draws what was an apparently obvious parallel between the eruptions of violence in prewar Europe and in Mexico.

Redondo's thinking is partly explained by a look at the historical developments in Europe and Latin America. Recent research shows that the Great War in Europe actually began before August 1914 with the fighting in the Balkans and in Africa.[1] At the same time, the Mexican Revolution in Latin America marked an outbreak of violence that fit into the larger global context of the time. This revolution was not one of many coups that Latin America had witnessed in the nineteenth century. Rather, with Porfirio Díaz, it toppled a dictator who seemed to have transformed Mexico into a model country of progress according to liberal European concepts. The uprising provoked a great deal of attention

[1] Janz, 14: *Der große Krieg*, p. 12.

in Latin America. While the public media had shown little interest in the region prior to 1910 (with a few exceptions such as the Spanish-American War in 1898–9), the Mexican Revolution became a continental media event. This was due not least to the sensationalistic reporting by the U.S. press, which had gained access to the Latin American media through its news agencies and associated the revolution with violence and chaos.[2] The common interest in the events in Mexico, which would also be expressed in diplomatic initiatives, helped to bring the Latin American public spheres closer together.

The social revolutionary demands that accompanied the developments in Mexico raised questions about whether the traditional social order as such was in jeopardy. Argentinians thus worried about social unrest and responded with a demand for either more police supervision or societal reforms.[3] The concerns were understandable, as the numerous factions fought a seemingly interminable bloody civil war that ultimately lasted for more than ten years and probably resulted in more than a million, mostly civilian, deaths. With casualties amounting to around 6.6 percent of the total population, Mexico – proportionally speaking – had to mourn much higher losses than the major powers did during the First World War.[4]

This order of magnitude of violence, unfamiliar to Latin America at that time, was clearly linked by contemporary observers to the global intensification of imperialistic rivalries up through the 1910s. In point of fact, the United States, the European powers, and even Japan sought to influence the course of the revolution. Especially prominent were U.S. officials, who had already played a dubious role in Mexico in its initial phase. Tensions came to a head after the inauguration of President Woodrow Wilson in March 1913. True to the Tobar Doctrine of 1907, which denied recognition to the Central American countries whose governments had come to power through violent means, Wilson refused to recognize putschist Victoriano Huerta and instead supported revolutionary leader Venustiano Carranza. At the same time, the German and Japanese governments, for instance, cooperated with the dictator Huerta.[5] Washington tried to dispel widespread fears in Latin America of U.S. expansion plans

---

[2] Yankelevich, *La revolución mexicana en América Latina*, p. 13.
[3] Yankelevich, *La diplomacia imaginaria*, pp. 70–7.
[4] Estimates vary considerably, which is also related to the fact that the end of the revolution is defined differently in the research. I follow here McCaa, "Missing Millions," p. 400.
[5] Yankelevich, *La diplomacia imaginaria*, p. 78. On the European and Japanese interests, see Katz, *The Secret War*, pp. 119–252, and Schuler, *Secret Wars*, pp. 67–82.

in Mexico by means of public pronouncements like those from journalist William B. Hale. Hale emphasized that his country had no such intentions, but stressed nonetheless that the United States had a duty to help the Latin Americans maintain "an orderly civilization" whenever they could not do so themselves.[6] South American powers Argentina, Brazil, and Chile, which followed the situation in Mexico with bated breath, adhered to the non-recognition policy, even though they feared that the United States simply wanted to give itself carte blanche for an armed intervention.[7]

The conflict between Mexico and the United States then actually culminated in the occupation of the port of Veracruz by U.S. troops in April 1914. A war appeared inevitable.[8] Argentina, Chile, and Brazil consequently seized the initiative, mediating at the conference of Niagara Falls in Canada in May and June.[9] This resulted in Huerta's resignation and a resolution regarding the withdrawal of American forces. Although this action did not entirely eliminate the threat of war, it showed the growing self-confidence of the participating Latin American governments in foreign policy. They ultimately managed to avert a conflagration through negotiation and dialogue. In response to the many pompous commentaries on the situation in Mexico in the European press, Argentinean intellectual Leopoldo Lugones wrote in July 1914 that the European powers had acted in the Balkans in a similar manner to the United States in Mexico, namely, by exploiting the unrest to their own advantage. What is more, Lugones argued, the Europeans had no reason to look down their noses so contemptuously at Mexico: "How is it possible that it seems so strange to Europe that Mexico has yet to civilize all of its Indios in its one hundred years of independence when the Albanian and Moroccan barbarity has been tolerated in the middle of Europe since antiquity?"[10]

POLITICAL CHALLENGES

Lugones' piece appeared after some delay on August 10 in the Buenos Aires newspaper *La Nación*. By this time, however, a war had long since broken out – a war, which due to the involvement of every major European

[6] Hale, "Our Moral Empire," pp. 54–5, quote p. 58.
[7] Yankelevich, *La diplomacia imaginaria*, p. 78.
[8] Katz, *The Secret War*, pp. 195–202. The action was a response to an arms shipment from the German Empire. See Baecker, "The Arms of the Ypiranga," p. 8.
[9] Solveira de Báez, *La Argentina*, p. 17.
[10] Lugones, "La viga en el ojo," in: *La Nación* (B. A., August 10, 1914), pp. 2–3.

power, represented an unprecedented challenge for Latin America. How were the governments to act toward the belligerent camps when they were connected to each side in a variety of ways, and also not be drawn into the maelstrom? What were the possible consequences of the conflict?

In political terms, there was no need to intervene on either side of the war in August 1914. After all, the conflict was being carried out between European powers. It was in the national interest of the Latin American states to maintain their vital economic ties as much as possible with all the warring parties by adopting a neutral stance. There were neither close political ties nor even alliance-like obligations with either the Allies or the Central Powers that would have otherwise made an overt taking of sides necessary or desirable. Indeed, such non-interference in European wars was consistent with Latin America's diplomatic tradition, which was further reflected by the notion of Pan-Americanism.[11] As a consequence, all the sovereign countries in Latin America wasted little time in declaring their neutrality.[12] In doing so, they invoked the Second Hague Peace Conference of 1907 and the Declaration by the London Naval Conference in 1909 concerning land and naval warfare and the applicable rights of neutral states, which specifically regulated the treatment of ships from belligerent states.[13]

In declaring their neutrality, Latin American governments followed the United States' lead, which, despite having great sympathy for the cause of the Entente, also wanted to stay out of the European conflict. And just as in the United States, neutrality in Latin American countries

---

[11] "O Brasil neutro," in: *Jornal do Commercio* (November 19, 1914), p. 3. Álvarez, *La Grande Guerre Européenne*, pp. 59–61.

[12] Neutrality statements were generally declared during August 1914. See, e.g., MRE, *Guerra da Europa*, pp. 5–8. *Memoria de relaciones exteriores 1913–1914*, pp. 168–70. Elizalde, *Circular al Cuerpo Diplomático*. Martin, *Latin America and the War*, pp. 1–4 and 9–11. On the reasons for Latin America's neutrality, see also Gravil, *The Anglo-Argentine Connection*, p. 112. Vivas Gallardo, "Venezuela y la Primera Guerra Mundial," pp. 114–5. P. Cavalcanti, *A presidência de Wenceslau Braz*, pp. 97–8. "Neutralidad del Ecuador," in: *El Comercio* (Quito, August 19, 1914), p. 1. However, there were undoubtedly expressions of sympathy. Thus, the Brazilian ambassador in Vienna indicated his understanding of Austria's behavior in July/August 1914. Brazilian Embassy to MRE (Vienna, August 3, 1914), in: AHI, Directoria Geral dos Negocios Políticos e-Diplomaticos. See also Ecuadorian Consulate General to the Ministry of Foreign Affairs (Hamburg, August 26, 1917), in: Ecuador, AMRREE, D.1.8.

[13] The detailed provisions put into place, inter alia, different lengths of stay in neutral ports for armed and unarmed ships, prohibited the use of wireless telegraphy, etc. See the itemized list in: Colombian Ministry of Foreign Affairs, Memorandum sobre declaración de neutralidad (Bogotá, undated), Colombia, AGN, MRREE, Serie Neutralidad, Caja 82. See also Neff, *The Rights and Duties of Neutrals*, pp. 128–39.

was a political imperative domestically. States with a high proportion of immigrants from Europe such as Argentina, Brazil, Chile, Paraguay, and Uruguay had a strong desire to guard against ethnic conflicts.[14] All the same, passions were ignited soon after the outbreak of war, especially in capital and port cities such as Buenos Aires, Santiago, São Paulo, and Porto Alegre, where crowds of demonstrators formed in the streets. In many places, Latin Americans heard spontaneous expressions of sympathy, for instance, when sympathizers sang the Marseillaise or the German national anthem in public.[15] The commentator of *La Nación* was thus already able to observe on August 5: "Our streets are now the forum of the war."[16] This is not surprising given that nine out of ten immigrants in Argentina, the Latin American country with the largest proportion of immigrants in its overall population, came from Allied states (including Italy).[17]

The European countries of origin attempted to call up potential conscripts among the emigrants in Latin America for military service. The consulates made public announcements in the numerous foreign press organs of immigrant communities urging local conscripts to sign up.[18] At first, these calls to action met with an overwhelmingly positive response. In cities such as Buenos Aires, Valparaíso, São Paulo, and Rio de Janeiro, the conscripts converged en masse. The press reported regularly on farewell parties for reservists who wanted to return to Europe.[19] There were also instances of violent clashes, however.[20]

In many countries of the region, the British set up small but well-organized communities that had numerous clubs, churches, and schools at their disposal. As the networking coincided with a high level of social control, this in turn benefited the conscription activities.[21] A large number of volunteers flocked to Great Britain from the colonies in the

---

[14] A survey of the population of Santiago de Chile showed the diversity of opinions depending on the country of origin: "Lo que piensan de la guerra," in: *Zig-Zag* (August 22, 1914).

[15] "Demonstrationen in den Theatern," in: *Deutsche La Plata Zeitung* (August 4, 1914), p. 2. "La guerra europea: la agitación en Santiago," in: *Zig-Zag* (August 8, 1914).

[16] "La conflagración europea," in: *La Nación* (B. A., August 5, 1914), p. 9.

[17] Otero, *La guerra en la sangre*, p. 23.

[18] See the advertisements in *Diario de Centro-América* (August 4, 1914), p. 2. See also *Activities of the British Community*, pp. 205–7. On recruitment in rural towns, see Compagnon, *L'adieu à L'Europe*, p. 111. Luebke, *Germans in Brazil*, pp. 85–7.

[19] "Homenaje a los reservistas franceses," in: *Caras y Caretas* (August 15, 1914).

[20] "Os reservistas das nações em guerra," in: *Correio da Manhã* (August 7, 1914), p. 1.

[21] For the case of Argentina, see Tato, "El llamado de la patria," pp. 276–81.

Caribbean.[22] In addition, the Panamanian government allowed the British to recruit around 3,000 men from the British West Indies, who lived on Panamanian territory. It also guaranteed that future veterans could return up to one year after the end of the war without having to prove they were in possession of a certain sum of money (which was otherwise obligatory).[23] Although these recruitment campaigns in neutral countries conflicted with rules of international law, as Chilean lawyer Galvarino Gallardo Nieto observed in hindsight, this did not detract from their success.[24] A special case was the small group of Jewish Argentines who volunteered for the British Jewish Legion in the context of the Balfour Declaration and, from 1917, fought in the Ottoman Empire.[25]

The starting point of the French who had immigrated to Latin America seems to have resembled that of the British. They, too, were quantitatively manageable communities, and the patriotic enthusiasm of the French in Buenos Aires, for example, could be seen everywhere. Those who lacked the requisite zeal were pressured by their French employers, who often put up the funds for the cost of the crossing. Those who stayed behind in La Plata founded aid organizations for the families of the men who had answered the call to arms.[26] There were clearly refusals as well, as the research of Hernán Otero has recently shown. Nevertheless, of all the foreign communities in the Argentine capital, the French would mourn the most war casualties.[27] Moreover, due to the marked Francophilia in almost all Latin American countries, a great number of volunteers was willing to fight for France. This included, for instance the famous Argentine flying ace Vicente Almandos Almonacid.[28] The government in Paris did not simply accept all comers, however. For example, the 200 Haitians who spontaneously reported in Port-au-Prince in 1914 to defend the former mother country were turned down with the explanation that President Oreste Zamor still had to pay the island's outstanding debts before they could enjoy the honor of wearing a French uniform.[29]

---

[22] Bras. Embassy to MRE (London, November 18, 1914), in: AHI, Directoria Geral dos Negocios Políticos e Diplomáticos.

[23] Garay, *Panamá*, p. 86.

[24] Gallardo Nieto, *Panamericanismo*, p. 231.

[25] For more on this, see Doron, *Legionarios de Argentina*.

[26] "Comité patriótico francés," in: *Caras y Caretas* (November 21, 1914).

[27] Otero, *La guerra en la sangre*, pp. 114–5 and 157. Sux, *Las voluntarios de la libertad*.

[28] Ribas, "Desde Paris: un aviador argentino en la guerra." See also Díaz Araujo, *Yrigoyen y la Guerra*, p. 215. Compagnon, *L'adieu à L'Europe*, pp. 84–8.

[29] Smith, *Jamaican Volunteers*, p. 37.

The diplomatic representatives of the German Empire were as busy as those of the Allies. Especially early on, conscripts of the German Empire and volunteers of German descent assembled above all in the heart of German settlement areas in Argentina, South Brazil, Chile, and Paraguay. These recruits who wanted to go straight to the front already crossed paths with the conscripts of their enemy on the way to the meeting places or at the latest in the port cities. In such encounters, dustups often went beyond the mere exchange of verbal abuse.[30] The large number of conscripts presented a particular challenge for the consulate in Buenos Aires, since they could not all be deployed on short notice. Up until October 1914, volunteers from the Río de la Plata reached the territory of the Central Powers by way of Italy. Thereafter, the Royal Navy also took control of Italian vessels, thus effectively blocking the way. In the cities, unemployed German men started to congregate. The efforts German associations made to relieve the situation had only limited success.[31]

From the perspective of the Germans, Italy's entry into the war on the side of the Allies on May 23, 1915, intensified the situation. Italian emigrants were especially well represented in the Río de la Plata and in southern Brazil, and the declaration of war inspired among them great patriotic fervor.[32] In Argentina above all, the Italian government maintained recruitment agencies that were especially successful at the outset.[33] Over time, however, the excitement gradually subsided and the conscription outcomes proved disappointing. Italian companies and institutions, such as the Italian Hospital in Buenos Aires, threatened to summarily dismiss any employee who did not report for duty. The German side also had to resort to similar measures.[34]

---

[30] A lively report was provided by German-Paraguayan Ernesto Gedult von Jungenfeld, *Aus den Urwäldern Paraguays*, pp. 51–3. On the voluntary registration of Brazilians of German descent, see Bonow, *A desconfiança*, pp. 98–9. Among them was also the occasional Latin American of non-German origin such as Venezuelan Rafael de Nogales, who originally intended to fight on the Belgian or French side, only to then take up arms with the German-Turkish side and serve in Arabia. Nogales, *Cuatro años*.

[31] Newton, *German Buenos Aires*, pp. 38–9. "O ministro allemão reune a colonia no Club Germania," in: *Correio da Manhã* (August 5, 1914), p. 4. Even in states with a small German community like Ecuador, mobilization efforts were in full swing: "Aviso a los alemanes," in: *El Comercio* (Quito, August 5, 1914), p. 4.

[32] "El patriotismo de los italianos," in: *Caras y Caretas* (June 5, 1915).

[33] Bonow, *A desconfiança*, p. 162. On Argentina, see also Tato, "El llamado de la patria," pp. 282–6.

[34] "Report on foreign and domestic propaganda in the Argentine Republic [...]" (April 9, 1918), NA, RG 165, MID 2327-L-1. Devoto, *Historia de los italianos*, pp. 318–21. Franzina, "La guerra lontana," pp. 64–77.

Patriotic parades on national holidays such as Bismarck's birthday or July 14, with the public singing of the national anthem, flag raising, and fundraising, repeatedly evoked the war at a time when Latin Americans had become more or less accustomed to events in distant Europe. Such methods were not effective in achieving larger mobilizations, however. This was the case even after Portugal's entry into the war in March 1916, which temporarily aroused tempers in Brazil. Among emigrants, the willingness to sacrifice proved rather limited after the initial euphoria, primarily to members of the middle class.[35]

The activities of the national minorities certainly had the potential to put the neutrality of the Latin American countries into question. That said, the fate of Latin Americans residing in Europe at the outbreak of the war also was not unproblematic. The consulates reported on foreign nationals who wanted to return to their home countries as soon as possible. One example concerned the estimated 5,000 Chileans, 10 percent of whom turned to their country's delegations for assistance. They had been imprisoned in England because of their German descent or were forcibly recruited elsewhere because of their ancestry.[36] In view of the advancing German armies in August 1914, many Latin Americans fled Paris in panic. Many moved temporarily to Spain, only to return shortly thereafter in 1915. Others stuck it out in Paris and served as war correspondents.[37] Still others reported for duty as volunteers and sacrificed their lives in the defense of France. Here, it was not only military men who signed up, but also in part more or less well-known intellectuals such as Peruvian José García Calderón, brother of the diplomat and writer Ventura, or Colombian Hernando de Bengoechea. On the whole, the originally comparatively high total number of Latin Americans in Paris declined greatly during the First World War.[38]

Due to the mass mobilizations in Europe, the numbers of conscripts and volunteers from Latin America were as slight as the number of Latin Americans who returned to their home countries. Nonetheless, they

---

[35] "Portugal na Guerra das Nações," in: *A Epoca* (March 15, 1916), p. 1. "Aufruf an die Deutschen in Argentinien," in: *Deutsche La Plata Zeitung* (August 8, 1914), p. 3. See also Cuenca, *La colonia británica*, pp. 2457. Bonow, *A desconfiança*, p. 163.

[36] Couyoumdjian/Múñoz, "Chilenos en Europa," p. 41. See also the depictions of Chilean student Eduardo Donoso, *Impresiones*. In Germany, Ecuadorians with English-sounding surnames were also detained: Ecuadorian General Consulate to MRREE (Hamburg, January 30, 1915), in: Ecuador, AMRREE, D.1.9.

[37] Thus, for example, "Un militar peruano," in: *La Crónica* (March 12, 1915), p. 1.

[38] Streckert, *Die Hauptstadt Lateinamerikas*, pp. 43–7. See also MRREE to War Department (Quito, June 8, 1915), Ecuador, AMRREE, I.1.10.1.

acted as witnesses and could report on their experiences. More directly affected from the start, by contrast, were the colonial possessions of warring European allies Britain and France in the Caribbean, Central America, and northern South America inasmuch as the dependent territories came into consideration as potential human repositories for the European battlefields. In fact, the imperial war rhetoric – according to which the fight against the Central Powers was a struggle for freedom – fell on fertile soil in the colonies. In response to the appeals made in the newspapers, which were largely directed at white landowners, many Afro-Caribbean men in Jamaica, for instance, came forward in both the cities and the countryside. Powerful motifs included the romantic masculine ideal of the self-sacrificing war-time volunteer, as well as the bond with the mother country and the monarch. At the same time, there was a strong desire to achieve participation by making a contribution to the war effort. Rumors of a supposedly imminent German invasion – fueled by certain sensation-mongering journalists – lent credence to a threat scenario that was taken at face value in many locations in the Caribbean. This even led to the internment of suspicious persons with German or German-sounding surnames.[39]

Despite the widespread anxiety, the Powers did not immediately institute a comprehensive recruitment program in their Caribbean colonies. Indeed, it was not until October 1915 that a regiment 15,000 men strong from the British West Indies was set up for deployment in Africa, the Middle East, Italy, and France.[40] This force consisted mainly of labor battalions, whose members contributed auxiliary services at lower wages and had to endure multiple forms of discrimination. In the jargon of the era, those who were "not of unmixed European blood" could not be promoted to become an officer in the British Army.[41] The French Caribbean also dispatched a contingent of 20,000 men to the European theater of war. Certainly, the segregation in the French Army was not as severe, yet there were also racially motivated disputes.[42]

Recruitment took place in immediate proximity to neutral Latin American states and had repercussions on the local communities. For instance, in 1916, Gallardo realized that the novelty of a global war also

---

[39] Smith, *Jamaican Volunteers*, pp. 4 and 38.
[40] On the reasons for the reluctance of the British, see Howe, *Race, War and Nationalism*, pp. 29–40.
[41] Quoted in Randall/Mount, *The Caribbean Basin*, p. 55. Howe, "West Indian Blacks," pp. 30–5.
[42] Fogarty, *Race and War in France*, pp. 95 and 298.

meant that a country's neutrality would have to take on a new form as well. To his thinking, the previously passive interpretation of neutrality needed to be replaced by an active one, for otherwise the belligerent nations would simply carry out their conflict in the neutral states in the guise of an economic and trade war.[43] As a consequence, it could hardly be said that Latin American countries remained passive toward the political challenge of the war in Europe. Already in 1914, for example, Chile and Argentina turned to the Pan-American Union in Washington, DC, to discuss the problems of neutrality. The Argentine ambassador to the United States proposed creating a commission, and the Ecuadorian government suggested that any encroachment of the neutral American territorial waters should be deemed an assault against all the American states and collectively avenged. While the Peruvian and the Brazilian governments concurred with this view, U.S. foreign minister William J. Bryan interjected that such a broad measure could take effect only after the war, for it stood to benefit at that point in time one side more than the other.[44] Venezuela subsequently proposed a resolution at the end of 1914 concerning a conference of neutrals, which eventually lost its impetus, however.[45] In 1915/16, the project of a league of neutrals was further discussed within a Pan-American framework. President Wilson strove for a treaty with all American states, which would guarantee political independence and territorial integrity, peaceful dispute settlements, and the non-recognition of revolutions. The common defense of neutrality, for which some Latin American countries had been pressing since 1914, was not contained in the proposal. The governments of Chile and El Salvador rejected these ideas in any case because they feared territorial claims from their neighbors.[46]

A form of international cooperation was initiated at first only within a smaller sub-regional framework. On May 25, 1915, Argentina, Brazil, and Chile, the three states participating in brokering the U.S.–Mexican conflict, concluded the so-called ABC Pact, which provided for compulsory arbitration by neutral commissions.[47] While the focus in May

---

[43] Gallardo, *Panamericanismo*, p. 203.

[44] Garay, *Panamá*, pp. 26–8. Compagnon, *L'adieu à l'Europe*, pp. 59–61.

[45] Delegation to MRREE (Caracas, November 26, 1914), in: Solveira, *Argentina*, Vol. 1, pp. 6–8.

[46] "Frente a la nota británica," in: *La Nación* (B. A., January 12, 1915), p. 7. Brit. embassy to Foreign Office (Washington, DC, February 25, 1916), in: *BD*, Part II, Series D, Vol. 2, p. 159. Gallardo, "Posición internacional de Chile," p. LXIX.

[47] British ambassador to the Foreign Office (Rio de Janeiro, April 26, 1915), BD, Vol. 1, pp 31. Guerrero, *Las conferencias del Niagara Falls*, p. 155. Yankelevich, *La diplomacia imaginaria*, pp. 91–114. See also Small, *The Forgotten Peace*. Ulloa, *La lucha revolucionaria*, pp. 212–24.

1914 was still on a method of peaceful dispute resolution that expressed Latin America's self-confidence via-à-vis the United States, the intention changed with the outbreak of war in Europe. The agreement aimed to secure the peace, but also to strengthen the neutral states' rights both in the Europeans' war and against the hegemonic claims of the United States. Consistent with the typical racist thinking of the time, Argentine diplomat Carlos Becú argued that the centers of the "white man" in Argentina, Chile, and Uruguay (although not involved in the agreement), along with Brazil (which may have been struggling still with the evil influences of the tropics, but supposedly had enough white elements to become a major power) were now apparently "blood brothers" who could collectively pursue their "own Monroeism."[48] The American continent would accordingly prove itself a model in contrast to bellicose Europe.[49]

However, criticism of the treaty was heard immediately from the non-participating Latin American countries. Uruguay thus rejected the associated claim to supremacy of the three neighbors. The Ecuadorian and the Peruvian press actually spoke of "megalomania," and the Bolivians wanted to oppose to it a kind of Andean Pact.[50] The treaty could not even reach majority support from within, for the Chilean and Argentinean parliaments failed to ratify it. The ABC Pact thus finally went nowhere.[51] Foreign-policy independence or even emancipation from the hegemony of the United States were not realistically to be achieved with this pact.

Neither U.S.-influenced Pan-Americanism, nor cooperation among the Latin American countries themselves gave rise to a mutual political stance with regard to the war or even to plans for a collective defense against attacks on neutrality and sovereignty in the course of combat operations. The political elites were well aware that one could not simply stand on the sidelines in this war given its new international dimensions. In a confidential memorandum of the Chilean Ministry of Foreign Affairs to its foreign delegations, it was pointed out that the war had put Latin America into a difficult spot, since the interests of the belligerent powers were not limited to Europe, but had rather global scale.[52] The truth

---

[48] Becú, *El A.B.C.*, pp. 11, 18–9, and 25.
[49] "La opinión americana sobre el A.B.C.," in: *La Prensa* (B. A., November 24, 1915), p. 3.
[50] Yankelevich, *La diplomacia imaginaria*, p. 121.
[51] "Tratado de solução pacífica de controvérsias entre o ABC (May 25, 1915)," in: Garcia, *Diplomacia brasileira*, pp. 376–8. See also: Ulloa, *La lucha revolucionaria*, pp. 227–51.
[52] MRREE, Circular confidencial No. 2 (Santiago de Chile, August 29, 1914), Chile, AMRREE, Vol. 479.

of this statement was already noticeable in the first months of the war, as the naval war brought the conflict to Latin American waters. Most Latin American countries were overwhelmed with the task of effectively policing their coastlines and ensuring that the belligerent powers did not violate their sovereign territory.[53]

At the Río de la Plata, the German military attaché had the passenger ship *Cap Trafalgar* of the Hamburg-Süd shipping line promptly converted into an auxiliary cruiser in August 1914. In September, a spectacular naval battle took place with an English auxiliary cruiser, which ended with the sinking of the German ship. The surviving crew members were detained on the island of Martín García in the Río de la Plata.[54] The use of a civilian ship lying in the neutral port for military purposes violated the neutrality rules and provoked protests from the Allies. The Brazilian government issued implementation provisions: Henceforth a written statement from the competent consul would need to be presented, confirming that a departure was for commercial purposes only.[55]

These requirements came too late, however, as the naval war in the South Atlantic had already assumed larger dimensions. Due to the Japanese declaration of war and the resulting loss of the Chinese supply station Tsingtau, the German East Asia Squadron under Vice-Admiral Graf Maximilian von Spee diverted its course across the Pacific and into the neutral waters of South America. Japanese and British warships also patrolled there, however.[56] Germans supplied themselves on Easter Island and at the Más Afuera, both Chilean possessions.[57] This unit met up with the light cruiser *Dresden*, which had been stationed along the Mexican Caribbean coast for the protection of nationals. It had also transported General Huerta of Mexico into exile in Jamaica at the end of July 1914. Finally the light cruiser *Leipzig*, originally stationed on the Pacific coast, joined the unit.[58] On November 1, the Germans were victorious in the Battle of Coronel against British warships off the Chilean

---

[53] Many cases had been reported on in the contemporary literature. See, e.g., Garay, *Panamá*, pp. 7–9.

[54] Newton, *German Buenos Aires*, p. 41.

[55] British ambassador to the Foreign Office (Rio de Janeiro, April 23, 1915), in: *BD*, Vol. 1, pp. 24–5.

[56] "La repercusión de la guerra," in: *Variedades* (Lima, December 26, 1914).

[57] This led to protests by the Chilean government: MRREE to the German delegation (Santiago de Chile, December 16, 1914), Chile, AMRREE, Vol. 471.

[58] The *Leipzig* obtained provisions on the Galapagos Islands, which led to protests by the Allies in Quito. "¿Buenos oficios," in: *El Comercio* (Quito, November 22, 1914), p. 1. Martin, *Latin America*, pp. 445–6. See also the correspondence with the German ambassador in Ecuador, AMRREE, B.1.2.

coastline, which the propaganda subsequently celebrated in grand style. The German warships then cruised into the port of Valparaíso. This gave rise to problems with the Chilean government, for the German units were supplied there with fuel and intelligence by the moored merchant ships of the Hamburger Cosmos line.[59] The Germans' behavior, along with the provisioning on the islands, was in violation of the neutrality conditions, which prohibited assistance to belligerent nations in neutral ports. In December 1914, the Chilean government thus decided to ban the release of large amounts of coal to vessels whose shipping companies impinged on these provisions.[60]

At first, though, the situation seemed to deescalate from the Chilean perspective. The German squadron, which had occasionally crippled British merchant shipping in the Pacific, was slowly making its way home via Cape Horn in the South Atlantic. When trying to destroy the British radio station in the Falkland Islands and to deploy German and German-born volunteers to the islands, Graf Spee blundered into a trap and superior hostile formations forced his hand. The conflict ended on December 8, 1914, in a devastating defeat for the Germans.[61] Only the *Dresden* managed to escape. In the weeks that followed, the ship – which was supported by German intelligence and German-born Chileans and had also reloaded with coal in the Chilean Punta Arenas – would inflict Allied merchant ships with several losses and continue to lurk for a while in Patagonian waters. Cut off from any supplies, the commander found himself faced with superior British forces in the Juan Fernández Islands on March 15, 1915, and ordered his own crew to sink the ship. The sailors were interned for the rest of the war on the Chilean island of Quiriquina.[62]

Because the military action had taken place in Chilean waters, the Chilean government complained in London – not least due to pressure from pro-German circles in the military – with a diplomatic memorandum on the violation of national sovereignty. However, the petition was dismissed with reference to the threat that the *Dresden* had posed. The

[59] "Los buques alemanes en Valparaíso," in: *Zig-Zag* (November 7, 1914). Leipold, *Die deutsche Seekriegsführung im Pazifik*, pp. 323–98. From the perspective of a marine commander, see Schönberg, *Vom Auslandsdienst in Mexiko*, pp. 133–74. See also Lascano, *Graf von Spee*, pp. 43–132. Fermandois, *Mundo y fin de mundo*, p. 78.

[60] Bravo, *La Primera Guerra Mundial*, pp. 69–71.

[61] "El combate naval de las islas Falkland," in: *Zig-Zag* (December 12, 1914). Strachan, *To Arms*, pp. 475–80. Leipold, *Die deutsche Seekriegsführung im Pazifik*, pp. 399–448.

[62] Strachan, *To Arms*, pp. 71–87. Leipold, *Die deutsche Seekriegsführung im Pazifik*, pp. 449–84.

ramifications in this instance were just as lacking as a few days earlier, when the illegality of the vessel's stay in front of the Juan Fernández Islands had been pointed out to the imperial government. These episodes demonstrated that the rights of neutrals did not figure into the warring powers' decision making. At least from the perspective of the government in Santiago with the loss of the German ships a dangerous source of friction at its very doorstep had evaporated. That said, the treatment of internees and the repeated escape attempts were to lead to diplomatic wrangling with the Allies in the future.[63]

With the elimination of the Pacific squadron, the Central Powers no longer had an opportunity to break through the Allied naval blockade in the South Atlantic. Using commercial or passenger ships as auxiliary cruisers or suppliers, which was common during the first months of the war, therefore made no sense. Consequently, the German merchant ships in the region allowed themselves to be detained in Latin American ports in order to avoid capture by the Allies. The issue of the use of the interned ships in Argentine, Brazilian, and Chilean ports, however, thrust a new source of conflict to the forefront. These ships represented considerable economic value and they acquired increasing importance due to the general lack of shipping space and the increase in cargo rates. The Allied objective was to induce the Latin American governments through diplomatic and economic pressure to confiscate the German merchant ships. Due to the naval blockade, the additional tonnage could only benefit the governments, either directly or indirectly. In the course of 1916, government representatives of Argentina, Brazil, and Chile expressed their interest to the German shipping companies and envoys in chartering the detained ships, while at the same time the threat of confiscation loomed over a possible refusal. The German leadership, however, succeeded time and again in putting off a decision.[64] At this juncture, no Latin American government was finally willing to face the consequences of an expropriation, which meant a break with Germany.[65]

In fact, the handling of ships in Latin American ports from belligerent nations remained a major sticking point. The inherent difficulties were made plain in November 1915, when British naval units captured the

---

[63] Dehne, "Britain's Global War." For instance, Lieutenant Wilhelm Canaris, who later became chief of the German counterespionage, managed to escape in August 1915.

[64] Thus, for example, in the case of negotiations with Brazil. Vinhosa, *O Brasil e a Primeira Guerra Mundial*, p. 47.

[65] See here the correspondence between the naval staff and the AA: BA, AA, 6685, the naval staff to AA (August 19, 1916); ibid., AA to Naval Staff (August 26, 1916).

Presidente Mitre, which had been sailing with a German-born crew on behalf of a German-Argentine company under the Argentine flag since before the war. The ship was only later returned following objections from Buenos Aires and under certain stipulations.[66] Again and again, the diplomatic representatives of the warring parties contended that the enemy's ships had received preferential treatment.[67] The Latin American governments responded to the numerous complaints of the respective diplomatic representations by referring to their interpretation of applicable law. Since issues like the length of stay of ships of belligerent states were ultimately legal gray areas, the European powers were nonetheless able to push through their positions by applying diplomatic pressure. The Allies had the upper hand in cases of doubt due to their control of the sea lanes.[68]

Ultimately, even the German measure against the blockade – unrestricted submarine warfare – did not change anything in this regard. The trade war with submarines was one of the new forms of warfare not regulated by the Declaration of London and it massively threatened the trade and maritime navigation of the neutrals.[69]

The controversial German retaliatory action of February 4, 1915, was heavily criticized in Latin America. After all, the German leadership had taken it upon itself to sink merchant ships without warning in its self-defined blockade area around the British Isles and Ireland and the English Channel. The imperial leadership had cautioned that this could also befall neutral ships in the case of mistaken identity. The timing of the declaration was hardly random as the shipment of the Argentine wheat harvest to Great Britain was slated for February.[70] The sinking of the *Lusitania*

---

[66] "Honi soit qui mal y pense," in: *Caras y Caretas* (December 11, 1915). "El vapor Presidente Mitre," in: *La Prensa* (B. A., November 30, 1915), p. 3. Díaz Araujo, *Yrigoyen y la Guerra*, pp. 21–3.

[67] See, for example, the complaint of the German ambassador in Montevideo to the Foreign Office on September 21, 1914, in: "Informes diplomáticos," pp. 181–2. German embassy to Uruguayan MRREE (Montevideo, November 30, 1914), Uruguay, AGN, PGM, MRREE, Caja 724. See also the Argentine records: *Memoria de relaciones exteriores, 1915–16*, p. VIII.

[68] MRREE to the German Ambassador (Bogotá, September 14, 1915), Colombia, AGN, MRREE, 00556, Trasf. 1, fol. 65.

[69] The Latin American press had already participated in these discussions early on. "Ao Redor da Guerra. Uso e abuso das minas submarinas," in: *Jornal do Commercio* (November 1, 1914), p. 3.

[70] "Ecos del día," in: *La Nación* (B. A., February 6, 1915), p. 8. "La lucha en los mares," in: ibid. (February 8, 1915), p. 6. "Ante el bloqueo," in ibid. (February 13, 1915), p. 7. For more context, see Hardach, *Der Erste Weltkrieg*, pp. 47–8.

on May 7, 1915, by a German submarine caused fierce indignation in
Latin America, not least because many of the dead were women and children.[71] The ensuing exchange of diplomatic notes between Washington
and Berlin was followed by the respective publics in Latin America with
rapt attention. There was a collective sigh of relief when U-boat warfare
was again provisionally restricted in September.

A year later, a purportedly Latin American ship was attacked for the
first time by German U-boats. On May 2, 1916, the steamer *Rio Branco*
was sunk. This event occurred in the context of the re-intensified submarine warfare under German naval command, which provided for the
sinking of armed merchant ships without warning. In Brazil, this ignited
a storm of indignation. However, it soon came to light that the *Rio
Branco* had been sold to Norway in November of the previous year and
was then chartered and armed by the British. The ship unlawfully flew
the Brazilian flag and, what is more, was carrying contraband.[72] For this
reason, the Brazilian government decided to not lodge an official protest.
In May 1916, the German Empire again curbed its use of submarine warfare under pressure from the United States following the sinking of the
passenger ship *Sussex*. The reactions from the public show that the topic
of submarine warfare was highly explosive and threatened the neutrality
of the Latin American countries.[73]

The German war effort was not only a constant stumbling block in
Latin America because of Germany's use of U-boats. Latin American foreign ministries were also already intensely debating the invasion of neutral Belgium. Belgian national Remy Himmer, who served as vice-consul
of Argentina, fell at the Massacre of Dinant in August 1914. Once his
fate became public, it consumed the Argentine press in November and
December.[74] The Foreign Ministry in Buenos Aires, however, finally ruled
out making a formal diplomatic protest.[75]

Germany's "global strategy," wherein Berlin wanted to confront
the British in their empire, was also supposed to bring the war to the
"informal empire," Latin America.[76] This approach assumed different

---

[71] "La catástrofe del Lusitania," in: *Caras y Caretas* (May 15, 1915). "El hundimiento del
Lusitania," in: *Zig-Zag* (May 15, 1915).

[72] "O Torpedeamento do Rio Branco," in: *Jornal do Commercio* (May 5, 1916), p. 2.
Vinhosa, *O Brasil e a Primeira Guerra Mundial*, p. 104.

[73] Martin, *Latin America and the War*, pp. 47–9. Hardach, *Der Erste Weltkrieg*, pp. 49–50.

[74] See the summary in Compagnon, *L'adieu à L'Europe*, p. 43.

[75] Solveira, *Argentina y la Primera Guerra Mundial*, pp. 55–101. See also the correspondence in Argentina, AMRREE, AH/00037/1.

[76] Strachan (*To Arms*, p. 694), which works out the strategy of the Reich, does not look at
the role of Latin America.

forms. The outbreak of war initiated a flurry of activity among German agents in the Americas. Numerous rumors of more or less utopian projects were in circulation, ranging from the recruitment of ethnic Germans in Chile for the campaign in the German colonies in Africa to the sabotage of the Panama Canal, but none of them was ever implemented.[77] More immediately, it was possible to pursue the idea of stoking the potential for social unrest in the colonies. Strategists therefore weighed the possibility of inciting riots in Jamaica.[78] The German efforts to encourage the uprising against the British in India are well known. These activities had an American dimension, for there was also talk about creating a Hindu republic in Trinidad and Tobago or in British Guiana, where many emigrants from India already resided.[79]

In addition to Germany's strategic maneuvering against the British Empire, the German war effort was also intent on tying up the United States in Latin America. Here, the primary setting was Mexico, where the German Empire had been conducting a secret war since 1910 that involved diplomats, agents, and even citizens of other European countries, and the United States. Mexico was of special interest for a number of reasons: first, because of its geographical proximity to the United States; second, because of the strategic importance of the Mexican oil wells; and, third, due to the uncertain political situation surrounding the revolutionary civil war. As historian Friedrich Katz has shown, the German national leadership made it a priority to promote the already-existing U.S.–Mexican tensions. With the provocation of a military engagement in Mexico, German officials wanted to divert U.S. President Wilson's attention from the European theater of war, halt the arms supplies to the Allies, and reduce the risk that the United States would enter the war on the side of the Allies.[80]

The Germans coordinated their intelligence work in Mexico from their embassy in Washington. They initially pursued the plan of bringing Huerta back from Spanish exile and then putting him back into power by means of a coup. Berlin rightly speculated that this would seriously undermine U.S.–Mexican relations. The plan failed because Huerta was arrested in transit by the U.S. Secret Service. The Mexican died in a prison in Texas in 1916.[81] Also connected with the intended overthrow was the

---

[77] Schuler attaches great importance to these plans, but cannot prove they existed. *Secret Wars*, pp. 96–7.

[78] Ibid., p. 97.

[79] Ibid., pp. 136–9.

[80] Katz, *The Secret War*.

[81] Ibid., pp. 364. Schuler, *Secret Wars*, pp. 112–3. Durán, *Guerra y revolución*, pp. 206–7.

so-called Plan of San Diego – a small town in Texas – from January 6, 1915. The document, whose authors are not known, called on Latinos, African Americans, and Asians to rebel in the former Mexican territories in the southwestern United States in order to establish an independent republic, which would then probably join Mexico. As part of this uprising – deliberately designated a "race war" – all "white" Anglo Americans over sixteen years of age were to be summarily executed. Indeed, from 1915 to 1917 there was a noticeable increase in the number of armed attacks in the region. To retaliate, a Law and Order League was organized that carried out lynchings of Mexican-born Americans. The U.S. tabloids variously attributed the attacks to the machinations of Germans and Mexicans. However, the extent to which the German secret service supported or, for that matter, was responsible for the Plan of San Diego is uncertain.[82]

The United States' officials were also in the dark. Secretary of State Robert Lansing stated in a personal memorandum from October 1915 that it appeared as though Germany was supporting all the revolutionary factions in Mexico with the aim of fomenting civil war and thereby weakening the United States.[83] At the beginning of 1916, the intelligence apparatus of the U.S. Navy stated that German meddling in Latin America had already led to numerous crises before the war. The polemics in the German press against the Monroe Doctrine, the pressure of the Reich government on the highly indebted Haiti, and the construction of wireless stations in the Caribbean were therefore the direct precursors to the aggressive Mexican policy.[84] To be sure, by the end of 1915, the German side sought a new ally in Mexico and found him in Carranza. The Mexican was interested in a limited cooperation with the German Empire against Mexico's powerful neighbor to the north. Toward this end, Carranza found that both Germany and Japan came into question. Yet, since the Japanese were only interested in the sale of arms and were otherwise focused on expansion in China, the German government proved the more attractive partner.[85]

---

[82] For the text of the Plan of San Diego, see: Mintz, *Mexican American Voices*, pp. 122–4. Johnson, *Revolution in Texas*, pp. 71–107. Lomnitz, *The Return of Comrade Ricardo Flores Magón*, pp. 450–1.

[83] Lansing, "Private Memorandum" (October 10, 1915), LC, Lansing Papers, Reel 1.

[84] Office of Naval Intelligence, "Foreign Relations Policies and Affecting the United States" (January 20, 1916), NA, RG 165, WCD, 9140-14, pp. 3–4.

[85] Katz, *The Secret War*, pp. 345–50. British intelligence had already concluded in 1916 that Carranza was acting in league with the Germans. Meyer, *Su majestad británica*, p. 243.

The correlation between the German and Mexican opposition to the United States became clear, on one hand, when Washington and Berlin stood on the edge of a war due to the U-boat question in 1915/16 and, on the other, when Mexico had turned into a flash point at the beginning of 1916. On March 9, 1916, Carranza's adversary and revolutionary leader of the north, Francisco "Pancho" Villa, attacked the U.S. border town of Columbus, New Mexico. The battle, which resulted in heavy causalities, gave rise to a punitive expedition under General John J. Pershing, who hunted Villa for nearly a year until February 1917. The condemnation of the punitive expedition was widely shared by otherwise opposing revolutionary factions, and hostile attacks against the policy of the United States in the Mexican press became the rule.[86] Numerous skirmishes took place, with the Battle of Carrizal on June 1916 between Pershing and Carranza's government forces proving especially important. Without an official declaration of war, a new low point had nevertheless been reached in U.S.–Mexican relations. Though the threat of war was palpable, in the end it was simply Wilson's concern about the developments in Europe that prevented the United States from formally taking up arms against Mexico. The events of 1916 reinforced the U.S. government's belief that there was a direct link between the problems in Mexico and the events in Europe. Germany was seen as a troublemaker.[87] Other countries in the region shared this impression, as press reports from South America show.[88]

This opinion was not entirely unjustified. Carranza actually sought closer collaboration with the Germans in the course of 1916, as another counterweight to the United States had not been forthcoming since the outbreak of the war. Despite its substantial oil interests in Mexico, Great Britain could ill afford the risk of pursuing its own policy given its dependency on supply shipments from the United States. The same was true for France.[89] Carranza and the German envoy met for talks at the end of the year. The head of state offered a new trade agreement that was advantageous for the German Empire and a submarine base. He asked in

---

[86] Gonzalo de la Parra, "Los cerdos que comercian con cerdos han ultrajado a mi patria," in: *El Nacional* (June 19, 1916), p. 1. See also Katz, *The Secret War*, pp. 303–14.

[87] Yankelevich, *La diplomacia imaginaria*, p. 142. Ulloa, *La lucha revolucionaria*, pp. 287–318. On the significance of the Mexican experience for Wilson's thinking on an intervention, see Knock, *To End All Wars*, pp. 24–30.

[88] See, for example, the comments of the correspondent for the Paraguayan *La Tribuna*, Pedro Sayé: Sayé, *Crema de menta*, pp. 129–34.

[89] Meyer, *Su majestad británica*, pp. 181–2. Durán, *Guerra y revolución*, pp. 171–88. Py, *Francia y la Revolución Mexicana*.

return for the deployment of German military instructors, experts for the construction of a munitions factory, and the supply of submarines and wireless stations.[90] As Berlin was still hoping to keep the United States neutral, the envoy remained noncommittal. This posture would change a few months later, however.[91] Carranza's overtures stemmed from his fear of an escalation of the conflict with the United States. The more or less known coup plots against him only added to his feeling of insecurity. Carranza's pro-German policy was thus quite understandable. Moreover, because it played well with the coup-ready, pro-German military, it had a stabilizing influence domestically.[92]

Mexico was not the only trouble spot where the interests of Europeans, the United States, and the affected countries clashed during the world war. With a view to Latin America, the conflict in Europe paved the way for unanticipated opportunities for the United States. Before the war, Washington had already firmly established itself as a protecting power and police force in both political and military terms, especially in Central America and the Caribbean. The strategic interest of the United States in its so-called backyard only increased with the opening of the Panama Canal on August 15, 1914. Arguing that it needed to protect the channel from encroachments by the warring parties and in light of the war-related absence of the Europeans, the United States could now assert its claim as a hegemonic power throughout the Western Hemisphere more openly and aggressively than ever. This was all the more vital when diplomatic relations with the German Empire reached a crisis in 1916.[93] The United States, for instance, occupied the Dominican Republic in 1916, where it established a military government and maintained a presence until 1924. Cuba, where the intervention began in 1917, and Nicaragua, which the United States had already invaded in 1912, also remained under U.S. control until 1922 and 1925, respectively. In these states, though, at least sovereignty de jure was preserved, in contrast to the Dominican Republic. In 1916, through the ratification of the Bryan-Chamorro Treaty, Washington secured exclusive rights in Nicaragua to build an inter-oceanic canal, along with the right to intervene in the case of internal disturbances and naval bases, inter alia, in the Gulf of Fonseca.

[90] Katz, *The Secret War in Mexico*, pp. 364–6.
[91] Meyer, *Su majestad británica*, pp. 245–6.
[92] Katz, *The Secret War*, p. 513.
[93] The objectives of U.S. policy are summarized in: Sec. of State Lansing to Woodrow Wilson (Washington, DC, November 24, 1915), NA, RG 59, M743, roll 1, pp. 70–3. See also Gilderhus, *Pan American Visions*, pp. 26–7.

In 1917, a few days before its entry into the war, the United States bought the then Danish Virgin Islands. President Wilson also tried by peaceful means and under U.S. leadership to expand on the economic and cultural relations of the Pan-American system, which had been loosely constituted since the 1890s.[94]

The first U.S. intervention after the outbreak of the world war occurred in 1915 in Haiti. Like Mexico, Haiti was located in the United States' immediate sphere of influence. And, also as in Mexico, the Americans feared that the small island state could fall under German control. Indeed, Haiti was viewed as having been greatly infiltrated and, what is more, with Môle St. Nicholas it offered a strategically located naval base overlooking the sea lanes to the Panama Canal.[95] In fact, traders from the German Empire had done a good deal of business in Haiti before the war.

This was also true for investors from France, which as a further competitor was also in the running for control of the country. Given the state's disintegration and its outstanding foreign debt, the German and French governments were able to exert considerable pressure on the country in 1914. True to the Roosevelt Corollary, U.S. foreign policy wanted to prevent Europe from increasing its influence in the Americas. The outbreak of war was therefore a very welcome turn of events for Washington. Now, the United States could pursue its own economic and military interests without concern for the Europeans. On July 28, 1915, the U.S. Marines invaded Haiti and would remain there until 1934.[96]

In addition to U.S. interventionism, war-related problems emerged for Latin American neutral states in another politically sensitive and militarily strategic area: wireless telegraphy. Shortly after the outbreak of war, the British Navy had severed the German transoceanic cable. Completely cut off from global news traffic, the German government sought to develop the new wireless telegraphy into a full-fledged replacement for cable and to break the news monopoly of the Entente. They thus pursued the goal of spreading German propaganda in the Americas, while also maintaining their communication ties with the German minorities there. This was the precise reason why the governments of the Allies urged Latin American countries to shut down their radio stations. They also

---

[94] Rinke, *América Latina y Estados Unidos*, pp. 121–3. Langley, *The Banana Wars*, pp. 49–160. Gonzalo, "Relaciones entre Estados Unidos y América Latina," pp. 181–242.
[95] On the rumors on German interests, see Smith, *Jamaican Volunteers*, p. 40.
[96] Renda, *Taking Haiti*, pp. 39–88. Schmidt, *The United States Occupation of Haiti*, pp. 42–81.

argued that the use of wireless telegraphy must be prohibited to all ships from warring nations anchoring in Latin American ports, for otherwise it would constitute a breach of neutrality.[97] Because of their maritime supremacy, the Allies could afford to dispense with the use of radio communication from neutral ports if necessary. The governments of the affected countries in Latin America responded by declaring the demanded prohibitions. However, in this modern sector that was hardly governed by any international agreements, there were frequently transgressions. Indeed, it was exceedingly difficult for the Latin American governments to effectively control where and how radio stations were operated on their territory. This was something the Allied diplomats also realized,[98] yet it did not dissuade them from protesting.[99]

At the same time, the center of transatlantic radio transmissions was not in Latin America, but in the United States. Of key importance were the Sayville and Tuckerton stations in Long Island and New Jersey, which the Telefunken-Gesellschaft had operated since 1912. They enabled communication between the Nauen Transmitter Station outside Berlin and the Western Hemisphere until the beginning of 1917. For transmissions between New York and the south, there had already existed a weaker Telefunken station in Cartagena, Colombia since 1912.[100] The agreement between the Colombian government and Telefunken stipulated that in cases of war or civil disturbance, the station could be used only under state supervision and control. The British legation concluded that this did not occur after the outbreak of the war because of a lack of adequate experts. As a result, in 1914, there was a temporary closure and the German technicians were dismissed. After the closure, however, the Colombians attempted to establish a new radio link via the United States in order to not have to rely on the Allies' cables for the transmissions of messages.[101] It was only when a Colombian expert was found who could take control of the Telefunken station that it could resume operations under censorship conditions.[102]

---

[97] Britische Gesandter an MRREE Costa Rica (Panamá, August 14, 1914), Costa Rica, ANCR, RREE, Caja 224:1.

[98] British envoy to the Foreign Office (Rio de Janeiro, April 23, 1915), in: *BD*, Vol. 1, pp. 25–6.

[99] On Colombia's confrontation with the English protests over this issue, see *Documentos relativos a la neutralidad*, pp. 3–21.

[100] *Informe del Ministerio de Relaciones Exteriores*, 1915, pp. 114–6.

[101] Colombian Ministry of Foreign Affairs to the legation in Washington (Bogotá, November 12, 1914), Colombia, AGN, MRREE, Caja 3, Carp. 19, Trasf. 5, pp. 10–4.

[102] MRREE to the English charge d'affaires (Bogotá, November 3, 1914), Colombia, AGN, MRREE, Caja 3, Carp. 19, Trasf. 5, pp. 10–4. MRREE to legation in Washington

Since the British protests persisted, the German envoy in Bogotá in 1914 recommended shutting down the station and waiving any claims for damages until the war was over. The Colombian government was happy to go along with the suggestion.[103] Following the closure of the station in Cartagena, which was in any case inadequate, German representatives looked for alternative solutions for its planned global radio network. According to the U.S. military attaché, Telefunken had already tried in vain in October 1914 to obtain a concession to build a wireless station in Guatemala.[104] The collaboration with the Netherlands proved more successful. As early as 1916, Telefunken erected stations in Java and in Dutch Guiana. After the U.S. government put Sayville and Tuckerton under the supervision of a censor in mid-1915, German interests took a highly active stance in Mexico via a U.S.-based front company. Telefunken aimed to expand the radio station that had been operated in Chapultepec since before the war. Mexico was to eventually become the new central switching point in the German radio network, which would comprise stations built in ten countries in Latin America alone. The Carranza government was keenly interested in this expansion, for it would make the country independent from the United States, whose news services had one-sidedly disseminated a negative image of the revolution. All the same, there were technical and financial problems. In addition to bridging 3,000 kilometers, the objective was to succeed in competition against English and American interests, who, just like the Germans, aimed for monopoly concessions to establish the new technology in Latin America. The German plans for a worldwide radio network could not be realized, however, until early 1917, not least due to technical difficulties.[105]

(Bogotá, November 12, 1914), Colombia, AGN, MRREE, Caja 3, Carp. 19, Trasf. 5, fol. 11–14.

[103] German legation to Colombian Ministry of Foreign Affairs (Bogotá, December 5, 1914), in: *Documentos relativos a la neutralidad*, pp. 27–9. On the British protests, see MRREE to the legation in Washington (Bogotá, December 1, 1914), Colombia, AGN, MRREE, Caja 139, Carp. 2, Trasf. 5, p. 108. Nervousness prevailed in the United States, which dispatched an expert at the end of 1915 to ascertain the existence of radio stations in the provinces near the Panama Canal. While he was officially commissioned by the Colombian government, he nonetheless reported directly to Washington. MRREE to Colombian envoy in Washington (Bogotá, December 3, 1915), Colombia, AGN, MRREE, Caja 3, Trasf. 5, fol. 2.

[104] U.S. military attaché (Guatemala, October 27, 1914), NA, RG 165, MID, 6370-26.

[105] Katz, *The Secret War*, pp. 417–9.

ECONOMIC THREATS

The greatest obstacle to Latin American neutrality existed less on the political than on the economic front. The war brought with it the collapse of the liberal world economy, which had shaped the period of globalization that began in the mid-nineteenth century. This had especially grave consequences for the countries of Latin America that depended on the world markets as exporters of raw materials.[106] Contemporary observers such as Chilean journalist Carlos Silva Vildósola therefore observed at the outbreak of the war that its effects needed to be taken seriously above all because Latin America had been dependent on European markets and capital since the nineteenth century.[107] The Brazilian envoy in London predicted already in mid-August 1914 that the war, however long it might last, would disrupt the world economy for decades to come and, by extension, also hit the Latin American economies hard.[108] In addition to the indirect repercussions of the war, the conflict's immediate impact had drastic economic consequences. It rapidly grew into a total war: The warring parties took the contest into the unprecedented territory of a global economic war, as they focused on the worldwide mobilization of all resources, including those in Latin America. What was economic development like under the conditions of a global war? And, more specifically, what effects did the economic war have on the region?

As early as 1912 and 1913, the reluctance of European investors to put their money in some countries such as Argentina and Brazil due to the Balkan crises had a noticeable dampening effect.[109] This uneasiness was eclipsed, however, in August 1914. The fear of the economic fallout of the war was a major reason for the mass rallies that took place in many cities in the first days. The dramatic news from Europe caused the general feeling of panic to spread. The collapse of commodity prices and lack of fuel led to the bottom falling out of business activity in a port city like Guayaquil in Ecuador.[110] The Argentine government responded to the acute crisis by implementing emergency measures, already decreeing bank holidays on August 3 to prevent a run. Furthermore, announcements

---

[106] On this topic, see also Dehne, "How Important Was Latin America," pp. 157–60.

[107] "El año financiero," in: *La Nación* (B. A. January 1, 1915), p. 7. Silva Vildósola, *Le Chili et la guerre*, p. 2.

[108] Bras. Legation to MRE (London, August 18, 1914), in: AHI, Directoria Geral dos Negocios Políticos e Diplomáticos.

[109] See, e.g., "Influencia nociva das noticias da guerra," in: *Correio da Manhã* (August 1, 1914), p. 1.

[110] "Crisis comercial en Guayaquil," in: *El Comercio* (Quito, August 7, 1914), p. 1.

were made regarding moratoriums on internal and external debt services and export restrictions, inter alia, on wheat.[111] Of the four South American countries investigated by Bill Albert, Brazil and Peru followed the Argentine example. Chile could do without it, although Santiago did declare a moratorium on gold payments.[112]

The moratoriums were also a response to the abrupt cessation of the capital inflows from Europe. Since their independence, Latin American governments had all more or less clung to the London Stock Exchange. In the course of the nineteenth century, direct and indirect investments also came from France and the German Empire.[113] In August 1914, however, it was suddenly no longer possible to issue new bonds. The warring governments canceled the pending loans and demanded their money back. The London Stock Exchange even shut down completely, only opening its doors again in January 1915 with severe restrictions.[114] The fact that the rescheduling of long-term government bonds was no longer possible was a painful reality that the Brazilian government had to accept.[115] Nonetheless, large debtor nations like Argentina and Brazil were hardly the only ones affected, for foreign capital was essential in all countries of the region. "All humanity constitutes a totality," commented *La Nación* in Buenos Aires on August 4. Indeed, from a financial perspective, "everyone was intertwined with everyone," which is what caused the paralysis brought on by the war to be all more acute.[116] Even in remote Paraguay, which had a relatively low degree of involvement in the world market, the economic effects of the war were felt immediately.[117]

What is more, the interruption of transport routes due to the British naval blockade led to a huge curtailment of trade relations with Europe. This was made painfully evident in the everyday economic life of Latin America. The ships for vital foreign trade did not come into port.[118] Immediately after the outbreak of war, German, Austrian, and French steamship lines at the La Plata canceled their service. In Buenos Aires'

[111] "Repercusion de la Guerra," in: *La Prensa* (B. A., August 4, 1914), p. 8. See also Weinmann, *Argentina en la Primera Guerra Mundial*, pp. 39–41.

[112] Gil Vidal, "Effeitos da guerra," in: *Correio da Manhã* (August 4, 1914), p. 2. "Os effeitos da conflagração européa no Brazil," in: ibid. (August 5, 1914), p. 1. "Os effeitos da conflagração européa no Brazil," in: *A Epoca* (August 13, 1914), p. 3. Albert, *South America and the First World War*, pp. 42–4.

[113] Rinke, *Historia de América Latina*, p. 112.

[114] Contreras, "La minería," p. 17.

[115] Compagnon, *L'adieu à L'Europe*, pp. 115–20.

[116] "Ecos del día," in: El momento financiero," in: *La Nación* (B. A., August 4, 1914), p. 8.

[117] "Ante la guerra," in: *El Diario* (August 4, 1914), p. 4.

[118] Albert, *South America and the First World War*, pp. 40–1.

harbor, for instance, an unusual silence took hold.[119] The German merchant ships, which had previously handled a large part of the trade of the neighboring states with Europe, took flight along the Pacific coast into neutral ports in order to avoid falling into the hands of the British. The absence of the German ships was quickly felt in a country like Venezuela, where trading houses from the Reich had played a central role.[120] The British again requisitioned numerous ships for military tasks. Besides this, there were restrictions that declared off limits the use of neutral European shipping capacity by war opponents.[121] The cargo room shortage would remain a serious problem until the end of the war.[122]

The impact on the foreign trade was initially catastrophic. Imports fell dramatically, variously due to the restrictions placed on exporters in Europe, the lack of shipping capacity, and the declining import capacity in Latin America. Domestic trade was hit hard overall. Even the few industrial companies that had formed, for instance, in some regions of Argentina, Brazil, and Chile suffered greatly because of the lack of raw materials, semi-finished goods, and capital from Europe. The export sector witnessed equally negative growth. From August 1914, the decline in the prices of export products such as coffee, sugar, and rubber resulted in noticeable problems in many economies, from Mexico to Central America and Brazil. This had direct consequences for countries such as Chile or Costa Rica, whose public coffers depended on import and export duties. No country in the region was spared government deficits and financial difficulties.[123]

The feeling of anxiety was palpable. In Argentina, the politicians already debated the crisis situation on August 2.[124] Basic necessities, such as the

[119] "La conflagración europea," in: *La Nación* (B. A., August 4, 1914), p. 9. "En la América del Sur," in: *La Nación* (B. A., August 5, 1914), p. 7.
[120] Velásquez, "Venezuela y la primera guerra mundial," pp. 28–9.
[121] In August and September 1914, Ecuador received offers from Danish shipping lines to handle the cocoa exports. Ecuadorian Consulate General to the Foreign Ministry of Quito (Hamburg, September 15, 1914), in: Ecuador, AMRREE, D.1.8. In early 1915, the Colombian government sought the shipment of goods via Belgium on a neutral ship, but the German government prevented it. MRREE to the legation in Berlin (Bogotá, January 22, 1915), Colombia, AGN, MRREE, tomo 00549, Transf. 1, fol. 15.
[122] Silva Vildósola, *Le Chili et la guerre*, p. 7.
[123] "Effeitos da Guerra sobre o Brasil," in: *O Imparcial* (September 2, 1914), p. 2. Albert, *South America and the First World War*, pp. 44–9. Alfredo González, "Mensaje del Presidente" (San Jose, May 1, 1915), in: Meléndez Chaverri, *Mensajes presidenciales* Vol. 4, pp. 254–6. Sandra Kuntz has recently demonstrated that the outbreak of the war greatly intensified the negative consequences of the revolution on Mexican foreign trade. Kuntz, "El impacto de la Primera Guerra Mundial," pp. 134–5.
[124] "Situación creada por la conflagración europea," in: *La Nación* (B.A., August 6, 1914), pp. 8 and 10.

capital's power supply, which had been provided by a German-Argentine electric company, were suddenly in doubt. In Brazil, the cabinet met with representatives of the banks to confer on countermeasures.[125] Ultimately, however, here as in most Latin American countries, one could only wait and see. Everywhere attempts were made to placate the enraged population, even if it meant using police violence. Buenos Aires' electric company thus announced that, if it had to, it could even meet the demand for fuel in the United States.[126] The daily *La Prensa* exhorted its readers to not lose their heads, for the government would act rationally. *El Día* in Montevideo also preached confidence in the government's actions, and the Brazilian *Jornal do Commercio* appealed to the patriotism of the people. The editorial in the Peruvian *La Crónica* even thought there was no cause for alarm, suggesting that the situation in Peru was not especially serious.[127]

The unemployed who assembled a few days later in front of the printing house to indicate the hopelessness of their situation had a more realistic take on things, however. The direct impact of the emergency measures was felt immediately. Since company owners had no money to pay salaries and maintain normal business operations, they responded with layoffs and hoped for better days.[128] All the industries of the Latin American economy tied to the export sector were hit by these near-convulsive shocks to the system.

This means that the problems extended beyond the port cities, and penetrated deep into the rural hinterland, where plantation and mining operations had to stop production.[129] Chile, where the dismissals mainly hit the workers in saltpeter mines in the northern desert, was particularly affected. Here as elsewhere, tens of thousands migrated to the capitals, and the social hardship continued to increase.[130] The violent tremors

[125] "A Repercussão da Guerra no Brasil," in: *Jornal do Commercio* (August 4, 1914), p 14.
[126] "La situación de Europa," in: *La Nación* (B. A., August 2, 1914), p. 9.
[127] "Cartera de Guerra," in: *La Prensa* (B. A., July 4, 1914), p. 5. "Del momento," in: *El Día* (August 24, 1914), p. 3. "A Repercussão da Guerra no Brasil," in: *Jornal do Commercio* (May 8, 1914), p. 3. "Sobre la guerra en Europe," in: *La Crónica* (August 4, 1914), p. 8.
[128] Albert, *South America and the First World War*, p. 44. "Sobre unas prisiones," in: *La Crónica* (September 13, 1914), p. 4.
[129] Brazil had thus recorded a trade deficit since 1913; see: Vinhosa, *O Brasil e a Primeira Guerra Mundial*, p. 129. Albert, *South America and the First World War*, pp. 37–8. For a description of the situation in Paraguay, see Gedult, *Aus den Urwäldern Paraguays*, pp. 30–5.
[130] Albert, *South America and the First World War*, pp. 49–50. "Salitre," in: *Zig-Zag* (September 5, 1914). On the problems of the cocoa plantations in Ecuador following the outbreak of war, see: MRREE to embassy in Washington (Quito, September 11, 1918), Ecuador, AMRREE, M.1.9.1. "20,000 hombres sin trabajo," in: *La Crónica* (August 15, 1914), p. 1.

resulting from the outbreak of war were thus hardly limited to the urban elite and the middle class. A cartoon from *Caras y Caretas*, published a month after the war had begun, captured the general uncertainty and anxiety about the economic crisis, which hung over the people like a sword of Damocles (see Figure 2.2).

The economic consequences of the war had varying intensity and were of different duration in the Latin American countries. The first measure taken was to cancel the bank holidays.[131] The resumption of the allocation of short-term trade credit resulted from the Allied demand for Latin American raw materials and had a stimulating effect on trade in the region.[132] In September 1914, newspaper articles already appeared in Argentina about potential profits for the neutrals as a result of the war. From December onward, the revitalization of activity could literally be heard in the streets of Buenos Aires.[133] Though much harder hit by the crisis, trade with Europe also picked up again in November 1914 in Brazil, albeit at very low levels.[134] Even the frightening rise in unemployment now appeared manageable, with commentators assuming that there would actually be a shortage of workers in the medium term due to the absence of immigration.[135]

While Latin American exports initially returned to their previous levels, various developments emerged from the turn of the year 1914/15 that depended on the demand of the Allies. As early as 1915, Latin American countries could point to positive trade balances and from 1916 the value of imports also increased. However, it was not a smooth recovery. The European defense industry needed strategically important goods such as copper, oil, tin, or saltpeter, and the diet of the armies depended on staple foods like sugar, wheat, and meat. Countries that produced these goods had a distinct advantage, while others stagnated.[136] On the other hand,

[131] "La guerra europea," in: *La Nación* (B. A., August 14, 1914), p. 8.
[132] Albert, *South America and the First World War*, pp. 177–9.
[133] Amarrete, "Los neutrales." See also: "Lo que mandamos a la guerra," in: *Caras y Caretas* (December 5, 1914).
[134] "O Commercio Brasileiro e a Guerra – A firma Germano Boettcher presta serviços incalculavéis ao nosso paiz," in: *Jornal do Commercio* (November 29, 1914), p. 12.
[135] "Ecos del día," in: *La Nación* (B. A., August 13, 1914), p. 7, 1914, i.e., before their own entry into the war, the Italian government had issued a warning about emigrating to Argentina because of low wages and high prices there. "Cómo se nos juzga en Europe," in: *La Vanguardia* (August 12, 1914), p. 2.
[136] Palacio, "La antesala de lo peor," pp. 101–34. Gravil, "The Anglo-Argentine Connection and the War of 1914–1918," pp. 61–70.

FIGURE 2.2 A feeling of crisis in Buenos Aires. Fears of the economy's collapse and unemployment seized Argentines everywhere.
Source: "Los efectos de la guerra en la Argentina," in: *Caras y Caretas* (September 5, 1914).

perceived luxury goods such as tobacco and coffee largely lost their target markets in Europe. Their providers had to find substitutes, as the Allies were not willing to make available the necessary shipping capacity.[137]

The impressions of the Argentine journalists were borne out, for the prices of wheat, animal hides, and meat did in fact rise. At the same time, the Argentine export sector benefited from the supply problems in Australia that were triggered by a poor harvest. Even meat from Uruguay and agricultural products from Paraguay found grateful buyers.[138] In 1914, the economic conditions in the Río de la Plata were already better than in the year that led up to the war, and in May 1916 a cartoon appeared for the first time in *Caras y Caretas* that depicted the Argentine Gaucho – alongside Uncle Sam – as a fortunate wartime profiteer (see Figure 2.3). The course of events also benefited sugar producers Cuba and Peru. The increasing demand for sugar was due to the loss of large parts of the European sugar beet harvest, whose growers had been called to the front. There was equally strong demand for commodities such as copper and rubber and alpaca wool from Peru. Peruvian exports were therefore able to show a similarly positive upward trend. In Cuba, layoffs in Havana's tobacco and cigar factories dampened spirits, yet the overall situation at the beginning of 1915 was better than before the war. This was due not least to the fact that its most important market, the United States, was still neutral. Chilean exports undoubtedly experienced the greatest fluctuations. When the demand for saltpeter collapsed due to the disappearance of the German market and the large stock levels in Europe, the initial feeling of shock was especially intense. By the same token, the incipient recovery in 1915 resulting from the enormous demand for nitrogen for the production of explosives in Europe was equally surprising.[139] In Brazil, whose main export coffee had endured a sales crisis for an extended period, the situation gradually improved, as demand in the United States at least partially made up for the loss of Europe.[140] The export boom even had a positive impact in revolutionary Mexico from 1915, where the demand for crude oil, copper, silver, and sisal rose sharply.[141]

---

[137] "Economic conditions in foreign countries" (May 8, 1915), NA, RG 151, General Records, Government Activities, Box 2925.
[138] Rivarola, *Obreros*, pp. 191–7.
[139] Albert, *South America and the First World War*, pp. 58–60.
[140] Ibid.
[141] Kuntz, "El impacto de la Primera Guerra Mundial," p. 126.

CARAS y CARETAS

LOS FAVORES DE LA FORTUNA

Nos fué su ayuda oportuna,
pues sin esperanza alguna
y a punto de perecer,
nos vino a favorecer
con su ayuda la Fortuna.

FIGURE 2.3 Lady Fortuna favored the wartime profiteers, the United States, and Argentina. Symbolically represented here, the former is bestowed with money, the latter a good harvest.

Source: "Los favores de la fortuna," in: *Caras y Caretas* (May 2, 1916).

But Latin America was not solely the object of good fortune, and in some cases economic success was only intermittent and superficial. The turbulence of the war was especially evident in the area of finance for a sustained period. There was a general shift in the orientation of the capital markets from London to New York, which, however, could not entirely replace the European lenders. The drying up of foreign capital meant the end of many public works projects as well as many direct investments, for example, in railway construction, as the case of the German company Orenstein & Koppel in Ecuador demonstrates.[142] Although the war from the beginning of 1915 filled the coffers of many exporters, they seldom used the proceeds to substitute for the lack of foreign capital. Instead, they continued to expand the export sector.[143] Even in a country like Uruguay, which was a direct beneficiary of European demand, the elites could not help lamenting the destruction of the global credit and trading system.[144]

The crisis triggered by the outbreak of war continued for many years, particularly in those countries that primarily exported tropical plantation products. Thus the cocoa producers in Ecuador and Venezuela experienced the same severe sales problems as the coffee exporters in Central America.[145] The decline in prices and export volumes led to massive budget deficits. As a consequence, there was no money for critical imports, which, moreover, became steadily more expensive. However, slight differences revealed themselves, depending on a country's import dependence and the strength of its ties to Europe. For example, the coffee exporters were more affected than the banana exporters, whose markets were mainly in the United States. The domestic political situation became very unstable in a country like Costa Rica, which was highly dependent on food imports, and even occasionally in Honduras. The countermeasures decreed by the governments to increase domestic production met with little success.[146]

[142] Martin, *Latin America and the War*, p. 439.
[143] Albert, *South America and the First World War*, pp. 177–9.
[144] "Los efectos de la guerra," in: *El Día* (April 8, 1915), p. 3. La situación financiera y económica," in: ibid., April 29, 1915), p. 3.
[145] Martin, *Latin America and the War*, p. 438. On Ecuador: "El malestar económico," in: *El Comercio* (Quito, May 11, 1915), p. 1. "Civilicémonos," in: *El Progreso* (January 16, 1917), p. 1.
[146] Notten, *La influencia*, pp. XV and 127–8. See also the annual report of the Costa Rican president: Alfredo González, "Mensaje del Presidente" (San Jose, May 1, 1915), in: Meléndez Chaverri, *Mensajes presidenciales*. Vol. 4, pp. 210–16.

There were drawbacks even for those countries that benefited from the export boom starting in 1915. As historian Bill Albert has demonstrated, the Allies' huge demand for Peruvian cotton from 1915 onward contributed to soaring prices. The producers responded, in turn, by expanding their areas under cultivation. The growing of food thus declined, which contributed to increased food prices and social unrest in Peru.[147] The lopsided dependence of Chile on the export of saltpeter was only intensified by the war boom, as nitrogen was an essential ingredient for the manufacture of explosives.[148] The industrial production of artificial nitrogen in Germany using the Haber-Bosch process was a great concern. Indeed, Chilean experts rightly assumed that the synthetic product would be a competitive threat to Chilean saltpeter after the war.[149] Everywhere in Latin America, the dependence on the warring nations was obvious, a fact increasingly criticized in newspaper commentaries.

As in many other regions of the world, for the broad mass of the population in Latin America the biggest problem brought on by the war was undoubtedly the unchecked rise in prices and the explosion of the cost of living. The inflationary trends triggered by the economic turmoil and emergency measures such as the issuing of fiat money would persist until the end of the decade. Above all, it was the continuous rise in food prices coupled with falling real wages that was responsible for the dramatic deterioration of the circumstances of the workers, but also the middle class. The increase in prices can be attributed to many factors. On one hand, imports effectively came to a halt, which sparked unfettered speculation in many places. This, in turn, caused the prices of basic staples to soar that were not considered imported goods – which the daily press vehemently attacked, albeit without any effect.[150] The tremendous increase in demand in Europe, for example, for corn from Argentina eased bottlenecks in meeting the needs of the local population from 1915.[151]

[147] Albert, *South America and the First World War*, pp. 110–1.
[148] Silva Vildósola, *Le Chili et la guerre*, p. 5.
[149] Alejandro Bertrand to Chilean ambassador Federico Puga-Borne (Paris, January 22, 1915), Chile, AN Siglo XX, Ministerio de Hacienda, 4714. Chil. Ambassador to MRREE (Berlin, April 7, 1915), Chile, AMRREE, Vol. 514.
[150] "Os géneros do consumo," in: *Jornal do Brasil* (August 7, 1914), p. 7. "O preço da carne," in: *Jornal do Brasil* (August 19, 1914), p. 5. "En Sud América," in: *La Nación* (B. A., August 3, 1914), p. 6. "Ecos del día," in: *La Nación* (B. A., August 11, 1914), p. 7. "El alza del azúcar," in: *El Comercio* (Quito, August 22, 1914), p. 1. See also Vinhosa, *O Brasil e a Primeira Guerra Mundial*, p. 136. On the global trends, see Tooze/Fertik, "The World Economy and the Great War," p. 225.
[151] "El pan sube," in: *Caras y Caretas* (March 13, 1915). See also Coke, "La vida cara," in: *Zig-Zag* (October 3, 1914).

The prices of other basic necessities, above all fuel, rose rapidly.[152] In Argentina this led, for example, to the expansion of oil production, though even this did not put significant downward pressure on prices. At La Plata, there was at least a political lobby for the workers in the form of the Socialist Party, which campaigned for a change of tariff policy and laws against usury. Government measures against rising prices generally remained ineffective, assuming they were undertaken at all or not finally counterproductive.[153] The plight of the working class was therefore a widely known problem that was much lamented in public and depicted in cartoons (see Figure 2.4).

The disastrous socioeconomic consequences of the war in much of Latin America were of course due not least to the current economic war. In fact, the war transformed into a world war because it was conducted as an economic war from the outset. The most important measure of the Allies was the maritime and commercial blockade, which gradually intensified over the course of the war and was accompanied by the mining of the North Sea.[154] Under international law, such an action against enemy coasts and ports as well as enemy ships and goods at sea was perfectly permissible according to the nineteenth-century rules of economic warfare. The Second Hague Conference of 1907 and the London maritime-law declaration of 1909 had specified the rules for the treatment of neutrals, even if there were conference participants – including the United Kingdom – who did not ratify it. These rules defined transported goods on neutral ships as contraband according to different categories and restricted, among other things, the possibility of seizing goods not vital to the war effort.[155]

After the outbreak of the war, both sides initially adhered to the maritime-law declaration, though, in the case of the United Kingdom,

[152] In Buenos Aires, coal prices rose between 1914 and 1918 by more than five times and crude oil prices by two and a half times. Compagnon, *L'adieu à l'Europe*, p. 124. Because of the sharp rise in paper prices, the price for printed matter of all kinds increased: "En la América del Sur," in: *La Nación* (B. A., August 4, 1914), p. 7.

[153] Thus, the Chilean government decreed at the outbreak of war a ban on exports of coal in order to prevent a shortage. The coal mines then reduced their production and laid off workers. "El carbón chileno," in: *El Mercurio* (October 22, 1914), p. 5 See also for the case of Peru, "La guerra en Europa," in: *La Crónica* (August 9, 1914), p. 3. On the topic of crude oil in Argentina: San Martín, *El petróleo*, pp. 20–1. The decreed limitations on the railways were also counterproductive, "Situación creada por la conflagración europea," in: *La Nación* (B. A., August 11, 1914), p. 5.

[154] As Dehne (*On the Far Western Front*, pp. 40–1) has shown, the initiative for the economic war originated with British businessmen living in Latin America.

[155] On the rights of neutrals in relation to the blockades: Hawkins, *The Starvation Blockades*, pp. 80–91.

CARAS y CARETAS

LA VÍCTIMA DE LOS ACAPARADORES

— ¿Y el pan? — Ha subido. — ¿Y la carne? — Ha subido. — ¿Y el azúcar? — Ha subido.
— ¡Caramba! Aquí todo sube, pero a esta mesa no llega nada.

FIGURE 2.4 The plight of the workers. Informed by his wife of the "increase" in bread, meat, and sugar, the desperate worker sighs that none of it will find its way onto his table. In the opinion of the cartoonist, he was a "victim of hoarders."
Source: "La víctima de los acaparadores," in: *Caras y Caretas* (August 26, 1916).

under a wider definition of contraband. Here, all foodstuffs were qualified as contraband – that is, the British government could decide on a case-by-case basis whether a shipment was contraband and whether it needed to be confiscated. Coffee was thus already impacted, for example, in November 1914. The government in London intended to strike a blow primarily against German coffee producers in Guatemala and Venezuela. Yet the provision also, of course, had negative consequences for Brazil and Costa Rica.[156] Certain critical war-related exports fell under the Allied export ban like coal, which was vital to Argentina (see Figure 2.5).[157] The measures were not least a reaction to the initial success of the German cruiser warfare, which had caused a great deal of apprehension among foreign-based British businessmen.[158]

As German trade at first continued to a limited degree via countries such as Denmark and especially the Netherlands, the British next tried to enforce regulations on the trade of neutrals, pressuring them to do business only with the Allies or with one another. In the initial phase of the war, measures were not yet coordinated systematically, however. London generated lists internally of companies that cooperated closely with the Germans and mediated the transfer of strategically important goods in order to then boycott them.[159] It was not until it expanded the blockade in March 1915 as a reaction against the first German declaration of unrestricted U-boat warfare from February 22 that the British government finally proceeded to alleviate these loopholes. German trade via neutral ports was hamstrung by import quotas established for the import of certain goods into neutral countries, in which the imported amount did not exceed the amount needed for self-subsistence. Further, the British consuls started to issue clearance certificates, so-called navicerts, to the exporters after inspections. To ultimately put downward pressure on the prices of critical imports, the Allied business interests in Latin America organized into trade committees (Comité Comercial de los Aliados or Comité de Compras), which held considerable sway over the market.[160]

Of course, the Latin American governments did not take this policy lying down. The public outrage over the measures of the Allies, which

---

[156] Vinhosa, *O Brasil e a Primeira Guerra Mundial*, p. 51. Embassy of Costa Rica to MRREE (London, January 4, 1915), Costa Rica, ANCA, RREE, Caja 230:1.

[157] Weinmann, *Argentina en la Primera Guerra Mundial*, pp. 46–7.

[158] Dehne, *On the Far Western Front*, pp. 44–7.

[159] Ibid., p. 51.

[160] Hardach, *Der Erste Weltkrieg*, pp. 19–25.

FIGURE 2.5 The Allies' economic war. There was a lot of criticism at La Plata in response to the audacity of the Allies, who essentially stole Argentinian goods under the motto "Your money or your life," while touting it as a good deed.

Source: "La bolsa o la vida," in: *Caras y Caretas* (January 8, 1916).

were a deep affront to national sovereignty, was palpable.[161] Former Foreign Minister of Brazil Amaro Cavalcanti voiced sharp criticism against the Allies in August 1916. In a lecture to the Brazilian Society of International Law, of which he was president, he accused the Allies of massive violations of the law.[162] Even within Britain itself, there were internal discussions about whether the measures did not actually violate the condition of neutrality and thereby especially risk provoking the powerful United States. Argentina, in particular, wanted to resist the blockade and turned to the United States for assistance.[163] Indeed, the United States lodged an official protest at the end of 1914, which, however, did not have the desired effect. Britain rebuffed the memorandums, referring to the exigencies of battle and the German U-boat war.[164]

Over the course of 1915, the Allied blockade measures became routine – until, that is, the British Parliament decided to extend the Trading with the Enemy Act in December and institute a Foreign Trade Department within the Foreign Ministry. It was on this basis that the British systematized the "blacklists," which were published biweekly. Appearing with increasingly frequency on the lists were companies from around the globe that either belonged to Germans or German descendants or cooperated with them. British citizens were forbidden from doing business with these companies. The Foreign Service was given the task of monitoring and enforcing compliance with these regulations, while British companies also provided assistance on site. The practice of coming up with "blacklists" was specifically aimed to permanently obstruct all German reinforcements and the supply of raw materials from overseas, with the long-term goal of ousting the German competition from the local markets. As historian Phillip Dehne has observed, this was part of a frontal attack against all German interests in the world, which also had major repercussions in Latin America.[165]

From the beginning, the measure hit many businesses hard. Some had to declare bankruptcy and lay off their workers. For German and ethnic-German workers, employment opportunities were now extremely hard to come by. As a precautionary measure to avoid attracting notice and

[161] "Ecos del día," in: *La Nación* (B. A., January 7, 1915), p. 7.
[162] Cavalcanti, *A neutralidade*, p. 7.
[163] Compagnon, *L'adieu à l'Europe*, pp. 57–8.
[164] "El comercio de los neutrales," in: *La Nación* (B. A., December 31, 1914), p. 6. Dehne, *On the Far Western Front*, pp. 65–6.
[165] Dehne, *On the Far Western Front*, pp. 71–3.

to evade the list, some companies let go their German workers.[166] Firms also re-incorporated as national enterprises or owners adopted Latin American citizenship, although these efforts at camouflage had only mixed success.[167] As a rule, the British tended to err on the side of over-listing companies rather than leaving off any that might be suspicious. Thus the Uruguayan firm Bonino & Schroeder found itself on the black-list, even though its partner Enrique Antonio Schröder, who was born in 1884 in Salto in Uruguay, abandoned his German citizenship in 1908 to escape German conscription.[168]

Even more devastating from the perspective of Latin American societies was the boycott against firms that provided basic services. For exam-ple, the suspension of coal supplies to the German electricity companies led to the outage of the street cars in Valparaíso and Viña del Mar and the power supply in Buenos Aires.[169] In Brazil, this caused considerable problems for the major coal-trading house Hoepcke in Santa Catarina, which, in turn, had harmful consequences for coastal and river naviga-tion. Responding to pressure from many Brazilian entrepreneurs, the government lodged a protest with the British Embassy in Rio de Janeiro in 1916.[170] In Chile, the closure of numerous German saltpeter plants led to unemployment and social tensions. This became a highly controversial issue among the Chilean public, and the pro-German forces repeatedly raised it as an argument against the British.[171]

The protests of the German diplomats against the actions of Allies were not long in coming. They found sympathetic listeners in urging Latin American governments to defend themselves against the new dimension

---

[166] In Buenos Aires, the German Benevolent Society tried to alleviate the suffering. Nonetheless, with around 60 percent unemployment among the Germans, it was hardly able make a meaningful dent in the problem. Newton, *German Buenos Aires*, pp. 41–4.

[167] Colombian Consul General to embassy (New York, September 22, 1914), Colombia, AGN, MRREE, Caja 94, Carp. 2), p. 81. For examples in Brazil, see also Vinhosa, *O Brasil e a Primeira Guerra Mundial*, p. 58. The British governmental authorities initially underestimated the problem: Dehne, *On the Far Western Front*, p. 131.

[168] Enrique Schröder to the Uruguayan MRREE (Montevideo, August 7, 1916), Uruguay, AGN, PGM, MRREE, Caja 735. See also the case of Ruete y Guyer in Uruguay: Brit. Foreign Office to Uruguayan ambassador (London, November 16, 1916), Uruguay, AGN, PGM, MRREE, Caja 735.

[169] U.S. Consul General to Dept. of State (Valparaíso, September 22, 1917), NA, RG 59, 625.119/48.

[170] Vinhosa, *O Brasil e a Primeira Guerra Mundial*, pp. 53–4.

[171] Even the Anglophile daily newspaper *El Mercurio* lamented the situation: "Las listas negras," in: *El Mercurio* (August 15, 1916), p. 2. "Las listas negras," in: *El Mercurio* (November 3, 1916), p. 3.

of economic war.[172] In Argentina, for instance, *La Prensa* complained in late November 1915 that any action that harmed Argentinean trade was de facto an action directed against their country. The newspaper further pointed out that all the warring powers were obliged to accept the country's neutrality.[173] A few months later, conservative MP Marcos Avellaneda even introduced a bill against the blacklist in the Argentine congress.[174] The *Correio da Manhã* in Brazil argued along the same lines as *La Prensa*. It chiefly railed against the trade restrictions among the neutral countries – as in the case of Brazilian coffee deliveries to the Netherlands – as an attack on Brazilian sovereignty.[175] The Brazilian Foreign Ministry shared this view and, in November 1916, instructed its delegation in London to take action against the prohibition of coffee exports in neutral ports. Brazilian diplomacy did not achieve a breakthrough, however.[176]

Along similar lines, in Chile, the Germanophile Gallardo characterized the war in October 1916 as an economic war over distant continents and called for South American solidarity against the blacklists. Citing numerous examples, he worked out the heavy price the Chilean economy had already paid due to the restrictions.[177] The blacklists, Gallardo observed, were a "sad example of the contempt that European countries, who invoked the sacred rights of the weaker nations, had for Latin American countries." This critique regarding the failure to act was directed against the United States, which, despite the Monroe Doctrine, refused to stand up to the Europeans.[178] The debates that went on in the Chilean senate about the implications of blacklists for state sovereignty ultimately fizzled out, however.[179] In the end, the Latin American governments had no

---

[172] MRREE to the legation in Berlin (Bogotá, September 1, 1916), Colombia, AGN, MRREE, tomo 00549, Trasf. 1, fol. 688. See also "Memorial que el alto comercio alemán presentó a S. E. el Presidente de la República el 28 de marzo," in: Gallardo, *Neutralidad de Chile*, pp. 99–107. Couyoumdjian, "En torno a la neutralidad de Chile," pp. 201–3.

[173] "El comercio argentino y la neutralidad," in: *La Prensa* (BA, November 29, 1915), p 3.

[174] Díaz Araujo, *Yrigoyen y la Guerra*, p. 245.

[175] "A lista negra," in: *Correio da Manhã* (June 1, 1916), p. 1. Garambone, *A primeira Guerra Mundial*, pp. 54–5.

[176] Brazilian embassy to MRE (London, August 31, November 15, December 8, December 21, 1916; January 22 and September 19, 1917), in: AHI, Directoria Geral dos Negocios Políticos e Diplomáticos.

[177] Gallardo, *Panamericanismo*, p. 210.

[178] Ibid., p. 219. Gallardo, "Posición internacional de Chile," p. LXIX.

[179] "Debate habido en el Senado de la sesión del 16 de agosto de 1916," in: Gallardo, *Neutralidad de Chile*, pp. 55–9.

choice but to come to terms with the practice of blacklisting, even if they continued to repudiate it on legal grounds.

Were the British, as the Allies' maritime leader, thus able to realize their war objective? The economic war in fact was not a complete success. After the war, an eyewitness from the southern Chilean city of Valdivia reported on three major shortcomings: First, those responsible for putting together the lists often had only limited knowledge of the local conditions; second, the blacklist had counterproductive effects, for it drove many Allied merchants who had lost their regular customers into bankruptcy; third, not all businessmen from the Allied countries adhered to the stringent guidelines.[180] What is more, despite the ongoing efforts, opportunities to trade continued to exist with the European neutral states and were pursued by, among others, major Argentine grain export houses with German roots like Bunge & Born and Weil Hnos. & Cia.[181] Such activity was carried out in the legal gray area of smuggling, which proved especially profitable for U.S. interests.[182]

To some extent, the British policy was also implemented ad absurdum, such as when the German-Argentine electricity company had to be removed from the list to keep the British railway lines running in Argentina.[183] At the end of the day, the Allies lacked the wherewithal to do what the British ambassador vehemently demanded in Brazil in April 1915, namely, that they seize the opportunity to expel the German competitors from among their ranks in Latin America once and for all.[184] The economic consequences of the lengthy war ultimately drove the Allies and most of all Great Britain to sell the lion's share of their Latin American securities to the United States, using the proceeds to pay for arms and ammunition purchases.[185]

[180] War Dept., Military Intelligence Division to the Bureau of Foreign and Domestic Commerce (Washington, DC, May 14, 1919), NA, RG 151, General Records, Government Activities, 841.

[181] Dehne, *On the Far Western Front*, p. 14. Gravil, *The Anglo-Argentine Connection*, p. 115.

[182] "Ao Redor da Guerra – A questão do contrabando do guerra," in: *Jornal do Commercio* (February 12, 1915), p. 3. "Notas Americanas," in: *Jornal do Commercio* (February 16, 1915), p. 2. Weinmann, *Argentina en la Primera Guerra Mundial*, pp. 69–70.

[183] Ibid., pp. 66–7.

[184] British ambassador to Foreign Office (Rio de Janeiro, April 23, 1915), in: *BD*, Vol. 1, p. 29. Dehne, *On the Far Western Front*, p. 103.

[185] This connection was recognized early on: "Os Estados Unidos e os Valores Sul-Americano," in: *Jornal do Commercio* (May 2, 1916), p. 3.

The United States, by contrast, was much better equipped to move into the areas that the Germans had abandoned in Latin America and, at the same time, to also push back the Allies. There was, accordingly, talk at the Department of State in November 1915 of a "golden opportunity" for expanding in Latin America and especially in the Caribbean.[186] The fact that the newly constructed Panama Canal was opened just as the war was breaking out in Europe was a historical coincidence. More than anything else, the canal symbolized Pan-American integration. Yet it also represented the United States' assertion of its superiority in the Americas, not only technologically, but also politically.[187] The U.S. economy harbored similar ambitions, as companies looked to do business in the south on a large scale.[188] Flanking policy measures such as the admission of foreign branches of U.S. banks proved crucial in this regard. In particular, the United States made use of its connections within the Pan-American framework, which it dominated. Washington wanted to give Latin Americans the sense that they were active participants in a fundamental realignment of the Western Hemisphere.[189]

On the other hand, the overtures were far from one-sided. Given the lack of investment capital from Europe, many Latin American governments had to turn to New York's capital market, where there were surpluses because of the war profits. For example, already in January 1915, the Argentine government took on a loan of 15 million pesos for the first time from the National City Bank in the United States.[190] Throughout the region, business relations with the United States acquired ever greater importance.[191] The Latin American consular services campaigned to increase the sales of export goods in the markets in the north. Even a country like Colombia, where anti-U.S. attitudes were

---

[186] Dept. of State, Memorandum: Our present opportunity in the Caribbean (November 30, 1915), NA, RG 59, 710.11/261.

[187] Salvatore, "Imperial Mechanics," pp. 667–72.

[188] Barrett, "Our Trade Opportunity."

[189] Especially important was the First Pan-American Financial Conference in Washington, DC, in May 1915, where agreements were settled on U.S. loans and the establishment of shipping lines. *Proceedings of the First Pan-American Financial Conference*, pp. 5–20. For the correlations, see especially Rosenberg, *World War I*.

[190] "Ecos del día," in: *La Nación* (B. A., January 5, 1915), p. 8.

[191] Even declared friend of Germany Dunshee de Abranches spoke out in favor of Brazilian–U.S. cooperation within the context of the Second Pan-American Scientific Congress in December 1915: Abranches, *Brazil and the Monroe Doctrine*.

especially pronounced due to the loss of the province of Panama, could not avoid going along with this trend, if only grudgingly.[192] This was also true for Mexico, whose imports were now even more focused on the United States, while Germany did not figure into the discussion.[193] In Central America and the Caribbean, the United States was the prevailing great power even before the war. Now, it attracted more coffee exports, which had previously been oriented toward Europe – a development that the Guatemalan dictatorship of Manuel Estrada Cabrera greeted with open arms.[194]

In general, however, the attempt at rapprochement with the United States was carried out of necessity and gave rise to concern. This was true not only for Great Britain, which hoped to secure the Latin American markets for itself, but also particularly for the affected countries of the region. The "commercial conquest" of the United States in Latin America was already a regular topic of conversation in the daily press in 1914.[195] The fear was that after the disappearance of Europe in Central America, now South America would also be ripe for the taking as the "war booty" of the United States.[196]

All the same, before 1917, the voices that predominated were those that perceived the rise of the United States to be only temporary and predicted that after the war there would be a return to the tried-and-true trade relations with Europe.[197] Some observers pointed out, with good reason, that, besides the United States, Japan as well as traders from the Middle East, the so-called *turcos*, had also established themselves in Latin America at the expense of the Europeans. What is more, the growing levels of trade within the region as well as the expansion of industrialization

---

[192] Colombian Ministry of Foreign Affairs to the legation in Washington (Bogotá, December 18, 1914), Colombia, AGN, MRREE, Caja 139, Carp. 3, Trasf. 5), p. 193. See also "El comercio interamericano," in: *La Nación* (September 5, 1914), p. 7.

[193] Kuntz, "El impacto de la Primera Guerra Mundial," pp. 127–31.

[194] "La guerra en Europa," in: *La Convención Nacional* (November 21, 1915), pp. 6–7.

[195] "La guerra europea," in: *La Nación* (October 1, 1914), p. 11. On the concerns of the British, see message to the Foreign Office (Washington, DC, June 8, 1915), in: *BD*, Part II, Series D, Vol. 1, pp. 31–2. "Latin American Notes," in: *The Times Supplement Trade* (October 1916), p. 12.

[196] "Sud-América como botín de guerra americano," in: *El Diario del Hogar* (September 22, 1914), p. 2. The fact that this was indeed the case was empirically demonstrated in 1919 by German-Argentine Ernesto Bott: Bott, *El comercio*.

[197] Foreign Office to British ambassador in Washington (London, March 15, 1916), in: *BD*, Part II, Series D, Vol. 2, p. 160. "Ecos del día," in: *La Nación* (March 19, 1916), p. 2. Silva Vildósola, *Le Chili et la guerre*, pp. 49–54.

in Argentina, Brazil, and Chile provided more than ample reason to be optimistic about the future.[198]

PROPAGANDA WAR

The twentieth century had already begun in the Americas with a propagandistic drumbeat in the form of the Spanish-American War in 1898–9. The First World War, however, brought with it an even more radical escalation of propaganda as a dimension of warfare.[199] Among the opposing camps, the totality of the war resulted in the creation of propaganda machines, which, as Michael Jeismann has shown, operated veritable "sense-making industries." The aim was to justify to the home front, as well as outwardly to other belligerents and especially to the neutrals, casualties running into the millions.[200] The propaganda portrayed the war as an ideologically charged all-or-nothing battle between fundamentally irreconcilable points of view. The alternatives were nothing less than victory or total destruction.

The propaganda war also took place on the two American continents precisely because they contained the largest number of the world's neutral countries. Although the Europeans were concerned primarily with influencing the public in the United States, the new world power, Latin America also came into focus. It was not exactly a fair fight, however. The Allies had open access to the communication links, whereas the German cable was severed at the start of the war and the new wireless technology still was not an adequate substitute. German foreign propaganda may have had a lot of catching up to do, but it nonetheless knew how to take the fight to the enemy.[201] During this period, discussion of propaganda – which the press compared to a new kind of armed services branch – typified public media throughout Latin America (see Figure 2.6).

Initially, the Latin American commentators and their media outlets wanted to remain out of the conflict, just as the governments wanted to keep out of the diplomatic struggles and businesses hoped to be spared

---

[198] Elliott, "South America and German Commerce," pp. 247–51. In contrast, the effects of industrialization failed to materialize in other countries. See Madueño, "La primera guerra mundial."

[199] Guthunz, "La construcción de imágenes." See also the essays in Hilton/Ickringill, *European Perceptions.*

[200] Jeismann, "Propaganda," p. 199.

[201] Notwithstanding the war, German foreign propaganda was also very active "overseas," contrary to the observation made in König/Neitzel ("Propaganda, Zensur und Medien," p. 128).

FIGURE 2.6 The significance of the propaganda war. In Latin America, the critical role that propaganda (the "sixth branch of the armed services") would play in this war was already evident in the first months of the conflict. The caption of this cartoon reads: "Victory will belong to whoever makes the best use of the telegraph." *Source*: Eduardo Álvarez, "La sexta arma," in: *Caras y Caretas* (December 19, 1914).

from the economic war. "Why should we work ourselves up about the czar or the emperor, these tragic playthings in the hands of fate? Who can say precisely who's to blame?" asked the editors of the Argentine cultural magazine *Nosotros*, socialists Alfredo A. Bianchi and Roberto F. Giusti, in August 1914. At that particular moment, they concluded, no one could justifiably wish for any one nation's victory, since none of them could claim to be civilization's sole arbiter.[202] Even the leading Chilean daily newspaper, *El Mercurio*, which would later unequivocally side with the Allies, was still on the fence in August 1914 since there were historical ties with both the German Reich and France and England.[203] Indeed, the Chilean ambassador in Paris warned the press that it should avoid partisanship, fearing that the Europeans would react sensitively to any opinions expressed on the war.[204] Yet, after the outbreak of war, it would soon prove very difficult to maintain such reticence because of the nature of the warfare and the intensity of the propaganda. This is evidenced by the grievances of the publishers of magazines such as the Chilean magazine *Zig-Zag*, whose readership complained about the publication's partisan reporting.[205]

A large portion of the elites who dominated the media landscape in Latin America shared a love for France, a country that not only had great economic influence in the region, but was also an important cultural touchstone. Members of the upper class often spoke French, and many had come to know the country personally on their travels or during their studies. French propaganda, therefore, had a distinct advantage when the war broke out. In addition, French foreign cultural and press policy had been very active in Latin America before 1914. The Comité France-Amérique founded in 1909 under the leadership of former Foreign Minister Gabriel Hanotaux brought together leading French intellectuals to strengthen ties with the Americas, and opened branches throughout Latin America.[206] During the war, the Comité intensified its efforts and successfully recruited members among the Latin American elites.[207]

The French Foreign Ministry and the General Staff also became actively involved in propaganda. They published books and pamphlets

---

[202] "La Guerra," in: *Nosotros* 8 (August 1914), pp. 118–9. This was also expressed a few months later by Basque intellectual Francisco Grandmontagne Otaegui, also known as Prudencio Amarrete, in "Las simpatías en la guerra."
[203] Couyoumdjian, "En torno a la neutralidad de Chile," p. 182.
[204] Chil. embassy to MRREE (Paris, January 15, 1915), Chile, AMRREE, Vol. 514.
[205] "Neutralidad," in: *Zig-Zag* (May 22, 1915).
[206] See epilogue in Silva Vildósola, *Le Chili et la guerre*, pp. 69–72.
[207] "L'Œuvre du Comité France-Amérique," *France-Amérique* 8 (November 1917), p. 29.

and distributed them across Latin America. The visual dimension of photos and films grew in importance. Before the war, French suppliers dominated the Latin American film markets, which the propaganda could easily build on. The weekly newsreels distributed by the company Pathé, which were presented before feature films, found a growing audience in the region. Eyewitnesses reported that audiences often responded very emotionally to the screenings.[208] Other elements of this policy included art exhibitions, lecture tours by famous French scholars, and a systematic "honoring policy," that is, the regular decorating of respected figures.[209] A high point was the "Latin America Week," held for first time in 1916 and then annually, which evoked the cultural and ideological unity with Latin America. At the same time, it was clear that France viewed itself as a kind of master teacher, as a "priestess of the sacred fire."[210] However, the ability to exert direct influence on the press remained decisive. Along with the daily newspapers of the French-speaking minority such as *Le Courrier de la Plata* and *Le Journal Français* in Buenos Aires or *Le Courrier du Mexique*, the propaganda focused on Latin American newspapers and also published writings in France like *Le Franco Americain* and *La Acción Francesa*.[211] It further benefited from the traditionally strong presence of the Havas intelligence service, which over time included radio transmissions broadcast from stations on the Eiffel Tower and in Lyon.[212]

The activities of the other Allies were similarly organized, though the work of the British was particularly significant. Their propaganda, too, put an emphasis on swaying the press and as a result of the influence their intelligence service and operations had on the market, they were able to force the printing of certain pro-British messages. Wherever there was a large enclave of British traders, there were also English-language newspapers such as the *South Pacific Mail* from Valparaíso. The specially issued monthly publications *La Guerra Ilustrada* and *América Latina* were read throughout Latin America.[213] The Italian propaganda, which played a particularly important role in Argentina and Brazil, leaned heavily on the

[208] Mont Calm, "La guerra y la paz," in: *Zig-Zag* (December 26, 1914). On the impact of film propaganda in Brazil, see Bonow, *A desconfiança*, p. 135.

[209] *L'effort politique et charitable de l'Amérique latine.* Bonow, *A desconfiança*, p. 169.

[210] Aillón Soria, "La política cultural de Francia," pp. 94–8.

[211] "Lo que costará la guerra" *El Mundo Ilustrado* (August 9, 1914), p. 1.

[212] Compagnon, *L'adieu à l'Europe*, pp. 76–8. Tato, "Luring Neutrals," pp. 328–30.

[213] Robert Cecil, "British Propaganda in Allied and Neutral Countries," TNA, Cabinet Papers, CAB 24/3/2. "South America and the War" (1918), NA, RG 63, Entry 132, Box 4, pp. 11–13. For Argentina, see Tato, "Luring Neutrals," p 325–8.

French propaganda and was widely disseminated.[214] Over the course of the war, the Allies developed some common propaganda strategies. For instance, in Santiago de Chile, they jointly published the magazine *La Patria de los Aliados*.

In line with the historically familiar opposition in Latin America between civilization and barbarism, the Allied propaganda portrayed the war against Germany as a conflict of basic principles. In this case, the Allied civilization allegedly faced a seemingly perverse German "culture" that had to be defeated.[215] According to the founder of the Radical Party of Argentina, Francisco Antonio Barroetaveña, France's battle with Germany resembled Athens' struggle against Sparta.[216] This was a common topos that Latin American intellectuals readily adopted and perpetuated.[217] Indeed, Colombian poet Eduardo Carrasquilla Mallarino, who resided in Argentina, published his poem "Canto de Guerra" from Paris in September 1914. It speaks about the struggle of the "Latin genius" who, led by the brave Gallic rooster, fought honorably, whereas the "satanic forces" of the "Germanic hordes" did not even restrain their destructive rage before women and children.[218]

For Francophile Latin Americans, there was no doubt, not least because of the idea of Latinity, that their own civilization was intimately connected to France. Shortly after the outbreak of the war, in a speech to the Brazilian Chamber of Deputies, delegate Irineu Machado invoked the "French blood" that pulsated in Brazilians' veins. A victory for France, Machado remarked, was synonymous with a victory "of our race."[219] In 1916, the famous poet and politician José de Medeiros e Albuquerque concluded: "Brazil is undoubtedly the most French of the republics of Latin America." Despite the fact that there were many more Italians and Germans living in Brazil, the French language was the most pervasive.[220] In Peru, Senator Mariano H. Cornejo recognized parallels between

---

[214] Piccione, La guerra ante la historia. "Report on foreign and domestic propaganda in the Argentine Republic" (April 9, 1918), NA, RG 165, MID 2327-L-1. Holder, Activities of the British Community.

[215] Piccione, *La guerra ante la historia*, p. 8. Bonow, *A desconfiança*, pp. 286–7.

[216] Barroetaveña, *Alemania contra el mundo*, p. 77.

[217] For numerous examples from Argentina and Brazil, see Compagnon, *L'adieu à l'Europe*, pp. 80–3.

[218] Carrasquilla Mallarino, "Canto de Guerra," pp. 58–64.

[219] "A Repercussão da Guerra no Brasil," in: *Jornal do Commercio* (August 9, 1914), p. 4.

[220] Medeiros e Albuquerque, "Le Brésil et la guerre," p. 35. See also "Razões contra a Allemanha. O Ponto de Vista Brasileiro (Conclusão)," in: *Jornal do Commercio* (February 26, 1915), p. 2.

France's struggle and Peru's own history, for Peru had also lost parts of its territory to an "imperialist aggressor," specifically, Chile.[221]

For countless pro-French thinkers in Latin America, the commitment to the "race latine" since the outbreak of war went hand in hand with the idea of a clash with a "Germanic" or "Teutonic" race. For example, a commentary in *Jornal do Commercio* asserted that Brazil had nothing Germanic in itself, but was instead thoroughly Latin. The Brazilian spirit was in fact diametrically opposed to the German spirit, so the editorial claimed.[222] The ideal conjured here of two brothers-in-arms logically culminated in a call to revoke the country's neutrality and to stand side by side with France, its Latin brother, in battle.[223]

The young Colombian journalist Alfonso Mejía Rodríguez, who had just returned from France, wrote this appeal in French. He was one of many educated Latin Americans and aesthetes who had experienced France for himself and fallen in love with it. Paris was the center of existence for many of these Latin American poets and writers, and it was the place where they penned their avowals of solidarity. They included, for instance, Peruvian writer-brothers Francisco and Ventura García Calderón and Chilean Alberto Mackenna, who also lived in Paris.[224] Often, they acted as war correspondents – like Argentine journalist Roberto Payró, who wrote for the *La Nación* and *Caras y Caretas* – and profoundly shaped public opinion back in their home countries.[225] The most influential eyewitness, heard throughout Latin America, was undoubtedly Rodó, who travelled to Europe as a correspondent for *Caras y Caretas* in 1916 and died in Palermo on May 1, 1917.[226] It is hardly surprising, therefore, that French observers had the impression that Latin America was more or less of one mind when it came to supporting France's war effort.

[221] Cornejo, *La solidaridad americana*, p. 32.
[222] "Contra o Germanismo. Carta a Certo Poeta," in: *Jornal do Commercio* (February 28, 1915), p. 2. See also "El gran conflicto," in: *La Nación* (B. A., January 9, 1915), p. 4.
[223] Mejía Rodríguez, *La France*, p. 14.
[224] Mackenna, *Le triomphe du droit*. Cited in Blancpain, Migrations et mémoire germaniques, p. 271. These views were collected and published in two volumes by the Groupement des universités et grandes écoles de France pour les relations avec l'Amérique latine: *L'Amérique latine et la guerre européenne*.
[225] Mejía Rodríguez, *La France* García Calderón, "Pourquoi nous sommes franco philes," pp. 61–7. Payró, *Corresponsal de guerra*.
[226] Rodó, "La solidarité des peuples latines," pp. 71–2. "La América latina y la guerra," in: *Los Aliados* (July 20, 1915), p. 34. Drews, "Estampas desde las trincheras," pp. 135–6. See also Corredor La Torre, "A nos grands frères," p. 36.

In fact, Francophile publications could be found throughout much of Latin America. The propaganda from Paris consequently benefited from especially fertile soil. French heroism and sacrifice were not only celebrated in the media, but also at public gatherings and rallies.[227] The Uruguayan government even declared July 14, 1915, a federal holiday. In most Latin American cities, the French national holiday served as an occasion for making declarations of solidarity.[228] Compagnon has identified three key aspects of Latin American Francophilia during this period: First, the idea that France and its revolution was the origin of all freedoms; second, the idea that France was the root of literature and the arts; and, third, the cult of the French capital, Paris.[229]

Regarding the attitudes of Latin Americans toward the other Allies, this conspicuous Francophilia had no equivalent. The British minister in Rio de Janeiro remarked in 1915 that while the Latin Americans respected England's commitment to the freedom of small nations, they held no great affection for the country.[230] The sentiment toward Belgium – the "country of martyrs" – represented an exception.[231] The small country's defensive struggle had been widely hailed as heroic, and in many Latin American countries, there were calls for donations and solidarity rallies.[232] The strong sympathy toward Belgium was due not least to the parallels Latin Americans recognized with their own situation in the international system. The attack on Belgium was also an attack on the principle of neutrality, and it was an attack of a major power on a small, weaker country. This was a constellation that Latin Americans, who faced U.S. imperialism in their own hemisphere, knew

---

[227] "El heroismo de Francia," in: *A.B.C.* (October 2, 1918), p. 5. Compagnon provides a comprehensive account of numerous Francophile demonstrations and statements ("1914–18," pp. 283–5).

[228] Buero, *El Uruguay*, pp. 215–22. For examples from Paraguay, see Sayé, *Crema de menta*, pp. 157–9.

[229] Compagnon, *L'adieu à L'Europe*, pp. 84–8.

[230] Brit. Envoy to Foreign Office (Rio de Janeiro, April 23, 1915), in: *BD*, Part II, Series D, Vol. 1, p. 29. Barroetaveña sums up Britain's positive aspects in: *Alemania contra el mundo*, pp. 97–106.

[231] Lugones, *Mi beligerancia*, p. 132. "La conflagración europea," in: *Variedades* (August 29, 1914), pp. 1143–5.

[232] "Em torno da Guerra – A historia epica dos Belgas," in: *Jornal do Commercio* (October 2, 1914), p 3. "¡Bravo belgas!," in: *El Abogado Cristiano Ilustrado* (October 15, 1914), p. 2 On solidarity: "Las damas uruguayas y el pueblo belga," in: *El Día* (November 6, 1914), p. 1. Vice Consulate to Paraguayan MRREE (Antwerp, November 20, 1916), in: Paraguay, AMRREE, Colección Política Internacional, Libro 70.

all too well. What befell tiny Belgium, Argentine intellectual Manuel Ugarte argued, could just as easily happen to the Latin Americans.[233]

Belgium's fate became a main weapon in the propaganda arsenal used against the German Reich. In 1915, well-known Colombian writer Santiago Perez Triana published an English-language essay titled "Why a Spanish American should not be Pro-German." He responded to the question raised in his title by making reference to the tragedy of Belgium, which was a "shame for the whole human race."[234] Pérez Triana not only meant here the German invasion itself, but also the German war crimes, which were promptly reported on in Latin America in considerable detail. The correspondents widely documented the destruction of villages and towns, and especially cultural treasures like the Library of Leuven or the Cathedral of Reims, at times even with photos, permitting Latin American readers to get a good handle on the events.[235] Even impartial commentators assessed the German actions as a betrayal of Germany's cultural heritage, while others spoke of a "violation of divine law."[236]

Reports of German massacres and atrocities in which Catholic priests, but also women and children, were killed, and, later on, that Belgian civilians were forced to work in Germany, elicited even greater disgust. Indignation was sparked above all by the subjective and emotional representations of eyewitnesses to the Germans' atrocities.[237] The distribution of this news was not limited to the urban press, for it was also disseminated in the Río de la

---

[233] Ugarte, *Mi campaña*, pp. 184–5. See also "A neutralidade belga e a invasão allemã," in: *O Imparcial* (August 27, 1914), p. 2. José Manuel Carbonell, "Alba de sangre," in: *El Comercio* (Quito, December 31, 1914), p. 1.

[234] Pérez Triana, *Some Aspects of the War*, p. 176. See also Rausch, "Colombia's Neutrality," pp. 107–8.

[235] See, e.g., "La guerra," in: *Variedades* (October 24, 1914), pp. 1358–9. "Os actos de barbarismo praticados pelos allemães na Alta Alsacia," in: *A Epoca* (August 17, 1914), p. 1. "Os horrores commettidos na Belgica pelos Invasores allemães," in: *O Imparcial* (September 16, 19, and 20, 1914), respectively, p. 1. Francisco García Calderón, "La guerra y los ideólogos," in: *La Nación* (January 11, 1915), pp. 3–4. Critical reports like these were found in all the examined press items of this period, from Mexico to Argentina. On the events related to the German march on Belgium, see Kramer, *Dynamic of Destruction*, pp. 6–30. Horne/Kramer, *German Atrocities*.

[236] Barroetaveña, *Alemania contra el mundo*, pp. 46–54. See also Del Valle, *La guerra europea*, pp. 33–4.

[237] "Em torno da Guerra – Impressoes de um estudante brasileiro em Liége," in: *Jornal do Commercio* (October 12, 1914), p. 3. See also "De nuestros corresponsales," in: *La Nación* (B. A., September 22, 1914), p. 6. Payró, *Corresponsal de guerra*, pp. 641–2. Del Valle, *La cuestión internacional*, p. 64. Mesquita, *A guerra*, Vol. 1, pp. 111–2. "Las deportaciones," in: *Zig-Zag* (December 16, 1916).

Plata region via the very popular dime-store magazines, which carried popular literature, poems, songs, and news and were also often read aloud in
public places. A good example of such a publication was the magazine published in Rosario in 1914 called *Los horrors de la guerra* (*The Horrors of
War*), with contributions such as "La vergüenza del ejército alemán" ("The
Shame of the German Army") and many succinct reports on documented
and invented German atrocities alike.[238] Attitudes seemed to be changing
even in a traditionally pro-German country like Chile.[239]

In light of the presented facts, it was not difficult for Allies' anti-
German propaganda to gain ground. It reached a high point with the
announcement of the sinking of the *Lusitania*, which was condemned
as a terrorist act by more than just anti-German observers.[240] A growing
number of the Latin American elites interpreted the individual war crimes
of the German troops as systematic in nature, which allegedly stemmed
from the Germans' inherently cruel character.[241] When Machado said in
his speech in early September 1914 that "Germany offended civilization
and humanity," he meant that the German people alone were to blame
for the war.[242] This statement came close to accusing Germans as such
of barbarism, of portraying them – as Pedro Sayé, the Paraguayan correspondent for *La Tribuna*, had – as the epitome of modern barbarians.[243]

The Allies utilized this equation of Germany with the heart of barbarism as an essential element of their propaganda in the Americas, and
encountered many sympathetic listeners.[244] But how could barbarism,

---

[238] *Los horrores de la guerra*, p. 3.

[239] Francophile Silva Vildósola claimed that this concerned all of Chile (*Le Chili et la
guerre*, pp. 44–5). See also Silva Vildósola, "Le Chili et la guerre européenne," p. 72.

[240] Mesquita, *A guerra*, Vol. 1, p. 207. "Os barbaros," in: *A Epoca* (May 12, 1915), p. 1.
"A guerra e a civilização," in: *O Imparcial* (May 12, 1915) p. 1. "El hundamiento
del Lusitania," in: *El Comercio* (Quito, May 11, 1915), p. 1. The fact that individual
Germans and German descendants in Brazil publicly celebrated the sinking only further
inflamed the situation. See "Destruição do Lusitania," in: *Jornal do Commercio* (May
29, 1915), p. 2. German-born Brazilian Foreign Minister Lauro Müller visited Porto
Alegre shortly thereafter and expressed pride in his ethnic roots, which also sparked
outrage. See Bonow, *A desconfiança*, pp. 179–82.

[241] García Godoy, "La France et Saint-Domingue," p. 96. On the topoi of French propaganda, see Krumeich, "Ernest Lavisse," pp. 143–54.

[242] Irineu Machado, "A Allemanha offende a civilisação e a humanidade," in: *A Epoca*
(September 3, 1914), p. 1. This was thus argued by Brazilian intellectual José Verissimo,
"Nós americanos e a guerra," in: *O Imparcial* (August 24, 1914), p. 2.

[243] Sayé, *Crema de menta*, p. 128. "As barbaridades allemãs," in: *O Imparcial* (March 24,
1915), p. 1. The Brazilian entertainment magazine *Fon-Fon* had remarked as early as
July 1914 that Europe was divided into "Latin, barbaric, and enslaved peoples." See
"Guerra!," in: *Fon-Fon* (July 1, 1914).

[244] This was true even for a colony like Jamaica, where Marcus Garvey declared his solidarity. Smith, *Jamaican Volunteers*, p. 44.

which in the racist European discourse had been traditionally located in the colonies or semi-colonies with their "colored" populations, now suddenly exist in the center of civilization among the "whites," who, according to the common view, were clearly responsible for the world's greatest cultural achievements? To resolve this dilemma and explain the discrepancy, commentators made a distinction between Germany and Prussia. For instance, the opinions of English writer and journalist Gilbert Keith Chesterton on the spirit and the philosophy of the German people gained wide acceptance. Chesterton concluded that the Prussian was intellectually inferior because his soul was inherently savage.[245] A commentary in the *Jornal do Commercio* from August 1914 adopted this line of reasoning and then expanded on it: The war, it opined, was a product of the Prussian spirit that held sway in Germany and encouraged greater brutality and aggression. The land of Goethe and Heine had been "Prussianized." This was the source of all evil.[246]

Nicaraguan writer and diplomat Santiago Arguello clarified how this Prussian barbarism was different from traditional barbarism.[247] The commentator of *Jornal* had already referred to the German Reich as a "modern-barbaric" empire. He later went one step further by speaking of a "wise barbarism" (*barbaria sábia*), of a kind of barbarism that would multiply by means of a highly cultivated, but cold and soulless (natural) science. According to critics, this attitude became dangerous when it was combined with a supremacy claim derived from the Nietzschean superman (*Übermensch*).[248] In the judgment of Guatemalan writer Enrique Gómez Carrill, who lived in Paris and was a Knight of the Legion of Honor, such a claim was unmistakably expressed in the so-called Manifesto of the Ninety-Three by German intellectuals in September 1914.[249] Demonstrating the effect of Allied propaganda,

[245] "Ao Redor da Guerra – Pontos de vista allemães", in: *Jornal do Commercio* (December 18, 1914), p. 2.

[246] "A obra do Germanismo", in: *Jornal do Commercio* (August 17, 1914), p. 2.

[247] Santiago Arguello, "L'opinion du Nicaragua sur la guerre européenne," p. 140.

[248] "A theoria do germanismo," in: *Jornal do Commercio* (April 3, 1915), p. 4. "Razões contra a Allemanha – Balanço da Cultura Moderna: Sciencia," in: *Jornal do Commercio* (February 14, 1915), p. 3. García Calderón, *Ideologías*, pp. 376–7. Argentine Raymond Wilmart, originally from Belgium, even cited the German language, which he felt was overly complicated, as evidence of German arrogance. Wilmart, "El ideal americano," pp. 369–85.

[249] Enrique Gómez Carrillo, "Los intelectuales alemanes y la guerra," in: *La Nación* (B. A., January 19, 1915), p. 4. See also Francisco García Calderón, "La teoría del Germanismo," in: *La Nación* (B. A., January 14, 1915), p. 4. García Calderón, *Ideologías*, pp. 309–10.

Gómez published his criticism in the Buenos Aires *Nación* immediately after the British *Reply to the German Professors by British Scholars* from October. As a collection of essays from Francophile Latin Americans and edited by Chilean poet Francisco Contreras (who was also based in Paris) shows, the attacks against the "Prussian barbarism" also contained genuinely Latin American elements. In the authors' repudiation of mindless German utilitarianism, they drew on the well-known topos that Rodó had already utilized in his acclaimed masterpiece *Ariel* from 1900 to warn readers about the United States.[250]

According to the Allied propaganda, Prussian-German barbarism found its most characteristic expression in militarism coupled with blind obedience. This argument, too, was broadly accepted in Latin America. As Barroetaveña observed, the Germans, like the Spartans, subordinated everything to military service and virtually enslaved their own people through Prussian discipline. Lugones, his compatriot, described "German militarism" as an extension of "ancient barbarism."[251] To his way of thinking, this explained why in the country previously known as a land of music, Krupp's "hell and death symphony" could succeed there.[252] These observers found especially worrisome the fact that German expansionism represented a threat to the entire globe. Independently, intellectuals like Barroetaveña or Brazilian journalist Lima Barreto realized to their dismay that the militarization of Latin American societies had already progressed because of this very danger.[253] *El Zorro*, the Buenos Aires satirical magazine, concluded that a German victory would make it necessary to emigrate to another planet, for "Who could endure being ruled by a people who behave like genuine cannibals in the middle of the 20th century?"[254]

For the tacticians behind the Allied propaganda, German Kaiser Wilhelm II was the personification of German barbarism. Biting satires and mischievous caricatures not only abounded in the decidedly propagandistic leaflets, but also in the Latin American press. *El Zorro*, for example, brought out a comic book series titled "Guillermo el macanudo" ("Wilhelm, the splendid"), which made the emperor a target

---

[250] Contreras, *Les Écrivains Hispano-Américains*, pp. 31–3.
[251] Barroetaveña, *Alemania contra el mundo*, pp. 66–7. Lugones, *Mi beligerancia*, p. 7.
[252] De la Guardía, "La redención," p. 66.
[253] Lima Barreto, *Marginália*, p. 46. See also "Razões contra a Allemanha II – A influencia mundial," in: *Jornal do Commercio* (February 3, 1915), p. 2. Barroetaveña, *Alemania contra el mundo*, p. 89.
[254] "La barbarie alemana," in: *El Zorro* (October 5, 1914).

of ridicule.[255] The criticism of the monarch also had serious undertones, however. For example, the comparison that Wilhelm had himself made to the Huns in his famous "Hun Speech" from 1900 was now used against him. Many anti-German observers argued that the struggle of the Western democracies against Asiatic despotism now needed to be fought against the German Kaiser, the new Attila, and his *kaiserismo*.[256] In order to find an explanation for such an anachronistic political system, some even insinuated that mental illness had put the emperor and his people on the path to barbarism.[257]

Belgian-born Raymond Wilmart, who had once traveled to Argentina as an envoy for Karl Marx and had lost a son in the war himself, simply characterized the emperor as the antithesis of the "American ideals." According to Wilmart, there was a duty to participate in the war against the emperor, for should the German Reich win, the neutrals would fall victim to the German megalomania. Wilmart complained most vocally about the infringement of all the principles of international law that had arisen in the age of globalization:

The international community took pride in its enormous interdependence, which globalized capital and production, and believed it was destined to create international institutions, whose need seemed to be obvious; it took pride in a humanitarian code that would eventually become even more humane; it took pride in the collectivity of the law, which, together with the common possession of the high seas, was the shared heritage of the international community. Today, the emperor has violated all of this. For him, there is no law beyond the fantasy of his backward-looking ambitions.[258]

As proof of the threat to the global order and of the putative German expansion strategy in Latin America, resourceful propagandists referred to the role of Germany in the Venezuelan crisis of 1902. They also repeatedly cited Friedrich von Bernhardi's book *Germany and the Next War* from 1912, which appeared during the war in Spanish translation.[259] They presented all-German Pan-Germanism as a particularly dangerous strain

---

[255] "Guillermo el macanudo," in: *El Zorro* (September 14, 1914), p. 3.

[256] "Ao Redor da Guerra. O Attila dos latinos e o Attila dos germanicos," in: *Jornal do Commercio* (May 22, 1915), p. 2. "Guilherme II, imperador dos bárbaros do Occidente?!" in: *A Epoca* (August 12, 1914), p. 1. See also: Lugones, *Mi beligerancia*, p. 40. Barroetaveña, *Alemania contra el mundo*, pp. 6–7.

[257] "A demencia germanica," in: *Jornal do Commercio* (November 9, 1914), p. 2. For a similar line of argument, see García Calderón, *Ideologías*, p. 311.

[258] Wilmart, "La guerra," pp. 514–5.

[259] Villanueva, "Le Vénézuela et la guerre européenne," p. 188. De la Guardia, "La redención," p. 68. See also Bernhardi, *Alemania y la próxima guerra*.

of pan-ideology since it involved an unbridled willingness to destroy.[260] As Gómez Carrillo argued in 1916, this imperialist domination would not even be reined in when it came to civilized Latin America.[261] As the clearest evidence of Germany's implicit contempt of Latin America, his Peruvian colleague García Calderón cited Germany's racism and the idea of Aryanism, as they were expressed in the writings of Josef Ludwig Reimer. If Reimer's vision of a Germanic empire ever actually came to fruition, García Calderón remarked, Latin America would be relegated to a slave state because of its "racial mixing."[262]

In Latin America, these ideas had considerable currency not least because the notion of the "German threat" had existed as a point of reference since the turn of the century. As evidence of Germany's ongoing ambitions, Allied propaganda distributed excerpts in Spanish translation of the text *Greater Germany: The Work of the 20ᵗʰ Century*, published in 1911 under the pseudonym Otto Richard Tannenberg. In the six-page pamphlet, which was printed in Paris, the author advocated the creation of a closed settlement area in southern Brazil, Uruguay, and Paraguay that would be supported by the German settlers already living there.[263] The fear that German descendants would infiltrate the country was very pronounced, especially in Brazil, and would play an important role in the war's further evolution.[264]

Against this backdrop, the German side found it difficult to defend its own cause. As a consequence, the lament the commentator of the *Deutsche La Plata Zeitung* voiced in Buenos Aires in November 1914 that there was a "lack of understanding for the German character abroad" was quite common.[265] By the same token, German propaganda was hardly idle, for it helped to fuel confrontations among opinion makers throughout Latin America on how to respond to the war. This aspect has so far been largely ignored in historical research, which has simply accepted Allied dominance in this area without further ado. The period's sources also often presented the pro-Allied utterances as reflecting

[260] "Ao Redor da Guerra – O programma pan-germanista", in: *Jornal do Commercio* (February 12, 1915), p. 3. "Pangermanismo," in: *La Prensa* (Lima, September 1, 1918), p. 3. Max Nordau, "Los Pan ... ismos," in: *La Nación* (B. A., January 15, 1915), p. 3.
[261] Gómez Carrillo, "Préface," p. 6.
[262] García Calderón, *Ideologías*, pp. 488–9.
[263] "Ambiciones alemanas en América del Sur," NA, RG 165 WCD, 6370-267.
[264] "Impressões do Sr. Graça Aranha," in: *Jornal do Commercio* (December 11, 1914), p. 4.
[265] "Das mangelhafte Verständnis für deutsches Wesen im Auslande," in: *Deutsche La Plata Zeitung* (November 8, 1914), p. 1. See also "Was ist die Wahrheit?," in: ibid., October 6, 1914), p. 1. Luebke, *Germans in Brazil*, p. 89.

genuine "public opinion," whereas the pro-German statements were dismissed as unrepresentative and the propagandistic lies of outsiders.[266]

Emulating France, German *Weltpolitik* (world policy) discovered foreign cultural propaganda for itself, although here Latin America played only a minor role.[267] The war propaganda was carried out by many military, civilian, and non-official agencies with little coordination until the Central Office for Foreign Service (Zentralstelle für Auslandsdienst) was created in October 1914. It issued Spanish-language publications produced in Germany, which – like the *Monitor Mercantil* in the guise of disinterested economic reporting – widely circulated war propaganda. In the neutral countries of Latin America, important propaganda actors included the not always very numerous, but nevertheless well-connected Germans and German descendants, that is, the "ethnic Germans," along with their clubs and churches. In countries such as Argentina, Chile, and Paraguay, the institutions merged into so-called peoples' federations (*Volksbünde*) in order to effectively organize all Germans during the war in a "overseas truce." Financially supported by foreign banks and companies, they founded their own Spanish-language newspapers and magazines, published pamphlets and books, and tried, partly through graft, to influence the local press.[268]

For the distribution of German propaganda in Latin America, the new medium of radio was of central importance. Shortly before the outbreak of the war, major German companies together with the German Foreign Office established the Transozean GmbH, which sent daily radio transmissions to Sayville and Tuckerton until 1917. From there, the reports were sent on to the German foreign newspapers and associations, which edited and translated the reports before then putting them out in the press locally.[269] From the recipient's perspective, the German intelligence service was preferable because, unlike the reports from Havas and Reuter, it was free.[270] By and large, the German propaganda was based on the news from Nauen near Berlin. This was then further supplemented by specially

---

[266] Barroetaveña, *Alemania contra el mundo*, p. 34. A good example of this kind of historiography is Michel, *L'Hispanisme*, pp. 50–1. Compagnon follows this line of thought in *L'adieu à l'Europe*.

[267] Kloosterhuis, *Friedliche Imperialisten*, pp. 251–2.

[268] Rinke, "The Reconstruction of National Identity," pp. 170–4. Luebke, *Germans in Brazil*, pp. 93–9.

[269] Katz, *The Secret War*, pp. 441–6. So far, there are only a few studies on the activities of German-language newspapers in Latin America during the war. On Buenos Aires, by contrast, see: Hoffmann, "¿Construyendo una 'comunidad'?," pp. 127–8.

[270] "La Germanofilia de El Nacional," in: *El Nacional* (May 17, 1916), p. 4.

prepared articles and reports from neutral Spain. Spain, in general, constituted a fundamentally important bridge to the Western Hemisphere for
the German operations.[271]

Given the massive criticism triggered by the invasion of Belgium,
German propaganda initially seemed flat-footed as regarded content.
The protests of ethnic German associations against the – from their vantage point – inaccurate portrayals were stultified by the Allied-friendly
press.[272] The activities of the Reich's diplomatic representatives proved
only marginally more effective. In any event, in Colombia, they prompted
Foreign Minister Marco Fidel Suárez to urge in a circular the editors in
chief of his country to reserve their criticism of the warring powers and
to respect the feelings of foreigners in view of the enormous influence of
the press in this conflict.[273] The Ecuadorian government warned its consuls abroad to not publish anti-German statements.[274] In Uruguay, the
intervention of the German envoy led to the punishment of anti-German
statements in the military and to a ban on anti-German satirical newspapers.[275] This changed nothing in terms of the government's fundamentally
pro-Allied stance. The German protests against the imposition of the holiday on July 14 thus ultimately went nowhere.[276]

Another aspect of German propaganda was to refute the Allies' alle-
gations and "unmask" them as "propaganda lies." Official agencies and
Germans living abroad repeatedly issued counter-statements, particularly
in the initial phase of the war.[277] The legations, for instance, distributed
the brochure "Noticias destinadas a propalar la verdad en el extranjero" ("Notes for spreading the truth abroad"), along with the Spanish

---

[271] Albes, *Worte wie Waffen*, p. 126. On the domestic Spanish disputes on the response to
      the war, see also Fuentes, *España en la Primera Guerra Mundial*.

[272] "Um protesto da colonia germanica," in: *Correio da Manhã* (September 21, 1914),
      p. 3. "O protesto dos teuto-brazileiros," in: *A Epoca* (September 4, 1914), p. 2. "Nós
      barbaros?!" in: *Jornal do Commercio* (January 15, 1915), p. 8.

[273] Foreign Minister Marco Fidel Suárez to the editors in chief of all Colombian periodicals
      (Bogotá, November 27, 1914), in: *Documentos relativos a la neutralidad*, pp. 22–4.

[274] German embassy to MRREE (Quito, January 2, 1916), in: *Ecuador*, AMRREE, B.1.2.
      MRREE to consuls abroad (Quito, February 7, 1916), ibid.

[275] Foreign Minister Baltasar Brum to Uruguayan Ministry of War (Montevideo, January 2,
      1915), Uruguay, AGN, PGM, MRREE, Caja 735. Montevideo embassy to AA (January
      5, 1915), in: "Informes diplomáticos," p. 183.

[276] Montevideo embassy to AA (July 19, 1915), in: "Informes diplomáticos," pp. 193–4.

[277] "Catecismo da germanophobia," in: *A Guerra: revista semanal* 5 (December 1914),
      pp. 3–4. Kuempel, *La guerra*, p. 1. See also Lorenz, "La gran guerra," p. 51. Scholz,
      Brasilien im Weltkriege, p. 7. Bonow, *A desconfiança*, pp. 166–7.

version of the German White Book and copies of the Kaiser's speeches.[278] From the beginning of the war, semi-official pamphlets were circulated to explain the "real causes of the war," often from the pens of supposedly neutral observers like Sven Hedin.[279] If the German war crimes were not simply denied, they were presented as acts of self-defense. Ultimately, however, there was only one perfectly valid counterargument that could be used against the accusation of "German threat," namely, the fact that Germany, unlike the Allies, had never had colonial possessions in America.[280]

The victimization strategy was quite central to German propaganda. Here, the German Reich was depicted as a "whipping boy" and the victim of a disgraceful smear campaign by way of overwhelming enemy propaganda.[281] Germany, so the argument went, had elicited the envy of other powers because of its rapid ascent, and now it faced a world of enemies from Europe, Africa, and Asia that only wanted to crush its economic might.[282] German propagandists took special pains to scandalize the other side's use of soldiers from the colonies, and also from Japan. In one of the many propaganda writings, the following could be read about the alleged terror of Asian and African soldiers: "These people, who grew up in countries where they continue to wage war in an even more abhorrent and barbarous manner, have brought the customs of their countries with them to Europe."[283] According to this rationale, the Allies were irresponsibly jeopardizing the "dominance of the white race" through

---

[278] See the numbers from September/October 1914 in Uruguay, AGN, PGM, MRREE, Caja 737. *Alemania ante el mundo*. See also: *Verletzung der Genfer Konvention durch französische Truppen und Freischärler*, Ecuador, AMRREE, B.1.2.

[279] Kaulen, *Las verdaderas causas de la guerra*. "Ao Redor da Guerra," in: *Jornal do Commercio* (January 31, 1915), p. 4. AA to Uruguayan MRREE (Berlin, August 21, 1914), Uruguay, AGN, PGM, MRREE, Caja 735.

[280] Thus, for example, "A Guerra (Um Ponto de Vista Sympáthico a Allemanha)," in: *Jornal do Commercio* (September 27, 1914), p. 2. Vial Solar, *Conversaciones sobre la guerra*, pp. 99–101.

[281] Niessen-Deiters, *Krieg, Auslanddeutschtum und Presse*, pp. 5 and 9–20. Ramos, "Alemania ante la guerra," p. 437. "Os Allemaes no Rio de Janeiro," in: *Jornal do Commercio* (September 22, 1914), p. 6. "Da Allemanha," in: *Jornal do Commercio* (November 1, 1914), p. 4. See also Tato, "Contra la Corriente," pp. 220–1.

[282] Ramos, "Alemania ante la guerra," pp. 428–9. Montoro, "Alemania y la guerra europea," p. 391. "Opinión de un americano sobre la guerra," in: *El Comercio* (Quito, November 25, 1914), p. 2.

[283] *Empleo, contrario al Derecho internacional*, p. 1. See also MRREE to the German Ambassador (Bogotá, November 17, 1915), Colombia, AGN, MRREE, 00556, Trasf. 1, fol. 147.

their use of colonial troops.[284] However, the use of this racist argument in Latin America cut both ways: It was certainly well received by large parts of the racist elites, yet it also implied a devaluation of their own ethnically heterogeneous continent.

Finally, the German propaganda strategists also focused on publicizing the Reich itself, for according to many Latin American observers, Germany and its achievements were still too little known. Thus the works of famous German thinkers quickly circulated in Spanish translation.[285] In terms of substance, this type of propaganda centered on military exploits, with German wartime bestsellers translated into Spanish that conveyed the linkage between modern weaponry and traditional notions of soldierly chivalry. In addition, the propagandists emphasized the technical, industrial, and military progress – in short, the power – of the German Reich.[286] Like the Allies, the German propagandists recognized that pictorial propaganda could be put to good use in Latin America at the cinema. Indeed, German newsreels were shown in many places during the war. The success was limited, however. Eugen Will, the legation councilor responsible for the coordination of the propaganda in Latin America, thus wrote in hindsight in 1918:

> Unfortunately, the films that were shown to us over there did not always meet with the audience's approval. Usually, too little emphasis was placed on variety and effective placement. Viewers were bored by the endless series of images, captured guns, and obliterated forts. Due to the lack of explanatory text, destroyed villages only seemed to confirm the enemy's lies about atrocities. The parade march looked ridiculous because of the rapid speed at which it had to be shown in the film.[287]

Offensive attacks against the enemy also did not markedly increase the effectiveness of German propaganda. That said, the most effective attacks were those against Russia, which many of the Allies' supporters considered the epitome of despotism.[288] The anti-British component, which was

---

[284] "Ao Redor da Guerra," in: *Jornal do Commercio* (January 31, 1915), p. 4. Ramos, "Alemania ante la guerra," p. 437. See also "A Inglaterra atraiçoa a raça branca," in: *A Guerra: revista semanal* 5 (December 1914), p. 11.

[285] Thus, for example, Troeltsch, *El espíritu.* See also the extensive collective edition: *Alemania y la guerra europea.* Tato, "Contra la corriente," pp. 207–10.

[286] Dohna Schlodien, *Las hazañas.* Spiegel von und zu Peckelsheim, *El submarino U 202.* Montoro, "Alemania y la guerra europea," pp. 378–9.

[287] PAAA, 121950, Eugen Will, "Bericht über die Bearbeitung der Presse und des Nachrichtenwesens" (June 6, 1918).

[288] Ramos, "Alemania ante la guerra," p. 443. See also Fernández Güel, *Plus Ultra,* pp. 5–7. "A missão da Russia prophetizada por Euclides da Cunha," in: *A República* (August 5, 1914), p. 1. Fóscolo, *Alemania ante la Guerra,* p. 19.

generally quite pronounced in German propaganda, was well received in countries like Mexico or Argentina that had experienced tensions in their relations with the island kingdom. In this context, as a topic of propaganda the Falklands/Malvinas conflict was as popular as British imperialism in general.[289]

The Latin Americans who were open to German propaganda, and indeed even helped to spread it, were conspicuously often personalities from the conservative end of the spectrum. Frequently, certain professions were represented. For instance, soldiers who were trained before the war in countries like Argentina or Chile by German military advisors and so were personally familiar with Germany were open to the arguments of the German side. Lawyers, philosophers, doctors, and Catholic clergy were also often sympathetic to Germany. Where the members of the first group had often studied in Germany, the latter were clearly moved by the anti-French sentiments.

The fulcrum of the German propaganda activities in Latin America was Argentina. Activists such as pedagogue Wilhelm Keiper and newspaper publisher Hermann Tjarks succeeded in building an extensive network that was subsidized by the German embassy. Its chief organ was the Spanish-language edition of the *Deutsche La Plata Zeitung* called *La Unión*, which started publication on October 31, 1914.[290] Like the German-language original, this paper struck a decidedly nationalistic chord that was a noticeable departure from the moderate style of the other German-language newspaper in Buenos Aires, the liberal *Argentinisches Tageblatt*, published by Theodor Alemann. Under the leadership of editor Belisario Roldán, *La Unión* reached a circulation of approximately 15,000 copies, making it by far the largest German propaganda sheet in the region. Its success was due in part to the fact that it did not present itself as a pure propaganda medium, but rather also contained general news items. The paper's influence extended beyond Argentina to Uruguay and Paraguay, where military circles and the entourage of President Eduardo Schaerer, whose parents came from Switzerland, ensured its further dissemination.[291]

---

[289] Fóscolo, *Alemania ante la Guerra*, pp. 3–5. "A Inglaterra," in: *Jornal do Commercio* (November 29, 1914), p. 10. Chavez, "L'opinion publique mexicaine," p. 113. Ramos, "Alemania ante la guerra," p. 439. See also Tato, "Contra la Corriente," pp. 212–13.

[290] "Eine spanische Ausgabe unserer Zeitung," in: *Deutsche La Plata Zeitung* (October 4, 1914), p. 2. "La Unión, die spanische Ausgabe unserer Zeitung," in: *Deutsche La Plata Zeitung* (October 25, 1914), p. 1.

[291] "Enemy propaganda in Argentina" (October 25, 1918), NA, RG 165, MID 2327 - B-108. Hoffmann, "¿Construyendo una 'comunidad'?", pp. 129. On the pro-German military context in Paraguay, see "Nuestro porvenir militar" in: *El Diario* (Asunción, August 8, 1914), p. 5 Brit. envoy, "Annual Report 1915," in: *BD*, Part II, Series D, Vol. 1, p. 50.

Given the widespread Francophilia in Argentina, it was important to convince at least some luminaries to take up the German cause and to defend it publicly. This included officer Emilio Kinkelin, who went to Germany shortly before the outbreak of war with the Argentine arms-procurement commission. Staying there as a war correspondent for *La Nación*, Kinkelin became a counterweight to those correspondents who were otherwise mostly critical of Germany. Another important voice from the military was José Félix Uriburu, who spoke out openly against the Allied propaganda and stressed the successes of German warfare.[292] Lawyers Alfredo Colmo, Ernesto Vergara, and Juan B. Ramos, and philosophers Josué A. Beruti and Coriolano Alberini also openly advocated for Germany.[293] Germanophile historian and sociologist Ernesto Quesada was especially active, attracting public attention already in 1914 with a book that defended Germany and experienced its second printing in the same year.[294]

In Brazil, public support for the Allies was even greater than in Argentina, and yet German propaganda developed here as well. With its activities, it primarily latched on to the propaganda network around Buenos Aires, such as by appropriating the news from *La Unión*.[295] Although the efforts to create a federation of ethnic Germans failed here, the latter nevertheless proved key propaganda actors due to the variety of clubs and the German press.[296] Since the first naïve published appeals to the Brazilian public's sense of fairness regarding the Germans had little resonance, they tried to gain the support of well-known personalities. Again, it was first and foremost military personnel who sided with the Germans, such as Lieutenant Pedro Cavalcanti de Albuquerque, who wrote a column in the *Jornal do Commercio* at the end of 1914 under the pseudonym Coronel Fix.[297] The faction of Germanophile physicians was strongly represented

[292] Uriburu, *La guerra actual*, pp. 3–4. On Kinkelin: "Tres meses y medio de guerra," in: *La Nación* (B. A. January 4, 1915), p. 4. Lorenz, "La gran guerra."

[293] Ramos' book was even translated into German by the German-South American Institute in Cologne: Ramos, *Die Bedeutung Deutschlands*. Newton, *German Buenos Aires*, p. 36. See also the work of lawyer F. Benavides Olazábal, *En el mundo de la filosofía y de la guerra*.

[294] Quesada, *La actual civilización germánica*. See also Quesada, "El 'peligro alemán,'" pp. 397–9.

[295] Bonow, *A desconfiança*, p. 161.

[296] On the failure of the ethnic federation efforts, see Rinke, "The Reconstruction of National Identity," pp. 173–4.

[297] "A Repercussão da Guerra," in: *Jornal do Commercio* (September 21, 1914), p. 2. "Um escriptor militar brasileiro," in: *A Guerra: revista semanal* 6 (December 1914), pp. 19–20. German-friendly voices could also be found in the military journal *A Defesa Nacional*. Bonow, *A desconfiança*, pp. 91–7.

in Brazil. One member of this group was Henrique da Rocha Lima, the cofounder of the Instituto Osvaldo Cruz, which enjoyed close ties with the Hamburg Institute of Tropical Medicine.[298] Fewer politicians and intellectuals stood up for the German Reich in Brazil than in neighboring Argentina. The deputy and chairman of the Foreign Affairs Committee, João Dunshee de Abranches, was a powerfully eloquent exception, however, as was writer José Bento Monteiro Lobato, whose Germanophilia was rather based on an attitude of non-conformism.[299]

From the perspective of German propaganda in Chile, the situation was much better. Founded in 1916, the German-Chilean Bund presented a well-organized propaganda hub with its local branches distributed throughout the country. With *El Tiempo Nuevo* and the *Revista del Pacífico*, it sporadically published Spanish-language newspapers as spin-offs of the *Deutsche Zeitung für Chile* in Santiago, which reprinted reports from *La Unión*. There were also newspapers like these in the provinces, such as the *Eco de la Guerra* in Punta Arenas. Well-known Germanophiles who expressed their views publicly could be found in many occupational groups due to the country's historically close ties to the German Reich. These included former Chilean War Minister Ricardo Cox Méndez, who traveled across Germany in 1915–16 and reported positively on his impressions, and diplomat Javier Vial Solar, lawyer Gallardo, and many others.[300]

There were even pro-German voices in the region of the North Andes with whom German propaganda could cooperate. They focused on the capital and port cities, where small but influential German communities existed. In Bogotá, they supported the newspaper *Transocean* edited by Francisco José Arévalo, the *Eco Alemán* in Caracas, the *Panorama* in Maracaibo, and *La Verdad* in Guayaquil. There was also a large number of short-lived newspapers and magazines.[301] But public advocates hoping for a German victory like Colombian nationalist Laureano Gómez, journalist Jenaro Guerrero, or the *Heraldo Conservador* in Bogotá were

---

[298] Lima, "Delenda est Germania," pp. 7–15.

[299] Abranches, *Porque devemos ser amigos da Alemanha*. Compagnon, *L'adieu à l'Europe*, pp. 190–3.

[300] "Lo que vió, oyó y observó don Ricardo Cox Méndez en la Europa en guerra," in: *Zig-Zag* (March 18, 1916). Cox, *A través de la Europa en guerra*, pp. 135–43. Gallardo, *Panamericanismo*. A list may be found in Blancpain, *Migrations et mémoire germaniques*, pp. 272–4.

[301] In Guayaquil, the publisher Gutenberg brought out monthly an uncommented compilation of articles containing translations from German publications on the war and from German-friendly Latin American publications. *La Guerra Mundial de 1914*.

rare, because here, too, the majority of the politically interested public sympathized with the Allies.[302]

The German propaganda work in Latin America was organized transnationally. In addition to Buenos Aires in the south, Mexico in the north served as a dissemination point, whose reach extended into the North Andes. Under Carranza, German activities could be carried out more or less uninterrupted. In the form of the daily *El Demócrata*, edited by Rafael Martínez (alias *Rip Rip*) – which, from 1916, had assumed a German-friendly stance on the orders of the revolutionary leader and was subsequently subsidized by the German delegation – German propaganda had an extremely effective mouthpiece.[303] It was able to get across its main points in provincial cities such as Mérida (*Boletín de la guerra*) or Monterrey (*El Heraldo Europeo*). From Mexico, the German services could reach Central America. Thus influential Germans in Guatemala founded the newspaper *El Eco Alemán* with the express approval of dictator Estrada Cabrera. German diplomats subsidized more short-lived publications in other countries of the region such as the *Amigo del Pueblo* in Honduras or *Diario de la Marina* in Cuba.[304]

The effects of the propaganda war in Latin America went far beyond the activities of the Germans and the Allies. Luminaries became involved on both sides, and, over time, disputes were increasingly played out in public. Sometimes they even got physical. For instance, despite President Suárez's admonition about maintaining neutrality, the Colombian police had to physically keep the quarreling parties in the Great Olympic Hall at arm's length in December 1914.[305] Incidents like this occurred with particular frequency among the immigrant communities of Argentina and Brazil, where debates on the war carried out in the media spilled over into public assemblies and manifested in demonstrations, protest meetings, and situational encounters on the street.[306] As one observer in Argentina noted in October 1914, suddenly there were "filos" ("friends") and "fobos" ("phobes") everywhere, who nervously followed the spectacle in Europe as if the war's opponents were directly tied to national

---

[302] Guerrero, *Alemania en la lucha*, pp. 5–46. On Gómez, see Rausch, "Colombia's Neutrality," p. 108.

[303] Katz, *The Secret War*, p. 448. Parra, "La Primera Guerra Mundial," p. 159.

[304] "Una palabra de introducción" and "Guatemala y la colonia alemana," in: *El Eco Alemán* (September 1, 1914), p. 1. Rivero/Gil, *El conflicto europeo*, p. 1. See also Schoonover, *Germany in Central America*, pp. 156–8.

[305] Rausch, "Colombia's Neutrality," p. 107.

[306] On the classification of the different forms of the public, see Bösch/Hoeres, "Im Bann der Öffentlichkeit," p. 15.

political parties.[307] In retrospect, one of the protagonists in Argentina, the nationalist intellectual and Ally sympathizer Rojas, observed that the war of opinion even occasionally took on civil war–like dimensions.[308]

Unsurprisingly, the media war was carried out in the foreign-language newspapers of immigrant communities. At the same time, the mainstream press was also affected. Argentine writer Juan Más y Pi, published an essay in *Nosotros* in December 1914 in which he unequivocally blamed the Central Powers for the war and argued that the neutrals had no alternative but to take the side of the Entente.[309] The article prompted the editor of the magazine to arrange for a survey among well-known public figures about the impact of the war on the future of mankind in general and Latin America in particular. The results confirmed in spectacular fashion the predominance of Argentine Francophilia.[310] By no means did this allay the disputes, however. On the contrary, the debates heated up so much in the following months due to intensifying propaganda activity that the editors of the *Revista Argentina de Ciencias Políticas*, for instance, prohibited the treatment of the subject in their publication at the end of 1915.[311]

At that time, numerous committees, leagues, and societies had already been formed in Argentina to support the Allies. Their members belonged to different social groups ranging from students to newspaper vendors. As historian María Inés Tato has demonstrated, the most important umbrella organization was the Comité Nacional de la Juventud (National Committee of Youth) founded in 1915, which had subgroups nationwide in the various districts of the capital, rural cities, and at the universities. Besides Barroetaveña, Lugones, and Rojas, its members included famous politicians and thinkers such as socialist Alfredo L. Palacios and poet Almafuerte (Pedro B. Palacios). They primarily organized mass demonstrations on the French national holiday, which inevitably gave way to disruptions of public order. The participation of women at these demonstrations was unprecedented. The arguments of the so-called Aliadófilos (Ally supporters) reproduced the propaganda of the Allies. They claimed that they represented the will of the people and the country's true interests. In order to save Argentina from the threat of international isolation,

[307] Castellanos, "Las consecuencias de la guerra."
[308] Rojas, *La guerra de las naciones*, p. 184.
[309] Más y Pi, "Con los nuestros."
[310] See various articles under the title "Nuestra tercera encuesta," in: *Nosotros* 8 (1914). See also Compagnon, *L'adieu à L'Europe*, pp. 69–71.
[311] "El tema de la guerra," in: Revista *Argentina de Ciencias Políticas* 11 (1915/16), p. 399.

the members of the committee made an appeal early on for renouncing neutrality.[312]

The Germanophiles and the proponents of maintaining neutrality, the so-called *neutralistas*, also made use of interest groups that were, nonetheless, much smaller than those of the Allies. The Liga Patriótica pro Neutralidad (Patriotic League for Neutrality), the Comisión Pro-Argentinidad (Pro-Argentine Commission), and the Comité Argentino (Argentinean Committee) were active in this regard. The dividing line between the two categories was not always clear, however. Inasmuch as the preservation of Argentina's neutrality was a distinct aim of German policy and propaganda, it was possible that a person who self-identified as a *neutralista* was in fact a staunch Germanophile. This was by no means true of all *neutralistas*, even though the pro-Ally forces increasingly made this allegation over the course of the war. In any event, the Federación Obrera Argentina, which condemned any form of militarism at its congress in April 1915 and threatened the country with a general strike should Argentina enter the war, was in no way sympathetic to Germany. The *neutralistas* included not only Ugarte, but other well-known personalities such as former Foreign Minister Estanislao Zeballos, popular writer Manuel Gálvez, and conservative politician Ibarguren.[313]

In Brazil, the domestic conflict also took on unexpected forms. It began with an exchange of verbal blows in the parliament between Machado and Dunshee de Abranches, who responded to Machado's pro-Ally speech with an impassioned appeal for the German Reich. In a country intent on neutrality, they both met with criticism due to their radical stances. Dunshee de Abranches had to vacate his post as chairman of the Foreign Committee, though he remained in the public eye in the following years with his pro-German writings.[314] In the press, statements were at first restrained. While there had been pro-Ally newspapers from the outset, like the *Correio da Manhã* by Liberato Bittencourt, both sides were allowed to have their say, for example, in the leading publication *Jornal do Commercio*. Magazines like *Fon-Fon* or *Careta* sought in the first months of the war to maintain a certain evenhandedness.[315]

---

[312] Tato, "La disputa por la argentinidad," pp. 233–42. Idem., "La contienda europea en las calles porteñas," p. 43.

[313] Siepe, *Yrigoyen*, pp. 64–6. Tato, "La contienda europea en las calles porteñas," pp. 56–9.

[314] Abranches, *A Allemanha e a paz*, p. 14. On the relationships, see Compagnon, *L'adieu à L'Europe*, pp. 44–6.

[315] Liberato Bittencourt, "Philosophia da guerra," in: *Correio da Manhã* (September 20, 1914), p. 3. Garambone, *A primeira Guerra Mundial*, p. 49.

The tone intensified, however, with the establishment of the Liga pelos Alliados (League for the Allies) in Rio de Janeiro on March 17, 1915, which sought to organize Brazilians who were on the side of Allies in the war. Writer José Pereira de Graça Aranha became president, and politician Rui Barbosa honorary president. Numerous well-known personalities were members of the League, including journalist and writer José Veríssimo, delegates Irineu Machado and Alexandre José Barbosa Lima, and sociologist Manoel Bomfim. The League's primary objective was the moral and material support of the Allies and it founded branches in all major cities of Brazil. In the period that followed, the League regularly organized press campaigns and rallies.[316] A popular target for attacks was Minister of Foreign Affairs Lauro Müller, who repeatedly found himself accused of partisanship because of his German ancestry. In this context, recourse was also taken to claims concerning the risk posed by the Germans in southern Brazil.[317] In this region above all there were increasingly violent clashes between German descendants and those who were citizens of the Allied nations. German specialists occupying Brazilian offices could no longer be sure of their posts.[318] In Brazil, just as in Argentina, dissenting and neutral voices such as that of nationalist Manuel de Oliveira Lima were soon suspected of being pro-German. The few unorganized Germanophile Brazilians had a hard time against the mass activities organized by groups such as the League, which claimed to speak on behalf of the national interest.[319]

The war in Europe confronted Latin Americans with significant challenges long before the first Latin American country was drawn into the conflict. New weapons and technologies, especially submarines and radio, gave rise to new spatial dimensions that could barely be controlled any longer with the traditional means of international law. The boundaries

[316] "Liga pelos Alliados," in: *Jornal do Commercio* (March 18, 1915), p. 3. On the individual members, see also Vinhosa, *O Brasil e a Primeira Guerra Mundial*, pp. 31–2. Compagnon, *L'adieu à l'Europe*, pp. 73–4.

[317] "A neutralidade brasileira," in: *Jornal do Commercio* (February 6, 1915), p. 6. Bonow, *A desconfiança*, p. 154 and pp. 174–87.

[318] Bonow, *A desconfiança*, p. 162. The dismissal of German educator Hans Heilborn at the Escola Normal in Rio de Janeiro in 1915 was intensively discussed in the press. "O caso da Escola Normal," in: *A Epoca* (June 17, 1915), p. 1. See also Luebke, *Germans in Brazil*, pp. 101–6.

[319] For a critique, see "Liga pelos Alliados," in: *Jornal do Commercio* (March 26, 1915), p. 2. The same newspaper had published a month earlier a series of articles titled "Arguments against Germany." See "Razões contra a Allemanha I – A responsabilidade," in: *Jornal do Commercio* (February 2, 1915), p. 2. On Oliveira Lima in detail: Compagnon, *L'adieu à l'Europe*, pp. 94–6. Bonow, *A desconfiança*, pp. 197–210.

between the civil and military spheres were now fluid, which was demonstrated not least by the brief but fierce naval war in South American waters and the belligerents' ships anchoring in neutral ports. Under these conditions, the most important political aim of all Latin American governments – the observance of neutrality while safeguarding the national sovereignty – was hardly achievable. In this regard, the new kind of warfare greatly exceeded the capabilities of the Latin American nation-states. Given the helplessness of the situation, their orientation toward the United States with regard to sensitive issues was quite understandable. At the same time, Latin Americans also recognized that Washington was a potential threat.

The major battlefields may have been far away, but they also cast their long shadows on Latin America and provoked a number of fundamental concerns. For instance, how were South American nations in particular to deal with the numerous ethnic minorities that had constituted the migration flows from the nineteenth century and whose countries of origin were now mercilessly at war with each other? As a result of their recruitment in the Caribbean, the roles of Britain and France as colonial powers also took center stage. Latin Americans experienced the conflict more directly when it came to the secret war and Germany's global strategy, which involved above all Mexico. The conditions of neutrality had changed fundamentally in this all-out war of global dimensions. It was no longer enough to simply keep a low profile or to remain on the sidelines.

The limitations placed on Latin Americans' room to maneuver became most apparent in the economic realm, which was of course intimately intertwined with the political. Here, the impact of the European upheavals on the Latin American economy could be detected everywhere. In August 1914, a proven decades-old system, in which the subcontinent had been permanently ensconced, suddenly collapsed. The shock waves caused by the outbreak of war were commensurately great, leading to the paralysis of the economy and dire social consequences. During this period, phenomena like unemployment and inflation were experienced throughout Latin America's export sector. The consequences were thus not limited only to the cities, but also felt in rural areas, raising concerns about the provisioning of basic necessities. The incipient recovery in many places from 1915 came at a high price, for it entailed Latin America's dependence again on Europe and its increasing reliance on the United States. The economic war, carried out in an international legal gray zone, was a painful reality, not least because of the loss of sovereignty due to the blacklists.

The war was also constantly present in the public debate in Latin America, especially in the south, because of the propaganda with its distortions and misrepresentations. Never before had an event overseas aroused such a response among the Latin American public. The war's tremendous effect in mobilizing the region was above all apparent in the interest people expressed for the belligerents' disputes. Although the focus was unmistakably on the capitals and port cities, the propagandists also sought to reach rural areas, which in the end was only partially successful. The fact that the pro-Ally voices clearly prevailed was not surprising given the initial situation of a deeply rooted Francophilia and the German war of aggression. In general, however, there were heterogeneous groupings on both sides with different motives that can be understood only in the local context. The propaganda war made one thing particularly clear, however: In this war, it was not possible to adopt a wait-and-see attitude. Gallardo was certainly right when he noted that the new war demanded an active neutrality. Still, it was difficult to put this demand into practice.

3

In the Wake of War, 1917

In January 1915, when it was already obvious that the war would take much longer than originally anticipated, the Argentine daily *La Nación* commented: "It is highly unlikely that this continent will be pulled into the vortex."[1] Two years later, this estimation would prove false. Actually, the war emanating from Europe had expanded into a global conflagration long before 1917. Latin America, which contributed to the conflict by exporting war-critical raw materials, was impacted in a variety of ways due to the economic and propaganda war. Nevertheless, the year 1917 would turn out to be an important milestone for the subcontinent: The United States, but also many Latin American countries, officially entered the war, which until then had taken place (if only officially) outside of their own hemisphere. Thereby Americans broke with the more than 100-year-old principle of Pan-American foreign policy to avoid entangling alliances. As a consequence, the war's ongoing pull on the whole of Latin America became much stronger. The political and socioeconomic problems apparent since August 1914 were exacerbated and the emotional character of the public debates gained in intensity. In addition, the events of 1917 gave rise to new fundamental questions about the relationship with the United States and the individual treatment of national minorities. Above all, however, Latin American countries faced the serious decision about whether to enter the war on the side of the Allies or to maintain their neutrality.

---

[1] Estlin Grundy, "La neutralidad sud americana," in: *La Nación* (B. A., January 28, 1915), p. 4.

SUBMARINE WARFARE AND THE UNITED STATES

The fact that this decision had to be made was due mainly to the radicalization of the German war effort by means of unrestricted submarine warfare against merchant ships in general. In 1915 and 1916, the German Reich had once again limited its use of submarines, primarily because of pressure from the U.S. government. When the hardliners prevailed in the German high command at the end of 1916 and not only ignored President Wilson's peace initiative in December, which had received wide approval in Latin America, but also once again took up a policy of unrestricted submarine warfare on February 1, 1917, the United States made good on its threat by breaking off diplomatic relations with the Reich two days later.[2]

Although this was still not a declaration of war, the U.S. diplomats gave an unambiguous signal to their counterparts in Latin America of what they now expected from them. Thus the U.S. ambassador in Buenos Aires, Frederic J. Stimson, remarked to the city's *La Prensa* that the United States hoped that the other American countries would follow their example out of solidarity, for "even those countries most distant from the conflict could not ignore the issues of international law raised by the war."[3] In fact, Washington immediately implemented military strategic security measures and focused on the Panama Canal. Together with Panama, whose government was dependent on the United States, the State Department unequivocally called on the Colombian government to begin to monitor the Gulf of Urabá, as it suspected the activities of German submarines there. At the same time, rumors emerged in the U.S. press of a German–Colombian alliance for the conquest of the Panama Canal, which, despite the insistence of the government in Bogotá to the contrary, were not easy to dispel.[4]

The German declaration of the U-boat war incited astonishment and criticism in Latin America. The reactions to the U.S. break of diplomatic relations were divided, however. For an Ally sympathizer like Lugones, the German declaration was evidence of the inhuman militarism of the

---

[2] On the contexts, see, e.g., Fiebig-von Hase, "Der Anfang vom Ende des Krieges," pp. 127–31. On the Latin American reaction to Wilson's initiative, see the correspondence in *FRUS 1917 Supplement I*, pp. 219–20. "El presidente Wilson, mediador de paz," in: *Zig-Zag* (January 6, 1917).

[3] "Alemania y los neutrales," in: *La Prensa* (B. A., February 8, 1917), p. 9.

[4] MRREE to the Ministro de Guerra (Bogotá, February 5, 1917), Colombia, AGN, MRREE, 00560, Trasf. 1, fol. 241. MRREE to the Ministro de Guerra (Bogotá, March 6, 1917), ibid., Fol. 249–50.

Germans.[5] The Brazilian daily *A Epoca* even printed the headline: "The Emperor has gone mad."[6] The Ally-friendly forces in Brazil demanded for moral and political reasons a close cooperation with the United States. In their view, the German submarines were also a threat to Brazilian navigation.[7] The *Liga pelos Aliados* criticized the Brazilian government's muted official response to the German declaration of submarine warfare as inadequate and overly careful and also urged the end of neutrality.[8] Argentine socialists made similar calls and demanded sanctions to put an end to "Germany's flagrant brutality."[9] A commentary from the Uruguayan newspaper *La Razón* summarized the main critiques of the submarine warfare. First, it was a blatant violation of the right of neutrals, which the Germans now for all intents and purposes treated as enemies; second, this kind of warfare represented an existential threat to neutral trade.[10] The Cuban and even the Mexican governments joined in the protests.[11] Bolivians could read in the press of La Paz that even a landlocked country like Bolivia should welcome the United States' move as it concerned the basic interests of all neutrals. Therefore, the government of General Ismael Montes suggested a joint declaration by all American states against submarine warfare, which, however, ultimately did not materialize.[12]

Still, the Brazilian government was not the only government to ignore the demand for clearer words of protest and active countermeasures. Although the foreign ministries sent more or less vigorous protest notes and expressed their solidarity with Washington in diplomatic language, Latin American nations remained otherwise tentative. The Paraguayan government hence communicated that while it was in complete agreement with the U.S. position, it nonetheless did not want to make this

[5] Lugones, *Mi beligerancia*, p. 156.

[6] "O Kaiser enlouqueceu," in: *A Epoca* (February 2, 1917), p. 1.

[7] "A guerra marítima e a sua repercussão no Brasil," in: *Jornal do Commercio* (February 8, 1917), p. 3.

[8] "A neutralidade Brasileira," in: *Jornal do Commercio* (February 5, 1917), p. 3.

[9] "Los neutrales y la guerra," in: *La Vanguardia* (February 4, 1917), p. 1. Geli, "Representations of the Great War," p. 211.

[10] "La actitud de Alemania," in: *La Razón* (February 8, 1917), p. 3. See also "EE.UU. y la ruptura," in: *El Siglo* (February 5, 1917), p. 3.

[11] U.S. envoy to Sec. of State (Panama, February 4, 1917), in: FRUS 1917 I, p, 222. See also Gutiérrez y Sánchez, *La neutralidad*, pp. 55–7. "El representante mexicano en Berlín protesta," in: *El Demócrata* (May 22, 1917), p. 1.

[12] "Bolivia y la guerra," in: *El Tiempo* (La Paz, February 5, 1917), p. 4. For a similarly worded commentary in Chile, see "El conflicto germano-americano," in: *El Mercurio* (February 7, 1917), p. 3.

officially known to the German Reich. The Argentine government similarly agreed in principle with the United States, yet was unwilling to follow State Department policy, since the rights of its own country had not yet been violated.[13] President Juan Luis Sanfuentes of Chile further explained to the U.S. ambassador in confidential talks that his country could not meet Washington's expectations because Chile was too small and had no problems with the German Reich.[14]

In many Latin American countries, the hope prevailed among the public that the war would not spill over to the Americas.[15] An opinion poll from *Caras y Caretas* of Argentine parliamentarians in February 1917 revealed that while a large number indeed continued to declare their sympathy for France, the vast majority nevertheless wanted to continue to preserve their neutrality, despite the U.S. entry into the conflict.[16] The general consensus seemed to be the economic and political interests of the country lay entirely in the Americas.[17] The political commentator of *La Prensa* wrote extensively about the situation. In his view, Argentina had completely different interests than the United States, if only because it did not have its own ships in the war zone and thus no losses to report. He vehemently criticized the notion that the United States might represent the ideal protector of all the neutrals. After all, European ships and a Brazilian ship had been sunk over the course of two years without Washington having done anything about it. The columnist appealed to his readers to not lose sight of the interests of their own country: "Our interests and our solidarity with the European civilization obliges us to uphold our moral authority in order to bring about peace, to maintain permanent neutrality, and, in addition, to avoid conflicts."[18]

The Ecuadorian newspaper *El Comercio* argued along similar lines in a series of articles titled "The new international conflict," published in four parts from February 7–10. The columnist stressed that the escalation of the U.S.–German tensions was more important for Latin America than the outbreak of war in 1914. Nevertheless, in this turn of events the subcontinent was by no means as prepared as their northern neighbor. Even though the United States' uncompromising course of action had

[13] U.S. envoy to Sec. of State (Asunción and B. A., ea. on February 8, 1917), in: *FRUS* 1917 II, pp. 225–6.
[14] Ambassador at Dept. of State (Santiago de Chile, February 10, 1917), NA, RG 59, M 367, Reel 32.
[15] "EE.UU. y Alemania," in: *El Diario Ilustrado* (February 4, 1917).
[16] "La Argentina y la guerra," in: *Caras y Caretas* (February 24, 1917).
[17] "Neutrales y beligerantes," in: *La Razón* (B. A., February 6, 1917), p. 3.
[18] "El polo de la paz," in: *La Prensa* (B. A., February 5, 1917), p. 5.

a tremendous impact on Latin America, the columnist complained, the government in Washington did not coordinate in any way with its partners. He further added that, despite its lofty Pan-American rhetoric, the United States ultimately only pursued its own particular interests (see Figure 3.1).[19]

In addition, proposals on mediation and peace initiatives were now voiced from a variety of corners in Latin America, beginning with the governments of Paraguay and Ecuador. Both countries suggested a peace congress of the American states that would declare the protection of the rights of neutrals a common goal.[20] Shortly thereafter, Mexico and Argentina took the lead on the initiative, redefining it as a general peace conference. This, however, found little support in Latin America. The United States did not welcome such Pan-American activity because it wanted to keep a free hand in the rapidly escalating conflict with the German Reich. Brazil and Chile also declined their support for different reasons: Brazil, because it did not want to submit itself to an initiative of the neighboring country and rival Argentina; and Chile, because it was wary of demands from its neighbors Bolivia and Peru at a continental congress.[21] The Chileans hoped rather for the revival of the exclusive A.B.C. for settling disputes.[22]

All these more or less half-hearted initiatives were dashed once a diplomatic cable that was severely compromising to Germany was simultaneously released in the United States and in Latin America on March 1, 1917. The Mexican *Universal*, one of the few openly pro-Ally papers in Mexico under publisher Félix Palavicini, thus published the full text of a telegram of German State Secretary of Foreign Affairs, Arthur Zimmermann, which would go down in world history as the Zimmermann telegram.[23] The content of this correspondence from the Foreign Office in Berlin in January – sent encrypted via the embassy in Washington to Mexico, but

---

[19] "El nuevo conflicto Internacional, parte I–IV," in: *El Comercio* (Quito, February 7–10, 1917), p. 1. See also "La lección de los hechos," in: ibid. (April 11, 1917), morning edition, p. 1. See also "Babilonias modernas," in: *El Progreso* (April 3, 1917), p. 1.

[20] U.S. envoy to Sec. of State (Asunción, February 15, 1917), in: *FRUS* 1917 II, p. 232. Ecuadorian envoy to Sec. of State (Washington, D.C., February 19, 1917), ibid., p. 233. MRREE to all foreign ministries in Latin America (Quito, September 11, 1917), in: Ecuador, AMRREE, U.8.

[21] U.S. ambassador to Sec. of State (B. A., February 27, 1917), in: *FRUS* 1917 II, p. 235.

[22] "Momento sudamericano," in: *La Nación* (Santiago de Chile, February 10, 1917), p. 3.

[23] Parra, "La Primera Guerra Mundial," pp. 162–3. See also "Declara el Secretario de Estado," in: *El Nacional* (March 1, 1917), p. 2.

El negocio en quiebra

Tío Sam.—Ya que he conquistado tantos dólares para mi bandera, es muy justo que consiga ahora unos cuantos laureles!....

FIGURE 3.1 Commerce is bankrupt. For the cartoonist of the Chilean magazine, the rupture with Germany by the United States was by no means solely attributable to noble motives. According to the caption, Uncle Sam wanted to decorate himself with military laurels after he had made enough money on the war. In February 1917, numerous caricatures like this one questioned the sincerity of the United States' motives.

Source: Luco, "El negocio en quiebra," in: *Zig-Zag* (February 10, 1917).

then decrypted by the British – was stunning. One could read, among other things:

We intend to begin unrestricted submarine warfare on February 1. The attempt will nevertheless be made to keep America neutral. In the event that this should not succeed, we will propose to Mexico that we enter into an alliance on the following basis: Joint warfare. A common peace agreement. Abundant financial support and consent on our part (which does not constitute a guarantee) to Mexico recapturing earlier lost territory in Texas, New Mexico, and Arizona (California will likely be reserved for Japan). Arrangement of the particulars will be left to Your Excellency. Your Excellency will want to divulge the foregoing under strict secrecy to the president once the war has broken out with the United States and encourage him to invite Japan to immediately enter the war of its own accord and at the same time to mediate between us and Japan. Please inform the president that unrestricted use of our submarines now offers the prospect of forcing the peace with England in a matter of months.[24]

What must have come as a terrible shock to uninitiated contemporaries made more sense within the context of Germany's efforts to align itself with Carranza. The idea of a joint German–Mexican military action was already secretly in the works in 1915/16 and was initiated by the Mexican side. In 1915, Carranza himself proposed cooperation for a joint attack on British Honduras and Guatemala and in the negotiations in 1916 the idea of a military collaboration remained on the table. Specifically, the Mexicans raised the possibility of a joint military action against the United States. The Zimmermann telegram was a response to these proposals that the German side had originally dismissed.[25] In addition, in 1916, the German Reich had sought a rapprochement with Japan, which shared Mexico's antagonism toward the United States and was in negotiations with the Mexican government. A Germany-supported Indian independence fighter like Manabedra Nath Roy was supposed to negotiate not only in Mexico with Carranza, but also with the Japanese. Mexico was increasingly becoming a main fulcrum for the German Reich's global strategy.[26]

This was the context in which Zimmermann's telegram was sent – a time when it was, moreover, already apparent that the U.S. entry into the war was imminent because of the U-boat warfare. Katz has rightly

---

[24] Quoted in Nassua, *Gemeinsame Kriegführung*, pp. 16–7.
[25] Schuler, *Secret Wars*, pp. 175–7.
[26] There were secret negotiations as early as 1916 in Stockholm between the German and Japanese ambassadors on a separate peace agreement. Katz, *The Secret War*, pp. 351–67. On Roy: Goebel, "M. N. Roy." On the negotiations between Carranza and Japan, see Schuler, *Secret Wars*, p. 156.

observed that "the alliance proposal was in reality a large-scale deceptive maneuver to incite Carranza to a suicidal attack on the United States."[27] In the event of Mexico's consent, Berlin would have let the Mexicans fight alone, since effective support would have been impossible and the German Reich also did not believe that Japan would be willing to get involved. On February 20, a conversation took place between the German envoy and Carranza, who rejected the proposal, even though there was no shortage of advocates within the Mexican government. Carranza cleverly avoided offending the Germans, and realizing he was dependent on weapons and money from abroad to stabilize his government, he also managed as a precaution to keep the door open to future negotiations.[28]

The lack of knowledge of these secret negotiations caused the publication of the Zimmermann telegram to explode in the public media. In Mexico itself, the Carranza-loyal press initially dismissed the publication as a typical hoax of the tabloids, commenting that the offer of an alliance seemed ludicrous.[29]*El Demócrata* remarked that even if the cable were genuine and meant to be taken seriously, the government could never agree to it, for Mexico was interested in promoting peace.[30] While the U.S. government took Carranza to task, he denied negotiating with the German Reich and even launched his own initiative to mediate between the United States and Germany.[31] In the United States, not only did the press take the Zimmermann telegram seriously, but so did government circles.[32] When Secretary of State Zimmermann confirmed the authenticity of the document on March 3, the initial doubts about the actual existence of the initiative, which were pervasive in Latin America, quickly dissipated.

The repercussions for U.S. Latin American policy were soon evident. The heightened anxiety that had taken root in the United States in the wake of the rising tensions was revealed by the internment of German sailors in Panama in mid-March, even before the official declaration of

[27] Katz, *The Secret War*, p. 353.
[28] Ibid., pp. 353–83.
[29] "El gran escándalo amarillista," in: *El Demócrata* (March 3, 1917), p 3.
[30] "Como pensamos," in: *El Demócrata* (March 3, 1917), p. 3.
[31] U.S. ambassador to Sec. of State (Mexico, April 3, 1917), in: *FRUS* 1917 II, p. 243. "La prensa sigue haciendo comentarios," in: *El Demócrata* (March 2, 1917), p. 2.
[32] Sec. of State Robert Lansing, Memorandum (Washington, DC, March 4, 1917), in: *The Papers of Woodrow Wilson*, Vol. 41, pp. 321–7. For a new detailed analysis of the reactions by U.S. citizens, see Boghardt, *The Zimmermann Telegram*.

war.[33] U.S. Secretary of State Lansing instructed envoys in March 16 per circular decree to regularly report on the activities of the Germans in their respective countries and the attitude of the governments toward the United States and Germany.[34]

The United States' official entry into the war took place on April 6, 1917. Strong reactions were triggered throughout Latin America. *La Razón* in Montevideo thus wrote: "America is no longer the continent of peace," and *El Comercio* in Quito spoke of a "black hour for Latin America."[35] As with the earlier rupture of diplomatic relations, opinions were thoroughly divided. The *Correio da Manhã*, for instance, called on Brazil to now stand alongside the United States against imperialism and for the values of the Americas, since Germany had proven itself an enemy of peace and, with its U-boat war, also threatened the sovereignty of their own country.[36] The *Jornal do Commercio* invoked the continental ideals of freedom, justice, and righteousness, arguing that they were worth fighting for.[37] In Argentina, there were massive demonstrations of support on the occasion of the U.S. entry into the war. Ricardo Rojas pointed to the new global dimension of the war, now that Canada, Australia, New Zealand, Transvaal, Egypt, India, China, Japan, and even the United States had become involved.[38] For both Argentina and the United States, moreover, the sinking of the countries' respective merchant ships by German U-boats played a major role.[39]

Other Brazilian newspapers such as *El Imparcial*, however, cautioned against overly harsh reactions, because national interests needed to take priority.[40] In Ecuador, the conservative press urged the country to maintain its neutrality, as it was too small and weak to interfere in a "Battle of the Titans."[41] In general, numerous editorials discussed the possible

---

[33] U.S. envoy to Dept. of State (Panama, March 17, 1917), NA, RG 59, M 336, Reel 45.

[34] Lansing to embassies and legations in Latin America (Washington, DC, March 16, 1917), NA, RG 59, M 336, Reel 45.

[35] "La guerra de América," *La Razón* (April 12, 1917) p. 1. "Ante el desastre humano," in: *El Comercio* (Quito, April 11, 1917) late edition, p. 1. See also "A intervenção americana," in: *Correio da Manhã* (February 4, 1917), p. 1.

[36] "O pan-americanismo," in: *Correio da Manhã* (February 5, 1917) p. 1. "A attitude brasileira," in: *Correio da Manhã* (February 6, 1917), p. 1. See also Garambone, *A primeira Guerra Mundial*, p. 84.

[37] "Varias Noticias," in: *Jornal do Commercio* (April 6, 1917), p. 3. There were also positive reactions in Uruguay: "Sucesos internacionales," in: *La Razón* (April 12, 1917), p. 2.

[38] Rojas, *La guerra de las naciones*, pp. 11–34.

[39] "Las cuestiones internacionales y la opinión pública," in: *Caras y Caretas* (April 28, 1917).

[40] "A attitude do governo," in: *O Imparcial* (February 6, 1917), p. 2.

[41] "La guerra," in: *El Progreso* (April 20 and May 1, 1917), p. 1.

consequences of the United States' move. Hence, the Mexican newspaper *Excelsior* suggested that while the active participation of U.S. troops in the European theater was unlikely, it was all the more probable that the United States would try to exert its influence in Latin America and especially in neighboring Mexico.[42] In particular, the commentaries in Latin America took stock of the economic consequences, given that the U.S. entry into the war meant that the last remaining neutral market in an industrialized country had been eliminated. This was a severe limitation for the agricultural exporters of the region.[43] In an interview with the *New York Times*, Chilean diplomat and international lawyer Alejandro Álvarez was able to concisely summarize the diverse range of opinions. According to Álvarez, the United States' entry into the war was a historic turn of events with crucial ramifications for the whole of the Americas. Even the most neutral states wished their neighbor to the north well out of a feeling of American solidarity. Still, Álvarez did not mention anything about Latin Americans' active support.[44]

The concerns of Latin American skeptics would prove valid. After entering the war, the United States immediately tried to disrupt the Germans' lines of communication by taking over the radio stations in Sayville and Tuckerton and tightening censorship. In addition, Washington exerted pressure on the Latin American governments to shut down radio stations with German stakeholders.[45] The anxiety around the strategically important Panama Canal and the Caribbean intensified because the U.S. government suspected that there were German U-boats operating in the region that could threaten the channel. The U.S. Office of Naval Intelligence took great pains to secure this territory by means of an intelligence network. For this purpose, the service used, among other things, discreet scientists. The intensive secret service operations that had been conducted since the outbreak of the revolution in Mexico were now expanded.[46] In addition, the Allies shared responsibility for guarding the Atlantic coast of the Americas. The French patrolled from the West Indies

[42] "México y la guerra germano-americana," in: *Excelsior* (April 5, 1917), p. 3. "La guerra contra los neutrales," in: ibid. (April 13, 1917), p. 3.

[43] "América y los submarinos," in: *La Prensa* (B. A., July 23, 1917), pp. 5–6. "El conflicto yanqui germano y sus prolongaciones en Sud América," in: *El Comercio* (Quito, April 20, 1917), p. 1.

[44] Martínez, "La entrada de Cuba en la guerra universal," pp. 9–10.

[45] U.S. consul at Dept. of State (Bluefields, May 18, 1917), NA, RG 59, M 336, Reel 45.

[46] Dept. of State to envoys in Chile, Colombia, Costa Rica, Ecuador, Guatemala, Honduras, Nicaragua, Peru, El Salvador, and Venezuela (Washington, DC, October 15, 1917), NA, RG 59, M 336, Reel 45. Harris/Sadler, *The Archaeologist*, pp. 2 and 38.

to Fernando de Noronha, and the British from Río de la Plata to Tierra del Fuego. The middle part between Fernando de Noronha and the Río de la Plata was guarded by the United States, which had sent a squadron to Brazil in June under the command of Admiral William B. Caperton, who had previously commanded the invasion of Haiti.[47]

The U.S. entry into the war was also of decisive importance for Latin America in economic terms. At one blow, the export of war-critical goods had become radically constrained. Since many infrastructure projects in the region depended on these supplies, which were now suddenly unavailable, work came to a halt and layoffs resulted.[48] Furthermore, the United States strengthened efforts to push out the Germans and promote its own businesses in the region.[49] Progressively developed warfare legislation gave the government broad powers, culminating in the establishment of the War Trade Board in October 1917. On October 6, supplementing the European Allies, the Board published for the first time its own blacklist, the Enemy Trading List, which would be updated and expanded several times by the end of the war. Not only that, the U.S. State Department urged Latin American governments to nationalize German properties or to put them up for sale to U.S. interests. Success was had particularly in the weak nations of Central America and the Caribbean that were dependent on the United States. The situation deteriorated markedly for the German economic concerns in the region.[50]

Another key area of U.S. warfare in Latin America was the propaganda war. Just one week after the United States entered the war, journalist George Creel founded the Committee on Public Information, known as the Creel Committee for short. The Committee was the central agency for U.S. propaganda worldwide. Latin America was a primary focus of its work, where it centered on influencing the press, distributing films, setting up reading rooms with U.S. literature, and organizing promotional trips for influential Latin Americans in the United States and vice versa. In addition, the Creel Committee operated offices locally, where it collaborated with long-standing English-language newspapers such as the *West*

---

[47] Weinmann, *Argentina en la Primera Guerra Mundial*, p. 125.
[48] Consul General to MRREE (New York, August 7, 1917), Colombia, AGN, MRREE, Caja 94, carp. 3, Trasf. 5, fol. 88–90.
[49] Thus, for example, through the Bureau of Foreign and Domestic Commerce of the Dept. of Commerce. US RG 151, General Records, passim.
[50] "Os bancos allemães," in: *Jornal do Commercio* (February 7, 1917), p. 8. U.S. War Trade Board, *Trading with the Enemy*, pp. 3–4. For various examples of diplomatic pressure, see Rosenberg, *World War I*, pp. 50–2.

Coast Leader in Lima.[51] The staff also took advantage of the business correspondence of U.S. companies to spread propaganda material and engaged commercial travelers to give them reports. Most important was undoubtedly the chance to use an up-to-date news service via the former German station in Tuckerton. News was transmitted wirelessly and then immediately disseminated by the Havas or Creel employees.[52]

Given the high rate of illiteracy and the lack of other forms of entertainment, especially in the rural areas of Latin America, the Creel Committee focused on image propaganda, which was very well received. The success was based on a detailed and systematic analysis of the cinema market with its distribution companies, production firms, and movie theaters. As it turned out, the audience was largely conservative, which meant that all films had to be strictly censored. Suggestive love or dance scenes were to be avoided. Low-quality films or those that criticized life in the United States were not allowed to be shown.[53]

A significant part of the Committee's work was dedicated to fighting against the German influence. If organizations were identified as pro-German or even as only critical of the Allies or the United States, they were placed – even when there was only the slightest suspicion – on the blacklist, and pressure was applied by depriving them of paper.[54] These actions successfully undermined the flow of German propaganda. A schematic diagram from 1918 shows that, through its censorship, the U.S. Postal Service could effectively inhibit the path of German propaganda as it traveled from Spain, Havana, and New York. Even German propaganda material sent to the south from Mexico and El Salvador could be intercepted and censored at the Panama Canal. However, the route from Spain to Buenos Aires and from there to Montevideo, Rio de Janeiro, La Paz, and Santiago remained open.[55]

---

[51] Mock, "The Creel Committee," p. 264. Creel, *How We Advertised America. Complete Report*, pp. 149–55.

[52] "Report on US Propaganda in the Argentine" (May 28, 1918), NA, RG 165, MID, 2327-12. "Universitarios chileno-yanquis," in: *El Mercurio* (Valparaíso, July 30, 1918), p. 5.

[53] "South America and the War" (1918), NA, RG 63, Entry 132, Box 4, pp. 19–22.

[54] "South America and the War" (1918), NA, RG 63, Entry 132, Box 4, p. 45. Dept. of State, Division of Latin American Affairs to Julius Klein, Chief Bureau of Foreign and Domestic Commerce (Washington, DC, October 31, 1917), NA, RG 151, General Records, 470. On the paper boycott in Mexico: Katz, *The Secret War*, pp. 454–5. See the numerous reports in NA, RG 63, Entry 209, passim.

[55] "German Propaganda Mail Routes" (undated), NA, RG 63, Entry 117, Box 1. On the role of Spain in German propaganda, see Albes, *Worte wie Waffen* On the lists, see NA, RG 63, Entry 117, Box 1. See also the reports of the U.S. censors. NA, RG 63, Entry 117.

Public relations activities were already evident in April 1917, as the agents of the Creel Committee promoted the cause of the United States in the Latin American press with numerous unattributed articles. Here, the United States was primarily portrayed as a powerful, indeed invincible nation. For reprinting the propaganda, the newspapers received financial or other benefits, such as paper allocations, which made the arrangement worthwhile (see Figure 3.2).[56] Furthermore, the Creel employees spread Spanish translations of speeches by President Wilson as well as pan-German fabrications like Tannenberg's *Groß-Deutschland* or even a map with a divided Latin America in the pamphlet *Ambiciones alemanas sobre América del Sur*, which referred to Tannenberg.[57]

U.S. propaganda was further reinforced through the involvement of prominent Latin Americans, such as those in the Latin American Committee in New York.[58] Deliberate efforts were made to recruit Latin American intellectuals and cultural elites. The Sociedad Panamericana de Señoras, founded by Lansing's wife, Eleanor Foster Lansing, was dedicated to soliciting the support of women. Through intensive Spanish and Portuguese language instruction and spreading mutual knowledge, the organization aimed to improve understanding between the Americas and mitigate concerns regarding U.S. imperialism. Contemporary observers, however, soon noted that the self-praise in the propaganda was often excessive and that the emphasis on the economic power of the United States actually aroused new fears.[59]

In fact, the German counter-propagandists seized on these very points. From the beginning of the United States' entry into the war, they latched onto the widespread anti-imperialist feelings in Latin America that had been chiefly directed against the United States since the Spanish-American War as a central element in their repertoire. In this regard, a multitude of already circulating critical writings on "Yankee Imperialism," such as those from Honduran poet Salvador Turcios, were helpful.[60] In particular,

---

[56] "1776-4 de julio – 1917," in: *Caras y Caretas* (July 7, 1917). "Los EE.UU. entran a la guerra," in: *Zig-Zag* (April 14, 1917). "Wilson, leader da politica da civilisação," in: *A Epoca* (March 22, 1918) p. 1. "La riqueza de EE.UU.," in: *El Mercurio* (Valparaíso, July 31, 1918), p. 3.

[57] *"Las intenciones de Alemania,"* in: Uruguay, AGN, PGM, MRREE, Caja 737.

[58] "El Comité latino-americano de Nueva York," in: *El Día* (Chillán, September 27, 1918), p. 1.

[59] See, for example, *La nueva interpretación de la Doctrina de Monroe*, pp. 11–13. Mann, *Kampf um den Kultureinfluss*, pp. 5–12. For this type of propaganda, see "El comercio marítimo," in: *La Unión* (Santiago, September 15, 1918), p. 1. "Los EE.UU. banqueros del mundo," in: *La Nación* (Santiago, September 20, 1918), p. 1. "Cuestiones económicas," in: *La Opinión* (October 9, 1918), p. 1.

[60] Turcios, *Al margen del imperialismo yanqui*.

FIGURE 3.2 The glorious United States. While the Chilean magazine still printed cartoons in April that were critical of the United States, propaganda from the north was predominant by the time of U.S. Independence Day in 1917. *Zig-Zag* received U.S. subsidies, although this did not prevent the magazine from publishing pro-German articles too.

Source: "En nombre de la civilización y de la libertad," in: *Zig-Zag* (July 7, 1917).

pro-German authors like the Chilean Gallardo or the Argentinean Vergara frequently criticized that while the United States warned about the "German threat," the United States itself was in reality the much greater danger to Latin America. Even decidedly less Germanophilic authors were convinced that Wilson's idealistic words were barely credible and that the United States' actual aim in entering the conflict was to displace the Europeans from the subcontinent in order to attain unchallenged economic and political supremacy there.[61] Although the anti-imperialist discourse took on a growing importance for Latin Americans, this should not belie the fact that it was finally only of limited benefit for German propaganda, whose situation became noticeably more complicated as a result of the United States' entry into the war.

SEVERED RELATIONS AND ENTRIES INTO WAR

The United States' entry into the war set into motion an undertow effect in the Americas that is not to be underestimated. At the same time, the attitude of the Latin American governments in early 1917 may not be simply reduced to the influence of Washington. The contexts and the reactions that crystallized over the course of the year were too distinct to reduce them to a common denominator (Table 3.1). Nonetheless, a look at the individual cases reveals five categories: first, the U.S. protectorates Cuba and Panama, which entered the war directly on the heels of the United States; second, the states of Central America and Haiti, which initially broke off relations with the German Reich only to then declare war shortly before the conflict ended in 1918; third, Brazil, which is the only South American country to not only sever ties with Germany, but to enter the war in 1917; fourth, the countries of South America, which only broke off relations with Germany, without entering the war (in practice, however, this meant abandoning neutrality, since they now treated the Allied powers as friendly nations and no longer imposed restrictions, e.g., as regards maritime traffic); fifth, the states that retained their neutrality throughout the war.

In the Dominican Republic, which stood under the military administration of the U.S. Navy and had completely lost its sovereignty with the intervention of 1916, Washington was able to enforce the same provisions of martial law from April 1917 that were in effect in the United States.[62] Furthermore, Secretary Lansing had categorically stated in a

[61] Gallardo, *Panamericanismo*, p. 136. Vergara, *Guerra de mentiras*, pp. 21–35.
[62] Moya, *The Dominican Republic*, p. 324.

TABLE 3.1. *The stance of Latin American countries in the First World War*

South America	Neutral	Severing of Relations	Entry into the War
Argentina	X		
Bolivia		April 13, 1917	
Brazil		April 11, 1917	October 26, 1917
Chile	X		
Colombia	X		
Ecuador		December 7, 1917	
Paraguay	X		
Peru		October 6, 1917	
Uruguay		October 7, 1917	
Venezuela	X		

Northern Latin America	Neutral	Severing of Relations	Entry into the War
Costa Rica		September 21, 1917	May 23, 1918
Cuba.		April 7, 1917	April 7, 1917
El Salvador	X		
Guatemala		April 27, 1917	April 23, 1918
Haiti		June 17, 1917	July 12, 1918
Honduras		May 17, 1917	July 19, 1918
Mexico	X		
Nicaragua		May 18, 1917	May 5, 1918
Panama		April 7, 1917	April 7, 1917

Source: Martin, *Latin America and the War*. Bailey, *The Policy of the United States towards the Neutrals*, p. 306.

letter to President Wilson on March 26, 1917, that Cuba and Panama were unlikely to remain neutral should the United States enter the war. Otherwise, both countries would offer, according to Lansing, ideal collecting points for German refugees and spies as well as submarine bases. In addition, Cuban and Panamanian neutrality would greatly restrict the U.S. military's freedom of movement with regard to the Canal and the naval base in Guantánamo. Lansing's conclusion was clear: Both countries, accordingly, also needed to enter the war. Tellingly, he added that he had the means to influence the respective governments.[63] In fact, Cuba and Panama entered the conflict just a day after the United States on

---

[63] Sec. of State Lansing to President Wilson (Washington, DC, March 26, 1917), NA, RG 59, M 743, Reel 59, pp. 352–3.

April 7, 1917, and one of the first measures was the internment of suspicious Germans and ethnic Germans.[64]

In Cuba, which had had the status of a protectorate since its independence from Spain in 1898, the controversial reelection of conservative President Mario García Menocal in 1916 led to a revolt on the part of the liberals. The declaration of war against Germany was therefore not only a response to the pressure from the United States, but, by making an appeal to patriotism, also a domestic political maneuver to curb the insurgency. To a certain degree, it succeeded. The Cuban government spared no effort to legitimize the island's entry into the war, invoking the noble ideals of struggle for national honor and against Prussianism. Beyond this, deputy Luis L. Adám Galareta made reference to the defense of civilization against barbarism and feelings of gratitude and solidarity with the Allies.[65] According to Adám, heroic Cuba, which had fought for many years for its own freedom, now joined with its allies to fight for the freedom of the world.[66]

The entry into the war had indeed taken the wind out of the Liberals' sails, but above all eastern Cuba with its sugar plantations remained highly contested, as the politically motivated rebellion there had devolved into a state of social unrest. This, in turn, gave rise to rumors about German sabotage activities. The United States therefore decided to intervene again. The first U.S. Marines arrived in the country in August 1917, officially at the invitation of Menocal, who in July had declared a state of emergency because of the alleged espionage threat and suspended basic rights. The troops were sent to protect the sugar harvest and defend against German secret service operations. By the end of 1918, the number of U.S. Marines was markedly increased because of the growing unrest. They would remain until 1922.[67]

In its war measures, the Cuban government followed the United States' wishes to the letter. Thus, Cuba was the first country to hand over – on the State Department's "suggestion" – four confiscated German steamers to the U.S. government in August 1917 for the purpose of alleviating the

---

[64] U.S. envoy to Sec. of State (Panama, April 19, 1917), in: *FRUS* 1918 Supplement 2, *The World War*, p. 235. The U.S. authorities succeeded in relocating the internees to New York to keep them even farther away from the danger zone, i.e., the Panama Canal.

[65] Adám Galareta, "Porque estamos en la guerra," pp. 7–8.

[66] Pardo Suárez, *Ladrones de tierras*, p. 129. On the Cuban context, see Perez, *Intervention*, pp. 65–87.

[67] Perez, *Intervention*, pp. 88–103.

shipping space shortage, which had been exacerbated by the submarine war.[68] The country also made an important contribution to the war effort through its sugar exports. These were mainly sold in 1917 to the Inter-Allied Sugar Commission and in 1918 to the United States well below the market price. The concentration of Cuban agriculture on the cultivation of sugar and tobacco proved problematic, for it meant that other foods had to be imported. Until 1917, such goods came primarily from the United States. Now, however, these imports were greatly reduced as U.S. production was increasingly dedicated to supplying the European Allies. The government tried to counter the shortage of food, inter alia, by establishing maximum prices, rationing and, above all, boosting domestic production. However, because of the dependence on the United States, meeting the basic needs of the population presented a significant challenge and put considerable pressure on the bilateral relations.[69]

In the course of 1917, Menocal managed to issue war bonds with the aim of sending a Cuban contingent of troops to Europe, despite the objection of the Liberals in Congress. The necessary preparations stalled, however, due to internal political disputes. Toward the end of 1917, the State Department considered calling on the Cuban government to send its own contingent of troops to the front. This would have allowed the approximately 2,000 Cuban volunteers in the armies of the United States and France to fight under their own flag, while also bolstering the position of President Menocal.[70] This particular step, however, was not yet possible in 1917.

Despite Cuba's modest military contribution, enthusiasm for the war took hold of the population. There was a certain degree of mobilization among the elites in particular, which found expression in prowar propaganda activity. Just a few months after Cuba's entry into the war, the Liga Anti Germánica de Cuba (Anti-German League of Cuba) was established, which mainly recruited from the upper class and drew attention to itself with numerous public events.[71] Female members were involved in the Cuban Red Cross and conducted fundraising campaigns for the Allies,

---

[68] Dept. of State to Cuban envoy (Washington, DC, September 23, 1917), in: *FRUS 1918* I, p. 725. Dept. of State to Cuban legation (Washington, DC, April 29, 1917), in: ibid. 1917 I, p. 270.

[69] Berenguer, *El problema de las subsistencias*, pp. 7–11. Martin, *Latin America and the War*, pp. 132–41.

[70] Dept. of State, Division of Latin American Affairs, Memorandum (Washington, DC, November 17, 1917), NA, RG 59, M 367, Reel 67.

[71] Díaz Pardo, *Cuba ante la guerra*, p. 5.

which enjoyed abundant success.[72] A year later, in May 1918, the propaganda work was bundled together in the Comisión Nacional Cubana de Propaganda por la Guerra y de Auxilio a sus Víctimas (National Cuban Commission for War Propaganda and War Victims). The senator for the province of Matanzas, Cosme de la Torriente, served as president, while the board was made up of other senior politicians. The Commission, which had local groups at its disposal around the country, organized cultural competitions and events, propaganda actions, and fundraising campaigns for the Red Cross, as well as publicity for U.S. war bonds.[73] In addition, Cuban writers and journalists such as Vicente Pardo Suárez and Fernando de Soignie made names for themselves with particularly harsh anti-German propaganda in their writings.[74]

Although there was hardly room for dissent in the heated atmosphere, there was nevertheless irony – if at times unintentional. For example, in May 1917, in the political magazine *Cuba Contemporánea*, journalist José Martínez wrote that Cuba's entry into the war was a serious matter, even if "certain Spanish newspapers" had made jokes about it. He added that it was also, but not only, an expression of Cuba's gratitude to their powerful northern neighbor, whose "attentiveness and devotion, whose eagerness to respond to our every need and selflessness in its political activities, was extraordinary."[75] Martínez, moreover, confidently pointed out that the United States needed Cuban ports for strategic reasons, specifically to safeguard the Caribbean. Liberal politician Horacio Díaz Pardo exhibited similar assurance, suggesting that the country was entitled to more autonomy because of its contribution to the "just war." Due to the ongoing presence of U.S. Marines, this turned out to be wishful thinking, however.[76]

Panama also hoped for more room to maneuver as a result of its role in the war. On February 4, the government of Ramón Maximiliano Valdés Arce already volunteered close cooperation with the United States to protect the Canal, which in any case was under U.S. control.[77] After the official announcement, the Valdés government declared war on Germany without hesitation. As the official word described it, Panama entered the war out of loyalty to its great protector, the United States, which

[72] Pardo Suárez, *Ladrones de tierras*, pp. 311–17.
[73] "Un aspecto de la propaganda," in: *Boletín de Información* 1 (September 1918), p. 2.
[74] Pardo Suárez, *Ladrones de tierras*. Soignie, *Crónicas de sangre*.
[75] Martínez, "La entrada de Cuba en la guerra universal," p. 7.
[76] Díaz Pardo, *Cuba ante la guerra*, p. 12.
[77] U.S. envoy to Sec. of State (Panama, February 4, 1917), in: FRUS 1917, I, p. 221.

was ultimately responsible for making the former Colombian province's statehood possible, and which continued to serve as a guarantor power.

The congress subsequently entrusted to the president extraordinary powers.[78] As a preemptive measure, the government detained suspect Germans on the Isla de Taboga, a move that prompted the German government to intern Panamanian students in return. Although Panama's actions were not consistent with the principles of international law, Panamanian observers were nevertheless convinced that the new global secret war involving acts of espionage and sabotage demanded novel countermeasures.[79] For the United States, the Canal was unquestionably the site in Latin America that had the most strategic importance. As a consequence, the Canal Zone remained under martial law from 1917 and the newly created Panama Canal Department organized its defense as a central authority. Panama was also important as a primary checkpoint for U.S. censorship. Numerous intelligence reports continued to stoke the fear of German U-boats in the region until the end of the war. Along with the increased presence of U.S. troops in the Canal Zone, the day-to-day problems with the Panamanians intensified. The troops' discipline was so wanting due to prostitution and alcohol that the military governor of the Canal Zone organized the seizure of all alcohol inventories in Panama City and Colón, that is, the entire Panamanian territory. The Panama government's desire to establish its own armed forces for self-defense, which it justified because of its entry into the war, was vetoed by the United States.[80]

The initial situation differed in the five other Central American republics compared to Panama because they were slightly less dependent on the United States. These states had more decision-making power as a result. Guatemala's move to break ties with the German Reich as early as April 27 was as swift as it was surprising, given that German coffee producers had played a central economic role there for decades. By the same token, it was because the German market had fallen off due the war that dictator Estrada Cabrera had reoriented his country toward the United States already before 1917. The decision to abandon the German market also went hand in hand with Panama's offer to allow the United States to use its ports and railways for the countries' common defense.[81] Besides the

[78] Garay, *Panamá*, p. 43.
[79] Ibid., p. 64. *Correspondencia relacionada con el internamiento de panameños.*
[80] Ibid., pp. 59–63. Conniff, *Panama and the United States*, pp. 74–5.
[81] Guatemalan ambassador to Sec. of State (Washington, DC, April 27, 1917), in: *FRUS* 1917 I, p. 271.

economic motive, the decision to change course also had a foreign policy dimension. Estrada Cabrera, namely, feared a hostile alliance involving the country's northern neighbor, the notoriously anti-U.S. Mexico, and its neighbor to the south, El Salvador. For Cabrera, the long-standing tensions with both countries made a close partnership with the United States seem especially advantageous.[82]

The State Department viewed the Guatemalan dictator's actions as exemplary for the whole of Central America. When the Nicaraguan ambassador to the United States asked his superiors in Washington how the Nicaraguan government should respond, they cited the example set by Guatemala.[83] This suggestion was received favorably in Nicaragua, which had been under U.S. occupation since 1912. The rupture of relations with Germany, accordingly, was carried out on May 21, 1917. Even though Nicaragua declared it was under a state of siege, the government nonetheless did not take any actions against Germans or ethnic Germans.[84]

The government in Honduras – where U.S. banana companies exercised strong influence – had already taken this step a few days earlier on May 17. At first, the Honduran government was interested in pursuing the idea of the conference of neutrals. Washington, however, signaled that such a meeting was unnecessary and, moreover, that it would be paying close attention to the country's actions. President Francisco Bertrand subsequently caved to the State Department. Honduras likewise contributed to the war effort through the delivery of Corozo palm nuts, used for the production of poison gas.[85] Finally, Haiti, which had been under the occupation of U.S. troops since 1915 like its neighbor the Dominican Republic, but still had its own government, did not break off relations with Germany until June 17, 1917. This was because the legislature initially refused to ratify the declaration of war from President Philippe Sudré Dartiguenave, who was appointed by the United States. In the end, ties were not severed with Germany until the parliament was on the verge of dissolution.[86]

---

[82] U.S. envoy to Dept. of State (Guatemala, March 30, 1917), NA, RG 59, M 336, Roll 60.

[83] Dept. of State to ambassador in Nicaragua (Washington, DC, May 11, 1917), in: *FRUS* 1917 I, p. 278.

[84] Schoonover, *Germany in Central America*, p. 163.

[85] Dept. of State to Honduras legation (Washington, DC, May 12, 1917), in: *FRUS* 1917 I, p. 279. Martin, *Latin America and the War*, pp. 503–5.

[86] Martin, *Latin America and the War*, pp. 517–19.

In Costa Rica, the political conditions were quite different. The wartime crisis had led to internal political turmoil, which culminated in a coup under Minister of War Federico Tinoco in January 1917. As in the case of Huerta in Mexico, U.S. President Wilson was no more inclined than the Allies or most Latin American countries to recognize the violently installed new head of state. All the same, in April Tinoco promptly offered the United States use of the Costa Rican ports, which the United States refused.[87] Indeed, the U.S. government repeatedly rejected Tinoco's proposal to terminate relations with the German Reich in exchange for Washington's official diplomatic recognition. The United States maintained its stance even after the dictator actually broke off relations with Germany on September 21, 1917. The U.S. government, in fact, successfully isolated the Tinoco regime, which worsened the country's economic situation and increased social unrest, which the strongman put down by force.[88]

To the Europeans, however, the Central American countries were little more than semi-sovereign satellites of the United States. From their perspective, the attitude of the major South American countries was a cause of greater concern. Brazil, for instance, had already attracted notice at the Peace Conference of The Hague in 1907 because of the actions of its representative Rui Barbosa. In April 1917, Brazil joined the United States in breaking off relations with the German Reich and, in addition, entered the war on the side of the Allies on October 26. Brazil's relations with the United States – which had been relatively close since the turn of the century compared to the other Latin American nations – unquestionably played a role. The context here, however, differed greatly from the one in Central America. The case of the *Rio Branco* in May 1916 certainly caused tempers to flare, yet it was the German submarine's sinking of the coffee-bearing merchant vessel *Paraná* of the Brazilian shipping line Commercio e Navegação on April 5, 1917, announced a day later, that resulted in the worst crisis to date between Germany and Brazil.[89]

Shortly before this, in March 1917, Rui Barbosa had once again inflamed public sentiment with a highly praised speech in the theater of

---

[87] Dept. of State to Sec. of the Navy (Washington, DC, May 2, 1917), in: *FRUS* 1917 I, p. 274. Aguilar, *Federico Tinoco*, pp. 57–103.

[88] Murillo, *Tinoco y los Estados Unidos.*

[89] "Um navio brasileiro torpedeado," in: *Correio da Manhã* (April 6, 1917), p. 1. "Torpedeamento do Paraná," in: *O Estado de São Paulo* (April 7, 1917), p. 3. See also Bras. Envoy to MRREE (Paris, April 10, 1917), in: MREE, *Guerra da Europa*, pp. 25–30.

Petrópolis.[90] The German attack on the ship seemed to bear out his arguments, sparking a storm of public protest, which the Liga Pelos Aliados gratefully acknowledged.[91] Mass demonstrations broke out in Rio de Janeiro on April 8 and 9 against German policy, and pressure on the Brazilian government to sever ties increased by the hour.[92] The commentators who spoke out on the *Paraná* case stressed that there had to be consequences. It was unanimously felt that the ship's sinking constituted a "brutal," indeed "barbaric," attack on the honor of the nation.[93] In view of the telegrams that were sent from Washington, Paris, New York, Havana, London, and Buenos Aires, the Brazilians found themselves at the forefront of the international community's attention and a coveted ally.[94] But when the government still had not responded four days after the sinking, the sense of outrage only intensified. By the time the government officially declared the severing of relations on April 11, Barbosa had already repeated his intention to give a speech that would publicly denounce the inaction of the cabinet and especially Foreign Minister Müller.[95]

Brazil's public media voiced nearly unanimous support for the government's move. Protest rallies were replaced by avowals of solidarity from students and mariners, as well as the local branches of the Liga pelos Aliados. Magazines like *Fon-Fon* published series of photographs showing the massive turnouts with war advocates.[96] The commentators' collective sense of relief was palpable: Brazil had at last put itself on the side of civilization and demonstrated that its honor was still intact.[97] In

[90] Barbosa, *Obras completas*, Vol. XLIV, 1917, Pt. 1, pp. 7–8. On Barbosa's foreign policy, see Vigevani, "Interesse nacional," pp. 17–23. Cardim, *A raiz the coisas*, pp. 225–37.

[91] "A espera do governo," in: *Correio da Manhã* (April 7, 1917), 1.

[92] "A conflagração," in: *O Estado de São Paulo* (April 8, 1917), p. 1.

[93] "Varias Noticias," in: *Jornal do Commercio* (April 7, 1917), p. 3. See also "O Torpedeamento do Paraná," in: *O Imparcial* (April 7, 1917), pp. 1–4. "A responsabilidade do governo," in: *Correio da Manhã* (April 8, 1917) p. 1. "Não mais delongas," in: ibid. (April 9, 1917) p. 1. "Está imminente o rompimento de relações com a Allemanha," in: *A Epoca* (April 8, 1917) p. 1. "O Brasil e a Allemanha," in: *O Estado de São Paulo* (April 10, 1917), p. 2.

[94] "A guerra – a conflagração na America," in: *Jornal do Commercio* (April 8, 1917) p. 1. "A conflagração," in: *O Estado de São Paulo* (April 8, 1917), p. 1.

[95] "Não mais delongas!" in: *Correio da Manhã* (April 9, 1917) p. 1. "Tortuosidades do Itamaraty," in: *O Imparcial* (April 10, 1917), pp. 2–3.

[96] "A moralidade da guerra," in: *Fon-Fon* (April 14, 1917). "O momento," in: ibid. (April 21, 1917).

[97] "O Brasil e a Allemanha," in: *O Estado de São Paulo* (April 10, 1917) p. 1. "Os apostolos da civilização," in: *O Imparcial* (April 11, 1917) p. 1. "O rompimento de relações entre o Brasil e a Allemanha," in: *Jornal do Commercio* (April 12 and 13, 1917), p. 3.

this context, the newspapers stressed again and again the importance of the country's close relations with the United States. The Allies, in fact, greatly approved of Brazil's decision, for it was another serious blow to German interests in Latin America.[98]

In the wake of its decision to sever ties with Germany, the Brazilian government immediately ordered the arming of the country's merchant ships.[99] Increased pressure was also placed on Foreign Minister Müller to enact tougher measures. His political adversaries openly referred to his German roots and even insinuated that he was colluding with Berlin. On May 3, Müller was forced to resign. His successor, Nilo Peçanha, announced right away that Brazil would cooperate more closely with the United States, especially as two more Brazilian ships, the *Tijuca* (May 20) and the *Lapa* (May 22), had been sunk by German U-boats.[100] In early June, the government rescinded its decree of neutrality in the war between the United States and Germany, and enacted a similar measure by the end of the month with regard to the other Allies. What is more, the country confiscated the German ships anchored in Brazilian ports. The anticipated upturn in coffee exports did not materialize, however, as Great Britain resisted relaxing its import restrictions.[101]

Immediately after Brazil broke off relations with Germany, a sizeable portion of the Brazilian press pushed the government to enter the war on the side of the Allies.[102] Rui Barbosa railed against neutrality in his speech at a mass demonstration in Rio de Janeiro on April 14, 1917, and deemed the country's entry into the war as inescapable.[103] To prevail, he stressed twelve days later in the Senate that Brazilians would have to reflect on the "power of the weak" and made an appeal to moral law. Rui Barbosa was certain that Brazil's inevitable entry into the war would usher in a new era

"A situação," in: *Correio da Manhã* (April 13, 1917) p. 1. "As manifestações das classes marítimas ao Sr. Presidente da República," in: *Jornal do Commercio* (April 17, 1917), p. 3.

[98] Vinhosa, *O Brasil e a Primeira Guerra Mundial*, p. 146.

[99] Ibid., p. 111.

[100] "A anomalia do Itamaraty," in: *O Imparcial* (April 13, 1917), p. 2. Vinhosa, *O Brasil e a Primeira Guerra Mundial*, pp. 85–6. On Müller's origin and career, see Luebke, *Germans in Brazil*, pp. 111–3 and 150–1.

[101] Ibid., p. 155.

[102] Garambone, *A primeira Guerra Mundial*, p. 91. See also Mesquita's article in: *O Estado Mesquita, A guerra*, Vol. 4, pp. 724–6.

[103] "Manifestação ao conselheiro Ruy Barbosa," in: *A Epoca* (April 15, 1917), p. 1. "O Brasil e a guerra," in: *O Estado de São Paulo* (April 16, 1917), p. 4. The speech is reprinted in Barbosa, *Obras completas*, Vol. XLIV, 1917, Pt. 1, pp. 45–58. Barbosa/Moacyr, *A Revogação da neutralidade*, pp. 10 and 39.

for the country, whose potential was virtually unlimited due to its enormous population and size.[104] Barbosa and his numerous supporters spoke out at a time when social conditions were becoming dire due to inflation and the ever-increasing cost of living. A general strike in São Paulo for better wages and working conditions in July paralyzed the entire city, and solidarity strikes formed in Rio de Janeiro. Brazilian officials suspected that the culprit behind these actions was German sabotage.[105]

Meanwhile, the Liga pelos Aliados and other nationalist forces, above all the Liga da Defesa Nacional, founded by poet Olavo Bilac in 1916, further mobilized Brazilian civil society. Voluntary military defense leagues (Tiros de Guerra) were thus organized in associations and schools. To arouse attention, they conducted a large parade in the capital on September 7, 1917. These Tiros de Guerra represented an alternative to the lowly regular army, in which members of the lower classes had traditionally served.[106] Even the women's movement got involved, as the Partido Republicano Feminino (Republican Feminist Party) used a military instructor to train its "Amazons." Many female volunteers also registered for the Red Cross and nursing school. Numerous workers' organizations were infected by patriotic fever. Labor unions, like the shoemaker's union, took collections for the Red Cross. Even some socialists now called for taking the fight to Germany.[107]

The military mobilization had a further domestic dimension, for the fundamental problem concerning the national affiliation of immigrants was more pressing than ever. Indeed, the more rapid the country appeared to be gearing up for the war, the more urgent the threat of the German-born settlers in southern Brazil seemed. In particular, nationalist Brazilian intellectuals held the view that the "settlement colonies" had essentially infiltrated and hollowed out the young nation-states, because the ethnic Germans there did not sufficiently integrate themselves and often did not even speak Portuguese. They identified the same problem in Argentina, Paraguay, Chile, and Uruguay. In their view, the threat regarding the plans for a "Pan-Germany" had grown considerably since the conflict began. They argued that an uncompromising *brasileirismo* needed to be opposed to the hostile *germanismo*. As in other countries, pro-Ally forces

[104] "O Brasil e a guerra," in: *O Estado de São Paulo* (October 28, 1917), p. 4.
[105] Lopreato, *A semana trágica*. Biondi, *Classe e nação*, pp. 316–26. Bandeira/Melo/Andrade, *O ano vermelho*, pp. 50–1.
[106] Bonow, *A desconfiança*, p. 283.
[107] Bandeira/Melo/Andrade, *O ano vermelho*, pp. 40–1.

deliberately fueled these concerns.[108] Here, they could exploit old stereotypes concerning the Germans' arrogance and the supposed danger of the isolated "German colonies" in the south. The public now evaluated elements of popular culture such as the rifle clubs, loved by ethnic Germans with their uniforms and massive celebrations, as a threatening display of German militancy within their own midst. Anxiety over the activities of the German secret service increased dramatically.[109]

In connection with the sinking of the *Paraná*, the pro-Ally press reported suspicious activities in the southern federal states.[110] Messages like these helped foment the violent riots that took place against German establishments in Porto Alegre and Pelotas after relations with Germany were cut off. Following the patriotic gatherings that had stirred up anti-German resentment, minor incidents sufficed to cause the powder keg to explode. From the night of April 14 to April 15, the mob raged for several days. The police found itself utterly overwhelmed, not least because the press had further agitated readers with sensationalism. Order was not restored until the military intervened on April 17. From the south, the anti-German riots also extended to other parts of the country, such as São Paulo.[111] After the unrest subsided, the U.S. Consul in Rio Grande do Sul observed that "the Germans" were now clearly keeping a low profile. In fact, the German-Brazilians reacted defensively, renamed their institutions, and tried to avoid provocations.[112]

Besides these domestic developments, Brazil's integration in the Allied defense system was carried out. The U.S. squadron for monitoring the South Atlantic under Admiral William B. Caperton visited Rio de Janeiro on July 4, 1917, which brought about large celebrations. It therefore seemed to be only a matter of time before the official declaration of

[108] Jose Verissimo, "Germanismo e Brasileirismo," in: *Jornal do Commercio* (May 31, 1915), p. 1. Vinhosa, *O Brasil e a Primeira Guerra Mundial*, p. 158.

[109] "O Perigo Allemão," in: *Jornal do Commercio* (February 14, 1915), p. 4. Luebke, *Germans in Brazil*, p. 124. Pro-Ally propaganda also spread the same line of reasoning against the German immigrants elsewhere, e.g., in Cuba (Pardo Suárez, *Ladrones de tierras*, p. 77) or in Chile (see the reporting in the Aliadophile journal *El Tanque*). On the perception of a German threat, see U.S. military attaché, "German Colonists" (Rio de Janeiro, November 20, 1916), NA, RG 165, MID, 6370-31.

[110] "Ultima hora," in: *O Estado de São Paulo* (April 8, 1917), p. 3.

[111] "Os acontecimentos de Porto Alegre," in: *Jornal do Commercio* (April 16, 1917), p. 2. "Todo o Rio Grande do Sul vibra de indignação," in: *A Epoca* (April 18, 1917), p. 1. "A agitação germanophoba," in: *O Imparcial* (April 18, 1917), p. 4. Bonow, *A desconfiança*, pp. 257–60. Luebke, *Germans in Brazil*, pp. 129–39.

[112] U.S. consul at Dept. of State (Rio Grande do Sul, April 28, 1917), NA, RG 59, 825.00/142. Luebke, *Germans in Brazil*, pp. 142–6.

war. This occurred on October 26, 1917, after another Brazilian ship –
the *Macau* – was sunk by a German submarine on October 18.[113] The
Brazilian public again responded with both approval and relief to what
many observers felt was long overdue.[114] Rui Barbosa, who had become
the undisputed leader of the War Party, thoroughly justified the historical decision in his speech before the Senate on October 26.[115] Given
the broad consensus among the elites, Dunshee de Abranches' insistence
on continuing to make pro-German statements was akin to committing
social suicide. He said it was an illusion to think that Brazil could truly
take part in the war as an equal partner. In the end, this was really only
a means for the Allies to colonize the country.[116] At this time, Abranches'
voice was in fact isolated, for the vast majority of the population welcomed the entry into the war. Brazil experienced a wave of national
enthusiasm. The striking workers returned to their jobs. Those who did
not go back willingly were further motivated to do so by the state of siege
that was declared on November 17.[117]

The reasons behind Brazil's entry into the war were diverse. Rui
Barbosa and other propagandists repeated appeals to patriotism and the
Brazilians' injured sense of justice due to the submarine warfare was,
in fact, only one side of the story. The traditional partnership with the
United States, which had often been stressed in the contemporary press,
the fear of isolation after the war, and the prospects of participating in the
peace conference on the winning side and obtaining reparations also did
not entirely explain the decision.[118] In view of the country's continuing
state of crisis, economic and social policy considerations played a prominent role. The country's commercial and financial dependence on the
Allies was beyond dispute. In joining the alliance, the government hoped
to obtain easier access to markets. This was sorely needed considering the

---

[113] "O Brasil na guerra," in: *O Estado de São Paulo* (October 27, 1917) p. 1. "O Brasil em
estado de guerra com a Allemanha," in: *Jornal do Brasil* (October 27, 1917), p. 1. "O
Brasil na guerra," in: *Revista da Semana* (October 27, 1917). For the diplomatic steps in
detail, see Vinhosa, *O Brasil e a Primeira Guerra Mundial*, pp. 91–128.

[114] Mesquita, *A guerra*, Vol. 4, p. 740. "O Brasil na Guerra," in: *Jornal do Commercio*
(October 27, 1917), p. 3. Jedo Luso, "Dominicaes," in: *Jornal do Commercio* (October
28, 1917), p. 1. "O grave momento nacional," in: *Correio da Manhã* (November 8,
1917), p. 1.

[115] Barbosa, *Obras completas*, Vol. XLIV, 1917, Pt. 1, p. 122.

[116] Abranches, *A illusão brazileira*, p. 11.

[117] Vinhosa, *O Brasil e a Primeira Guerra Mundial*, pp. 152–3. On the state of siege, see
also "O grave momento nacional," in: *Correio da Manhã* (November 11, 12, and 13,
1917), in each instance p. 1.

[118] Vinhosa, *O Brasil e a Primeira Guerra Mundial*, p. 122.

decline in coffee prices stemming from the combatants' trade restrictions and record harvests. Only the export of agricultural products such as meat, rice, sugar, and beans, as well as natural resources such as manganese, lessened the predicament somewhat. The fear of social destabilization, which was already apparent during the great strike, was widespread among the elites. In their view, the entry into the war offered the appropriate pretext for forcibly tackling the issue and for construing the experienced deprivations as a patriotic duty.[119]

Bearing witness to the instability was the riots that were inflamed again after the entry into the war in October against the establishments of Germans and ethnic Germans. This time, however, the unrest originating in Curitiba became much more pervasive than in April. It held the country under its spell until the beginning of November, when Brazilian ships fell victim to German submarines once more. The coastal towns were affected above all. The police decided not to intervene against the "mob" consisting mainly of students, young people, and members of the lower classes.[120] President Brás did his part to stir up the war hysteria with his appeal to the nation on November 1, in which he warned of espionage and sabotage. The statements from this period suggested that the enemy within was more dangerous than the enemy without. Along with the German-born population, domestic enemies included anarchists and socialists who threatened the social order and whom the bourgeois press had implied were in league with the Germans. Even the government of the state Rio Grande do Sul under Antônio Borges de Medeiros, known for his cautious attitude toward the large ethnic German group, was suspected of "Germanism."[121]

By Brazilian standards, the measures against the German minority were therefore quite severe. Cultural restrictions were already put into place even before the country entered the war. The state of Santa Catarina stood out in particular as a primary location of German settlement. After the new education law was passed there in the beginning of October 1917, future lessons had to be taught in Portuguese. Many schools in the German community perceived this as a threat. The restrictions also affected churches, whose services had to be held in Portuguese. Later, the activities of German associations became strictly regulated. Rifle clubs were forced to disband.[122]

[119] Ibid., p. 134. Compagnon, *L'adieu à l'Europe*, p. 127.
[120] "A destruição do germanismo," in: *Correio da Manhã* (November 17, 1917), p. 1. Luebke, *Germans in Brazil*, pp. 164–73.
[121] Bandeira/Melo/Andrade, *O ano vermelho*, p. 70. Bonow, *A desconfiança*, pp. 314–21.
[122] Luebke, *Germans in Brazil*, pp. 162, 174–90.

After it declared war, the Brazilian government wanted to keep the German minority in check by imitating the methods of the United States. First, the police registered all German nationals living in Brazil. The measures implemented against this group gradually intensified in November as the war hysteria grew. The government had some 700 Germans – mostly reserve officers and sailors of the seized ships – interned at various *campos de concentração* (concentration camps) throughout the country. The treatment of the prisoners, however, was so good in places that Medeiros e Albuquerque complained.[123] The measures directed against the Germans and ethnic Germans came to a head with the passing of martial law on November 16 (*lei da guerra*). The law enabled the government to declare a state of siege, void contracts with citizens of enemy states, seize property, and liquidate companies.[124] At the same time, the government took advantage of the law's wide-ranging powers far less than the Allies would have liked. German businesses had actually already been under government control since the beginning of August, with the banks falling under the policy in October. Still, businesses as a rule were allowed to continue to operate in secret in order to prevent further strain to the country's already ailing economy.[125]

In addition to its raw materials, Brazil had another war-critical resource at its disposal: the German ships which had sought safe harbor after the war broke out. In July 1917, the Navy Department in Washington had already pondered how the Brazilian government might be persuaded to confiscate the vessels and charter them to the United States. Navy strategists argued that chartering the ships lay in Brazil's national interest, for it meant that the United States could better supply the country with necessary imports.[126] When Brazil entered the war, the conditions were in place for confiscating the ships. The government in Rio de Janeiro proposed first having the German vessels sail under the flag of Lloyd Brasileiro in regular service to the United States and Europe, which the Allies rejected. There were conflicting ideas among the latter about who should take over the ships, for even the British and French asserted claims. Great Britain,

---

[123] U.S. envoy to Sec. of State (R. d. J., 11.5.1917), NA, RG 59, M 336, Roll 64. "O Brasil na Guerra," in: *Jornal do Commercio* (November 18, 1917), p. 2. Bandeira/Melo/Andrade, *O ano vermelho*, p. 43. Luebke, *Germans in Brazil*, pp. 164–74. On the orientation toward the model of the United States, see U.S. ambassador to Dept. of State (R. d. J., 10.27.1917), in: *FRUS 1918* Supplement 2, *The World War*, p. 341.

[124] Pinheiro, *Problemas da guerra e da paz*, pp. 9–32.

[125] Ibid., pp. 32–50. Dehne, *On the Far Western Front*, pp. 178–80.

[126] Sec. of Navy to U.S. Shipping Board (Washington, DC, July 10, 1917), NA, RG 31, 555-3.

for its part, promised Brazil it would relax the ban on imports of coffee, while the United States insisted on the importance of American solidarity. After lengthy negotiations, the Brazilian government finally decided in December 1917 to charter the vessels to France. This exposed the limits of U.S. diplomacy, not to mention the considerable mistrust between the Allies over how to deal with their new partner.[127]

Other than the United States, Brazil was the only country in the Americas to take part in the war militarily. Being present on the battlefield seemed important to Brazil if it wanted to play an active role in the peace negotiations later on. There was already a Brazilian representative at the Inter-Allied Conference in Paris, which took place from November 20 to December 3, 1917. Senior military officials traveled to Europe and the United States to explore the country's options. In the end, Brazil volunteered to send to Europe a Marine division, a group of airmen, and a medical mission. The ground forces remained at home, however, in order to root out the "German threat" in southern Brazil.[128]

After Brazil entered the war, the Brazilian Navy actually immediately reinforced Caperton's squadron to protect the Atlantic coast against German submarines.[129] The decision was then made at the end of 1917 to deploy a naval division under Admiral Pedro Max Fernando de Frontin, which was to navigate to Gibraltar and put itself under British supreme command. The Brazilian units were understood to be part of a joint American fleet.[130] It took a long time, however, before the obsolete ships could be made seaworthy. And after they finally set out in May 1918, the crew got caught in the grip of the world's rampant flu epidemic during a stopover in Dakar. The depleted unit did not actually make it to Gibraltar until the fall, when the war was already over. The mission of the Brazilian aviators fared no better, for the British had no interest in

---

[127] Barbosa, *Obras completas*, Vol. XLIV, 1917, Pt. 1, pp. 193–4. "Vao a ser cedidos á França trinta navios," in: *Correio da Manhã* (December 5, 1917), p. 1. On the negotiations, see U.S. ambassador to Dept. of State (R.d.J., 06.02.1917), U.S. ambassador to Dept. of State (London, June 13, 1917), Brit. ambassador to Dept. of State (Washington, DC, August 19, 1917), Dept. of State to Embassy of R. d. J. (Washington, DC, September 29, 1917), in: FRUS 1917 I, pp. 293–4, 297, 318, and 332. See also Foreign Minister Nilo Peçanha to London legation (R.d.J., June 1, 1917), in: MRREE, *Guerra da Europa*, p. 129.

[128] Bras. Embassy to MRE (London, December 26, 1917), in: AHI, Directoria Geral dos Negocios Políticos e Diplomáticos. Vinhosa, *O Brasil e a Primeira Guerra Mundial*, p. 158.

[129] Vinhosa, *O Brasil e a Primeira Guerra Mundial*, p. 168.

[130] Sec. of State to embassy in Rio de Janeiro (Washington, DC, January 26, 1918), in: *FRUS* 1918 Supplement 1, *The World War*, Vol. 1, p. 663.

using them. Ultimately, a compromise was worked out that allowed the Brazilian government to save face. Thus only Brazil's medical mission in France finally made a real contribution to the war. The effort, though, was not one that might be expected to earn Brazil much gratitude from the Allied forces.[131]

On April 13, 1917, Bolivia also broke off relations with the German Reich, just one day after Brazil. The decision came as a surprise for many observers. The country, after all, was relatively closely linked to Germany economically, and German army consultants, who remained in Bolivia until after the start of the war, had successfully reformed the military.[132] Beyond this, Germans and ethnic Germans in La Paz and other cities had occupied influential positions. At the same time, the Montes government had expressed its fundamental opposition to German submarine warfare early on. The press in the capital, further, emphasized the noble goals of the government in its struggle for justice against the "monstrous" conduct of the German Reich.[133] President Montes' move was also influenced by an interest in securing the economic and political support of the United States. On one hand, the government was dependent on U.S. capital during the war-related crisis. On the other hand, Montes hoped that the United States would lend its diplomatic backing after the war with regard to neighboring Chile. Bolivia continued to dispute its loss of direct sea access in the War of the Pacific.

Similar motives figured prominently in Peru's decision to sever ties with Germany, which, however, did not occur until October 6, 1917. The elite in Peru were much more disposed to France and the United States than they were in Bolivia. The previous sinking of the cargo ship *Lorton* in neutral waters by German submarines on February 4, 1917, was yet another factor. This brought about intense diplomatic negotiations with the German government, with the Peruvian side demanding an apology and compensation.[134] Berlin was initially slow to respond, however, and even later argued that the transport of contraband, specifically saltpeter, had justified the sinking. As the negotiations continued to drag on, the United States entered the conflict. The pro-Ally newspaper *El Comercio* declared its support for the United States, but also noted that it could do

---

[131] Vinhosa, *O Brasil e a Primeira Guerra Mundial*, pp. 169–73. See also Streeter, *Epitácio Pessoa*, pp. 66–70. On British Admiral Lloyd Hirst's derogatory remarks about the Brazilian units, see Dehne, *On the Far Western Front*, p. 175.

[132] Bieber, "La política militar alemana en Bolivia," p. 88.

[133] "La ruptura," in: *El Diario* (April 16, 1917), p. 3.

[134] Lavalle, *Las negociaciones de Berlín*, p. 7.

little more than profess Peru's sympathy given the relative insignificance of its own country.[135]

Not all Peruvians saw it this way, however. Senator Cornejo was one of the officials who called for taking a harder stance toward Germany. The senator asked how the America of Simón Bolívar could remain on the sidelines if even China was entering the war.[136] Cornejo justified his demand with geostrategic arguments: If Latin America did not want to sink to the status of a "Western China" and be informally exploited, then it needed to stand on the side of the only possible victors, the Allies. He imagined, quite pragmatically, a postwar order in which the border issue – which Peru still hotly contested – could be reopened with Chile. This made sense given that the Allies were fighting for the inviolability of territorial integrity, the same ideal that Peru had invoked against its neighbor.[137] The final straw, however, that led Peru to sever relations with Germany was the fact that the government in Berlin was not prepared to extend to Peru the same diplomatic goodwill it had shown toward Argentina following the sinking of the *Toro*.[138]

After the unsuccessful initiative to organize a conference of American neutrals in February 1917, Peru's neighbor Ecuador took no further actions and decided to cling to neutrality. Public pressure on the government to join the Allies – if only indirectly by rupturing ties with Germany – grew over the course of the year, especially from those circles concerned with export. Thus officer and former consul Nicolás F. López wrote in June 1917 in an article published in a pamphlet in Quito that the country soon had to decide and that it moreover needed to stand on the side of the democracies. According to Washington's diplomatic representative in Quito, anti-German sentiment had also intensified.[139] By the middle of the year, however, the Foreign Ministry was still not prepared to be a "puppet" of the United States and its allies.[140] Only reluctantly did the government succumb to the external and internal pressure and close ranks with the Allies. It allowed the British to build radio stations and dismissed a German expert from the Construction Ministry. In the

[135] "El Perú y la Guerra," in: *El Comercio* (April 20, 1917), p. 1.
[136] Cornejo, *La Solidaridad americana*, p. 36.
[137] Cornejo, *La Intervención del Perú*, pp. 3–20.
[138] *Ruptura de relaciones diplomáticas*, pp. 71–87 and 138. See also Lavalle, *El Perú y la gran guerra*, pp. 18–50.
[139] López, "The Attitude of Ecuador," p. 27. Consul General at Dept. of State (Guayaquil, October 16, 1917), NA, RG 59, M 336, Roll 63.
[140] MRREE to embassy in Washington (Quito, May 29, 1917), in: Ecuador, AMRREE, M.1.9.1.

end, it was officially a matter of diplomatic protocol that proved the decisive factor in the severing of relations with Germany on December 7, 1917.[141] The actual reasons, however, were altogether different. Although *El Comercio* initially cited the united struggle against German militarism as the real impetus for the rupture, the press was more explicit on this point shortly thereafter. In short, the newspapers admitted with resounding candor that it was less noble ideals that motivated the decision than a concern about cocoa exports to the United States, which were critical for government revenue.[142]

The government of Uruguay had already laid out its more or less pro-Ally neutrality before 1917. It was therefore hardly surprising that the German declaration concerning submarine warfare encountered swift and unanimous criticism.[143] A debate was kindled, nevertheless, about what steps needed to follow. In this regard, the postures of the two major neighboring countries, Brazil and Argentina, had an influential role. Former foreign minister Antonio Bachini, for instance, stressed in a newspaper editorial in mid-April 1917 that while he wished the United States and Brazil well, their conduct nevertheless did not imply perforce how Uruguayans should proceed in their own country. On the contrary, Bachini argued that the case of Argentina showed that Uruguay could maintain neutrality in good conscience because Germany did not actually constitute an imminent threat.[144] Nonetheless, the majority of the media pleaded like *La Razón* on behalf of American solidarity with Brazil and the United States, who were like "big brothers" to Uruguay.[145] The government of President Feliciano Viera, however, declared its neutrality

---

[141] MRREE to embassy in Washington (Quito, May 16, 1917), in: Ecuador, AMRREE, M.1.9.1. MRREE to War Office (Quito, December 13, 1917), in: ibid., I.1.10.1.

[142] "Ruptura de relaciones," in: *El Comercio* (Quito, December 12, 1917), p. 1. "Las ventas de cacao," in: ibid. (December 21, 1917), morning edition, p. 1. The opposition press in Cuenca also sharply criticized the Baquerizo government, "Los limpiabotas del Tío Sam," in: *El Progreso* (December 11, 1917), p. 2. The liberal press, by contrast, expressed hope for a relatively speedy resumption of relations: "Ecuador y Alemania," in: *El Tren* (December 20, 1917), p. 1.

[143] Buero, *El Uruguay*, pp. 325–6.

[144] Antonio Bachini, "Conceptos sobre la actitud argentina," in: *El Diario del Plata* (April 15, 1917), p. 3.

[145] "La solidaridad americana," in: *La Razón* (April 16, 1917), p. 4. As Dehne has recently explained, contemporary observers and later many historians interpreted Uruguay's attitude as a quasi-association with the Allies. That said, they overlooked the critique relating to the British economic war, which at least partly explains the decision to postpone the rupture of relations with Germany. Dehne, *On the Far Western Front*, p. 183.

when the United States and Cuba entered the war. At the same time, it jointly pursued with Argentina the goal of a Pan-American conference to discuss the hemisphere's common stance toward the war.[146]

By May, however, Viera had already made wide-ranging concessions to the United States. Especially significant was the government's statement on June 18, 1917, which stipulated that Uruguay would not treat any American country at war with non-American powers as a belligerent state. In other words, when it came to the United States, the legal obligations of neutrals pertaining to combatants would no longer apply. Montevideo justified the measure by citing the demands of continental solidarity. In essence, this meant the end of Uruguayan neutrality, even though the German charge d'affaires was allowed to remain in the country. The government communication was unprecedented and created quite a stir in Latin America. Peru and Bolivia immediately voiced their support for the spirit of the statement. Guatemala, Ecuador, and Costa Rica followed suit shortly thereafter. Already in July, the Uruguayan government welcomed Caperton's squadron as if it were on a goodwill tour.[147] In September, despite the protests of the German representative, the Uruguayan military seized the eight German vessels anchored in the port of Montevideo, for there was concern that their crews might destroy them. The ships were designated to sail under the Uruguayan flag until the war's end.[148] A few days later, the press argued that the continuation of neutrality had become impossible because of the ongoing attacks on neutral ships and that the threat from Germany extended to South America. The rupture of relations with Germany took place on October 7.[149] Four days later, the supporters of this decision held a large demonstration in Montevideo, which was intended to be a declaration of the people's solidarity with the government. There were also speakers from Buenos Aires such as Lugones.[150] Uruguay was able to make a significant contribution to the war in the ensuing period through its livestock and agricultural exports, for which the government granted the Allies generous loans.

---

[146] Martin, *Latin America and the War*, pp. 360–2.
[147] "La doctrina Uruguaya," *La Razón* (July 13, 1917), p. 1. Martin, *Latin America and the War*, pp. 362–8.
[148] *Requisición de los vapores alemanes*, pp. 19–23.
[149] "La neutralidad imposible," in: *El Día* (October 5, 1917), p. 6. "La ruptura de relaciones con el imperio alemán," in: ibid. (October 9, 1917), p. 3.
[150] "La ruptura de relaciones con el imperio alemán," in: *El Día* (October 11, 1917), p. 3.

THE NEUTRALS

While Uruguay's northern neighbor, Brazil, was a point of orientation for the Latin American countries that entered the war or severed ties with Germany, its neighbor to the south, Argentina, was a model for those countries that clung to their neutrality. This stance was fiercely contested, however, especially in 1917. As with Brazil and Peru, a German submarine attacked a ship from Argentina's merchant navy – the *Monte Protegido* – in early April. When the news of the sinking was made public in Buenos Aires ten days later, it sparked a storm of protests and intense rioting that resulted in injuries and the destruction of a number of German establishments. The mass demonstrations in the capital spread rapidly to the countryside. The police struggled to bring the situation under control.[151] Even the newspapers, which had aggressively voiced their views leading up to that point, appeared to be shocked by the events and called for calm and nonviolence.[152]

Everyone turned to the new government under President Hipólito Yrigoyen with bated breath. He had just won office in October 1916 and his election is recognized as a turning point in Argentine history insofar as it brought the Radical Civic Union to power, a party that was receptive to the concerns of the middle class and workers. The *Monte Protegido* incident was the government's first major foreign policy challenge. Argentina's Foreign Ministry took the view that only an apology, the punishment of those responsible, and compensation could still prevent a rupture of relations. On April 22, the Foreign Ministry handed the German chargé d'affaires the official word of protest.[153]

On the same day, the pro-Ally forces staged a large rally at the Frontón in Buenos Aires, which yielded a massive crowd. The audience spilled out into the street to listen to the speakers. Among them were the well-known names like Alfredo L. Palacios, Francisco A. Barroetaveña, and, finally, Ricardo Rojas. They all demanded the rupture of relations with the German Reich, the *ruptura*. Rojas called neutrality a "cowardly peace"

---

[151] "Hundimiento de una barca con bandera argentina," in: *La Prensa* (B. A., April 14, 1917), p. 8. "Asuntos internacionales", in: ibid. (April 14 and 15, 1917), p. 9. "El hundimiento del velero Monte Protegido," in: *La Época* (B. A., April 14, 1917), p. 1.

[152] "¡Calma!," in: *La Época* (B. A., April 14, 1917), p. 3. "Serenidad" and "Excesos," in: *La Vanguardia* (April 15, 1917), p. 1. Del Valle, *La cuestión internacional*, pp. 104–25.

[153] Restelli, head of Divisón Asuntos Políticos y Comerciales, memorandum (Buenos Aires, April 15, 1917), in: Solveira, *Argentina y la Primera Guerra Mundial*, Vol. 1, pp. 224–8. *Memoria de relaciones exteriores* 1917, pp. 56–8.

(*"paz cobarde"*) and, in actual fact, a "hidden form of Germanism."[154] After Rojas' speech, a large demonstration formed that made its way to the Plaza de Mayo. Participants sung the Marseillaise and cried out, "We don't want neutrality."[155]

The other side did not remain idle, however. On behalf of upholding neutrality, the Liga Patriótica Argentina under Alberto J. Grassi also organized a major event two days later, involving leading figures such as Belisario Roldán. After speeches at numerous public locations, the demonstrators marched under police protection from the Congress to the Plaza de Mayo. The speakers stressed again and again that they were not concerned about Germany, but only what was best for Argentina. The general tenor of the speeches was that the country's entry into the war would be a crime against the nation. Counter-protesters tried unsuccessfully to disrupt the demonstration. The day ended with an appeal to President Yrigoyen to preserve neutrality at all costs.[156]

In reality, the *Monte Protegido* case was no more a *casus belli* than the sinking of the *Oriana* on June 6 or the *Toro* on June 22. Whereas the *Oriana* had been carrying contraband and was, for all intents and purposes, not entirely an Argentine possession, the sinking of the *Toro* once again ignited major protests and anti-German riots.[157] In this instance, the German government responded to the Argentinean demands. Berlin offered the desired compensation, part of which, however, was to be paid after the war. In return, the Argentine government ensured that no more of its ships would sail into the contested submarine warfare zones. To secure the neutrality of this critical Latin American country, Germany's leadership was prepared to yield this concession. This is the only time it would do so in the entire course of the war.[158]

Here, too, Germany pursued its own interests. In April 1917, the U.S. military attaché already reported on the Germans' efforts to establish a radio receiving station, which, however, had run into technical

---

[154] Díaz Araujo, *Yrigoyen y la Guerra*, p. 220. Rojas, *La guerra de las naciones*, pp. 8–10 and 21.

[155] "Por la causa de los Aliados," in: *La Prensa* (B. A., April 23, 1917), p. 5. See also Tato, "La contienda europea en las calles porteñas," pp. 39–41.

[156] "En favor de la neutralidad," in: *La Prensa* (B. A., April 25, 1917), p. 11.

[157] On the riots from a German perspective: Ibero-American News and Archive Service (June 18, 1917), PAAA, 21900.

[158] Hermann Weil to AA (Frankfurt am Main., April 28, 1917), PAAA, 21899. This led to internal tensions between the Naval Staff and the Foreign Office, which was able to prevail on this issue. Doß, *Schülersche Reform*, pp. 26–9. Siepe, *Yrigoyen*, p. 23.

difficulties.[159] Following Brazil's entry into the war and Uruguay's decision to rupture relations, Mexico gained importance as a bridge to
Argentina for news and technical materials from Germany. Due to the
vast distance, it was not possible to establish a direct wireless connection
by the end of the war. All the same, representatives of Siemens-Schuckert
remained in contact with government agencies as proxies of Telefunken
and negotiated over licensing. German propaganda, at any rate, continued to operate from its central hub at *La Unión*, even though the newspaper was repeatedly the target of vandalism.[160]

According to Tato, the demonstrations of April 1917 represented a
shift in the internal Argentinean disputes over the issue of neutrality.
From this point forward, the pro-Ally forces were the *rupturistas*, and
their opponents the *neutralistas*. Both sides claimed that they were acting
in the best interest of the nation. They were, nevertheless, highly heterogeneous groups with different motivations and objectives.[161] Hence,
among the *rupturistas* there were conservatives who favored a military
acid test for Argentina, but also pacifists and socialists who only wanted
to enter the war in order to defeat imperialism and its wars of conquest
once and for all. Among the *neutralistas* there were Germanophiles who
supported neutrality to help the German Reich, anti-imperialists, who
warned about the influence of the United States on Argentina in case
of war, pacifists who were fundamentally opposed to the conflict, and
internationalists, for whom solidarity to the working class in other countries was more important than any national interests.[162] The division of
Argentine society cut across class and political affiliation. British ambassador Reginald Tower observed that it was precisely the old rulers who
were trying to push their way back into power and using their pro-Ally
stance to stir up public opinion against the president. President Yrigoyen's
decision against entering the war, therefore, is also to be understood as a
domestic political statement.[163]

The example of the Socialist Party of Argentina clearly illustrates the
divisiveness of the debates on the stance toward the war. Thus, while
the party had organized a big peace demonstration in Buenos Aires in

[159] U.S. military attaché to War College Division (B. A., May 5, 1917), NA, RG 38,
20950-876.
[160] "Telefunken," in: *La Unión* (B.A., July 24, 1918), p. 1. See also ONI to Director of
Naval Communications (Washington, DC, August 1, 1918), NA, RG 38, 20950–1025.
Katz, *The Secret War*, pp. 421–2.
[161] Tato, "La disputa por la argentinidad," pp. 230–1.
[162] See, e.g., Díaz Araujo, *Yrigoyen y la Guerra*, pp. 202–29.
[163] Goñi Demarchi/Scala/Berraondo, *Yrigoyen y la Gran Guerra*, p. 136.

February after the sinking of the *Monte Protegido*, it was primarily the leadership and the parliamentary faction under party head Juan B. Justo who did an about-face by explicitly embracing the position of the *rupturistas* and sharply criticizing the Germans' "Hun-like" warfare.[164] With the party newspaper *La Vanguardia*, these forces had an influential press organ at their disposal. These socialists were especially critical of the Yrigoyen government's supposedly too half-hearted response to the German provocation, which threatened Argentine trade.[165] At the same time, there was also a strong fundamentalist opposition to this attitude within the party, which appealed to the original ideals of socialism. A party congress convened on April 27 and 28, 1917, to settle the dispute. Heated debates culminated in a crucial vote in which the *neutralistas* prevailed by a narrow margin. In the immediate aftermath, Justo and many other well-known *rupturistas* expressed a desire to leave the party, only to then reconsider and continue the ideological struggle.[166]

After the April crisis, the quarrels persisted between the *rupturistas* and *neutralistas*, not only among the socialists, but throughout the Argentine public. Each side accused the other of being controlled from abroad.[167] Public appearances by intellectuals such as Lugones and his compatriot José Ingenieros ensured that the arguments of the pro-Ally forces were not forgotten. In their eyes, neutrality meant isolation and decline. By contrast, rupturing relations with Germany served a cause which, now that the United States had entered the war, stood for higher ideals.[168] The public embraced this stance during the visit of the U.S. squadron in Buenos Aires, when a large crowd appeared to cheer on the sailors.[169] Shortly thereafter, on July 14, the *rupturistas* held another mass rally in the Plaza del Congreso in the city center that was attended by numerous organizations.[170] The *rupturistas'* visibility in the media created the impression that they unilaterally dominated public opinion.

---

[164] "Neutralidad mal entendida," in: *La Vanguardia* (April 16, 1917), p. 4.

[165] "Ante el conflicto," in: *La Vanguardia* (April 13, 1917) p. 1. "La cuestión internacional," in: ibid. (April 18, 19, and 20, 1917), in each instance p. 1. "Hablemos claro," in: ibid. (April 25, 1917), p. 1. See also José Rouco Oliva, "La cuestión internacional," in: ibid.

[166] Siepe, *Yrigoyen*, pp. 70–1. "La neutralidad y la opinión," in: *La Vanguardia* (April 29, 1917), p. 1.

[167] Colmo, *Mi neutralismo*, pp. 6–14.

[168] Lugones, *Mi beligerancia*, p. 205. Ingenieros, "La significación histórica," p. 378. See also Díaz Araujo, *Yrigoyen y la Guerra*, p. 222. Compagnon, *L'adieu à l'Europe*, pp. 246–8.

[169] Admiral Caperton, *Memorandum* (Washington, DC, September 17, 1917), NA, RG 59, 835.00/144.

[170] Tato, "La contienda europea en las calles porteñas," p. 43.

That said, the *neutralistas* also did not miss any opportunities to publicly express their views. Vergara, for instance, defended the German war effort in the Teatro Coliseo a few days after the pro-Ally demonstration. He took on every single one of the *rupturistas'* arguments, which, to him, were all part of a "war of lies."[171] By mid-1917, his faction was very large, but also very heterogeneous. Unlike the cosmopolitan and liberal-oriented *rupturistas*, the *neutralistas* mainly recruited from the conservative and nationalist milieu. The appeal to national pride and foreign policy autonomy resonated as much with them as the motto: "Better to live in the Fatherland than to die for strangers."[172] With their widely dispersed local groups, the *neutralistas* had approximately the same number of organizations at their disposal nationally as their opponents. The Liga Patriótica Argentina pro Neutralidad (Argentine Patriotic League for Neutrality) was the primary umbrella organization. In the press, only *La Época* and, of course, the propaganda newspaper *La Unión* might be deemed pro-German. By the same token, *La Prensa* and *La Razón* also were inclined toward neutrality but did not spare their criticism of Germany.[173]

In their published memoirs after the war, many *rupturistas* wrote retrospectively as if all the major intellectuals had been on the side of the Allies. This is understandable given the war's outcome. Above all, the Germanophile faction among the *neutralistas* had been repudiated in the wake of Germany's defeat. Still, a closer look at the sources shows that this faction was not as small or insignificant in Argentina as some historians suggest. This reality on the ground is further substantiated when accounting for the difference between the city and the countryside. Thus, although a majority probably spoke in favor of the rupture with Germany in major cities, it was very much the reverse in the hinterlands. There, a disproportionate number advocated keeping the peace at any price.[174]

The violent clashes also left their mark on Argentinean politics. Despite increasing hostility, however, President Yrigoyen held fast to his stance in favor of neutrality. In response to domestic political pressure, he further launched his own initiative in May 1917 to organize a conference of Latin American countries with the aim of preserving neutrality

[171] Vergara, *Guerra de mentiras*, pp. 3–5.
[172] Tato, "La disputa por la argentinidad," pp. 236 and 243–7. Compagnon, *L'adieu à l'Europe*, pp. 246–8.
[173] Tato, "La disputa por la argentinidad," pp. 233–4.
[174] Díaz Araujo, *Yrigoyen y la Guerra*, pp. 212 and 232.

and, in connection with the activities of the Pope, of facilitating peace. Unsurprisingly, the Argentinian president's actions were met with harsh criticism from the United States.[175] What is more, the response across Latin America was also not entirely positive. By July, only the governments in Colombia, El Salvador, and Mexico had announced their support for the conference.[176] *La Prensa* nevertheless defended the president's policies, suggesting they were evidence of Argentina's independence and that of Latin America in general. They were likewise a step toward a necessary emancipation from a unilateral Pan-Americanism aimed at the economic interests of the United States.[177] The conference, however, ultimately remained up in the air until the end of 1917.

In early September, the atmosphere in Argentina was so caustic that the slightest spark was enough to cause it to explode. As it turned out, it was much more than just a spark. On September 9, *La Prensa* published the texts of three telegrams of the German chargé d'affaires, Karl Graf von Luxburg, to the Foreign Ministry in Berlin that the Allies deciphered. In them, the diplomat pushed for a total onslaught against Argentine ships, called Argentine Foreign Minister Honorio Pueyrredón a "notorious ass and Anglophile," and characterized the people in South America as deceiving "Indios."[178]

The Argentine government reacted swiftly: Three days later, on September 12, Luxburg received his passports and was declared persona non grata. Street rallies and demonstrations immediately followed. The episode, however, only escalated. At night, there were violent riots against German establishments, which were partly burned down and looted. The buildings of *La Unión* and the German Club were especially hard hit. In light of the scale of the destruction, the press suspected that the protesters had been well equipped. The police, who tried to subdue

---

[175] Rosenberg, *World War I*, pp. 15–7. The preparation of the démarche had already begun in the press in April: "El punto de vista sudamericano," in: *La Nación* (Santiago de Chile, April 15, 1917). In mid-May, Buenos Aires felt compelled to explain its position to the U.S. government in order to avoid any "misunderstandings" in their relations. Argentine ambassador to Dept. of State (Washington, DC, May 17, 1917), in: *FRUS* 1917 I, p. 283.

[176] Argentine ambassador to MRREE (The Hague, August 10, 1917), in: Solveira, *Argentina y la Primera Guerra Mundial*, Vol. 2, p. 19.

[177] "La posición de la República Argentina de Sud América," in: *La Prensa* (B. A., June 8, 1917), p. 5. "Panamericanismo y panhispanismo," in: ibid. July 3, 1917), p. 5.

[178] "Despachos reservados del Conde de Luxburg," in: *La Prensa* (B. A., September 9, 1917), p. 5. The complete telegrams have been reprinted in: Solveira, *Argentina y la Primera Guerra Mundial*, Vol. 2, pp. 100–27.

the "mob," became embroiled in all-out street battles.[179] The incident led
to the public's further polarization and intensified the accusations from
both sides.[180] While the pro-Ally newspapers felt justified in their condemnation of "German barbarity," now even the magazine *Nosotros*,
which had called for calm in April, forcefully insisted on severing ties
with Germany.[181] The repercussions of the events in Argentina were felt
in neighboring Uruguay and even in Chile. The diplomatic cooperation
of the German leadership, which on September 15 had vowed to spare
Argentine ships going forward, did nothing to change the fact that the
calls for resolute action against the German Reich had become louder
everywhere (see Figure 3.3).[182]

Now, the vast majority of the public was clearly for breaking ties with
the German Reich. This became apparent when, after long debates in
both chambers following the hearing of Foreign Minister Pueyrredón on
September 19 and 22, the Argentinean congress announced its support
for the move. The deputies and senators who spoke in favor of the rupture affirmed that the honor of Argentina had been attacked and also
raised economic considerations. While the congress debated, the Comité
de la Juventud chaired by Mariano Villar Sáenz Peña organized another
mass rally, where Rojas and Lugones, among others, demanded that relations be severed with Germany. Amidst all the turmoil, the message from
Berlin that the imperial government distanced itself from Luxburg's statements received little notice.[183] In October, the violent attacks on German
property spread to the interior of the country, including Mendoza, Bahia
Blanca, Santa Fe, and Rosario.[184] At the same time, foreign policy pressure continued to increase on the Yrigoyen government.

---

[179] "Las manifestaciones callejeras de ayer," in: *La Prensa* (B. A., September 13, 1917), p. 8.
See also the photo reportage: "El caso de Luxburg," in: *Caras y Caretas* (September
22, 1917).

[180] Tato, "La contienda europea en las calles porteñas," p. 42.

[181] "América en la guerra," in: *Nosotros* 11 (25/1917), pp. 433–6. "Hacia la ruptura," in:
ibid, p. 11 and (27/1917), pp. 5–7. See also "Bellezas diplomáticas," in: *La Vanguardia*
(September 10, 1917), p. 1.

[182] "La publicación de los despachos," in: *Diario del Plata* (September 11, 1917), p. 3.
"El caso Luxburg," in: *El Día* (September 14, 1917), p. 2. "El pangermanismo en
América," in: ibid. (October 30, 1917), p. 3. "El asunto Luxburg y nosotros," in: *Zig-
Zag* (September 29, 1917). On Germany's softening of its tone regarding the subma-
rine question, see "Un triunfo de nuestra diplomacia," in: *Caras y Caretas* (September
15, 1917).

[183] "Congreso: sesión de ayer" and "Asuntos internacionales," in: *La Prensa* (B. A.,
September 23, 1917), pp. 3–7. Siepe, *Yrigoyen*, pp. 13–14.

[184] Tato, "La disputa por la argentinidad," p. 233.

TODO NOS UNE,
NADA NOS SEPARA

El dragón de la perfidia
usó en vano su rencor;
que lo que ha *unido* el amor
no lo *separa* la insidia.

FIGURE 3.3 An appeal for South American solidarity. The solidarity of Argentina, Uruguay, and Brazil in the face of the "treacherous dragon" remained an unfulfilled dream of the *rupturistas*.

Source: "Todo nos une, nada nos separa," in: *Caras y Caretas* (October 27, 1917).

The Luxburg affair renewed the inner-party clashes. Senator Enrique del Valle Iberlucea, the publisher of *La Vanguardia*, openly spoke out against the "Teutonic imperialism" in his speech before the Senate on September 19. Conversely, the *neutralista* faction of his own party, which had had its own mouthpiece with the newspaper *La Internacional* since August 1917, accused him of warmongering.[185] The right-wing members of the party, in turn, criticized these voices as "German agents" and pushed for their expulsion from the party. The quarrel did not come to an end until the socialists who supported neutrality decided to split off from the party on January 5, 1918, as the Partido Socialista Internacional (Internationalist Socialist Party). This move carried with it a message of solidarity to the Russian revolutionaries and the demand for an immediate end to the war.[186]

Despite the developments among the socialists, in September 1917, virtually all political actors anticipated that there would be a rupture of relations with the German Reich. Indeed, it seemed as if it was only a matter of time before President Yrigoyen would take this step – and yet, he did nothing of the sort. Faced with enormous pressure from the opposition and many of his own party members, he stayed the course on neutrality. The *neutralistas*, further, took advantage of Día de la Raza (Day of the Race) – the new holiday Yrigoyen introduced to commemorate the discovery of America in Buenos Aires on October 12 – to organize a counter-demonstration at the official events.[187]

Researchers have long puzzled over why a politician would cling to neutrality, despite opposition from the majority of the population, including the parliament. It was in this vein that contemporary observer and scholar Julio S. Storni from Corrientes meticulously recorded the surrounding circumstances in a press report that was already published on October 3, 1917. In Storni's assessment, the German apology was sufficient. Argentina now had to act in its own interest. Neutrality, he further offered, was not a sign of weakness, but rather proof of Argentina's self-confidence. Beyond this, neutrality also made sense from an economic and industrial point of view. The war, on the other hand, seemed absurd and criminal. For Storni, Argentina had only one unresolved issue with Europe and that concerned the possession of the Malvinas/Falkland

---

[185] Del Valle, *La cuestión internacional*, p. 127.
[186] Ibid., pp. 251–3. Corbière, *Origen del comunismo argentino*, pp. 26–45. Compagnon, *L'adieu à l'Europe*, pp. 130–1. In 1920, the party merged with the Communist Party of Argentina.
[187] Díaz Araujo, *Yrigoyen y la Guerra*, p. 208.

Islands.[188] Even if President Yrigoyen was not a Germanophile like Storni, whose book also contains an apologia for German policy, he probably shared Storni's views nonetheless.

Besides Yrigoyen's nationalistic posture, which was likely influenced by financial contributions from German sources, other factors played a role.[189] For instance, Argentina had more bargaining power with the Allies than its neighbor Brazil, because it could supply raw materials that were vital to the war effort.[190] As historian Sérgio Bagú has demonstrated, Argentina's entry into the war was not, in fact, necessarily in the interest of the British government, as critical deliveries of Argentinean wheat would have been even more under threat by German submarines. It also would have meant that the United States would have greater access to Argentina, as in Brazil.[191] Finally, Argentina viewed its stance toward the war in the context of the country taking a leadership role in Latin America. Its own neutrality, as a consequence, was to be understood as a counterweight to Brazil's participation in the war.[192]

The public debate over the response to the war was more intense in Argentina than in any other neutral country. There were, however, also clashes between opposing interests in the other neutral states, although it was least evident in landlocked Paraguay. The country's own orientation in relation to neighboring Argentina was clear when a large pro-Ally rally was organized at the National Theatre of Asunción on July 7, 1917. Attended by many of the leading politicians from the country's major parties, it was striking how all the speakers, including former President Cecilio Báez, emphasized the importance and the idealism of the United States in its fight against the aspirations of militaristic empires to dominate the world. According to Báez, President Wilson's famous speeches were the new "gospel of free peoples."[193] Rallies like this were not least attributable to the rising economic importance of the United States in Paraguay. They remained a rare occurrence, however. Neither did they have an impact on the liberal governments under Schaerer and

---

[188] Storni, *Mi opinión sobre la neutralidad*, pp. 10–19.

[189] On the money flows, see the report of the U.S. intelligence service: "Report on foreign and domestic propaganda in the Argentine Republic ... " (April 9, 1918), NA, RG 165, MID, 2327-L-1.

[190] Compagnon, *L'adieu à l'Europe*, p. 143.

[191] Bagú, *Argentina en el mundo*, p. 78.

[192] Compagnon, "Si loin, si proche ...," p. 85. Dehne's contention that neutrality should be understood as a protest against the blacklists is not entirely convincing. *On the Far Western Front*, pp. 162–3.

[193] *En favor de los aliados*, p. 15.

his successor, Manuel Franco, which held fast to neutrality. The Allies consequently assessed them as pro-German.[194]

Chile was similarly deemed pro-German, even though there were also heated debates over the stance toward the war in response to the United States' entry into the conflict and the unfettered German submarine warfare. In August 1917, the magazine *Zig-Zag* even wrote in verse about the "war mania" that broke out early one morning among the newspaper's readers on the trolley. A German with a heavy accent had quarreled with passengers who were pro-Ally, which resulted in everyone arriving late for work.[195] This short satirical poem is the work of an attentive journalist who was able to capture the fraught atmosphere that prevailed in his country. The Chilean Ministry of Foreign Affairs had already been trying to strengthen ties with the United States since March 1917, since the U.S. markets were needed more than ever. Additionally, power-political considerations played a significant role. The Chilean diplomats clearly recognized that the United States was the dominant force in the Americas. They also knew that Chile needed to be on good terms with its northern neighbor if it wanted assert its own regional supremacy over the long term. It was also important to avoid reopening the dispute over the northern border with its neighbors Peru and Bolivia, which were now making demands.[196]

In October 1917, the Chilean ambassador in London, Agustín Edwards McClure, thus urged his country's explicit solidarity with the United States and Brazil. He further noted that future cooperation, especially with the United States, was unavoidable.[197] The pro-Ally voices were convinced that Brazil's example was worth imitating, for it showed how taking sides with the Allies could result in a substantial gain in power.[198] Among the press, *El Mercurio* in Santiago founded by Edwards was especially forceful under editor-in-chief Silva Vildósola in advocating for Chile's entry into the war on the side of the Allies. At the same time, it actively sought to stir up sentiment against Germany. These arguments were aired publicly, above all, on U.S. and French national holidays.[199]

---

[194] Ibid., passim. On the assessment of the government's stance, see anonymous reports of Paraguay (September 9 and 12, 1918), NA, RG 165, MID, 2048–72.

[195] Robin, "¿Aliadófilo o germanófilo?," in: *Zig-Zag* (August 4, 1917).

[196] Chil. Embassy to MRREE (Washington, DC, October 5, 1917), Chile, AMRREE, Vol. 613.

[197] Quoted in Fermandois, *Mundo y fin de mundo*, p. 84.

[198] "La cooperación del Brasil en la guerra," in: *El Mercurio* (July 3, 1918), p. 1.

[199] "Horrores de la invasión," in: *El Mercurio* (April 16, 1917), p. 2. Donoso, "Nuestra Francia."

These favorable accounts, in part taken directly from Allied propaganda, were only one side of the coin, however. In fact, many reservations persisted about the U.S. policies, even if they were often only expressed indirectly.[200] For their part, Chilean conservatives made no secret of their pro-German attitude. Their newspaper *El Diario Ilustrado* remained an important counterweight to the press of the Edwards Group. Authors like Gallardo and Roberto Huneeus Gana became involved in editorial clashes with Ally supporters. Pointing to the important contribution from German immigrants in building up the Chilean nation, they warned against hate propaganda that sought to propel the country into a war that did not concern Chile.[201]

Ultimately, the majority in Chile, including those who sympathized with the Allies, felt that neutrality should be maintained as long as the country was not directly affected. The Sanfuentes government could preserve this attitude relatively easily, despite external political pressure. After all, unlike Brazil, the Chilean government was a supplier of coveted raw materials such as saltpeter and copper and had even made an important contribution to the war.[202] As the government newspaper *La Nación* remarked in mid-April 1917, neutrality made sense for Chile in particular and the Americas in general because – regardless of the preference for one warring side or the other – it meant that civilization and peace could be preserved in this part of the world.[203]

From the United States' perspective, the neutrality of two countries, Venezuela and Colombia, was a particular source of irritation. Due to their central geostrategic location in the Caribbean and their proximity to the Panama Canal, they both had a special significance in Washington's military planning. The attitude of Venezuela was essentially due to the will of dictator Juan Vicente Gómez, who ruled the country from 1908 to 1935. Although Gómez certainly sought rapprochement with the United States in an economic sense, he was also an admirer of the Prussian-German military. This attitude was reinforced by an influential group of German merchants, who cultivated close ties with him. The opposition to Gómez increased rapidly during the war and came partly from those in exile. They seized on his Germanophilia as a target for fierce criticism.

[200] Embassy to Sec. of State (Santiago, July 5, 1918), NA, RG 59, 825.911/1.
[201] "Un juego peligroso," in: *El Diario Ilustrado* (April 16, 1917). Gallardo, *Panamericanismo*, p. 104. Huneeus, *Por amor a Chile*. "Tres años en Alemania," in: *Zig-Zag* (November 24, 1917).
[202] "Guerra de comunicaciones," in: *El Diario Ilustrado* (April 7, 1917).
[203] "La doctrina Wilson y Sud América," in: *La Nación* (Santiago, April 17, 1917), p. 3.

From exile in London, Rafael de la Cova thus accused the dictator of heavily promoting the Germans in Venezuela and brutally suppressing pro-Ally voices. On the other hand, the Germans in Venezuela supposedly used every opportunity they had to spread the rumor that their opponents were planning a coup, which hit a real nerve with Gómez. Overall, Venezuela lacked the willingness and the ability to effectively monitor the long coastline for German submarines. This would have been necessary in the event of war, however. The preservation of neutrality, therefore, followed from entirely rational considerations.[204]

The Colombian decision to not enter the war against Germany should be understood against the backdrop of the country's highly strained relations with the United States since Panama's separation. From the perspective of the major newspapers in the capital, neutrality was necessary to avoid being caught in the grip of "Yankee" power. As journalist Manuel Alberto Vergara remarked, the United States' entry into the war demonstrated that the North Americans must be very certain of their control over Latin America, otherwise they would not have taken the risk. Yet, for their own region, it represented a tremendous threat that could be averted only if Latin Americans did a better job of banding together.[205] At the same time, voices like that of governmental adviser Julio Villar Vale, who insisted in an open letter to Foreign Minister Marco Fidel Suárez that cooperation with the United States was the only way to avoid suffering the consequences after the war, remained few and far between.[206]

As with Venezuela, the stance of the Colombian government raised hackles in Washington. The U.S. press repeatedly published reports that Colombia was cooperating with the German Reich, an assertion President José Vicente Concha was forced to deny.[207] To help dispel the accusations, he even sent a government commission to the Darién region to prove that there were no German submarine bases. Suárez, further, called on the press to show restraint in their reporting on the events of the war, and the Colombian parliament spoke out against submarine warfare.[208]

---

[204] De la Cova, *Venezuela ante el conflicto europeo*, pp. 6–7. On German propaganda in Venezuela, see U.S. consul to Sec. of State (Maracaibo, September 22, 1918), NA, RG 195, MID, 35-19-2.

[205] Manuel Alberto Vergara, "Defensa latinoamericana," in: *Sur América* (Bogotá, January 26, 1918), p. 1.

[206] Charge d'affaires to Dept. of State (Bogotá, September 1, 1917), NA, RG 165 WCD, 6393-23.

[207] *Informe del Ministro de Relaciones Exteriores 1917*, pp. 101–3.

[208] "Una entrevista con el General Ortiz," in: *El Diario Nacional* (Bogotá, November 20, 1917), p. 1. Rausch, "Colombia's Neutrality," pp. 109–11.

The U.S. concerns were not entirely unwarranted, however. The German Reich was very active in Colombia, both in terms of propaganda and behind the scenes. Berlin, for instance, promised it would purchase coca leaves in the postwar period as a stimulant for German soldiers.[209] In Bogotá, the propaganda newspaper *Transocean* continued to published undeterred and worked closely with the German intelligence service in Mexico. In general, the Mexican government's unyielding attitude toward the United States was appreciated and even characterized by a number of newspapers as a "lesson worthy of imitation."[210] In the final analysis, as the foreign minister summed up in a memorandum, Colombia's neutral stance throughout the war was due to a combination of the public's critical attitude toward the United States and the simple lack of a *casus belli*.[211]

Colombia was not the only country where Mexico served as a role model in the course of 1917. Its independence-oriented, nationalistic policy vis-à-vis the dominant United States was apparent from its attitude toward the war. The Mexican Constitution of 1917 took effect on February 5, 1917, almost simultaneous to the U.S. decision to break off relations with the German Reich. The constitution proclaimed a new kind of social legislation and, above all, the nationalization of natural resources. At bottom, this was a direct assault on the interests of the major powers, which depended on the oil supplies from Mexico during the war more than ever. It was hardly surprising, therefore, that statements of solidarity with the United States from Mexico were few and far between. On the contrary, Mexico embraced a literal interpretation of the idea of active neutrality, already submitting a concrete proposal for a peace initiative to the neutral countries of the Americas and Europe on February 12. In the memorandum from Foreign Minister Cándido Aguilar, it was argued that the neutrals had contributed to prolonging the war because of their resources. They now needed to come together to bring the conflict to an end. The Mexican government's proposal had revolutionary undertones. The neutrals were to suspend their trade with

[209] MRREE to the Ministro de Guerra (Bogotá, March 6, 1917), Colombia, AGN, MRREE, 01060, Trasf. 1, fol. 253–4.

[210] "Lección digna de imitarse," in: *Ecos Mundiales* (Cúcuta, September 14, 1918). Supplement to U.S. consul Sec. of State (Maracaibo, September 22, 1918), NA, RG 165, MID, 35-19. See also "Lógica y patriotismo," in: *Transocean* (Bogotá, November 6, 1917), p. 1.

[211] MRREE to Colombian envoy in Washington (Bogotá, August 18, 16), Colombia, AGN, MRREE, Caja 02040, Trasf. 1, fol. 19.

all combatants until peace finally prevailed. Although this was a completely novel measure in international law, Aguilar also explained that as the global war itself was new, extreme steps were justified and seemed necessary to finally end it.[212] Even though the Mexican memorandum did not receive much of a response, the Carranza government nonetheless devised a new initiative after the United States entered the war to mediate conflict with Germany. Washington, however, brusquely turned down the suggestion.[213]

Certainly, Carranza's foreign policy can only be understood against the backdrop of the extremely strained relations with the United States since the Pershing expedition. In the Mexican press, anti-U.S. comments dominated and pro-German statements were now more frequent. Carranza's government newspaper *El Demócrata* contributed a great deal to this general orientation.[214] By contrast, the number of those speaking out in favor of a rapprochement with the United States remained relatively small. Publisher Félix Fulgencio Palavicini, who founded his own anti-Carranza newspaper in 1917 with *El Universal*, was undoubtedly the most prominent voice to openly campaign in Mexico on behalf of the Allies. In this context, marine engineer Miguel Rebolledo published an intriguing article in June 1917. He believed that Mexicans needed to seek better relations with the United States for practical reasons. This was especially urgent due to the global dimensions of the war:

The almost universal character of the current struggle cannot leave unfazed even the most insignificant countries, the barbarians and the savages. Many of [these countries] are involved in the fighting! The crisis is so terrifying that all humanity has been swept away by its deadly current.[215]

In December 1917, considerations like these informed a petition in the Mexican Senate, proposing that the country's neutrality should be changed – in line with the Uruguayan model – into a kind of benevolent neutrality toward the Allies. A large majority rejected this proposal, however. The consensus was that Mexico did not have the means to make a

---

[212] Mexican Foreign Minister C. Aguilar, circular (Querétaro, February 12, 1917), printed in: Garay, *Panamá*, pp. 13–15.

[213] Secretary of State to the Embassy in Mexico (Washington, DC, April 21, 1917), in: *FRUS* 1917 I, p. 261. See also U.S. ambassador to Sec. of State (Mexico, April 3, 1917), in: *FRUS* 1917 II, p. 243. "La prensa sigue haciendo comentarios," in: *El Demócrata* (March 2, 1917), p. 2.

[214] Katz, *The Secret War*, p. 459. In 1919, the British government honored Palavicini for his pro-Ally stance. Meyer, *Su majestad británica*, p. 249.

[215] Rebolledo, *México y Estados Unidos*, p. 163.

meaningful war contribution, and that the country would humiliate itself by taking such a step.[216]

Given this state of affairs, Allied policy toward Mexico remained in disarray and lacked coordination. In a first response to the Mexican peace initiative and the constitution of 1917, London and Washington contemplated intervening militarily to secure the country's all-important crude oil.[217] The British military, in particular, pushed for taking an aggressive stance toward Carranza. The English petroleum companies, however, insisted on a more cautious approach, as they were concerned about their investments.[218] As in Argentina, a view in favor of upholding Mexican neutrality eventually prevailed, since it was thought to be the only way to keep U.S. influence in check. Paradoxically, this was more or less the interest of Washington, which mainly wanted to keep Mexico "quiet" for the duration of the U.S. war effort on the battlefields of Europe.[219]

This was no easy task, however, due to the propaganda and secret service war in Mexico. The Allies here played an active role.[220] The U.S. boulevard press, above all, engaged in repeatedly publishing sensational reports on German intrigues there following the Zimmerman telegram scandal. Among other things, they incited fear concerning an ad hoc alliance between German spies and anarchists to commit acts of sabotage in the oil region around Tampico. When the workers there went on strike to enforce better working conditions, even the Brazilian press immediately suspected that the German secret service was behind it.[221] In the United States, worries about espionage gave rise to the implementation of security matters against Mexican migrants.[222]

The Mexican press deplored these measures as much as it did the United States' foreign trade restrictions. News editorials pointed out that Mexico had long supplied critical war products such as crude oil, without, however, receiving its due recognition.[223] This, however, did not sway the U.S. government, which instead looked with concern at Mexican policy toward Central America with its anti-Guatemala thrust.

[216] "El fracaso de le neutralidad benevola," in: *El Nacional* (December 22, 1917), p. 3.
[217] Meyer, *Su majestad británica*, p. 231.
[218] Gerhardt, "Inglaterra," p. 128.
[219] Katz, *The Secret War*, p. 460.
[220] Py, *Francia y la Revolución Mexicana*, p. 211.
[221] "Um exército allemão concentrado no México," in: *A Epoca* (March 12, 1917), p. 1. Durán, *Guerra y revolución*, pp. 156–7.
[222] "Una barrera para los germanos," in: *Excelsior* (December 5, 1917), p. 1.
[223] "Memorandum," in: *El Demócrata* (March 6, 1918), p. 3.

The Mexican propagandists, in any event, noticed that the U.S. influence on the Central American press had increased tremendously since the
United States entered the war. Moreover, it was hardly possible to spread
anti-U.S. and pro-Carranza articles any longer because of the increased
costs. On the contrary, Carranza was now maligned in many places as a
Germanophile.[224]

Ironically, it was the success of German propaganda in Mexico that
made this assessment seem credible to many contemporaries. After the
United States entered the war, Mexico became a focal point of the German
intelligence and propaganda work in northern Latin America more than
ever before. Thus, alongside India and the Middle East, it was a key part
of Berlin's strategy to revolutionize and thus destabilize its enemies' colonial empires.[225] The expelled Telefunken workers from Tuckerton and
Sayville moved their headquarters to Mexico.[226] This move made sense
given that the Mexican radio station, which had already been upgraded
for some time, could now be turned into a hub of German communication. From 1917 onward, there was regular radio traffic between Nauen
and a new station that was now located in Ixtapalapa, a suburb of the
capital. Across this connection, even coded messages could be received
since the Mexican government had imposed no restrictions. With a view
to the importance of Mexico for the project of a world radio network,
the German leadership swept aside the financial concerns expressed only
a few months earlier against the undertaking. On this basis, publisher
Carl Düms was able to operate his own news service with *Informaciones
Inalambricas*, which he published as a newspaper from 1917.[227] Beyond
this, the German side hired a gifted propagandist, journalist Manuel
León Sánchez, who succeeded in reaching a large audience with his anti-
imperialist writings directed against the United States and its Monroe
Doctrine.[228]

---

[224] "Il ya fagot et d'étranges neutralités," in: *Le Courrier du Mexique* (November 1, 1917),
p. 1. Yankelevich, *La revolución mexicana en América Latina*, pp. 114–20.

[225] Meyer, *La marca del nacionalismo*, p. 23.

[226] Katz, *The Secret War*, pp. 441–6.

[227] Katz, *The Secret War*, pp. 419–20. U.S. Consul to Dept. of State (Veracruz, March 10,
1917), NA, RG 59, 812.74/61. U.S. military attaché to War College Division (Mexico,
August 21, 1917), NA, RG 38, 20950-876.

[228] León's speeches and translations of German propaganda literature were published in the
series *Boletín de la Guerra*: León, *La guerra mundial*, p. 3. Idem, *Si el Ejército alemán
llegase a México*, pp. 4–5. Idem, *Noticias falsas*, pp. 3–4. Idem, *Los submarinos y las
listas negras*, pp. 16–20. See also Katz, *The Secret War*, pp. 450–3. Gerlich, "La política
norte-americana y la doctrina de Monroe," p. 35.

Carranza himself responded to the pressure from the outside with a flexible policy. On one hand, he continued to work towards bolstering relations with the German Reich; on the other, he avoided making overly dramatic provocations with respect to the Allies. At the same time, he declined any further requests for support.[229] With his peace initiative, Carranza underlined Mexico's aspiration to lead in Latin America under the auspices of the country's revolutionary nationalism. He skillfully took advantage of the anti-U.S. resentment, which predominated throughout the region. He also portrayed his country as an alternative to the regimes of the old elites, which did not stand up to the hegemony of the north. Carranza's approach proved quite successful for Mexico, for he kept his country out of the war. That said, he failed to inspire many countries in his own backyard to follow his lead. The dominance of the United States in Central America was too great.

El Salvador remained a conspicuous exception in the region. As regards Germany, there was neither a rupture of relations here, nor a declaration of war. This was due not least to the fact that the coffee export and subsistence economy was far less under U.S. influence than the banana production in neighboring countries. Furthermore, under Carlos Meléndez (1913–18) the country experienced a period of relative domestic political stability. The fact that El Salvador did not seek a partnership with the United States after the war-related loss of European markets, as, for instance, Guatemala had done, was not because of its particular sympathy for Germany, as some Allied propagandists charged. Rather, the country was afraid of losing sovereignty like Nicaragua. One particular stumbling block was the U.S. naval base in the Gulf of Fonseca. Claiming ownership of the region, El Salvador lodged a complaint against the Brian Chamorro Treaty before the Central American court, which was upheld on March 2, 1917. Because the United States ignored the ruling, Meléndez was only willing to consent to a "friendly neutrality" with Washington. This meant that while the U.S. Navy could sail in Salvadoran waters, the blacklists and other anti-German measures were ignored in El Salvador. The Meléndez government could stick to its guns, because the absence of foreign capital was at least partially offset by a policy of rigorous austerity. Meléndez not only cultivated ties with Mexico, but he continued to advance the cause of Central American integration. Thus, as far as Washington was concerned, the neutral El

---

[229] Buchenau, *In the Shadow of the Giant*, p. 129. Fabela, *La política interior y exterior de Carranza*, pp. 215–6.

Salvador and Mexico continued to be the "troublemakers" in the region until the end of the war.[230]

In 1917, the war was no longer simply present in Latin America due to the economic and propaganda war. The war's political dimension also pulled the subcontinent along in its wake. For the first time in their history, Latin American countries entered into a war that was being fought outside of the Americas. And they did so, according to their own rhetoric, in order to contribute to the struggle for world freedom. The fact that many small states in the Caribbean and Central American region followed the example – or, more precisely, the demands – of the United States, and had to follow it, emphasizes the power-political dominance that Washington had had in the region since the beginning of the twentieth century. At the same time, these entries into the war were tied to hopes of loosening the grip of the "big brother" at least somewhat, even in the case of Panama and Cuba. The contribution to the world war was supposed to be the basis for more state sovereignty and equal treatment, which had been witnessed in the case of Brazil's entry into the war under entirely different circumstances. Factors figuring into the decision of whether to enter the war, or even to only suspend relations with Germany, were, on one hand, German submarine warfare, and, on the other, economic and political calculations.

By 1917, no Latin American government could ignore the provocation of the war. The situation was urgent even for a number of neutral countries, like Argentina, where neutrality could no longer simply be maintained by decree. The pressure coming from the streets, as well as from pro-Ally propaganda and its Latin American advocates, was too strong. In actual fact, the decision to stick with a strategy of nonintervention had diverse reasons. The explanations many contemporary observers and some historians thus cited relating to Germanophilia or anti-U.S. attitudes played only a subordinate role. Ultimately, the vast majority of Latin American governments pursued their own national interests when making the decision for or against joining the war.

---

[230] Conversely, the United States contributed only very limited humanitarian aid when a violent earthquake and volcanic eruption devastated the capital and the western part of the country on June 8, 1917. Suter, *Prosperität und Krise*, pp. 36–51. See also Notten, *La influencia*, p. 38.

4

Turbulent Paths into a "New Era," 1918–1919

The hope for a rapid end to the war, which some Latin Americans thought possible after the United States entered the conflict, dissipated by the end of 1917. The war was now a world war in every respect and no resolution was in sight. Latin America found itself increasingly more dependent on its demands. In many places, there were supply shortages. This gave way in 1918 to unrest that spread across the entire subcontinent. The revolt not only had domestic causes, for the threat posed by the revolutionary wave in Russia was increasingly felt in the region, too. The radicalization of social conflicts influenced the attitude toward the end of the war, which Latin Americans far and wide certainly welcomed enthusiastically. At the same time, the war's culmination in the Treaty of Versailles and the League of Nations also soon gave way to a sense of disillusionment.

THE "SUBTLE WAR" FOR REGIONAL HEGEMONY

"South America today is a vast battleground in which a subtle war is being fought for public opinion and commercial supremacy."[1] When the officials of the U.S. Creel Committee arrived at this conclusion in its activity report in mid-1918, they highlighted two dimensions that in fact remained critical for Latin America's involvement in the war. In the propaganda war, the Allies kept the upper hand in most countries of the region and drove out German activities. In the warring countries of Latin America, this propaganda was intended to stoke hatred of the Central Powers in order to divert attention from the hardships that the

[1] "South America and the War" (1918), NA, RG 63, Entry 132, Box 4, p. 1.

war brought with it or to make them more palatable. On the other hand, in those countries where governments had only severed relations or remained neutral in 1917, campaigns on behalf of entering the war persisted. Especially in the neutral countries, German propaganda continued to fight back intensively even in the last year of the war. The Allies were thus in no way able to realize their ambitious goal of motivating all of Latin America to enter the war.

The work of the Creel Committee was undoubtedly an asset for Allied propaganda in Latin America. Apart from the dissemination of its own material, which the committee boosted significantly in 1918, the monitoring and influencing of the Latin American media had top priority. For instance, when it recognized that newspapers in Peru like *El Comercio*, *La Crónica*, and *La Unión* were more or less pro-German in their reporting, it undertook a two-pronged campaign against these newspapers. The English-language *West Coast Leader* published counter-statements, and in the background the staff made sure that the advertising revenue of *Crónica* dramatically declined. Subsequently, the Peruvian newspaper radically altered its reporting – so much so that it was praised a few months later for being especially helpful toward the Ally cause.[2] Otherwise, the Allied propaganda turned to proven resources. What is more, in the wake of the separate German-Russian Treaty of Brest-Litovsk, it could now more persuasively make the case for the struggle of democracy against imperialism.[3]

The Allies' propaganda machine, however, encountered hurdles wherever neutrality remained in effect. Hence, U.S. observers reported from Colombia in private that the hatred of the United States there was so great that their own arguments mostly fell on deaf ears.[4] In Venezuela under Gómez, according to the New York-based exile newspaper *La Joven Venezuela*, there were no longer any pro-Ally publications in 1918 because they had all been persecuted by the censor.[5] In Chile, in turn, where quite a few pro-Ally voices were heard, the Allies could not silence the powerful German minority, which had organized itself into a

---

[2] C. N. Griffis, "Allied Propaganda – Lima Peru (January 11, 1918), NA, RG 63, Entry 117, Box 2. Dept. of Commerce to Committee on Public Information (May 11, 1918), ibid., Box 3.

[3] Ferrara, "América Latina y la Gran Guerra," pp. 8–9.

[4] U.S. ONI to MID, Conditions in Colombia and Venezuela (April 23, 1918), NA, RG 165 MID, 35-4-1.

[5] Legation to Sec. of State (Caracas, July 28, 1917), NA, RG 59, 710.11/334. U.S. Postal Censorship, Index No. 90642 (August 26, 1918), NA, RG 63, Entry 117, Box 1.

nationwide peoples' federation (Deutsch-Chilenischer Bund) and continued to pursue its own propaganda activities.[6] In the view of the Allies, one particular sore spot was the fact that German propaganda materials continued to make their way via Spain into countries such as Cuba, despite the enormous efforts to censor them until the end of the war.[7]

German propaganda continued to have especially favorable conditions in Mexico. While French propaganda activity remained active here with its pamphlets and the Creel Committee also paid Mexico intensive scrutiny, the attitude of nearly the entire Mexican press left much to be desired from the perspective of the Allies.[8] In particular, the government newspaper *El Demócrata* stayed on the side of the Germans. Still in October 1918, a committee of Mexican journalists was founded (Comité Neutral Paulista de Periodistas Mexicanos), which aimed to defend the country's neutrality.[9]

In Buenos Aires, the pressure from the Allies steadily increased against neutrality in 1918.[10] Yet the financially strong German companies in the region guaranteed the continuation of German activities.[11] The Creel Committee acknowledged in its reporting that the editor of *Deutsche La Plata Zeitung* was still pulling strings. Having already established his own news service, the Prensa Asociada, in 1917, he had a structure in place through which the news from newspapers of German nationals living abroad and *La Unión* could be further disseminated. In order to disguise their own propaganda, German actors deliberately had chosen a name similar to that of the famous U.S. news agency Associated Press.[12] The fact that there was still news from the German Reich coming in was attributable to the gradual improvement of radio communications. *La Unión* was thus able to report as late as August 1918 that it could receive radio messages from Nauen without difficulty, although this was

---

[6] Agent 140, Report (July 9, 1918), NA, RG 38, 20288–864. "La propaganda del jermanismo," in: *El Sur* (September 30, 1918), p. 3. On the attitude of the so-called German nationals living abroad (Auslandsdeutsche), see Rinke, "The Reconstruction of National Identity," pp. 174–7.

[7] U.S. envoy to Dept. of State (Havana, May 9, 1918), Appendix: "¡Yanquis alerta!" NA, RG 59, M 336, Roll 62.

[8] Adam, *A los intelectuales de México*, pp. 5–13. *Los ideales de México y la guerra europea*, pp. 1–8. "Propaganda Manual Mexico," [1918], NA, RG 63, Entry 133 m.

[9] "Procalama patriótica," in: *El Nacional* (October 14, 1918), p. 3.

[10] U.S. Marine attaché to MID (March 26, 1918), NA, RG 165, MID, 2048-12.

[11] "Report on foreign and domestic propaganda in the Argentine Republic … " (April 9, 1918), NA, RG 165, MID 2327-L-1.

[12] "South America and the War" (1918), NA, RG 63, Entry 132, Box 4, pp. 8–9 and 41–7.

undoubtedly an exaggeration.[13] Just the same, the radio traffic was at least reliable enough to supply even the hinterland with news out of Buenos Aires.[14]

In addition to its disparagement of the European allies and their American collaborators – which was met with winking approval in Argentina in the form of criticism against Brazil – German propaganda took pains until the end of the war to bolster the public's faith in the victory of the Central Powers.[15] In Buenos Aires, for instance, the propaganda film *The Great German Offensive on the Western Front* was still playing in the Germania-Halle in May 1918. The film sparked great enthusiasm among its viewers even though most were themselves Germans and ethnic Germans.[16] German activists, moreover, used anti-imperialist rhetoric to mobilize Argentine supporters to fight the blacklists. In 1918, the Liga pro Libertad de Comercio (the League for Freedom of Trade) introduced a corresponding bill in Congress, which, in the end, was no more successful than the associated calls for mass demonstrations.[17]

This did not mean, however, that the internal struggle in Argentina over the stance toward the war had subsided. To be sure, the openly pro-German voices had lost their relevance. Still, the camp of the *neutralistas* with representatives like Roldán, Zeballos, Quesada, Colmo, the newspaper *La Época*, and various associations such as the Asociación Argentina pro Neutralidad or the Unión Patriótica Argentina continued to be influential. Furthermore, the *rupturistas*, who fought to sever relations with Germany, were very active with their Comité pro Ruptura or the Comité Nacional de la Juventud, and numerous rallies. They claimed members of the ruling party, including Pueyrredón, as well as socialist parliamentarians. As Compagnon has shown, this demonstrated the large degree of openness relative to other countries in Latin America that provided room for free speech and, to some degree, even violent conflict.[18]

---

[13] "Comunicaciones radiotelegráficas," in: *La Unión* (August 30, 1918), p. 4. See also "German telegrams in South America," in: *The South Pacific Mail* (Valparaíso, May 2, 1918), p. 3. "German information agencies at Buenos Aires" (Washington, DC, August 30, 1918), NA, RG 165, MID, 10987-197.

[14] "Report on German propaganda in Argentina" (April 22, 1918), NA, RG 165, MID, 10987-200.

[15] "El Brasil en la guerra," in: *La Unión* (B.A., February 13, 1918), p. 1.

[16] Ralph B. Boss to U.S. military attaché (B. A., May 18, 1918), NA, RG 63, Entry 209.

[17] "Anti blacklist propaganda" (Washington, DC, February 10, 1918), NA, RG 165 MID, 10987-346.

[18] Compagnon, *L'adieu à l'Europe*, pp. 149–52. Goñi Demarchi/Scala/Berraondo, *Yrigoyen y la Gran Guerra*, p. 163.

The pressure on the Yrigoyen government to abandon neutrality certainly increased in 1918, especially in the Argentine press (see Figure 4.1). The ambassador in Washington, Rómulo S. Naón, even tried to unilaterally change the country's foreign policy.[19] In addition, influential groups such as the Italian community regularly organized mass rallies, where the chief demand was to terminate relations with the German Reich.[20] As Cuban journalist Orestes Ferrara remarked in *Nosotros*, active participation in the war was essential for preserving autonomy from the all-powerful United States in the postwar world. According to Ferrara, Latin America should not retreat to a "castrated neutrality." It was on the basis of these nationalist and anti-imperialist arguments that *rupturistas* countered Yrigoyen's own line of thought.[21] These efforts proved futile, however. Naón was forced to resign and Argentina remained neutral.

Quite to the contrary, Yrigoyen continued to pursue his project of a conference of neutrals, for, according to the official justification, neutrality was not a passive state, but an active political statement. The original invitation in May 1917 had provided for holding the conference in Buenos Aires in early January 1918. In the meantime, the Peruvian government – in consultation with Brazil and the United States – had taken a step that was supposed to undermine Yrigoyen's objectives. The Peruvians made their participation in the conference contingent upon the addition of a new first point on the agenda that would center on the rupture of relations of all Latin American countries with the German Reich.[22] Such a discussion, however, ran counter to the spirit of the initiative, which was precisely about strengthening the position of neutrals, and was therefore unacceptable. Ultimately, in mid-December 1917, only a Mexican delegation came to Buenos Aires and Paraguayan President Manuel Franco advocated forcefully for the solidarity of the Americas. The continental pact of neutrals Yrigoyen had sought did not

[19] Ibid., pp. 175–200. "Naon going to Argentina," in: *The New York Times* (January 16, 1918), p. 9. U.S. envoy and Secretary of State (Buenos Aires, March 26, 1918), in: *FRUS 1918 Supplement 1, The World War*, Vol. 1, p. 678.

[20] Devoto, *Historia de los italianos*, pp. 325–6. Goñi Demarchi/Scala/Berraondo, *Yrigoyen y la Gran Guerra*, p. 166.

[21] Ferrara, "La América latina y la Gran Guerra," p. 11.

[22] "Solidaridad americana," in: *La Razón* (B.A., October 1, 1917), p. 3. Dept. of State, Memorandum (Washington, DC, November 29, 1917), in: *FRUS 1917 I*, p. 377. Díaz Araujo, *Yrigoyen y la Guerra*, p. 240.

FRENTE A FRENTE
DEFINIENDO LA LUCHA

FIGURE 4.1 Democracy against autocracy. Since the loss of Russia, Allied propaganda used the argument of the struggle for freedom and democracy. The press in neutral Argentina also adopted this trope.

Source: "Frente a frente," in: *Caras y Caretas* (November 2, 1918).

materialize. The criticism of his policy in the Allied countries, however, increased markedly.[23]

The pressure on the governments in other neutral countries also grew. One example is Colombia. The leading Colombian newspaper *El Tiempo* contended that the country needed to move closer to the United States, despite the sensitivities stemming from a self-interested, but well-understood patriotism.[24] *El Heraldo Conservador* reacted vehemently against this proposal. It expressed the widespread view among conservatives that a rapprochement with the United States would result in Colombia's descent to colonial status, as in the case of Nicaragua and Cuba.[25] In the final analysis, despite the increasing hostility of the clashes, Colombia remained in the camp of the neutrals.

From the perspective of German propaganda, the neutrals were at any rate at the vanguard of Latin America, while those who had broken off relations or declared war were nothing more than lackeys of the United States that deserved to be ridiculed.[26] There were ample opportunities for this from the end of April 1918, as the Central American governments that had previously only cut off relations with Germany had now entered the war. Guatemala got the ball rolling once again on April 23. The Estrada Cabrera government had already had the Germans officially monitored in the country since relations were ruptured with the Reich. After the declaration of war, the regulations were tightened.

While the government did not carry out the expropriation of all German property as the United States had demanded, it nonetheless came to an arrangement with Washington. Estrada thus confiscated the utilities companies in German possession, first and foremost the electricity company, and put them under the administration of a U.S. overseer. He had to continue to work with the German staff, however, since no other

[23] U.S. ambassador to Sec. of State (B. A., December 28, 1917), in: *FRUS* 1917 I, p. 394. Siepe, *Yrigoyen*, pp. 41–4. Díaz Araujo, *Yrigoyen y la Guerra*, p. 164. Goñi Demarchi/Scala/Berraondo, *Yrigoyen y la Gran Guerra*, pp. 247–9. On the stance of Paraguay: *El Estado General de la Nacion*, Vol. 1, p. 336. U.S. chargé d'affaires to Secretary of State (Asunción, April 2, 1918), in: *FRUS* 1918 Supplement 1, *The World War*, Vol. 1, p. 681. For a critique of Yrigoyen in the United States, see: Argentine Ambassador Naón to MRREE (Washington, DC, December 22, 1917), in: Solveira, *Argentina y la Primera Guerra Mundial*, Vol. 2, pp. 95–6.
[24] "La actitud de Colombia ante los EE.UU." and "Dos orentiaciones para nuestra política exterior," in: *El Tiempo* (Bogotá, March 12, 1918), p. 3.
[25] "El mal que nos hacen," in: *El Heraldo Conservador* (March 14, 1918), p. 1.
[26] "Nicaragua" *Transocean* (May 10, 1918), p. 1.

qualified workers were available. The dictator also had German plantation owners expropriated in the coffee sector.[27]

The governments of Nicaragua and Haiti, which U.S. Marines still occupied, followed the example of Guatemala on May 8 and July 12, 1918, although Haiti put German property into the hands of a state administrator.[28] Costa Rica's outlaw dictator, Tinoco, declared war against Germany on May 23. In order to curry favor with the U.S. government, he even offered 10,000 troops to protect the Panama Canal. But this offer was to no avail, much like the press campaign Tinoco orchestrated in the United States.[29] The last Latin American country to enter the war was Honduras on July 19, 1918. Washington had already complained at the end of 1917 about the ongoing presence of a German coastal freighter business, which supplied the Pacific port of Amapala.[30] The U.S. government refused to accept President Bertrand's claim that the company was harmless and had peacefully pursued its operations in Amapala for thirty-five years. The United States was ultimately able to prevail through diplomatic and economic pressure, as the German company was transferred to U.S. ownership. In September, the German property was placed under the administration of a specially designated expert of the U.S. War Trade Board.[31]

Cuba and Panama, which had already been at war since 1917, continued to sharpen their measures against German property and German nationals in 1918.[32] The U.S. diplomats instructed the governments more or less explicitly on what individual steps to carry out.[33] Conversely, the U.S. government refused the request of the Cuban government to

---

[27] Dept. of State to Colonel M. Churchill, Military Intelligence Branch (Washington, DC, July 20, 1918), NA, RG 165, MID, 10987-246. Dept. of State to Cuban legation (Washington, DC, September 18, 1918), in: *FRUS* 1918 Supplement 2, *The World War*, p. 370. Schoonover, *Germany in Central America*, pp. 163 and 165. Buchenau, *In the Shadow of the Giant*, pp. 130–1.

[28] Martin, *Latin America and the War*, pp. 519–20.

[29] "Mensaje del Presidente" (San José, May 1, 1918), in: Meléndez Chaverri, Mensajes presidenciales, Vol. 5, p. 9. Federico Tinoco, decree (San José, May 26, 1918), ANCR, RREE, Caja 241: 30. See also the excerpts included there from the U.S. press.

[30] U.S. consul to Dept. of State (Amapala, November 23, 1917), NA, RG 59, M 367, Roll 264. Memorandum, Amapala situation (Tegucigalpa, December 27, 1917), ibid.

[31] U.S. chargé d'affaires to Dept. of State (Tegucigalpa, September 16, 1918), in: *FRUS* 1918 Supplement 2, *The World War*, p. 396. Legation to Dept. of State (Tegucigalpa, August 24, 1918), NA, RG 165, MID, 10903–14.

[32] Martin, *Latin America and the War*, pp 118–23.

[33] Dept. of State to U.S. legation in Cuba (Washington, DC, December 28, 1917), in: *FRUS* 1918 Supplement 2, *The World War*, p. 357. U.S. ambassador to Dept. of State (Panama, November 5, 1918), in: ibid., p. 398.

buy weapons to fend off German submarines.[34] The United States did, however, continue to support President Menocal's efforts to establish the country's own fighting force for the European battlefield. In mid-1918, Menocal was able to win out against the liberal opposition. With a lot of patriotic pomp, Cuba introduced conscription on August 2, 1918, as a "school of the nation and democracy."[35] When the preparations for the deployment of troops were almost complete a month later, Washington changed its mind because of the lack of transport capacity. It ordered the Cubans to instead use the available troops to defend their territorial waters.[36]

At the same moment, the secret war continued in Mexico. Mexico persisted in its efforts to cooperate with the Indian nationalists and to strengthen its ties to Japan. Where it seemed feasible, the German agents supported revolutionary movements in Central America.[37] On the other hand, Allied intelligence services were relatively unsuccessful in enforcing the blacklists but did a little better at unmasking German spies. Another objective was the destruction of the German radio station, whose signals had been received in Spain since 1918, and were sent from there to Nauen.[38] While this plan could not be implemented, the German side also failed to set up new radio stations in El Salvador and Argentina. The couriers on board Spanish vessels thus remained important, although they were diligently pursued by the U.S. censor.[39] The Mexican–Argentine rapprochement over the issue of the neutrality conference and the propaganda activities of the Mexican delegation in South America, after the completion of its mission at La Plata, intensified the antipathy that Washington, London, and Paris felt toward the Carranza government.[40]

While the Allies were stretched to their limits in pursuing their war aims in Mexico, they could in the last year of the war exert enormous pressure

---

[34] Cuban ambassador to U.S. Secretary of State (Washington, DC, June 15, 1918), in: *FRUS 1918* Supplement 1, *The World War*, Vol. 1, p. 704.

[35] "A los cubanos de edad militar," *Boletín de Información* 1 (October 1918), p. 47.

[36] Pardo Suárez, *Ladrones de tierras*, pp. 307–8. Martin, *Latin America and the War*, pp. 141–55. Díaz Pardo, *Cuba ante la guerra*, p. 38.

[37] Katz, *The Secret War*, pp. 411–16 and 423–33.

[38] Ibid., pp. 433–41.

[39] Ibid., pp. 420–2. A German radio technician was also employed in Paraguay, only to be replaced in 1918 by a Paraguayan under pressure from the United States. U.S. military attaché to MID (Asunción, June 12, 1918), NA, RG 165, MID, 127-1-163.

[40] Goñi Demarchi/Scala/Berraondo, *Yrigoyen y la Gran Guerra*, p. 113. U.S. envoy to the Secretary of State (Buenos Aires, January 25 and February 9, 1918.), in: *FRUS 1918* Supplement 1, *The World War*, Vol. 1, pp. 662 and 665. Rosenberg, *World War I*, pp. 26–8.

on the neutrals with their economic power and thereby settle an issue that, until then, had remained unresolved in many places. Specifically, the Allies were able to seize German ships in Latin American ports for the purpose of mobilizing as much tonnage as possible for the transportation of troops, weapons, and ammunition to Europe. Washington consequently negotiated the chartering of these ships, and it exerted pressure in the process by restricting oil supplies and commercial traffic.[41] When negotiations came to a positive conclusion in the case of Chile, the German crews destroyed the ships in September 1918 in a cloak-and-dagger operation, causing a severe diplomatic crisis in German–Chilean relations.[42] Less problematic was the takeover of the German ships detained in Uruguay and Peru. Both governments seized the ships in February 1918 and rented them out in May and September, respectively, to the U.S. Emergency Fleet Corporation after long negotiations.[43]

ECONOMIC RIVALRIES AND PERSPECTIVES

The struggle for economic dominance and control of Latin American raw materials was the second dimension in the fight for regional hegemony, and one which proved increasingly more important over the course of 1918. The Allies waged this confrontation on two levels: on one hand, they reinforced the economic war against the Germans on the ground; on the other hand, they also competed against one another. The latter level was connected to the planning for the postwar period. At least in this

[41] "El arrendamiento de los vapores alemanes," in: *Zig-Zag* (June 29, 1918). U.S. envoy to Dept. of State (Santiago, September 24, 1918), in: *FRUS* 1918 I, p. 726. Couyoumdjian, "En torno a la neutralidad de Chile," pp. 197–8. Brazilian coffee and cocoa were especially affected by the restrictions. Secretary of State to the U.S. envoy in Rio de Janeiro (Washington, DC, April 15, 1918), in: *FRUS* 1918 Supplement 1, *The World War*, Vol. 1, p. 684.

[42] "Vapores alemanes" and "Las naves alemanas en Corral," in: *El Mercurio* (Santiago de Chile, September 5, 1918), pp. 3 and 18. "Ceguera en el gobierno," in: ibid. (September 18, 1918), p. 3. "La cuestión de los barcos alemanes," in: *La Nación* (Santiago, September 27, 1918), p. 3. U.S. Shipping Board, circular (Washington, DC, October 10, 1918), NA RG 32, 555-5. "South America and the War" (1918), NA, RG 63, Entry 132, Box 4, p. 126. Couyoumdjian, "En torno a la neutralidad de Chile," p. 199.

[43] Secretary of State to the Peruvian ambassador (Washington, DC, February 14, 1918), in: *FRUS* 1918, Supplement 1, *The World War*, Vol. 1, p. 666. U.S. envoy to Dept. of State (Lima, September 7, 1918), in: *FRUS* 1918 I, p. 718. Lavalle, *El Perú y la gran guerra*, pp. 86–105. *Requisición de los vapores alemanes*, p. 117. Secretary of State to Uruguayan ambassador (Washington, DC, February 26, 1918), in: *FRUS* 1918, Supplement 1, *The World War*, Vol. 1, p. 670.

area, there was a clear winner: the United States. However, the goal of totally displacing German interests was overly ambitious.

This was surprising, for due to the political developments, the situation of German business interests in Latin America deteriorated significantly in 1918. The Allies dramatically stepped up the blockade through improved cooperation, and in January they released the U.S. blacklists for the whole of Latin America.[44] These mutual arrangements did not proceed as a matter of course, however. Behind the scenes, there were heavy clashes between the British and U.S. partners. The U.S. companies harbored a deep distrust of their long-established British rivals. They also suspected, rightly, that the British wanted to once again push them out of the lucrative market that had just opened up through their own interpretation of the blacklists.[45]

Just the same, the governments of the warring nations in Latin America were not about to have the Allies impose their blacklists on them. Brazilian diplomats, for example, had been insisting since 1917 that a blacklist was not necessary for their country, as they had already implemented the measures against enemy property. For the British, however, these steps did not go far enough. They, therefore, upheld their restrictions for Brazil, despite their ally's protests. In the blacklists published by the United States in 1918, companies even appeared that were purely Brazilian in origin.[46]

The same problem existed in the neutral countries, as the case of Chile shows. Here, the German propaganda newspaper *El Tiempo Nuevo* relished in publishing the complaints that emerged in the Chilean press.[47] An informant told U.S. intelligence in hindsight of friction within the Comité Comercial de los Aliados (Trade Committee of the Allies), as competing businessmen from different countries were now suddenly expected to cooperate. The members repeatedly fought over who was on the blacklist; and the list itself was criticized for being put together by people who had little knowledge of the region. Finally, the informant

---

[44] Secretary of State to embassies in Latin America (Washington, DC, January 7, 1918), in: *FRUS 1918*, Supplement 1, *The World War*, Vol. 2, p. 1013. Summary of blockade Information March 22–April 4, 1918 (London, April 5, 1918), in: TNA, War Trade Intelligence Department, Blockade Information, CAB 24/47.

[45] Dehne, *On the Far Western Front*, pp. 134–5 and 144.

[46] Ibid., pp. 174–6. Bonow, *A desconfiança*, pp. 294–5. Vinhosa, *O Brasil e a Primeira Guerra Mundial*, p. 61. Secretary of State to U.S. War Trade Board (Washington, DC, February 25, 1918), FRUS 1918 Supplement 1, *The World War*, Vol. 2, p. 1020.

[47] "EE.UU. implanta las listas negras," in: *El Tiempo Nuevo* (November 3, 1917), p. 1.

noted that the effects were actually somewhat counterproductive, since even Allied firms suffered when their regular customers vanished.[48]

Shortly after the war, the U.S. military intelligence compiled reports to document the remaining German assets – not only in Chile, but nearly everywhere in the region. These documents clearly show the obstacles that arose in the implementation of the economic war. Assuming the reports are credible, the boycotted German trading companies in Argentina appear to have been well stocked with goods and also to have continued to receive further supply contracts for war-related raw materials such as rubber and nickel. These companies bypassed the blacklists by forming a circle of interests and establishing dummy companies. The close cooperation with the Argentine Ernesto Tornquist & Co., as well as the "Turkish" company Ini Hermanos & Tawil, proved particularly effective. Some also had success cooperating with Scandinavian and Dutch houses, while yet others diversified or relocated their facilities by, for example, selling shares to Allied companies and using the proceeds to enter into the crude oil business in Comodoro Rivadavia.[49]

The German-born community often even remained unaffected in the countries at war, despite the state of martial law. This was due not least to the fact that Germans living abroad controlled economically important areas in many Latin American countries, were highly respected, and networked well. One example is Peru, where the Bremen-based company Gildemeister operated the largest sugar plantation in the country, the Casa Grande. On the basis of the blacklists, the operation was no longer able to receive money for financing its sale of sugar, which plunged the whole region and around 16,000 workers into turmoil and meant a painful loss of tax revenue for the state. The U.S. government pressed the Peruvian government to purchase the company, but the owners in Bremen were not ready. The situation ultimately remained unresolved until the end of the war, at which point Gildemeister continued its operations.[50]

---

[48] "Operation of the black list in southern Chile" (Washington, DC, April 20, 1919) NA, RG 165, MID, 10921-304.

[49] "Special report on expansion of trade in Argentina" (1918), NA, RG 165, MID, 10987. "German scheme for developing oil properties in Argentina" (London, August 7, 1918), NA, RG 165 WCD, 6370–22533. Kinkelin was involved in establishing initial business contacts: "Emilio Kinkelin," in: *La Unión* (B.A., August 18, 1919), p. 2. The report from Brazil was similar: "Special report on expansion of German trade in Brazil" (December 8, 1918), NA, RG 165, MID, 10987-413.

[50] "El asunto de la negociación Casa Grande," in: *La Prensa* (Lima, May 22, 1918), p. 3. U.S. envoy to Dept. of State (Lima, May 27, 1918), NA, RG 59, M 367, Roll 265. Peruvian envoy to Dept. of State (Washington, DC, July 27, 1918), in: *FRUS 1918*

In the Brazilian coffee trade, Theodor Wille & Co. occupied a similarly strong position to that of Gildemeister in Peru. The company was so closely intertwined with the Brazilian economy that the government could not break it up without serious repercussions. This was also true, if to a lesser extent, of German banks and companies in Brazil such as the brewery Companhia Antártica Paulista, which enjoyed a near monopoly in the beer market of São Paulo.[51] In Brazil, many German companies survived the war relatively unscathed because the government dealt with them leniently. Despite pressure from the Allies, many were able to continue operating, and some, such as Wille, even made good profits, which they reinvested in Brazilian production.[52] German interests were thus impacted relatively little by the formation of another Liga de Resistência Nacional in Porto Alegre in September 1918 or the ongoing mob activities against German property. Overall, the mass rallies dwindled considerably due to the rapidly spreading flu epidemic and the fervent anti-German sentiment of the previous year died away.[53]

The Allied war objective of eradicating German interests in Latin America was not achieved anywhere. Even if the Germans living abroad did not by any means adhere to the "overseas *Burgfrieden*" that interest groups repeatedly invoked, they nonetheless showed, in economic terms, an amazing knack for surviving. In many places, the companies founded German chambers of commerce, disguised their possessions by adopting the legal form of their host country, utilized foreign intermediaries –in particular, the so-called turcos from the Ottoman Empire – and benefited from their close ties to the Latin American elites. By the end of the war, financially powerful German companies in particular had adjusted to the conditions of the economic war.[54]

Through the support of the German diplomatic missions in Latin America, many companies invested in war-critical raw materials only to then deny them to the Allies and make provisions for the postwar period. The supply problems of the Allies in fact intensified in 1918, and Latin American raw materials and foodstuffs became all the more important.

Supplement 2, *The World War*, p. 411. On Gildemeister after the war, see Rinke, "Der letzte freie Kontinent," pp. 64–5.

[51] Vinhosa, *O Brasil e a Primeira Guerra Mundial*, p. 57.

[52] Luebke, *Germans in Brazil*, pp. 175–95. Vinhosa, *O Brasil e a Primeira Guerra Mundial*, p. 145.

[53] Bonow, *A desconfiança*, pp. 299 and 329.

[54] Rinke, "Der letzte freie Kontinent," pp. 45–7. For the case of Argentina: Dehne, *On the Far Western Front*, pp. 147–57.

The Brazilian president therefore repeated his appeal to the population to produce and to save more so that exports could flow in greater abundance to languishing Europe.[55] British and U.S. economic interests were themselves active in the region to safeguard vital raw materials for the war. In Chile, they established in February 1918 the Nitrate of Soda Executive to control the purchase of saltpeter, which was so vital to the conflict. This resulted in a price collapse that triggered resentment in Chile. In protracted negotiations, the Chilean government was able to push through a better price, but the delivery had to be transported on Chilean warships to the United States.[56]

The Allies used their willingness to compromise to apply additional pressure regarding the issue of the interned German vessels. They were also concerned about the lawsuits that the German saltpeter producers in Chile, Sloman, and Gildemeister had brought against U.S. crude oil suppliers. In a first instance, German companies won their case against the boycott before the Chilean court. The U.S. companies lodged an appeal in response and the case went before the Supreme Court. The pressure on the Chilean government increased. In fact, it volunteered its "good offices" in influencing the judges, which the State Department gratefully accepted. Chile was thus effectively compelled to take the side of the Allies in terms of its economic policy. By delivering its raw materials on Allied terms, the country made a decisive contribution to the prolongation of the war.[57] This decision was even easier to make once the Chilean government discovered to its horror how rapidly synthetic nitrogen was being developed in the German Reich. Even the promise of the German Foreign Office in Berlin to switch back to saltpeter after the war could not allay the Chileans' concerns. The Chilean ambassador in Berlin suggested Chile demand a purchase guarantee for Chilean saltpeter in exchange for maintaining neutrality, along with Germany's suspension of government incentives for industrial nitrogen production. Given the circumstances, however, this finally remained wishful thinking.[58]

---

[55] "Brazileiros!" in: *Revista da Semana* (January 25, 1918).

[56] Couyoumdjian, "En torno a la neutralidad de Chile," p. 199.

[57] War Trade Board, Memorandum, (Washington, DC, July 10, 1918), NA, RG 182, No. 11. U.S. Dept. of State to Chilean ambassador (Washington, DC, March 18, 1919), in: Chile, AM-RREE, Vol. 743. Rosenberg, *World War I*, p. 29.

[58] Chil. ambassador to MRREE (Berlin, March 12, 1917 and August 21, 1918), in: Chile, AMRREE, Vols. 604 and 669. The German Foreign Office only met the Chileans halfway insofar as it stated that "German agriculture also intends to use Chile saltpeter again in the future." See legation councilor Count of Welczeck, memorandum (Berlin, December 29, 1918), in: *Akten zur deutschen auswärtigen Politik, 1918–1945*, Series A, Vol. 1, p. 153.

The course of events in Argentina was similar. While Yrigoyen officially stuck to neutrality, the implications of the country's foreign economic policy in 1918 indicated otherwise. Due to the abundant wheat harvest, warehouses were bursting to capacity. As a consequence, the government permitted the hoarding of grain in order to support prices.[59] At the same time, Argentine wheat supplies became more crucial to the Allies, for the loss of Russia following the Treaty of Brest-Litovsk caused a critical supply shortage. On January 14, Yrigoyen signed an agreement with the European Allies, in which Argentina sold off all of its surplus grain, while granting customers credit to the amount of 100 million pesos. In exchange, Argentina once again obtained extremely critical coal deliveries from England and France, as well as a guarantee for the transport of its exports.[60] Thus, Argentina, too, had de facto abandoned its economic neutrality, as its grain and meat nourished the Allied troops on the battlefields of Europe. On the other hand, unlike Chile, the country was not forced to requisition German ships.[61] The firmness of this new direction was first witnessed by the Mexican delegation for the failed neutrality conference. Despite a friendly, if equivocal, reception, it soon left Chile empty-handed.

If only economically, the Allies succeeded in bringing into line Argentina and Chile, two major neutral states that had placed great importance on keeping their political independence. They reached their limit even in this respect, however, when it came to Mexico. According to Katz, the especially intense secret war of 1918 being carried out there for economic concessions was tied to the interest in Mexican raw materials, chiefly crude oil. Carranza continued to negotiate with both sides in order to gain the most latitude. His financial needs were unquestionably great in view of the ongoing domestic crises, but he was not ready to accept a U.S. offer of credit under the condition of severing relations with Germany. On the other hand, his plans for obtaining a German loan did not come to fruition either.[62]

The more the war seemed to be nearing its conclusion because of the U.S. involvement on the battlefields of Europe, the more the rivalries among the Allies came into view. They all vied for the optimal economic starting position in the postwar period. Even in the United States, the

---

[59] "South America and the War" (1918), NA, RG 63, Entry 132, Box 4, p. 39.
[60] Siepe, *Yrigoyen*, p. 107. On the agreement, see also Convenio 14 de enero 1918, in: Argentina, AMRREE, AH/00069/1.
[61] Weinmann, *Argentina en la Primera Guerra Mundial*, p. 143. Dehne, *On the Far Western Front*, p. 167.
[62] Katz, *The Secret War*, pp. 403 and 408–10.

largest economic beneficiary of the war in the Americas, interest groups called for taking a systematic approach to trade propaganda for the sake of the postwar period. They argued that the country had to defend the gains and continue to fend off the still-intense anti-U.S. attacks.[63] The Europeans, for their part, were very much aware that the United States had drastically increased its presence in the Latin American markets at their expense. France's former diplomatic representative in Rio de Janeiro, Baron Albert d'Anthouard, observed in mid-1918 that while his country's propaganda efforts in Latin America were impressive, they were nonetheless insufficient for intensifying the economic exchange after the war or, more particularly, for winning out against the German interests over the long run.[64] As a consequence, the French government sent military missions to the region immediately after the war's ceasefire to boost arms exports and gain influence on the Latin American armies, which before the war had often been trained by Germans.[65]

British activities were primarily motivated by a strong sense of rivalry toward the United States with respect to the Latin American markets, an attitude which was already manifested in the early years of the war. Diplomatic representatives and British firms on site in Latin America had pushed the government leadership in London to adopt more vigorous economic policies as early as 1915. These efforts only intensified further after the United States entered the war.[66] In mid-1918, the government in London officially sent Maurice de Bunsen, a senior diplomat, to South America with the task of improving the effectiveness of the economic war. Unofficially, he was also charged with laying the groundwork for retaking in the postwar period the terrain lost during the conflict. Warmly welcomed by the governments of the countries he visited, the local representatives of the United States interpreted Bunsen's mission, which they had not been consulted on in advance, as an unfriendly act. In fact, it contributed to exacerbating the British–U.S. trade rivalry in Latin

---

[63] "Organization amongst Americans for combating anti-American propaganda" (October 10, 1919), NA, RG 165, MID, 2515-O-2.

[64] D'Anthouard, "La politique française au Brésil," p. 228. The Brazilian ambassador in Paris sent a similarly argued article from *La Petite République*, published October 8, 1918, titled "L'Amérique latine et nous." See Bras. Legation to MRE (Vienna, September 4, 1918), in: AHI, Directoria Geral dos Negocios Políticos e Diplomáticos.

[65] Brazilian Legation to MRE (Vienna, November 18, 1918), in: AHI, Directoria Geral dos Negocios Políticos e Diplomáticos.

[66] Brit. Embassy to the Foreign Office (Rio de Janeiro, April 23, 1915), in: *BD*, Part II, Series D, p. 26.

America. The competition between the two competitors, which did not go unnoticed to Latin American observers, would eventually shape the postwar period. At the same time, the United States, which benefited from its progress during the war years and its financial clout in most countries of the region, had a clear competitive advantage.[67]

The speculation about the postwar order and the efforts to create favorable starting conditions also set the tone for the discussions in Latin America. In January 1918, the rumor of an imminent peace agreement incited a panic in the stock market in Santiago de Chile.[68] This reaction showed just how fragile the export-based bull market actually was. Unlike the United States, which over the course of the European war had developed from a debtor to a creditor nation, the war gains in Latin America were shorter lived and did not lead to structural change.[69] In mid-1918, in a three-part essay for *Nosotros*, Argentine economist Ernesto J. J. Bott focused on the economic consequences of war for belligerent nations, in the past and present. He noted how now, due to the increasing "internationalization," everything was interconnected. Therefore, the economic ruin of the conquered nations would necessarily plunge the global economy into a deep crisis. With regard to Argentina, Bott thus argued, the outlook was anything but rosy.[70] Indeed, the decline in U.S. demand for raw materials from Latin America immediately following the war was to lead to deep economic problems in the region.

THE END OF THE SOCIAL TRUCE

The pessimistic prognoses of Latin American experts like Bott were due not least to what they viewed as troubling social developments. While the war yielded enormous profits for a small, export-oriented upper class, the broad mass of the population, especially in the cities, found

---

[67] "South America and the War" (1918), NA, RG 63, Entry 132, Box 4, p. 5. Memorandum, War Trade Board (June 26, 1918), NA, RG 38, 21036–1267. U.S. envoy to Sec. of State (Santiago, November 4, 1918), NA, RG 59, 825.6374. 430. Arg. envoy to MRREE (Rio de Janeiro, May 18, 1918), in: Solveira, *Argentina y la Primera Guerra Mundial*, Vol. 2, p. 161. See also the correspondence in Argentina, AMRREE, AH/00034/1 Brazilian legation to MRE (Paris, May 11, 1918), in: AHI, Directoria Geral dos Negocios Políticos e Diplomáticos. Buero, *El Uruguay*, pp. 363–4. Dehne, *On the Far Western Front*, p. 145. Rosenberg, *World War I*, p. 54.

[68] "Falsos rumores de paz que originan un pánico bursatil," in: *Zig-Zag* (January 19, 1918).

[69] This was also pointed out by the Argentine press in 1917: "El capital extranjero," in: *La Prensa* (B. A., August 5, 1917), p. 4.

[70] Bott, "Los efectos económicos II," p. 31.

itself confronted with immense challenges in meeting its basic needs.[71] Accordingly, the readiness to heed the calls for national unity under the banner of the war-related crisis decreased, especially among the urban working class. While the size and the extent of the strikes had already greatly increase in 1917, this trend continued to accelerate in 1918/19. The Allies concluded that the strikers were being influenced by German propaganda and spies who, the presumption was, partly orchestrated labor conflicts using Spanish middlemen in order to interrupt supply.[72] A closer look, however, reveals that the social unrest had far deeper causes, with domestic and transnational factors playing a role.

At the transnational level, one event above all must be cited that actually took place in 1917, but was not perceived in its world-historical importance in Latin America until 1918: the Russian Revolution. Of course, the Latin American left was interested in the events in the Russian Empire already before the war, especially the revolt of 1905, but the country did not become a focal point until 1917. Havas and Reuter distributed their coverage of the revolutionary events in the Latin American press, providing one-sided, negative accounts because of the German support for the Bolsheviks and Russia's exit from the military alliance. As a result of their revolutionary missionary activity and pan-European, indeed, global networks, many Latin American observers viewed the Bolshevik movement as a threat. Thus the state and nationalist paramilitary organizations responded to it with particularly brutal repressive measures.[73]

Despite – or perhaps because of – the negative reporting in the bourgeois press, the October Revolution mobilized the left all across Latin America.[74] In Argentina, commentators were already speculating in March 1917 about the course of further developments. As early as mid-March, Del Valle put the Russian Revolution on a par with the 1789

---

[71] Examples included, for instance, Cuba and Ecuador. See Berenguer, *El problema de las subsistencias*, pp. 7–10. "Las subsistencias," in: *El Progreso* (March 12, 1918), p. 2. "Al pueblo de Azogues," in: *El Tren* (January 10, 1918), p. 2. "La patria está en peligro," in: ibid. (August 29, 1918), p. 1.

[72] For an explanation of the strikes from the side of the Allies, see, e.g., "Report on foreign and domestic propaganda in the Argentine Republic ... " (April 9, 1918), NA, RG 165, MID, 2327-L-1.

[73] Pardo Suárez, *Ladrones de tierras*, p. 120. Lugones, *Mi beligerancia*, pp. 224–6. "Maximalismo: un cancer social," in: *Zig-Zag* (December 21, 1918). "Cossacos e Bolcheviques," in: *Correio da Manhã* (December 31, 1918), p. 3.

[74] Albert, *South America and the First World War*, p. 271. For the example of Brazil, see Bandeira/Melo/Andrade, *O ano vermelho*, p. 33. For individual press releases, see ibid., pp. 73–113. For Argentina, see Geli, "Representations of the Great War," p. 203.

French Revolution and spoke of the triumph of the international proletariat.[75] Mexican anarchist Ricardo Flores was particularly full of hope. As he saw it, the entry of the United States into the war was an important step toward world revolution, which he had been anticipating for a long time. He further suggested that the overthrow of the czar and the famines observed around the world were crucial signs of the beginning of global anarchy and that his revolutionary country was leading the way forward.[76]

The debates picked up again, in particular after the Bolsheviks' October Revolution. The revolutionaries' willingness to end the war was a signal that the anarchists in Latin America enthusiastically welcomed.[77] Revolutionary leader Emiliano Zapata also recognized in February 1918 that there were parallels between the Russian and the Mexican Revolutions. Flores Magón encouraged this view a short time later – in fact, he even equated the Russian Revolution under its new leaders Lenin and Trotsky with the promise of world revolution.[78] When they learned about events in Russia, workers, mainly in the cities, but also in the countryside, adopted the positive evaluation for themselves. Many leftist intellectuals in Latin America drew a connection between Mexico and Russia, and, in the period that followed, moved to Mexico. Joining them were the many conscientious objectors from the United States, the so-called slackers. To the outside world, they all helped to turn Mexico into a kind of brother state of Bolshevik Russia.[79]

But the news of the Bolshevik victory also spread quickly elsewhere. For example, despite martial law and a government ban, rallies making demands for peace and social revolution took place on May 1, 1918, in Rio de Janeiro.[80] On November 1, 1918, in Porto Alegre, the União Maximalista (Maximalist Union) called on workers to fight against the bourgeoisie.[81] These influences were the strongest in Argentina. In an

---

[75] Del Valle, *La cuestión internacional*, p. 89. See also Iaroschewsky, "La revolución en Rusia," pp. 289–83.

[76] Ricardo Flores Magón, "Rumbo a la anarquía," in: *Regeneración* (February 12, 1917), p. 2. Idem, "El mundo marcha," in: ibid. (February 24, 1917), p. 2. Idem, "La revolución mundial," in: ibid. (March 24, 1917), p. 1 See also Lomnitz, *The Return of Comrade Flores Magón*, p. 448.

[77] Geli, "Representations of the Great War," p. 203.

[78] Ricardo Flores Magón, "La revolución rusa," in: *Regeneración* (March 16, 1918), p. 1.

[79] Spenser, *Los primero tropiezos*, pp. 67–77.

[80] Bandeira/Melo/Andrade, *O ano vermelho*, pp. 115–20. "Report on foreign and domestic propaganda in the Argentine Republic … " (April 9, 1918), NA, RG 165, MID, 2327-L-1.

[81] Bandeira/Melo/Andrade, *O ano vermelho*, pp. 363–7.

essay for *Nosotros* about the "historical significance" of Maximalism, Ingenieros wrote that the war led to the suicide of feudal autocracies and that the revolutions were by no means merely controlled by the German secret service. They were rather a sign of a world-historical turning point that was sure to ultimately take hold in all of Europe.[82] Indeed, the transformation could not even be halted in his part of the world. Here, Russian immigrants from various socialist and anarchistic movements, including many Jewish activists, founded the Federación Obrera de Sudamérica Rusa (Russian Workers' Federation in South America).

At a mass rally in Buenos Aires on November 24 to celebrate the first anniversary of the October Revolution, the speakers of this association outlined the program of the Russian Communists, the "Maximalists." The internationalist wing of the Argentine socialists joined this movement and received an invitation from Moscow in late 1918 to become a founding member of the Third International.[83]

The appeal of the new ideas from Russia was partly due to the catastrophic social situation in many Latin American countries. In the case of Argentina, wages fell by about 38 percent during the war, while the cost of living rose by 71 percent. While it was the price of food and textiles that exploded in particular through 1917, the rapidly increasing rental rates in 1918 made the social conditions for many city dwellers even worse. Real wages fell even further in 1918, although the economy had recovered thanks to the wheat export business.[84] One result was the large mobilization of workers, which developed since 1916, when the dockworkers came out on strike, into progressively more intense strike activity. In Buenos Aires alone, the number of strikes and strike participants rose, respectively, from 80 and 24,300 in 1916 to 367 and 309,000 in 1919. Most strikers were organized in the Federación Obrera Regional Argentina (FORA), which, however, remained weak because of the great number of seasonal workers and day laborers. The government was nevertheless worried about the impact of the strikes on production in the meat-packing plants and in the transport sector. The Allies, who suspected the involvement of German secret-service activities, greatly upped the pressure on Yrigoyen.[85] Until the end of the war, however, the president nonetheless rarely used police or military against the strikers in

[82] Ingenieros, "Significación histórica," pp. 380–6.
[83] Kersffeld, "El activismo judío," pp. 152–4. Kersffeld, *Rusos y rojos*, pp. 70–104. Spenser, *Los primero tropiezos*, p. 29.
[84] Bilsky, *La Semana trágica*, pp. 63–4.
[85] Díaz Araujo, *Yrigoyen y la Guerra*, pp. 233–9. Caruso, "La huelga general marítima," p. 2.

comparison to previous regimes and instead tried to mediate. The labor unrest repeatedly resulted in deaths and injuries, whose numbers are not known. In addition, employers now organized themselves in order to systematically disrupt the strikes and fight against the trade unions.[86]

The situation came to a head in 1918. In March, the workers of the British-owned railways went on strike, severely impacting wheat deliveries and thus the supply from the Allies.[87] In response to a Bolshevik mass rally on November 24, the bishop of Córdoba issued a pastoral letter the very same day against Maximalism. In early December, even the police in Rosario threatened to strike over unpaid wages. From the perspective of *Review of the River Plate*, the Sovietization of the country was already at hand. By the end of the year, the fear of revolution among the elite could hardly have been greater.[88] During the so-called Semana trágica (Tragic Week), which began on January 7, 1919, tensions erupted into a veritable orgy of violence.

During this period, civil war–like conditions developed not only in the capital, but also in several rural towns, and claimed countless deaths and injuries. In response to the overwhelming pressure, the president called on the military to take on the strikers, but also to neutralize the rebellious tendencies within the armed forces themselves. The unions reacted by calling a general strike. Especially brutal were the attacks against Russian and Jewish immigrants, who were seen as instigators of the unrest.[89] Emilio Kinkelin, who had returned to his homeland from Germany, recognized parallels to the German Spartacist uprising he had a chance to witness before his departure. According to Kinkelin, total chaos was only avoided in the end because of the military.[90]

Violent conflict resolution also became increasingly necessary in Chile as the social situation came to a head due to the war. The weakness of the trade unions at the outbreak of the war helped to inhibit large labor disputes. As in Argentina, the strike actions began in 1916. They grew dramatically over the course of 1917 due to the cost of living, which had risen by about 140 percent between 1913 and 1919. Especially the

---

[86] Ibid., p. 11. Deutsch, *Las derechas*, pp. 113–15. Dehne, *On the Far Western Front*, p. 161.

[87] "Report on foreign and domestic propaganda in the Argentine Republic ... " (April 9, 1918), NA, RG 165, MID 2327-L-1. Goñi Demarchi/Scala/Berraondo, *Yrigoyen y la Gran Guerra*, pp. 122–3.

[88] Kersffeld, "El activismo judío," pp. 152–4.

[89] Bilsky, *La Semana trágica*, pp. 96–7 and 205. Deutsch, *Las derechas*, pp. 115–8.

[90] Kinkelin, *Los estragos del hambre*, pp. 3–4.

strike of the dockworkers in Valparaíso, which had spread over the whole country by April, as well as the work stoppages in the saltpeter territory in August, offered a preview of what was to come. After the socialists had assumed leadership within the trade union umbrella organization Federación Obrera de Chile (Workers' Federation of Chile, FOCh) in 1917, the scale of the labor disputes accordingly increased in 1918, as did the intensity of the crisis stemming from the end of the saltpeter boom following the armistice in Europe. On November 22, the FOCh organized the until-then largest mass protest in Chilean history in Santiago. It was attended by different political forces, including Social Catholics and women's and youth organizations. Even the press in the capital praised the peaceful conduct of the demonstrations and basically validated the workers' demands. *El Mercurio*, for example, remarked that a starving population cannot have patriotic feelings and loses its respect for the government.[91]

The government responded, nevertheless, by taking repressive measures. In December 1918, it passed a law that was supposed to make it easier to identify the so-called unwelcome troublemakers and to prevent their migration. At the same time, this threat was negligible in Chile given the small number of left-wing immigrants. The emerging xenophobia was fueled by the border dispute with Peru, the so-called Tacna-Arica question, which flared up again after the end of the war. It was in this context that a vigilante group – the Liga Patriótica Militar (Military Patriotic League) – was founded, which formed local groups across the country and further fueled nativist sentiment.

There were attacks on Peruvians and Chilean workers, who were thought to be under foreign influence.[92] The magazine *Zig-Zag* commented in this context that, if push came to shove, the Chilean people would defend the nation against the Red menace, since there were no anarchists or communists in Chile itself.[93]

The warring nations were equally susceptible to the fear of social unrest and the new ideology coming out of Russia. In Brazil, where the cost of living had also tripled since the outbreak of war, the wave of strikes reached its first climax in 1917. In period that followed, however, the government resorted to martial law to crush the labor movement,

[91] "Carestía de los artículos de consumo," in: *El Mercurio* (November 23, 1918), p. 17. See also "La manifestación popular de ayer," in: ibid., p. 3.

[92] Deutsch, *Las derechas*, pp. 89–91. Albert, *South America and the First World War*, pp. 283–7. Pinto, "Crisis salitrera," pp. 70–80.

[93] "Los deberes de la hora presente," in: *Zig-Zag* (November 30, 1918).

which it suspected of being infiltrated by foreign agitators.[94] Particularly intense clashes did not take place again until November 18, 1918, in Rio de Janeiro. The situation for the lower classes had worsened due to increasing food shortages, triggered not least because of the exports going to the Allies. The government, in any case, had tried to implement countermeasures and ensure a more equitable distribution through state intervention.[95] By the end of the war, the social situation in Brazil ultimately resembled that of Argentina and Chile. At the same time, the actual tensions were obscured in the interim due to the war's favorable outcome.[96]

This phenomenon, in which social conflicts escalated to a breaking point around the end of the war, was observable nearly everywhere in Latin America. It remained relatively quiet in Peru until 1918, when a wave of strikes – in contrast to those in neighboring countries – started to spread from the countryside. By the end of the year, the labor movement widened its activities. On January 13, 1919, the general strike gave rise to a surge of clashes throughout the country. Although the uprising initially brought about some reforms, it was finally brutally repressed in May.[97] In Mexico, strikes had repeatedly flared up since 1917 in the oil-producing area around Tampico and were directed in particular against the British company El Aguila. As with the major railway strike, suspicion fell on German intelligence officials who were accused of collaborating with anarchists and Russian Bolsheviks to cripple the Allied war machinery.[98] Intense labor disputes, some of which extended into 1919, also took place in Colombia, Ecuador, Bolivia, Paraguay, Uruguay, and Cuba. The reasons were always the same, namely, the revolutionary impetus coming from Mexico and Russia, as well as the crisis of international capitalism the war had caused.[99]

The fact that the social tensions escalated everywhere was due in no small measure to the spread of the flu epidemic, which Allied propaganda designated the "Spanish flu." The naming was an attempt to conceal the

[94] Deutsch, *Las derechas*, pp. 145, 149. Albert, *South America and the First World War*, p. 267.
[95] Bandeira/Melo/Andrade, *O ano vermelho*, pp. 128–9. Vinhosa, *O Brasil e a Primeira Guerra Mundial*, pp. 154–5. Freire, "Guerra e alimentação nacional," p. 285.
[96] Albert, *South America and the First World War*, p. 266.
[97] Ibid., pp. 295–301.
[98] Ackerman, *Mexico's Dilemma*, pp. 68–9. Meyer, *Su majestad británica*, p. 199.
[99] Albert, *South America and the First World War*, pp. 236–7. Spalding, *Organized Labour*, pp. 1–51. Woodard, *A Place in Politics*, pp. 79–87. Rivarola, *Obreros*, pp. 215–21 and 242.

true extent of the flu and its origin in the military camps of the United States, but also to do harm to allegedly pro-German Spain. The second wave of the epidemic, which claimed around 15 million lives world-wide in 1918–19, also spread in Latin America from September 1918. By October, already around two-thirds of the population in the Brazilian capital was suffering and the rate of mortality exploded. Due to lack of a national health care system, public life collapsed in Rio de Janeiro and in many other Brazilian cities soon thereafter. The press was relatively forthcoming in documenting the disaster. Soon, rumors even circulated that the Germans were engaging in bacteriological warfare.[100]

In countries like Mexico, where the population was already in an en-feebled state and the hygiene standards had declined markedly because of the long civil war and the related typhus epidemics, the flu epidemic was also devastating.[101] In neighboring Guatemala, an earthquake on Christmas Day in 1917 caused severe devastation that still had not been alleviated when the flu epidemic struck in August 1918. The outbreak claimed a high number of casualties, in particular among the indigenous population.[102] The leaders were helpless to respond wherever the epi-demic hit, and all over Latin America the sense of crisis only got worse.

FROM ARMISTICE TO "WILSONIAN DISAPPOINTMENT"

The armistice in Europe seemed to reconcile the conflicting parties, at least for the short term, and thus put to rest any concerns or ominous feelings. In the days leading up to November 11, the atmosphere in many cities of Latin America was fraught with anticipation. In response to the protracted negotiations between the warring parties, the Mexican daily newspaper *Excelsior* demanded "peace at any price" on November 9.[103]

---

[100] "A epidemia da 'grippe' toma cada vez maior vulto," in: *Correio da Manhã* (October 13, 1918), p. 1. "A quinzena trágica," in: *Fon-Fon* (November 2, 1918). Goulart's assertion that the press did not report on this because of censorship regulations cannot be con-firmed ("Revisiting the Spanish Flu," p. 3). On the spread of the flu in other regions of Brazil, see Souza, *A gripe espanhola na Bahia*, p. 325. Bertucci, *Influenza*, pp. 90–172. Bertolli Filho, *A gripe espanhola em São Paulo*, pp. 70–7. Olinto, "Uma epidemia sem importância," pp. 285–303.
[101] Cuenya, "Reflexiones."
[102] McCreery, "La pandemia de influenza en Guatemala," p. 111.
[103] "La paz a toda costa," in: *Excelsior* (November 9, 1918), p. 3. See also "Os alliados assignaram o armisticio," in: *Correio da Manhã* (August 11, 1918), p. 1. Idem, "La contienda europea en las calles porteñas," p. 49.

The news of the successful brokering of the ceasefire aroused elation throughout Latin America. For the majority of commentators, the end of hostilities was, as the Uruguayan *Día* remarked, a "triumph of humanity."[104] Many observers during this period also described a feeling of connectedness to people from all parts of the world who also celebrated the end of the war. According to *Revista do Brasil*, November 11, 1918, would go down in history as an extraordinary day for all mankind.[105]

The news coverage reflected the city street scenes that were initiated by the announcement of the armistice. On November 11 and 12, spontaneous public celebrations were the order of the day. The fact that the flu epidemic could spread again via the mass rallies did not dampen the euphoria because of the absence of information.[106] In Buenos Aires, for instance, the employers gave their workers the day off, enthusiastic crowds paraded through the streets, and entire boulevards were festively decorated.[107] The ecstasy that people felt over the end of hostilities was intermingled with delight over the Allies' victory. It was a "triumph of civilization."[108] Even in neutral countries such as Argentina, there was a palpable enthusiasm for the victors, as the English, French, and Italian immigrant communities took the lead in organizing public celebrations and triumphal marches.[109]

In the days that followed, the celebrations took on an official character, with the emphasis now clearly being placed on the Allied victory. Uruguay's government declared November 13 a national holiday, and Argentina did the same for November 14. In Chile, the president even took part in the capital's cathedral in a solemn Te Deum for the triumph of the Allies – indeed, as if his country had fought on their side.[110] War

---

[104] "El triunfo de la humanidad," in: *El Día* (November 12, 1918), p. 3.

[105] "A paz," in: *Revista do Brasil* 3 (1918), p. 245. See also "O mundo inteiro vibra com a victoria dos alliados," in: *Correio da Manhã* (November 13, 1918), p. 1.

[106] Bandeira/Melo/Andrade, *O ano vermelho*, p. 122.

[107] "Júbilo popular," in: *La Prensa* (November 12, 1918), p. 9. Tato, "La contienda europea en las calles porteñas," pp. 49–51.

[108] "A victoria da civilisação," in: *O Imparcial* (November 13, 1918), p. 4. "Celebración del triunfo de los aliados," in *El Mercurio* (November 14, 1918), p. 5. "A Victoria dos Alliados. Manifestações Populares – As Acclamações á Belgica foram Delirantes," in: *Jornal do Commercio* (November 16, 1918), p. 4.

[109] "Entusiasmo popular por la victorias aliadas," in: *La Prensa* (November 11, 1918), p. 7. "The armistice," in: *South Pacific Mail* (November 14, 1918), p. 3. "Celebrating the Allies' victory," in: ibid. (November 28, 1918), p. 15.

[110] "El homenaje nacional," in: *El Día* (November 13, 1918), p. 2. *Memoria de relaciones exteriores, 1918–19*, p. 23. "La celebración del triunfo de los aliados," in: *Zig-Zag* (November 23, 1918). See also Cámara de Senadores de la República Oriental del Uruguay, *Versión oficial de la sesión extrodinaria*.

participants like Brazil received congratulatory telegrams from neighboring countries and proudly counted themselves among the victors. In Havana, the magazine *Social* published a photo collage of the major personalities who had made the "triumph of freedom" possible. They ranged from Wilson, Lloyd George, and Poincaré to Cuban President Menocal.[111] In addition to conveying a larger sense of unity with the triumphant part of humanity, the commentaries about what had transpired also spoke of a spirit of Latin American solidarity, especially among those states that had contributed to the war effort in one way or another.[112]

At the same time, the enthusiasm was relatively muted in some countries such as Mexico or Colombia, where the proponents of neutrality defended their position despite the war's outcome. In Mexico's Monterrey, those who were affiliated with the victorious powers even had to forgo their triumphal parade because public opposition was too great.[113] In neutral Argentina, the obvious jubilation was interspersed with criticism of the Yrigoyen government. The pro-Ally voices used their triumph as an opportunity to vigorously attack the president for clinging to neutrality. For speakers like Ricardo Rojas, Yrigoyen was to blame for the fact that the country had lost prestige in the world. Public demonstrations once again led to violent confrontations between the president's supporters and his opponents.[114]

The Germans and ethnic Germans, not to mention the pro-German groups, had no cause for celebration. On the contrary, their disappointment, indeed shock, was immense. The propaganda coming from the Reich had continued to proclaim the invincibility of the German troops until the very end. The response to the news of the armistice and its harsh conditions was, consequently, disbelief. The German ambassador in Mexico even denied the news in the local press.[115] Coming to terms with the defeat was all more difficult because Germany now found itself exposed to ridicule and hostility in the press. Even previously neutral newspapers like *Zig-Zag* assigned all the blame to the Prussian-German

[111] "Um dia de gloria e alegria," in: *A Epoca* (November 13, 1918), p. 1. "A victoria do ideal," in: *Fon-Fon* (November 16, 1918). "Un coup de chapeau a estas personalidades," in: *Social* (January 1919), pp. 36–7.

[112] "O Brazil na guerra," in: *A Epoca* (October 28, 1918), p. 1.

[113] Meyer, *Su majestad británica*, p. 249. Matiz, *Amistad Colombo Germana*, p. 8.

[114] Rojas, *La guerra de las naciones*, pp. 73–82. Tato, "La contienda europea en las calles porteñas," pp. 4951. See also "La acción argentina per aliados," in: *Caras y Caretas* (November 16, 1918). González, "La paz internacional," p. 283.

[115] Katz, *The Secret War*, p. 451. Rinke, "Der letzte freie Kontinent," pp. 368–9.

emperor (see Figure 4.2).[116] The victory – as Rui Barbosa, and along with him the Brazilian press, saw it – was a moral triumph over the spirit of conquest and destruction. It was also a successful defense of civilization against Pan-Germanism and barbarous autocracy.[117]

However, there was also concern in Mexico about the news of the revolutionary chaos prevailing in Germany, as a slide into Bolshevism could not be ruled out.[118] Due to the chaotic situation in Europe, this threat appeared to be a general danger at the end of 1918. Fears were amplified even more when countries looked at their own circumstances on the ground. In a lecture before the Instituto Histórico y Geográfico (Historical and Geographical Institute) in Montevideo on July 17, 1918, Uruguayan intellectual Octavio Morató had a comparatively positive outlook for Latin America during the war. Still, he also warned of the new challenges peace would bring.[119] On the opposite side of the La Plata estuary, the editors of *Nosotros* tempered their elation over the ceasefire – which they saw as the culmination of the French Revolution in the struggle against the autocratic monarchies – with a warning to the victorious powers. They needed to create a lasting and just peace on the basis of Wilson's 14 Points, or else face the threat of Maximalism, as in Russia.[120] In anticipation of the peace conference, Argentine intellectual Augusto Bunge wrote in January 1919:

If the imminent peace for the civilized world does not bring with it a fundamental solution to the problems that disturb it today, it will be only a truce, during which the war will continue with other, but no less destructive, means than those of armed conflict, and perhaps lead to even more appalling confrontations.[121]

As in the rest of the world, the people of Latin America were riveted by the peace conference, which began in Paris on January 18, 1919. Eleven Latin American countries officially took part in the conference: the war

---

[116] "El final de la guerra," in: *Zig-Zag* (November 16, 1918).

[117] "O grande momento histórico," in: *Jornal do Commercio* (November 13, 1918), p. 3. See also Victor Viana, "A derrocada allemã," in: ibid. (November 12, 1918), p. 3. "A derrota da Allemanha," in: ibid., p. 5.

[118] "El derrumbamiento de un gran imperio," in: *Excelsior* (November 12, 1918), p. 3.

[119] Morato, *América del Sur*, p. 14. Similar reasoning can already be found in "Guerra europea," in: *El Comercio* (Quito, January 12, 1918), p. 1.

[120] "Nueva era," in: *Nosotros* 12 (115/1918), pp. 365–73. See also "EE.UU. y la Liga de las Naciones," in: *El Sur* (September 30, 1918), p. 1. In Peru, the discussion even turned once again to the vanquished. Since the emperor and the nobility had dishonorably fled their country, Germany would now need to be quickly re-integrated: "Alemania y el fin de la guerra," in: *El Comercio* (November 12, 1918), p. 3.

[121] Bunge, *El socialismo y los problemas de la paz*, p. 5.

FIGURE 4.2 Blaming the Kaiser. In the press of many Latin American countries, the question of guilt was clearly established: The German emperor was at fault.
Source: "Made in Germany," in: *Caras y Caretas* (November 16, 1918).

participants Brazil, Guatemala, Haiti, Honduras, Cuba, Nicaragua, and Panama, as well as Bolivia, Ecuador, Peru, and Uruguay. The neutrals, too, demanded a seat at the negotiating table when it came to discussing their rights. Nevertheless, they remained excluded.[122] Only the major powers Britain, France, the United States, Italy, and Japan were involved in organizing and directing the course of the conference. It was only when their own concerns were at issue that they invited the delegations of other states. As a consequence, the "small" nations felt disadvantaged. Yet instead of displaying solidarity with each other, they gave way to a veritable pecking order. The victors ultimately established three categories in response to the question of how the Latin Americans were to be treated in Paris, which caused a great deal of resentment in the run-up to the conference. The first category was reserved for the aforementioned major powers; the second category included warring nations with limited interests, such as the Central Americans and Brazil; and, finally, the third category contained states that had only broken off relations.[123]

While the Central American countries in the second category followed the U.S. government, the Brazilian delegation held a privileged position. This reinforced the irritation of the Hispano-American representatives, who were relegated to extras. As a result, the representatives from Latin America were, for all intents and purposes, barely involved in the proceedings.[124] The Brazilian press, however, had already lauded the participation at the Inter-Allied Conference from November 29 to December 3, 1917, where a Cuban representative was present, too, as a great success and proof of the country's new international standing.[125] In Paris, the Brazilian representatives already counted themselves as part of the "Latin Group," which, as the envoy in London observed, was competing with the Anglo-Saxons. In the diplomat's view, the latter were more powerful and their striving for world dominance was a cause of concern for Brazil.[126] In order to substantiate its claims, therefore, the Brazilian government published its own "color book" – the "Green Book" – in 1918.[127]

[122] "Los derechos de los neutrales," in: *La Unión* (January 4, 1919), p. 1.

[123] Streeter, *South America*, pp. 85 and 93–6.

[124] Fischer, *Die Souveränität der Schwachen*, pp. 85–93. The Guatemalan government instructed its delegation to observe Washington's terms: Secretaría de RREE, Decree (Guatemala, February 4, 1919), in: Guatemala, AGC, MRREE, Legajo B5922.

[125] "O Brasil e os alliados," in: *Correio da Manhã* (November 16, 1917), p. 1. Brazilian legation to MRE (Paris, November 30 and December 5, 1917), in: AHI, Directoria Geral dos Negocios Políticos e Diplomáticos.

[126] Brazilian Legation to MRE (London, December 27, 1917), in: AHI, Directoria Geral dos Negocios Políticos e Diplomáticos.

[127] *Brazilian Green Book* MRREE, *Guerra da Europa*.

Rui Barbosa, the leading spokesman of the War Party, was originally picked to head the Brazilian delegation to the peace conference a year later. However, he turned down the commission following a period of internal squabbling, which left the opportunity open for future president Epitácio Pessoa.[128] Even before the conference, tensions emerged with the Allies over how many Brazilian delegates should be allowed to attend. It was only after Wilson intervened that the Brazilian delegation was permitted to nominate three representatives to the negotiations, as many as attended from Belgium and Serbia.[129] This aroused indignation in the former mother country Portugal, which was awarded only one delegate. Pessoa and his companions fought, first and foremost, for the national interests of Brazil. These included financial demands concerning the German Reich, as well as a seat in the future League of Nations. In addition, Pessoa pushed for a more appropriate level of participation for the smaller states. He achieved some notable successes, no less with the backing of the U.S. delegation.[130]

Despite the United States' backing of the Brazilians, Latin American observers viewed its role in these months with ambivalence. Already at the turn of the year 1916/17, the columnist at the daily newspaper *O Imparcial* expressed his skepticism about Wilson's pronouncement concerning each nation's right to self-determination. He welcomed the ideal, but noted that it also raised questions about whether the Allies would also accept the principle for Ireland or India.[131] This mixture of hope and skepticism would persist over the course of the next two years. In Latin America, Wilson was himself taken to be a great idealist. From the time the United States entered the war, its propaganda was specifically geared toward transmitting this image. There were many professions of sympathy between the time of the truce and the start of the Peace Conference, which were coupled with the hope of a new world order of equality and

[128] Garcia, *O Brasil e a Liga das Nações*, pp. 28–9. "A conferencia da paz," in: *Correio da Manhã* (January 19, 1919), p. 1.

[129] "Em consideração ao Brazil serão admittidos tres delegados seus á confencia da paz," in: *A Epoca* (January 15, 1919), p. 1. Vinhosa, *O Brasil e a Primeira Guerra Mundial*, p. 191.

[130] MRE to Brazilian legation (R.d.J., December 11 and 30, 1918), in: AHI, Directoria Geral dos Negocios Políticos e Diplomáticos. MRE, memorandum, Situação juridica e politica (Rio de Janeiro, June 1919) and Memorial sobre as reclamações brasileiras (Rio de Janeiro, October 25, 1919), in: ibid. See also Neves, *O Brasil e as espheras de influencia*, pp. 201–5. Garcia, *O Brasil e a Liga das Nações*, pp. 36–43. Streeter, *Epitácio Pessoa*, pp. 81–119. Vinhosa, *O Brasil e a Primeira Guerra Mundial*, p. 210.

[131] "O Ponto de vista americano" in: *O Imparcial* (February 3, 1917), p. 2.

international legitimacy.[132] For *Nosotros*, the name Wilson connoted nothing less than the promise of a "new era" and a "peaceful revolution," which would bring about a more equitable distribution of landownership and the improvement of living standards of all people.[133] The signing of the peace treaty on June 28, 1919, was the culmination of the dream for a better world.[134]

All the same, many commentators were by no means this optimistic. In the region, there was considerable distrust about the imperialist intentions of the victorious powers and in particular those of the United States that rested on specific experiences. Already in February 1917, one pundit in *Caras y Caretas* complained that the "preacher Wilson [preached] one policy for Europe and [practiced] another for America. The little American peoples do not arouse the same interest in him as the little European peoples."[135] These reservations were even quite pronounced in Brazil. Lima Barreto noted in April 1919 that the imperialistic attitude of the Europeans had not changed, although they did let "Senegalese, Gurkhas and Annamites" fight for them. He judged the work of the peace conference negatively: "The conference is not creating a new future; what it is doing is simply mixing together the garbage of the past in a new way."[136] It is unclear to what extent the German war-guilt propaganda that followed on the heels of the armistice, and which was specifically directed at Iberian countries, had already affected voices such as that of Lima Barreto.[137]

The Treaty of Versailles seemed to bear out the critics. A disenchanted Monteiro Lobato commented that this agreement was a confirmation of egoism that prevailed on the international stage.[138] In fact, Brazil's demands were of secondary importance to the major powers. The British and French even separately claimed the requisitioned German ships

---

[132] Ingenieros, *Los tiempos nuevos*, p. 27. Bunge, *El socialismo y los problemas de la paz*, p. 5. Huidobro, *La paz europea*, p. 9. Geli, "Representations of the Great War," p. 212. For more on such propaganda, see, e.g., Wilson, "El programa de la paz."

[133] "Nueva era," in: *Nosotros* 12 (115/1918), pp. 365–73.

[134] "Cinco annos depois," in: *Correio da Manhã* (June 29, 1919), p. 1.

[135] Allande, "Comentarios irreverentes." See even earlier, in 1916, the Chilean Borquez, "Hexametros a Wilson."

[136] Lima Barreto, *Feiras e mafuás*, p. 143.

[137] Examples of this include the following pamphlets: David, *¿Quien es el culpable de la guerra?*, pp. 41–3. Kinkelin, *Los estragos del hambre*, p. 4. Bose, *Lo que he visto en Alemania*, pp. 4–30. On the contexts, see Rinke, *"Der letzte freie Kontinent,"* pp. 492–3.

[138] Lobato, *Críticas*, pp. 230–1. See also "O tratado de paz," in: *Revista do Brasil* 4 (1919), pp. 193–4. This opinion was shared by the Brazilian military: "Parte editorial," in: *A Defeza Nacional* (December 10, 1918), pp. 81–4.

as part of the reparations.[139] The other Latin American delegates also assessed the outcome of the peace negotiations critically. Bolivian delegate Ismael Montes reported in a letter from Paris to the Foreign Office in La Paz that the Allies and especially France had lost a lot of sympathy because of their tough stance toward Germany: "The peace agreement has not yet been signed and you can already recognize the seeds of the next war. The hatred growing in the vanquished countries might prove stronger than all the means that were applied to defeat them."[140]

Accompanying the signing of the peace treaty was the adoption of the charter of the League of Nations. The eleven Latin American signatories were to become founding members, along with the invited neutral countries Argentina, Chile, El Salvador, Colombia, Paraguay, and Venezuela, as well as Costa Rica, which was approved for the first plenary meeting in November 1920. Ultimately, only revolutionary Mexico was excluded for the time being due to pressure from Britain and the United States. Of the forty-two original members of the League of Nations, as many as eighteen came from Latin America. This strong numerical presence gave rise to the hope that the ideal of international equality would actually be realized.[141]

But was there truly an expectation of "universal brotherhood for the world," as a Brazilian commentator remarked in his initial burst of exuberance?[142] Undoubtedly, since the Hague Peace Conference of 1907, many Latin American countries recognized the principle of peaceful arbitration as an ideal. This conference was also essentially viewed as the beginning of eye-level negotiations for the diplomats of the region. Colombian intellectual Santiago Pérez Triana already implored for a return to these ideals from his permanent residence in London.[143] The League of Nations, however, was first and foremost a matter of prestige that Brazilian policy makers thought they could exploit. Brazil's old rival Argentina, on the other hand, was skeptical about the new organization precisely because of its neighbor's special role and thus very quickly withdrew again.[144] The other Latin American governments typically joined the League of Nations with exaggerated expectations, hoping – in the wake

[139] For a detailed discussion, see Garcia, *O Brasil e a Liga das Nações*, pp. 36–43. Streeter, *Epitácio Pessoa*, pp. 81–119. On the Brazilian demands from the perspective of an eyewitness, see economist Pinheiro, *Problemas da guerra e da paz*, pp. 91–104.
[140] Quoted in Streeter, *South America*, p. 110. See also Lobato, *Críticas*, pp. 227–9.
[141] Rinke, *"Der letzte freie Kontinent,"* p. 177.
[142] "Finis Germaniae," in: *O Imparcial* (June 29, 1919), p. 1.
[143] Pérez Triana, *The Neutrality of Latin America*, p. 10.
[144] Rinke, *"Der letzte freie Kontinent,"* pp. 177–8.

of Wilson's pronouncements – for resolutions to a number of disputes, some of which had been long-standing. This was the case for Bolivia and Peru, for instance, with regard to the contentious border issue with neighboring Chile involving the provinces of Tacna and Arica, as well as for Ecuador in its border dispute with Peru.[145]

That said, in the view of many Latin American diplomats and international law experts, the most important question in the longer term was the degree to which the League of Nations could serve as a counterweight to U.S. hegemony in the Americas. This Latin American interest was recognized early on in the United States, where young State Department official James G. McDonald anticipated many fundamental problems in a prescient memorandum from January 1918. According to McDonald, the demand for the absolute equality of all sovereign states was not achievable. This was due not least to the fact that countries such as Argentina, Brazil, or Chile were not willing to put themselves on a par with their weaker neighbors. For Latin America as well as for the United States, a tense relationship consequently developed toward the new global organization. The diplomat accordingly recommended that Washington's policy should aim to separate Pan-Americanism and inter-American relations from the context of the League of Nations. The discussion of contentious issues – McDonald cited the Panama Canal, Cuba, Puerto Rico, and Haiti – should be avoided whenever possible.[146]

From a Latin American perspective, the Monroe Doctrine was another sensitive issue because the U.S. government had repeatedly used this doctrine and its amendments to legitimize its interventions in Latin America since the turn of the century. U.S. interventionism, moreover, had experienced a revival especially under Wilson. The dogma actually made its way into Article 21 of the League of Nations' charter under pressure from the United States and was thus more or less validated before the world community. This met with harsh criticism in Latin America,[147] where the League of Nations was believed to have had an ominous start. Among the optimistic intellectuals of the region who had put their faith

---

[145] Streeter, *South America*, pp. 93–6. For the contemporary Chilean point of view, see, e.g., Rocuant, *La neutralité du Chili*, pp. 5–8. On Peru, see: Lavalle, *El Perú y la gran guerra*. On Ecuador, see: Ecuadorian Ministry of Foreign Affairs to embassy in Paris (Quito, April 8, 1919), in: Ecuador, AMRREE, M.1.23.4.

[146] James G. McDonald, Memorandum on Latin America and a possible peace conference (Bloomington, IN, January 19, 1918), NA, RG 256, Reel 8, No. 103, p. 2.

[147] Streeter, *South America*, p. 133. Streeter, *Central America*, p. 99. Fischer, *Die Souveränität der Schwachen*, pp. 278–89. The government of neutral El Salvador took a critical stance: Meléndez, *Las relaciones*.

in Wilson, the father of the League of Nations, disappointment began to spread from mid-1919 in response to the "decepción wilsonista," as the Argentine Ingenieros called it.[148] This "Wilsonian disappointment" was one aspect of the Latin American experience of the last year of the war and the war's end. Undoubtedly, the subcontinent had never been so caught up in the mechanisms of the conflict. Now, it also affected neutral countries like Chile and Argentina, who kept the Allies' war machine running with their exports. In view of the resources of the American continent, the Allied triumph was only a matter of time. The more imminent the German defeat seemed, the easier it was to detect the rivalries among the Allies. In 1918, they were already jockeying for position in anticipation of the competitive struggle of the postwar period, and paid little consideration to their confederates in the process. Latin Americans looked forward eagerly to the end of the war, but at the same time were still concerned about their future prospects. The economic and social developments gave cause for worry. In particular, the major disturbances from 1918/19 throughout much of the region were an indirect consequence of the war in Europe. In addition, they were the result of long-standing social problems and international events, including, first and foremost, the Russian Revolution. The euphoria which the end to the war had sparked in Latin America quickly turned into disappointment. The war, which ended in 1918/19, also cast long shadows on Latin America's future. The arrival of the "new era" that many Latin American commentators identified with this moment was full of uncertainties.

---

[148] Funes, *Salvar la nación*, pp. 109 and 220–1.

5

The Demise of a World

The confrontation with the First World War in Latin America went far beyond the exclusive spheres of the diplomats or the elites involved in the propaganda war. In Latin America, the war was above all a highly mediatized event. Although the upper classes produced most of the available sources, these sources nevertheless show that the conflict had an astonishingly wide social impact in many parts of Latin America, especially in its urban areas. These developments attest to changes in perceptions about the world, which were at once immediately connected to, but also greatly transcended, the reception of the war's progress and its tangible repercussions. As a "global media event,"[1] the war affected the global consciousness of many Latin Americas. Through news reports and their own firsthand experience, they developed a stronger sense of the entanglements and the various dependencies that impacted their region of the world. In discussing the war, Latin Americans participated what for the first time became a global public sphere. A form of symbolic delimitation took place that radically reduced, if not entirely eliminated, the distance between the region and the battlefields. The war was thus also a world war because it permeated the everyday lives of many Latin Americans.

THE WAR IN EVERYDAY LIFE

In the Latin American press, the outbreak of the war in August 1914 was the event that overshadowed everything else and filled up the gazettes'

---

[1] Jeismann, "Propaganda," p. 208.

columns.[2] In Latin America's urban centers, the reports could reach a huge audience because the newspaper industry had experienced a genuine explosion in the 1910s. Unlike in the nineteenth century, their readership was by no means limited to members of the national elites, but rather also increasingly attracted readers from the working class and the growing middle class. Even in civil-war-torn Mexico, newspapers like the *El Imparcial* already had full-page spreads on the events in Europe on August 1.[3] The cables from the news services in Europe followed in rapid succession. The reports, however, did not stay current for even a day and there was a voracious appetite for the latest news. Consequently, the papers in Buenos Aires printed three, sometimes even four, editions daily.[4] Innumerable photographs depicting modern weaponry, military maneuvers, and the European aristocracy heightened interest. Although the swift deployment of the belligerents' propaganda was highly noticeable, the press and public in Latin America were hardly as naïve as some European strategists believed.

This was partly due to the fact that the correspondents reported directly from the theater of the war. These war reporters acted in a wider Latin American context. In the leading Brazilian newspaper *O Estado de São Paulo*, these included diplomats and intellectuals like Manuel de Oliveira Lima, who reported regularly on the conflict in his column "Ecos da guerra" ("War Echoes"). The founder of modern Brazilian journalism, Júlio Mesquita, similarly wrote a weekly chronicle, Boletim Semanal da guerra.[5] In the Argentine *La Nación*, well-known intellectual figures like Lugones, but also Kinkelin, regularly informed the paper's readers. *Caras y Caretas* immediately dispatched its correspondent Javier Bueno and illustrator Federico Ribas to the Allied front. Beginning in December 1914, they both reported on the adventures that journalists could go on given the numerous colorful uniforms from around the world. In the years that followed, the magazine printed reports from up

---

[2] La contienda europea," in: *La Nación* (B. A., August 2, 1914), p. 6. "Notas chalacas," in: *La Crónica* (August 2, 1914), pp. 1–2. "Conflagración europea," in: *El Comercio* (Quito, August 2, 1914), p. 1. Compagnon ("Si loin, siproche ...," p. 79) speaks of a "relative absence of war" in the press of Argentina and Brazil when the conflict began. This finding is not supported by the sources.

[3] "La situación europea se agrava," in: *El Imparcial* (Mexico, August 1, 1914), p. 1.

[4] German emigrant Ernesto Gedult von Jungenfeld, who wanted to make his way from Paraguay to Germany, provides a vivid description of this. Gedult von Jungenfeld, *Aus den Urwäldern Paraguays*, pp. 70–1.

[5] Mesquita's reports were reissued in a four-volume edition: Mesquita, *A guerra, 1914–1918*, Vols. 1–4. See also Compagnon, "Si loin, si proche ...," pp. 82–3.

to five correspondents stationed at the various fronts and, in this way, offered its readers an immediate impression of the fighting.[6] The appeal of this reporting and the fascination with the new profession was so great that *Caras y Caretas* expressly introduced a picture story from Manuel Redondo, titled "Sarrasqueta en guerra." Its main character was a war reporter who had to endure all kinds of daring escapades between the fronts.

The war coverage could occasionally take on comical proportions because of the low credibility of the reporting from Europe. The Peruvian and Cuban press doubted the veracity of the telegrams from Europe, which only transmitted the Allies' reports of success, as early as mid-August 1914.[7] Vague and conflicting reports ensured that confusion predominated everywhere. "Absolute ignorance" even prevailed among the correspondents near the battlefields about what actually went on.[8] Observers were convinced that this was mainly due to censorship and the tendency to misreport Allied victories, which primarily Havas transmitted to Latin America.[9]

This was a godsend for cartoonists and satirists.[10] Argentine playwright Emilio Dupuy de Lôme made this confusion the subject of his one-act monologue "¡No me hable de la guerra!" ("Don't talk to me about the war!"), which premiered at the Teatro de la Comedia in Buenos Aires on November 9, 1914. The protagonist bemoans his torment:

Gosh, did you see what nonsense *La Prensa* wrote today? But it was less egregious than what was in *La Nación*, where there's a telegram that refutes it; though I tend to believe what *La Mañana* claims, *La Razón* says the exact opposite, and yet *El Diario* seems to confirm it. In order to know what to believe the best thing to do is to wait for *Última Hora* or *Crítica*, although *La Vanguardia* in fact writes ... "[11]

---

[6] Lorenz, "La gran guerra vista por un argentino," pp. 48–65, here p. 49. Kinkelin published his contributions after the war in two volumes: *Mis correspondencias*.

[7] "Se duda de la veracidad," in: *La Crónica* (August 15, 1914), p. 3. Rivero/Gil, *El conflicto europeo*, pp. 10–1.

[8] Pele-Mele, "Al margen de la guerra," in: *La Crónica* (September 8, 1914), p. 12. See also "A victoria da Triplice Alliança?," in: *Jornal do Commercio* (February 8, 1914) p. 17. "La guerra en Europe," in: *Variedades* (August 22, 1914), p. 1120. Castex, "Verdades y mentiras."

[9] "La conflagración europea," in: *El Abogado Cristiano Ilustrado* (August 20, 1914), p. 512 Mesquita, *A guerra*, Vol. 1, pp. 63–4. "Mirando a otros horizon," in: *El Mundo Ilustrado* (September 20, 1914), p. 17. See also Germanophile Argentine Vergara (*Guerra de mentiras*, p. 3) or the report from the Ecuadorian Consul General to the Ministry of Foreign Affairs in Quito (Berlin, August 14, 1914), in: Ecuador, AMRREE, D.1.9.

[10] See, for instance, the following edition of *Cara-Dura* (February 23, 1915).

[11] Dupuy de Lôme, *¡No me hable de la guerra!*, p. 7.

The Latin American newspapers reacted differently to the mass deceit. Lacking alternatives, most continued to reprint the telegrams, although some were not willing to let the propaganda lies pass without comment. For example, in response to criticism of alleged false and one-sided reporting on European events, *El Imparcial* from Mexico announced in early August that it would not take sides and from that moment would offer its pages to anyone who had verifiable news.[12] The Mexican rival paper *El Nacional* titled its cable and correspondent section about the war "Mentiras y Verdades" ("Lies and Truths") and, in Colombia, sensational success stories from the front wound up in the humor columns.[13]

Despite strong doubts about the validity of the news agencies' reports, the interest in the war remained huge. The press continually reported on the many contexts in which men and women from different social strata eagerly received the news about the war. To some degree, the war brought people together and created new forms of public spheres, as in the case of Los Pocitos, a suburb of Montevideo.[14] Undoubtedly, it aroused particularly intense interest where larger national minorities of the warring powers lived together side by side, as in the port cities and the settlement centers of South American immigrant communities.[15] At the same time, the news of the outbreak of war altered the lives of many people, even in some of the more remote regions.[16]

The satirists of *Caras y Caretas* soon made the Buenos Aireans' "obsession" with the war a target of their ironic commentary (see Figure 5.1). Julián Castex thus related in a fictional tale how a man no longer asks for his usual *mate* upon hearing his morning alarm clock, but instead the latest news on the war. When strolling through the city, he does not walk through the park as he did before. He rather determinedly heads off to the large newspaper houses where huge maps of Europe portray the course of the war. Castex' character observed that the insatiable thirst for news from Europe, even in the lower classes, had led to an increase in

---

[12] Note from publisher, in: *El Imparcial* (September 8, 1914), p. 1.

[13] "Verdades y mentiras," in: *El Nacional* (May 10, 1916), p. 4. "Minutos de humor: estos alemanes," in: *ABC* (Quindío, July 20, 1916), p. 3. "Conflicto europeo," in: *El Tren* (September 3, 1914), p. 1.

[14] "Los estudiantes y la guerra," in: *Caras y Caretas* (December 19, 1914). Castellanos, "Las consecuencias de la guerra." Bouret/Remedi, *Escenas de la vida cotidiana*, pp. 48–9. "Guerra europea," in: *El Progreso* (December 5, 1916), p. 3.

[15] Compagnon has rightly pointed out that interest in the war, for instance, in the north and northeast of Brazil, was far less pronounced than in the south (*L'adieu à L'Europe*, p. 111).

[16] Woodard, *A Place in Politics*, pp. 71–2.

FIGURE 5.1 The carnival parade in Europe. The cartoon shows unperturbed neutral states enjoying themselves in watching the battles.
Source: "El corso en Europa," in: *Caras y Caretas* (February 20, 1915).

historical and geographical knowledge. Even the poorest people listened to the news criers in the public squares, and shoeshine boys had to have a solid knowledge of the war's progression in order to keep their customers up to date and accordingly promote their business.[17] On the other hand, as numerous cartoons on the election campaigns from that period show, war metaphors found their way into characterizations of domestic policy.[18]

The experiences of Dupuy's protagonists were quite similar to that of Castex: "I can no longer walk into the street without immediately stumbling into a dear-friend who … thinks he has to bring me up to date on the war and gives me a speech which almost always lasts more than a couple of hours." Dupuy detected a full-blown "war mania" ("bélico-mania") with characters like the map fanatic, the prophet, and the military expert. Even the goods of the street traders, who now sold colored maps and contraband raincoats, had changed. Bemused, Dupuy reported on the heated discussions in the trams. He was, however, unnerved by the dumb war jokes, all of which he already knew.[19] As some of the cartoons show, these jokes were often quite crude. The black humor, which spared none of the warring countries, indicates that Europe had lost much of its prestige and that little of the great respect that had existed for the Old World remained.

The "war mania" was highly welcome to a kind of journalism that increasingly relied on images and sensations and thus came to resemble the U.S. boulevard press. The new form of sensationalism is well illustrated by the magazine *Revista da Semana*, which promised its readers on August 1, 1914, that it would report extensively "on every disaster" in Europe.[20] The ingenuity of the press was put on display when *La Prensa* devised a highly visible color signal system for the roof of its building in August 1914. For a victory of the Central Powers, it indicated the color red with a white circle, for the Allies, the color green with a white circle. In addition, the newsroom revved a siren each time an important new telegram came in. The fact that people waited for these signs from war with bated breath is demonstrated by the many photos that appeared in the press at the time. Pictures of massive crowds standing before the newspaper building were, indeed, a way for the press to tout its own success.[21]

[17] Castex, "La emoción de la guerra."
[18] Alonso, "Estrategia radical," in: *Caras y Caretas* (March 6, 1915).
[19] Dupuy de Lôme, *¡No me hable de la guerra!*, pp. 6–7.
[20] "Os Successos," in: *Revista da Semana* (R.d.J., August 1, 1914), p 2.
[21] Tato, "La contienda europea en las calles porteñas," p. 35.

The press underscored the spectacle of the war with photos and drawings of supposedly picturesque scenes from the events.[22] Full title pages showing military parades, modern aircraft, and gigantic cannons were emblematic of the fascination many Latin Americans still had with Europe. Judging from the number of media images, the Latin American public was especially enthusiastic about new weapons systems, such as aircraft, airships, submarines, and tanks.[23] Of course this was due in no small measure to the influence of propaganda, as most images were aimed at demonstrating the power and superiority of the respective warring parties.[24] Based on troop levels and economic resources, several statistics-obsessed editorial boards tried to calculate exactly which side would emerge at the end of the conflagration as the victor.[25]

An "exotic" element that attracted particular attention in the press was the deployment of troops from the colonies to the European theater of war (see Figure 5.2). The commentaries demonstrate the degree of the racism that existed among Latin American elites. For instance, reports on the contribution of China to the war hewed closely to the racist views of the Europeans, in which Chinese were supposedly better suited for menial tasks. A front-line soldier described in his memoirs his African comrades' method of fighting as especially barbaric and cruel.[26] A respected thinker like Ingenieros was also convinced that the "white race" had repeatedly proven its superiority in this regard over the centuries.[27]

A new feature involved directly engaging the readers. The newspaper *Jornal do Brasil*, for instance, called on its readership in September 1914 to participate in a sweepstakes: The readers were supposed to plot how they thought the borders in Europe would look by the time of the war's generally anticipated conclusion in January 1915.[28] The press not only wanted to arouse interest among the traditional male readers, but they now turned increasingly to women and even to children as new target groups. In September 1914, *Caras y Caretas* announced a prize for the most beautiful child's drawing. The submissions reflected how much

[22] "Notas pintorescas del ejército aliado," in: *Caras y Caretas* (November 14, 1914).
[23] See, for example, "A guerra nos ares," in: *O Imparcial* (R.d.J., August 5, 1914), p. 1. Abaca, *La guerra europea*, pp. 15–16. "Los modernos elementos de guerra," in: *Caras y Caretas* (August 29, 1914).
[24] "Escenas británicas de la guerra," in: *El Mundo Ilustrado* (September 13, 1914), p. 6.
[25] "Austria-Hungria, Rusia, Francia," in: *Caras y Caretas* (August 8, 1914).
[26] "La China en la Guerra Mundial," in: *Zig-Zag* (September 8, 1917). Homet, *Diario*, pp. 59–65.
[27] Ingenieros, "La formación de una raza argentina," p. 468.
[28] "Concurso intellectual," in: *Jornal do Brasil* (R.d.J., September 6, 1914), p. 7.

Ayer era negro, hoy me han hecho blanco de las balas enemigas.
Dib. de Redondo.

Ayer era rajá de la Katapulka, hoy soy
carne de cañón.

FIGURE 5.2 An "exotic" war. Cartoonists responded to the participation of soldiers from the colonies on the European battlefields with more or less racist depictions like this one.
Source: "Cambios bruscos a causa de la guerra," in: *Caras y Caretas* (February 20, 1915).

boys in particular grappled with the war, while girls preferred to focus on other issues.[29]

The role of women in the war was a topic that magazines gladly seized upon. In Latin America, these portraits also tended to put a spotlight on women as nurses and benefactors. The newspapers stressed their sense of duty in service to the fatherland, be it on the part of the Entente or the Central Powers.[30] In general, the now traditional use of women as metaphors of the nation again became increasingly important in the context of the war. For instance, the organizers of a demonstration of the *neutralistas* in Buenos Aires had an automobile with three young women clad in white, each wearing a sash with the national colors, lead the procession.[31] Representations dominated that reproduced gender stereotypes, such as those on "wartime fashion." Women's magazines like the Cuban *Social*

[29] Compagnon (*L'adieu à l'Europe*, pp. 117–18) even discovered a board game for children that appeared in Argentina in 1917, *Juego de la guerra europea*.
[30] Di Carlo, "La caridad y la guerra." Zarraga, "El amor y la guerra," p. 8.
[31] "En favor de la neutralidad," in: *La Prensa* (B. A., April 25, 1917), p. 11.

spread these images and the subject of war also appeared, for example, in advertisements.[32] Eventually, the belligerent states became interested in mobilizing women for fatigue duty and even for armed service, although the latter was characterized as a violation of the "unwritten laws of logic."[33] The images the press transmitted emphasized that the role of women in war was the self-sacrificing servant and caregiver who makes the warrior's existence more tolerable. Women represented the ideal of humanity, which, despite the atrocities of warfare, had to remain intact.[34]

It was not only with regard to female customers that advertisers in Latin America's slowly evolving consumer societies recognized the war as a potentially stimulating subject. Whether it was alcohol, fashion, or medicine, allusions – not infrequently with humorous undertones – were made to the war nationwide in the newspapers and magazines and on public advertising spaces in the modernizing major cities (see Figure 5.3). Regional firms and in particular those U.S. companies that were rapidly expanding in Latin American markets exploited this promotional strategy. The latter, such as the shoe manufacturer Regal, indicated that the fashion trends once set by the Europeans were no longer valid and that the yardstick had now been established by the United States.

The war entered the imagination of the general population as a global event of unprecedented proportions in a variety of ways. In Brazil, the genre of "Literatura de Cordel," which published folk literature in small booklets and was especially widespread in the north and northeast of the country, embraced the topic. In Argentina, Tango poets like Alejandro Bustamente or Eduardo Arolasalso found the subject attractive.[35] Beyond this, at La Plata, the popular "Literaturagauchesca" or "criollista," which the German anthropologist employed in Argentine service, Robert Lehmann-Nitsche, methodically collected during the war years, was receptive to the war theme. It was mainly dealt with in verse form, wherein the horrors of war were highlighted as much as heroic deeds. The poets were mostly self-taught, such as a certain Abaca who in a moment of reflection apologized for his "humble" text. All the same, this kind of folk literature that was printed in cheap booklets of ten to thirty pages

---

[32] "Modas de la guerra," in: *Caras y Caretas* (January 2, 1915). See, e.g., the ads in the issues of *Social* from March and April 1917.
[33] "El feminismo en acción," in: *Caras y Caretas* (July 3, 1915).
[34] "La mujer en la guerra," in: *El Día* (October 5, 1914), p. 3.
[35] Compagnon, *L'adieu à l'Europe*, pp. 117–8.

FIGURE 5.3 The war in product advertisements. Product advertising profited from the general fascination with the war.

Source: "Ginebra Bols," in: *Caras y Caretas* (September 19, 1914).

became a veritable mass medium in a mostly illiterate country, as it was publicly performed in a range of contexts, even in the hinterlands.[36]

In one of the booklets, a "Sargento Salomon" from Rosario sang in verse about, inter alia, the battle victories of the French, the defeats of the Germans, and the bravery of the Belgians. Sargento wanted his text "Italia Neutral" to be set to the music of the anarchist anthem "Hijos del Pueblo."[37] Frequently, the booklets contained short one-act plays like Tito Livio Foppa's *Mambrú se fue a la guerra*, which premiered in Buenos Aires on October 30, 1919, and dramatized the love of a returning soldier. Another was the tragedy *Después de la guerra* by Leron Vieytes, in which an old man and a dying soldier disclose their suffering to each other.[38] In 1917, Argentine writer Belisario Roldán published the dime novel *Unamadre, en Francia* as part of the series "La novelasemanal." The story concerned the transformation of a mother from war-damning anarchist to ardent patriot.[39] Often the authors would combine the sad fate of the war heroes who returned as invalids with tragic storylines of lost love. In this way, they could portray the cruelty of the war to a wide audience on the basis of the fate of a single individual.[40]

In narratives like these, the horror and fascination of the war were difficult to separate. Shocking tales in magazines, like the one about looters who robbed the dead, seem to have been very popular. Indeed, versions of them were published again and again.[41] The reader mainly became acquainted with the suffering of the soldiers through the reports of the war correspondents (see Figure 5.4). However, the testimonial literature of an Argentine volunteer in French service, Juan B. Homet, conveyed this as well. Homet's book, whose publication had probably been supported by German propaganda, depicted the terror and the brutality of the war from the perspective of a simple soldier on the front line. Arguably more than any other Spanish-language book before 1919, it exposed the state of its protagonist's disillusionment and severe disability upon returning home in 1917. As Homet writes: "Today, I recognize the terrible lie of this war." He continued:

Here, there are no more civilized people. They're all savages, worse than savages. And I unfortunately let myself get caught up in the story, for I was deceived,

---

[36] Rey de Guido, *Cancionero rioplatense*, pp. XX–XXV. Chicote, "La cultura de los márgenes," pp. 103–20. Examples from the Lehmann-Nitsche collection: Ariyaga/Firtuoso, *La guerra europea*. Abaca, *La guerra europea*.

[37] Salomon, *La guerra europea*.

[38] Foppa, *Mambrú se fue a la guerra*. Vieytes, *Después de la guerra*.

[39] Roldán, *Una madre en Francia*.

[40] González Cadavid, *El héroe*.

[41] Marthur, "Los buitres."

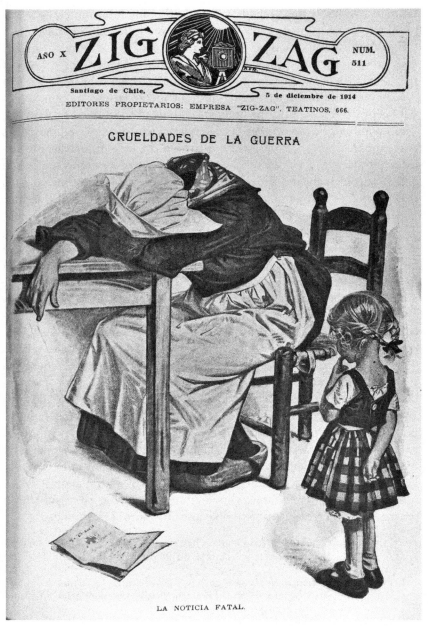

FIGURE 5.4 The inhumanity of the war. Images like these appealed to the viewer's emotions.

Source: "Crueldades de la guerra," in: *Zig-Zag* (December 5, 1914).

dragged away, and corrupted by them. They even made wild beasts out of good-natured people. Down with the war! A thousand deaths to the war![42]

The lament about the futility of war spread and found its way, for instance, into the poetry of Chilean Vicente Huidobro.[43] Venezuelan intellectual Pío Gil, who escaped the Gómez dictatorship by fleeing to Paris, also disputed the myth of the just war that had become common currency due to the propaganda of the warring states.[44] Dime novels invoking Leo Tolstoy offered biting ironic criticism of the war coupled with an entreaty for the return of love and peace.[45] It was hardly a coincidence that the classic work from 1870 by Argentine Juan Bautista Alberdi, *El crimen de la guerra* (*The Crime of War*) was reprinted in 1915. In the book, the great intellectual categorically rejected the legitimacy of the war as a political instrument.[46]

In particular, the industrial character of the killing in trench warfare on the Western Front sparked revulsion, but also simultaneously fascination. Military officers like Kinkelin or Uriburu tried to draw lessons from this in order to prepare for future wars.[47] An article published in *Caras y Caretas* already alluded to the ambivalence in August 1914. The atrocities of the war were juxtaposed with soldiers' heroism and self-sacrifice. With his "Poetry in Red," Uruguayan poet Angel Falcó artistically treated the "the tension between heroism and horror.[48] By the time the whole truth became known at war's end, however, no room was left for romanticizing. As Ibarguren expressed to his readers in 1919 on the basis of diaries of French soldiers, the idea of the noble war portrayed in paintings of battle and beautiful museum sculptures was obsolete: "The overall conception is exasperating: The enemy doesn't appear, and yet perfidious death lurks everywhere."[49]

This negative impression solidified the more became known about the fate of the civilian victims in the occupied areas. Not only did the public

[42] Homet, *Diario*, p. 69. See also Compagnon, *L'adieu à L'Europe*, pp. 176–82. Tato, "Luring Neutrals," p. 339.

[43] Ellis, "Vicente Huidobro," pp. 333–45. León, "La presencia de la Gran Guerra." Even a military officer like Kinkelin occasionally came to this realization: Kinkelin, *Mis correspondencias*, Vol. 2, p. 233.

[44] Gil, *Diario íntimo*, p. 24.

[45] Ariyaga/Firtuoso, *La guerra europea*, p. 3. Abaca, *La guerra europea*. See also "La guerra europea: lecciones y enseñanzas," in: *La Defensa* (September 10, 1916), p. 2.

[46] Alberdi, *El crimen de la guerra*, p. 55.

[47] Kinkelin, *Mis correspondencias*, Vol. 1, p. 83.

[48] "El horror de la guerra," in: *Caras y Caretas* (August 8, 1914). Falcó, *Troquel de fuego*.

[49] Ibarguren, *La literatura y la gran Guerra*, pp. 130–1. Lorenz, "La gran guerra," pp. 62–3.

find out about the abuses in Belgium early on, but Allied propaganda referred to them repeatedly as an example of German barbarism. At the same time, news about the violence against civilians in other theaters of the war went beyond anything known before.[50] Popular writers Vicente Ariyaga and Julio Firtuoso from Argentina concluded with outrage:

Educated people climb into aircraft and, brimming with enthusiasm, drop bombs on the enemy city. The bombs fall and explode. Their shrapnel kills men, women, and children. Innocent victims – but victims who would have done the same thing as the pilot. The pilot, who was the instrument of death, receives commendations. The people to which he belongs, distinguishes him. If he kills a lot of people, they build a statue of him, and the government of the country in which he was born renames streets in his honor.[51]

The monstrous events were not unfolding in remote parts of the world, but rather in the place that Latin Americans of all social strata so far had admired as the heart of civilization.

THE END OF CIVILIZATION

In light of the reporting on the tensions and the outbreaks of violence at different venues, the upper and middle classes in Latin America were, as in other regions of the world, fairly well informed about the affairs in Europe. The crises in the Balkans from 1912–13 had foreshadowed what was to come. The impending war dominated editorials and the front pages of the press throughout Latin America. Nevertheless, as evidenced by the countless sensational news reports, the transition to the hot war in August 1914 came as a shock. The global dimension of the outbreak of hostilities – the connection between European and regional events – seemed undeniable. In the eyes of many contemporaries, what was taking place in Europe meant the demise of a world. Was civilization coming to an end? This is the question that many Latin American politicians, intellectuals and journalists obsessively reflected on during the war years.

The great concern about the developments in Europe that had gripped the whole world was already apparent in July 1914. On August 5, a dispatch out of Paris at the end of July from Julio Piquet was published in Buenos Aires' *La Nación*. In the report, Piquet speculated about whether the catastrophes that transpired in June were an ominous sign. Despite the enormous progress the Europeans had made, there could be no certainty

---

[50] Chil. ambassador to MRREE (Berlin, March 12, 1917), in: Chile, AMRREE, Vol. 604.
[51] Ariyaga/Firtuoso, *La guerra europea*, p. 2.

of or guarantee for the "armed peace," which seemed increasingly tenuous.[52] "Uncertainty, mistrust and fear" were the three concepts, according to the columnist at the Peruvian *La Crónica*, that best described the situation.[53] At the same time, even in late July, there still seemed reason to hope. Hence, *El Diario* in Asunción wrote optimistically about the "universal solidarity" that could prevent the war.[54] A Brazilian commentator, by contrast, remarked that the people themselves seemed to be chomping at the bit even more than their rulers, who had much to lose. For this reason, he thought there remained a chance for peace.[55] Given the enormous progress and the global entanglements, the notion of war breaking out in Europe remained inconceivable.[56]

When the situation nonetheless came to a head in early August and news spread rapidly in Latin America about the eruption of hostilities, the sense of surprise in the media did not last long. Indeed, the media adjusted to the new reality quickly. The Paraguayan *Diario*, for instance, which had issued its hopeful plea just a week earlier, now spoke of the war's inevitability. Making war, the commentary further noted, was after all a human instinct and when an appeal is made to patriotism, everyone signs up for military service. In the columnist's opinion, the visions of the pacifists were utopian. The war rather played an essential role in the rivalry between the nations, while peace was only a temporary lull before the next conflict, in which the losers would avenge themselves.[57] Although this radical, social Darwinist commentary remained a minority point of view, many skeptical observers now felt vindicated. As they saw it, the harmony in Europe had long been hanging by a thread. Now, what they had expected to occur for some time was finally taking place.[58] Forty years of militarism in Europe had supposedly prepared the nations for the war, which could not be circumvented in the end.[59] Despite the peace

---

[52] Julio Picquet, "Una tormenta mortifera," in: *La Nación* (B. A., August 5, 1914), p. 5. See also "La situación de Europa," in: ibid. (August 2, 1914), p. 9.

[53] "Sobre la guerra en Europa," in: *La Crónica* (August 4, 1914), p. 8.

[54] "¿Conflagración?," in: *El Diario* (July 27, 1914), p. 1.

[55] "Ainda uma esperança," in: *Correio da Manhã* (August 1, 1914), p. 2.

[56] According to Chilean Pedro Subercaseaux Errázuriz, cited in: Couyoumdjian/Muñoz, "Chilenos en Europa," p. 43. See also "A maior guerra da história," in: *Fon-Fon* (August 8, 1914).

[57] "Ante la guerra," in: *El Diario* (August 4, 1914), p. 1 and 4. See also "A hora da guerra," in: *A Careta* (August 8, 1914).

[58] "Mirando a otros horizontes," in: *El Mundo Ilustrado* (August 2, 1914), p. 3.

[59] "Chronica," in: *Revista da Semana* (August 8, 1914), p. 5. In Peru as well observers were of the opinion that the "armed peace [had] failed." "La conflagración europea," in: *Variedades* (August 8, 1914).

conference in The Hague, the pacifist rapprochements, and the efforts at international arbitration, the war remained a "merciless divinity," as the Chilean Gallardo wrote.[60]

In addition to the fatalism of many comments, the reports usually expressed dismay. The outbreak of the war seemed to be a tremendous jolt that carried with it potentially bitter after-effects for Latin America. The recurring reference to Greek antiquity in texts and images shows that the foundations of European civilization had been upended. Everywhere, the media now used the term "catastrophe," the result of which was undoubtedly a "hecatomb," that is, the downfall of the entire world, for victors and vanquished alike.[61] With a keen sense of the mood of the population, Ariyaga and Firtuoso wrote:

The most frightening catastrophe has befallen mankind. The nations that were the pioneers of modern civilization are rushing to war. Destruction has opened its maw and is getting ready to thrust its fangs into mankind. Poor Europe! Poor humanity![62]

The journalists drew on natural metaphors, without, however, finding an explanation for the incomprehensible events. They did not refrain from using superlatives to emphasize the historical uniqueness of the war and thus to anchor its significance as a global media event.[63] The editorial of the leading cultural magazine *Nosotros* from Buenos Aires observed that the "terrible conflagration" was "one of the worst catastrophes in millennia"; it had "struck like a bolt of lightning, suddenly and ... unexpectedly."[64] Already in August, an astonishing number of commentaries referred to an epochal shift and the beginning of a new era of history.[65] Not even two weeks after hostilities erupted, the consul of Venezuela in Genoa, Raúl Crespo, reported:

We're falling back into barbarism, just like one of those fires in our tropical forests, in which the all-consuming fire destroys everything. The farmer can then

---

[60] Gallardo, *Neutralidad de Chile*, p. CIII.

[61] Enrique Jauregui, "Hecatombe," in: *La Nación* (B. A., August 4, 1914), p. 3. "A repercução do conflicto no Brazil," in: *A República* (August 4, 1914), p. 2. Ramos, "Alemania ante la guerra," p. 427. Brull, "La ansiedad del mundo." Ingenieros, *Los tiempos nuevos*, p. 15.

[62] Ariyaga/Firtuoso, *La guerra europea*, p. 2.

[63] Ramos, "Alemania ante la guerra," p. 427. "A repercução do conflicto no Brazil," in: *A República* (August 4, 1914), p. 2. Montesa, "La guerramás grande de los siglos." On the theory of world events, see the discussion in Morgner, *Weltereignisse und Massenmedien*, pp. 168–9.

[64] "La Guerra," in: *Nosotros* 8 (August 1914), p. 117.

[65] "La guerra europea," in: *Caras y Caretas* (August 8, 1914). See also Ibarguren, *La Literatura y la gran guerra*, p. 8.

clear off the blackened soil and sow the new seeds in the fertile interior, which will yield the blessed fruit.[66]

Of course, the question was how things had gotten that far. The newspapers analyzed the historical development of French-German "enmity" and France's aspiration for revenge.[67] Commentators also cited Pan-Slavism, the British hegemonic striving, Germanism with its claim to world power, the colonial conflicts, and imperialism in general as causes for the outbreak of war. Typically, they would emphasize one aspect over the other, depending on their inclination.[68] They all agreed that the nations had been pushed to the brink of war because of the enormous military buildup since 1871 and secret diplomacy.[69] Observers were mystified by the European foreign ministries publication of color books to elucidate their respective points of view on the causes of the war, which were actually a woeful attempt to put the blame on the enemy.[70] The war was characterized here as a war of civilizations or the "races" – between Slav and Teuton, Latin and German.[71] The columnist at *El Día* from Montevideo hit the nail on the head when he complained that the European powers had all accused each other of having started the war, even though it was ultimately irrelevant for the world as a whole. The war's terrible truth was that it would cause Europe to hemorrhage and leave the world impoverished as a result.[72] From this perspective, the war reflected a failure of European diplomacy *in toto*. In fact, it was a crime, "a monstrous attack on human civilization."[73]

---

[66] Velásquez, "Venezuela y la primera guerra mundial," p. 31.

[67] "A França, 44 annos depois de Sedan, intenta a sua revenge," in: *O Imparcial* (August 3, 1914), p. 1. Yañez, "La Guerra Europea," pp. 441–8.

[68] Alberto de Carvalho, "A miragem dos imperios," in: *A Epoca* (August 4, 1914), p. 1. "As grandes causas da guerra," in: *Jornal do Commercio* (August 6, 1914), p. 3. Barés, "Delenda Germaniae," pp. 227 and 38–53. Barroetaveña, *Alemania contra el mundo*, p. 5.

[69] Bertrán, "La conflagración europea," p. 87. "A victoria da Triplice Alliança?," in: *Jornal do Commercio* (August 2, 1914) p. 17. "El secreto de las relaciones exteriores," in: *La Vanguardia* (August 24/25, 1914), p. 1. Even Malthus' ideas on the population problem were raised in this context: Bonet, "Malthus y la guerra," pp. 51 and 58.

[70] Amarrete, "El libro gris."

[71] Montoro, "Las causas de la guerra," p. 147. "Alemania y la guerra," in: *La Nación* (B.A., September 19, 1914), p. 5.

[72] "La culpa de la guerra," in: *El Día* (August 5, 1914), p. 3.

[73] "Las terribles consecuencias de la guerra en el porvenir," in: *La Crónica* (September 13, 1914), p. 6. This is also unmistakable in the commentary in "La gran desgracia," in: *El Economista Paraguayo* (August 8, 1914), p. 1. For the critical reactions, see also Bonow on example of the press in Porto Alegre (*A desconfiança*, p. 83) and Garambone for Rio de Janeiro (*A primeira Guerra Mundial*, pp. 57–75).

Not only the bourgeois, but also the labor press dealt intensively with
the outbreak of the war in Europe. In Argentina, the Socialist Party newspaper *La Vanguardia* wrote of a foreseeable event, which could also be
felt in the Americas because the massive development of communications
and diverse relations had made it possible for a close and permanent contact to emerge between the Old and the New Worlds. All the same, the
paper further noted, the dimensions of the eruption went well beyond
what anyone could have imagined.[74]

Anarchist journalist Antonio de Pío Araujo from Mexico shared this
opinion, but was nonetheless able to see a silver lining in the conflict. This
was because the "war of races and religions," which merely concerned
the competing interests of the bourgeoisie and capital, would sooner or
later transform into a war of united laborers against their oppressors.
He believed that the great world revolution was close at hand.[75] Flores
Magón was even more enthusiastic, writing: "Long live the war! May the
war continue! May the entire globe become a battleground!"[76] This conflagration, he further remarked, would cause capitalism to devour itself.
Certainly, he was disappointed by the nationalist fervor of the masses,
but he trusted in the power of mobilized workers who would need to ensure that this was the final capitalistic war:

> If this conflict fails to bring about the death of the right to property, the eradica-
> tion of the principle of authority, and the extinction of religion in the conscience
> of mankind, then we will have to accept the fact that humanity has become so
> degenerate that it will still require hundreds of years before it experiences a
> renewal.[77]

Even though anarchism never represented a majority opinion inside the
Latin American labor movement, the words of Flores Magón were nonetheless entirely part of the *zeitgeist* to the extent that the global dimension
of the war figured prominently in commentaries and debates from the
outset. The centrality of the war was summed up as early as August 2,
1914, by the columnist of *La Nación*, who described the events in Europe
as a "drama of all mankind" in which there could be no spectators.[78] Even

---

[74] "Dura lección," in: *La Vanguardia* (August 6, 1914), p. 1.
[75] Antonio de Pío Araujo, "La catástrofe mundial," in: *Regeneración* (August 22,
1914), p. 1.
[76] Flores Magón, "La crisis mundial," in: *Regeneración* (September 29, 1914), p. 1.
[77] Ricardo Flores Magón, "La Gran Guerra Europea," in: *Regeneración* (August 8,
1914), p. 1.
[78] "Ecos del día: La catástrofe," in: *La Nación* (B. A., August 2, 1914), p. 1.

at this early stage, there was talk about how the war was not European, but universal, for it severed all ties between people.[79] This aspect was even more evident 1917 when Latin American countries began to enter the war. Whereas the Europeans previously did not see the value of having weaker states participate in their disputes, or even arrogantly rejected it, they were now confronted with a truly international conflict that involved all countries (see Figure 5.5).[80] Ricardo Rojas spoke of a "civil war of mankind" that had indeed begun as a local matter, but then quickly took on a global dimension that had universal ramifications.[81]

For Rojas' countryman Juan P. Ramos, the war was about nothing less than the whole of humanity: "The victory of one side or the other may bring with it fundamental changes in the political organization of nations and especially in the inner life of all constituted societies."[82] All nations of the earth were closely intertwined, so even if only five states took up arms against each other, as in August 1914, the world would still be shaken in its economic foundations. "The same can also occur tomorrow to the moral order, the political order [and] the spiritual order."[83] The Argentine socialists made a similar observation when they connected the serious crisis in the subcontinent to a plight concerning "the entire civilized world," even the remotest regions. *La Vanguardia* further remarked that the war appeared to have expanded geographically and was now even felt in Asia and Africa.[84] Spanish-Mexican poet Amado Nervo thus observed that the human race needed to realize that nations could no longer isolate themselves.[85]

These comments alluded to the reality of the grave social and economic dislocations that the war had unleashed all over Latin America. The sense of one's personal dismay and one's own direct involvement in world events was palpable because the consequences of the war had become an all-too painful reality. Observers were unanimous that 1914 was generally a bad year for humanity – indeed, an unparalleled

---

[79] "Chronica," in: *Revista da Semana* (August 8, 1914), p. 5.

[80] Cornejo, *La intervención del Perú*, p. 42.

[81] Rojas, *La guerra de las naciones*, pp. 66–7. See also "A conflagração europea," in: *A Epoca* (August 4, 1914), p. 1.

[82] Ramos, "Alemania ante la guerra," p. 442.

[83] Ibid. See also Fernández Güel, *Plus Ultra*, pp. 5–7. Eduardo Navarro Salvador, "Fuerzas y alianzas," in: *El Demócrata* (Mexico, October 17, 1914), p. 3.

[84] "Dura lección," in: *La Vanguardia* (B. A., August 6, 1914), p. 1. See also Antonio de Pío Araujo, "La catástrofe mundial," in: *Regeneración* (Mexico, August 22, 1914), p. 1.

[85] Amado Nervo, "Ante la catástrofe," in: *La Nación* (B. A., October 6, 1914), p. 5.

FIGURE 5.5 The world on the brink. Famine and pestilence looked forward to feasting on the entire planet, prepared for them by the god of war.
Source: "A beira do abysmo," in: *Careta* (August 15, 1914).

catastrophe originating on European soil had upset the whole world.[86] Many columnists thus contemplated just how long the war could last. As in Europe, there was an initial hope for a quick end following a decisive battle.[87] However, in mid-August 1914, there was already widespread speculation that it could have a longer duration, as war in the twentieth century appeared to have an utterly different form. By the beginning of 1915, speculation had nearly transformed into outright certainty.[88] The longer the war went on, the more disappointment and frustration took hold in response to the numerous failed peace initiatives (see Figure 5.6). After a year of war, the columnist of the Brazilian pro-ally *Correio da Manhã* made an urgent appeal to all combatants to finally make peace.[89]

This assessment was particularly ominous, because the media thought it could identify a clear pattern of global violence, which was first witnessed in Latin America in 1910 with the outbreak of the Mexican Revolution and had now grown into an "immense horror" because of the war in Europe. "The human beast," Ramos wrote, "claims its forgotten rights, and, angrily and pridefully, towers above the colossal pyramid of bodies from the battlefields."[90] This richly evocative, expressionistic language could be found in many newspaper commentaries, which further claimed to recognize the demise of all moral values, indeed a "Dantean inferno":

People are killing each other, on all the seas and in all the lands; millions of soldiers are simply out to kill or be killed; it's raining fire and steel; huge battle cruisers are sinking; cities are burning and fields are being destroyed; everywhere there is murder, immolation, plunder, violence; the only law calls for destruction and death; mankind has stepped aside for the lecherous and savage gorilla.[91]

The relapse into barbarism was especially disturbing in view of the progress that had already been achieved (see Figure 5.7). According to Nervo, "The horror and the atrocities of the war of today [surpassed] all notions

---

[86] "O anno que passa," in: *Correio da Manhã* (R.d.J., January 1, 1915), p. 1. "El nuevo año," in: *Zig-Zag* (January 2, 1915).

[87] "Triple Alianza y Triple Entente," in: *La Nación* (B. A., August 3, 1914), p. 4.

[88] "La duración de la guerra," in: *La Nación* (B. A., August 16, 1914), p. 5. "La duración de la guerra," in: Ibid. (January 21, 1915), p. 7.

[89] "Paz!," in: *Correio da Manhã* (August 1, 1915), p. 1.

[90] Ramos, "Alemania ante la guerra," p. 426. See also "La guerra," in: *Variedades* (September 19, 1914).

[91] "La Guerra," in: *Nosotros* 8 (August 1914), p. 118.

FIGURE 5.6 The endless war. While cartoonists in 1915 saw the theater of war moving in the direction of peace, if only at a snail's pace, the outlook in 1917 was far gloomier, as the god of war continued to lash out at the whole world in vengeance. *Sources* (left to right): "A paso de tortuga," in: *Caras y Caretas* (January 16, 1915) and "Esfuerzo de Marte," in: Ibid. (August 11, 1917).

FIGURE 5.6 (*continued*)

(Dibujo de Moraima)

¡Al primer tapón... zurrapas!

FIGURE 5.7 Barbaric Europe. From the perspective of the Chilean cartoonist, Europe had quickly shed its cloak of civilization and now showed its true barbaric face.

Source: Moraima, "Europa y la civilización," in: *Zig-Zag* (September 29, 1914).

of barbarism."[92] For Nervo and other Latin American intellectuals, it was particularly frightening to see that men of letters did not shun the violence. In fact, many were voluntarily and enthusiastically pulled into the trenches. Their deaths, however, also meant the loss of an intellectual elite.[93] Showing less elitism, the socialists argued:

[E]normous masses ... clash in these moments to sow death into Europe's soil and destroy it. The youth of the nations is being ground into a powder in the war. ... Many months or years, which will seem like centuries to us, the work of millions of men will be interrupted, replacing it with calculated savagery and the academic cruelty of technologies of destruction.[94]

"THE HOUR OF AMERICA"

What conclusions did Latin America draw from these distressing events? After all, many still considered Europe the center of civilization and a guiding force. A survey by *Nosotros* demonstrated this when it asked intellectuals in Latin America in October 1914 about the effects of war for humanity and for Latin America in particular.[95] This civilization, founded on reason and materialism, appeared to be moving rapidly toward its own extermination. This was in fact a *topos* borrowed from the discourse in Europe, where intellectuals had voiced a similar complaint before the war.[96] But what conclusions might be drawn from it? Was this "the hour of America" that Angel Falcó praised in his poems?[97]

New was the bluntness of the engagement with Europe, Latin America's formerly idealized model during its period of state emergence following independence. Journalists now openly discussed the barbarization of the Old World. The England correspondent of *Jornal do Commercio* reported on the nightly blackouts in London, which reinforced the signs of disintegration and left a deep impression on the psyche of the nation.[98] According to the commentators, the civilization in a supposedly highly cultivated Europe was bankrupt. The most complicated and modern

---

[92] Amado Nervo, "Ante la catástrofe," in: *La Nación* (October 6, 1914), p. 5.
[93] E. Gómez Carillo, "La vida trágica," in: *La Nación* (December 24, 1914), p. 5. "La literatura después de la guerra," in: *La Prensa* (B. A., November 18, 1915), p. 5.
[94] "¡La guerra!," in: *La Vanguardia* (August 2, 1914), p. 1. See also Geli, "Representations of the Great War," p. 204.
[95] "Nuestra tercera encuesta," in: *Nosotros* 8 (October 1914), p. 164. See also Compagnon, *L'adieu à L'Europe*, p. 203.
[96] Rojas, *La guerra de las naciones*, pp. 289–90.
[97] Falcó, *Troquel de fuego*, pp. 261–72.
[98] "As finanças da Guerra," in: *Jornal do Commercio* (November 26, 1914), p. 2.

technology was now being used to kill with greater efficiency and to serve the self-enrichment of unscrupulous economic elites.[99] Ingenieros wrote in September 1914: "Old feudal Europe has chosen to die like all desperate souls: by committing suicide."[100]

Of course, criticism of Europe was raised even before the outbreak of war.[101] By August 1914, however, the furor about the betrayal of civilization, of which Latin America clearly considered itself a part, came to a head. In particular, the failure of the jointly codified regulations of warfare, the countless war crimes, and the disregard for the treaties bitterly offended many commentators, who further emphasized Latin America's contribution to these civilizational achievements. Occasionally, disillusionment turned into compassion. Europe appeared as a lamentable "old continent," which was being set back centuries on its progressive march and brought to ruin.[102] It was in this vein that Ariyaga and Firtuoso eloquently wrote: "Barbarism grows. Civilization weeps. The instinct of the beast triumphs."[103] This quote expresses the dismay over having lost Europe as a cultural reference point, a status it had held for Latin American intellectual elites for some time (see Figure 5.8).[104]

At the same time, however, the columnists also did not hide their scorn. According to Brazilian historian and geographer Basílio de Magalhães, where his country was still in puberty, Europe had already reached menopause.[105] The Mexican newspaper *El Demócrata* ironically noted the arrogance of the Europeans toward Latin America and diagnosed its own region's "underdevelopment." When it came to militarism and brutality, the Old World stood head and shoulders above the rest, while the extent of the bloodshed in its own civil war paled in comparison. "Thank God," wrote the columnist, "we're not as developed here as the Europeans."[106] His colleague from *El Diario del Hogar* observed that

---

[99] "La guerra," in: *Variedades* (September 19, 1914). Melgar, *La bancarrota de una civilización*, p. 11 Lugones, *Mi beligerancia*, p. 10. For a critique of the unscrupulous elites, see also Compagnon, *L'adieu à l'Europe*, pp. 188–90.

[100] Ingenieros, *Los tiempos nuevos*, p. 15. See also Taborda, *Escritos políticos*, p. 4.

[101] Devés Valdés, *El Pensamiento latinoamericano*, pp. 44–5.

[102] "A victoria da Triplice Alliança?," in: *Jornal do Commercio* (August 2, 1914) p. 17. "La pobre Europa," in: *Zig-Zag* (August 8, 1914).

[103] Ariyaga/Firtuoso, *La guerra europea*, p. 2.

[104] Funes, *Salvar la nación*, p. 26.

[105] Skidmore, *Black into White*, pp. 165–6.

[106] "La guerra de Europa y nuestra revolución," in: *El Demócrata* (September 25, 1914), p. 2. See also Chavez, "L'opinion publique mexicaine," p. 111.

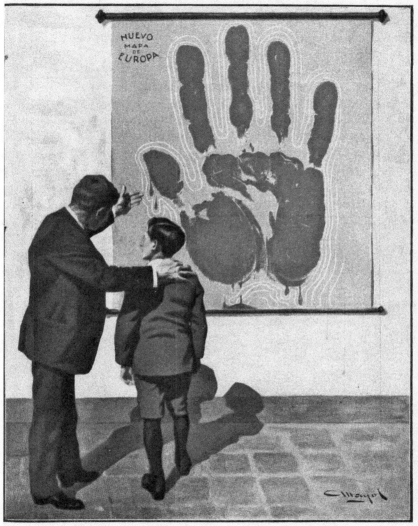

OCTUBRE
17
1914.

CARAS Y CARETAS

AÑO XVII.
NUM.
837.

LA NUEVA GEOGRAFIA

— ¿Por qué ha cambiado de ese modo el mapa de Europa?
— Esa es una de las reformas que impone la civilización.

FIGURE 5.8 The bloody map of Europe. When the student asks why the new map of Europa now looks like this, the teacher replies that civilization demands it.
Source: "La nueva geografía," in: *Caras y Caretas* (October 17, 1914).

although old Europe had always deemed Mexico barbaric, it was now fighting a much bloodier battle for far pettier motives. A war incited by the greed and envy of diplomats and aristocrats was being fought in the name of civilization. At home, at least, the focus continued to be on social reform and social equality.[107] Lugones argued along similar lines and concluded already in the face of the European crisis in July 1914, shortly before the war broke out: "We are ourselves entirely the masters of our fate.... The New World has a new civilization as its foundation and it is already fully under way."[108]

In fact, countless observers agreed that the future of civilization now lay in the Americas. "The free, robust Americas will be the refuge of European civilization. Europe itself does not offer a safe haven any longer," wrote Argentine Jaime Brull in an early 1915 edition of *Caras y Caretas*.[109] After the European purgatory, this civilization would be revived across the Atlantic like the phoenix from the ashes and the Americas would shine forth as a beacon like "Mount Ararat."[110] In his speech before the senate on May 31, 1917, Rui Barbosa argued that Europe had ceased to be the instructor. Now the Americas had to defend the values of civilization, because "America does not just belong to the Americans. America belong to humanity."[111] For the columnist of Uruguay's *La Razón*, whose writing was also marked by the enthusiasm surrounding the entry of American states into the war, the continent had in fact already asserted its calling and was now the model for future mankind.[112] Even the decidedly Ally-friendly Argentine poet Pedro Bonifacio Palacios, aka Almafuerte, admitted that civilization was

---

[107] "Historia de la actual guerra en Europa," in: *El Diario del Hogar* (Mexico, October 7, 1914), p. 2.

[108] Lugones, "La viga en el ojo (Paris, July 1914)," in: *La Nación* (B. A., August 10, 1914), p. 3.

[109] Brull, "La ansiedad del mundo."

[110] "America, Ararat as civilisação," in: *A Epoca* (September 9, 1914), p. 1. The metaphor of the "city upon a hill" can already be found in Julio Picquet, "Unatormentamortifera," in: *La Nación* (B. A., August 5, 1914), p. 5. See also Morató, *América del Sur*, p. 92. On the phoenix metaphor, see Velásquez, "Venezuela y la primera guerra mundial," p. 31. See also "La neutralidad americana," in: *Diario de Centro-América* (August 25, 1914), p. 1. "Interesante entrevista con don Alejandro Álvarez," in: *Zig-Zag* (February 20, 1915). Lugones, *Mi beligerancia*, p. 161. Ugarte, *La patria grande*, p. 118.

[111] Barbosa/Moacyr, A Revogação da neutralidade, p. 103. See also "América en marcha," in: *La Razón* (April 17, 1917), p. 3.

[112] "América en marcha," in: *La Razón* (April 17, 1917), p. 3.

no longer tied to a particular country or continent, but had to involve "the civilization of mankind."[113]

The war, Bunge wrote in his response to the *Nosotros* survey, offered a unique opportunity to break free from dependence on the Europeans and to destroy the power of foreign monopolies.[114] Mexicans shared this viewpoint,[115] as did Chilean officer Ernesto Medina, who anticipated that there would be many European emigrants after the war who could help Latin America advance.[116] Overall, the published opinions testified to a confidence about the future of one's own country, when it would gain prestige at the expense of the Europeans and assert itself in the circle of the "civilized" powers (see Figure 5.9).[117] Medina's compatriot, the international law expert Álvarez, was certain that all of the states in the Americas would increase in importance if they oriented themselves toward the achievements of civilization and restored the old values after the war.[118] Argentine educator and university reformer Saúl Taborda declared:

Europe has failed. It can now no longer lead the world. The Americas, which understand its developmental process as well as the reasons for its failure, can and must kindle the sacred fire of civilization with the lessons of history.[119]

Observers were in agreement, however, that the future looked bleak for Europe. Bunge was particularly discerning in his assessment, writing that the war raised much bigger problems for the Europeans than the individual countries could solve. The enormous costs of the devastation and warfare, in his opinion, would spell the end of classical liberal capitalism and bring about Europe's impoverishment. In general, it was predicted that the working class would ascend politically and that the state would strengthen its power.[120] Often prognoses also spoke of the fall of European dynasties and of social revolutions. While all of these predictions, of course, entailed great upheavals, they also ultimately implied

[113] Almafuerte, *Almafuerte y la guerra*, p. 5.
[114] "Nuestra tercera encuesta," in: *Nosotros* 8 (October 1914), p. 144. See also the commentary from zoologist Clemente Onelli, ibid., p. 169.
[115] "Horizontes abiertos," in: *El Demócrata* (Mexico, April 4, 1917), p. 3.
[116] "El conflicto europeo," in: *Zig-Zag* (August 8, 1914).
[117] This is the conclusion of the survey: "Nuestra tercera encuesta," in: *Nosotros* 8 (October 1914), p 161.
[118] "Interesante entrevista con don Alejandro Álvarez," in: *Zig-Zag* (February 20, 1915).
[119] Taborda, *Escritos políticos*, p. 97.
[120] "Nuestra tercera encuesta," in: *Nosotros* 8 (October 1914), pp. 140–2.

FIGURE 5.9 Europe's death, the Americas' life. In the confrontation with Europe, a spotlight was put on the contrast between life and death, fertility and destruction, youth and age. Vitality and civilization, symbolized here by the bees, are looking for a new start in the Americas.

Source: José Foradori, "Mors tua, vita mea," in: *Zig-Zag* (October 24, 1914).

that there would be more freedom.[121] This freedom was something that new social actors in Latin America also wanted to fight for.

As a result of its murderous conduct, the Old World soon lost its exemplary status in Latin America. Deeply ingrained was the shock at the scope and global dimension of the violence, the attack on a common civilization and Europe's demise, the revolutionary potential fueled by the war, and, finally, the sense of outrage that the Europeans had let things get so out of hand. On the other hand, the diverse reactions also demonstrated how embedded Latin American observers were in European discursive patterns. In the minds of Latin Americans, the world war was a singular, sensational event whose underlying tragedy could not be escaped. The catastrophe had a profound significance for Latin America and for the

[121] "La guerra," in: *Nosotros* 8 (August 1914), p. 118. "Nuestra tercera encuesta," in: Ibid, p. 159. Bertrán, "La conflagración europea," p. 91. Lavaerd, "Después de la guerra," p. 445.

whole world, with which there was greater sense of connection than ever before due to the war. Progress and peace turned into ruin and death. At the same time, America was able to rise as the new beacon of civilization. The repercussions of the war, which were already felt with full force in the region in the beginning August 1914, showed unequivocally that Latin America would face new challenges that would significantly affect the future.

6

Nation and Trans-nation

According to the perceptions of many intellectuals and journalists, the center and the yardstick of civilization had shifted to the Americas due to the war. They were of the opinion that it was not enough to merely preserve the prewar European values and norms, but that fundamental change was needed. The *topos* of international equality, which had been in circulation before the war, and that of the self-determination of peoples, which Lenin and Wilson had helped spread globally since 1917, ignited a lively discussion in Latin America about the future. In 1918, the Peruvian Cornejo put in a nutshell the expectation that accompanied the debate: "By entering the war, the South American states [would] gain the price of admission to world politics."[1] But what did this mean for a nation and its citizens? What role should and could the continent now play in the global context?

THE RISE OF NATIONALISM

When Flores Magón addressed the positive effects of the Russian February Revolution in March 1917, he referred in the first place to the downfall of nationalism, which the masses had become disgusted with after the many years of war. Flags, the anarchist argued, would soon be found only in museums as souvenirs of barbarism.[2] Flores Magón, however, would prove mistaken. Significantly more accurate was the prognosis from Augusto Bunge three years earlier when responding to a

---

[1] Cornejo, *La intervención del Perú*, p. 42.
[2] Ricardo Flores Magón, "El suicidio," in: *Regeneración* (March 24, 1917), p. 2.

survey from *Nosotros* on the effects of the First World War for humanity and for Latin America in particular. According to Bunge, the war had unleased the genie of nationalism from its bottle, which was stronger than all of the spirits together in *Thousand and One Nights*. Taming this spirit, he asserted, would be a nearly impossible task.[3] Indeed, the rise of nationalism had made such an impression on the members of the U.S. Creel Committee in 1918 that they reported: "The South American today demands as his natural right what he would have hesitated to request as a special favor five years ago."[4] Undoubtedly, as Latin American observers noted, the war had boosted nationalism everywhere.[5]

Certainly, the pursuit of a strong nation was centrally important, just as national power seemed to increase as a result of the war. Especially common among countries participating in the war such as Brazil was the belief that the war was bringing forth a new generation of "energetic men and noble women" poised to lead the country to a better future.[6] At the same time, in neutral Argentina, José Ingenieros suggested in a series of articles for *Caras y Caretas* in 1914 that it was possible to draw lessons from the war. He recommended that his nation reflect on its "own values" in order to overcome a decades-long moral crisis. Toward that end, a well-contemplated and deliberate commitment to one's own nation was in no way to be confused with xenophobia. Instead, Ingenieros averred, it emphasized the spirit of sacrifice for the commonweal.[7]

The guarantor of this positive development was a strong state. Military officers and politicians called for defending against the encroachments on national sovereignty that had become ever-more frequent over the course of the war, as well as for a new policy of independence from foreign powers.[8] While demands like these were in the air before the war, now decidedly nationalistic parties were being founded in countries like Chile (1913) and Peru (1915). The discussion, moreover, included the appeal for government intervention in socially relevant issues, for, in the view of many contemporaries, laissez-faire capitalism had become outdated.

[3] "Nuestra tercera encuesta," in: *Nosotros* 8 (October 1914), p. 142.
[4] "South America and the War" (1918), NA, RG 63, Entry 132, Box 4, 1.
[5] García Calderón, *Ideologias*, p. 350.
[6] "A geração nova," in: *Revista da Semana* (January 19, 1918).
[7] Ingenieros, "Patria y cultura" and "El nuevo nacionalismo."
[8] Arturo Alessandri, "Defendamos nuestra soberanía," in: *La Nación* (February 26, 1917), p. 3. "Defensa de la economía nacional," in: *La Prensa* (B. A., February 2, 1917), p. 6. More than a decade after the war, the captain and instructor at the Escuela Superior de Guerra, Juan Perón, drew similar lessons from the war: Perón, *Guerra Mundial 1914*, p. 103.

Costa Rican president Alfredo González, for instance, made such a statement in his annual address from 1916.[9]

Participants in this public debate concurred that the only way a nation could achieve a basis for the expected or already existing strength was to be true to itself. Just what this was supposed to mean, however, in the immigrant countries of South America or other ethnically heterogeneous societies remained unclear. Answers to this question were provided in some of the recognized classics of the national literature on authenticity that appeared during the war years. For example, Ricardo Rojas published his manifesto *La Argentinidad* on the occasion of Argentina's centenary celebration of national independence in 1916. Here, Rojas appealed to Argentina's heroic history and to the "collective memory." By the same token, Rojas explained that Argentine nationalism was still evolving.[10] This view was shared by his compatriot Lugones, who was also responsible for some of the seminal works of this genre during the war years.[11] In Brazil, on the other hand, physician and intellectual Afrânio Peixoto insisted on a national identity for all Brazilians in his 1916 classic *Minha terra e minha gente* (*My Country and My People*). Unlike his intellectual predecessors, Peixoto and his comrades at *Revista do Brasil* did not accept that the country was doomed to backwardness because of its climate and racial makeup. On the contrary, they recognized its potential to evolve.[12] Similar arguments were made by leading voices in other countries, such as Mexican Alfonso Reyes, who had published his work *Visión de Anáhuac* in 1917 while in exile in Spain. Ultimately, the concern was with how individual interests could be subordinated to the national ideal.[13]

The debates continued to be influenced by the European discourse on race, especially in the immigration countries. For instance, according to Ingenieros, the European members were still the basis of the "Argentine race" – even though the circumstances on the ground had led to the formation of national peculiarities.[14] Examples of the pride in the *raza*

---

[9] Alfredo González, "Mensaje del Presidente" (San José, May 1, 1916), in: Meléndez Chaverri, *Mensajes presidenciales* Vol. 4, p. 260.

[10] Rojas, *La argentinidad*, p. 2. See also Rojas, *La guerra de las naciones*, pp. 87 and 91.

[11] For Lugones' observations on the nation, see Funes, *Salvar la nación*, pp. 85–8.

[12] Skidmore, *Black into White*, pp. 169–70. Bonow, *A desconfiança*, pp. 187–95. See also the reflections of Monteiro Lobato, *Críticas*, p. 231.

[13] Cornejo, *La solidaridad americana*, p. 12. For the overall context: Miller, *Reinventing Modernity in Latin America*.

[14] Ingenieros, "La formación de una raza argentina," p. 464. Jacques Petiot, "Del Brasil," in: *La Nación* (B. A., October 1, 1914), p. 5. Ecuadorian Gabriel Villagómez saw the war in a traditional manner as an opportunity to attract "good immigrants" from Europe.

that resonated among the Argentineans could equally be found in Chile or Brazil.[15] The sentiment was combined with the typical contemporary racist feeling of superiority vis-a-vis supposedly "inferior" peoples such as the Asians.[16] It also gave way to demands for sealing off the border to supposedly "useless" immigration, which commentators in Argentina, for instance, ascribed to war invalids, Africans, Chinese, and Indians.[17] On the other hand, the world war also stimulated the discussion on the so-called race question, as, for example, in Brazil, where intellectuals like Elysio de Carvalho and Álvaro Bomilcar called for recognizing nationality as directly linked to ethnic heterogeneity.[18]

However, just who was ultimately able to claim this nationality and, consequently, receive citizenship remained very much in dispute during the war years. In the warring nations of Latin America, nationalization measures directed against the ethnic German population proved effective. Even neutral governments made efforts to promote the nationalization of the education sector and prohibited the exclusive use of foreign languages in immigrant schools. In general, the improvement of education was considered a key factor for the formation of a national consciousness. Peixoto, for example, who personally looked to "Greco-Latin culture" and "Lusitanian traditions," saw a better education system as critical for fostering the Brazilian identity.[19] Another highly touted "school of the nation" was the military. The demand to introduce or implement conscription was high on the agenda, for instance, in Brazil and Cuba. The issue at hand was not simply defense against external enemies, but first and foremost the stabilization of the nation.[20]

In Latin America – as in many other parts of the world, especially in Europe – the world war encouraged radical right-wing nationalist thinking, which became especially widespread in the military. Officer Kinkelin, for example, adopted the militaristic, anti-Semitic, and racist ideology of the German right during the war. He subsequently brought it back with

Gabriel Villagómez, "La inmigración en el Ecuador," in: *El Comercio* (Quito, November 11, 1914), p. 2.

[15] Gallardo, "Posición internacional de Chile," p. X. Lima, *Na Argentina*, pp. 24–43.

[16] "O perigo amarello," in: *O Imparcial* (March 13, 1917), p. 2.

[17] Morató, *América del Sur*, pp. 62–7. Funes, *Salvar la nación*, pp. 193–5.

[18] Compagnon, *L'adieu à l'Europe*, pp. 254–5.

[19] Peixoto, *Minha Terra*, pp. 228–30. See also Woodard, *A Place in Politics*, pp. 74–5.

[20] "Editorial," in: *A Defeza Nacional* (September 10, 1914), pp. 1–3. A. Amaral, "O problema da defesa," in: *Correio da Manhã* (June 2, 1916), p. 1. See also Woodard, *A Place in Politics*, pp. 76–7. Bonow, *A desconfiança*, p. 157. Skidmore, *Black into White*, pp. 152–5.

him to his native Argentina, where he carved out a career as a military advisor with the Legion Cívica Argentina (Civil Argentine Legion) and became Uriburu's right hand after the military coup of 1930.[21] In these circles, war was thought to be an adequate means of regeneration and the military an internally oriented protector of the nation. These were decisive steps for the military's new, active role in politics.[22]

Besides the population, the economy was considered a sector that urgently needed to be nationalized. Throughout Latin America, those in charge were frustrated about the dependence on foreign trade, which turned out to be fatal when catastrophe hit in 1914, exposing the nations' impotence. Politicians called for government intervention in the economy for the development of native resources, with priority to be given to the domestic population.[23] Related demands were aired within a matter of days after the outbreak of war. Hence, the editorial of *La Prensa* from August 5, 1914, commented:

The economic solidarity of the world has been destroyed. Each market is withdrawing into itself, where it confronts and determines its own destiny and ignores the others, without following any other criteria than the basic demands of its own survival.... Today, we must share the motto of the great financial powers: Every man for himself![24]

Taborda called on all Latin Americans to make good on their independence once and for all by overcoming Europe's commercial dominance.[25] Emancipation from foreign rule was the watchword of the day.[26] The Latin Americans who took part in these debates did so in the knowledge that the continent had access to resources from which it could profit. It became quickly apparent that the European superpowers could continue their war only with raw materials from Latin America.[27] The export boom, which began for many countries of the region in 1915, engendered self-confidence and urged the better exploitation of relative strengths (Figure 6.1). The generous concessions granted to foreigners were to be

[21] Lorenz, "La gran guerra," pp. 59–61.
[22] Compagnon, *L'adieu à l'Europe*, pp. 260–7.
[23] Albert, *South America and the First World War*, pp. 53–4. Compagnon, *L'adieu à l'Europe*, pp. 268–71.
[24] "Ruptura de la solidaridad económica," in: *La Prensa* (August 5, 1914).
[25] Taborda, *Escritos políticos*, pp. 7 and 9.
[26] Alfredo González, "Mensaje del Presidente" (San José, May 1, 1916), in: Meléndez Chaverri, *Mensajes presidenciales* Vol. 4, pp. 260–1.
[27] "Ante la realidad," in: *La Nación* (B. A., February 9, 1915), p. 7.

LA SOLUCION

Al ver su hacienda medrada
y su comercio quebrado,
su agricultura explotada
y su crédito agotado,
haciendo una gran gauchada
la crisis ha dominado.

FIGURE 6.1 Overcoming the crisis. Symbolizing Argentina, the cartoon shows a proud gaucho who has managed to overcome the economic crisis on his own. *Source*: Alonso, "La solución," in: *Caras y Caretas* (January 22, 1916).

critically examined in the future, while national citizens were to be given preference in the exploitation of natural resources.[28]

Although foreigners remained important because they brought capital into the country, it was thought that they needed to be more involved in the development of national production sites. Following the United States' lead, the neighbors to the south also wanted to take advantage of the war economy. In Brazil, for example, the idea of exploiting the existing iron ore to build up heavy industry there won its share of supporters.[29] For the development of domestic industries, the proponents of nationalization advocated above all those areas where, as in Argentina, Brazil, and Chile, attempts had already been made.[30] The Carranza government in Mexico was especially persistent in implementing economic nationalism. Here, the president's goal was to force foreign companies to pay higher taxes, to restrict their political influence, and to establish national sovereignty over natural resources. The constitution of Mexico contributed at least in theory to the realization of these objectives. The reverberations in Latin America showed commensurate enthusiasm.[31]

Finally, culture in the broadest sense was also touched by the nationalistic zeal. The establishment of the so-called Generation of 1915 (or the "Seven Sages") in Mexico underscores this, for example. An eye was cast on a glorious history, an endeavor the first national congress of historiand in Brazil in 1914 undertook professionally. It was allegedly possible to discover authentic musical and artistic forms of expression from the past such as in folklore.[32] The world war even inspired avant-garde circles to create new forms of unambiguously national art. The most famous example is without a doubt Brazilian painter Emiliano Augusto Cavalcanti de Albuquerque Melo, aka Di Cavalcanti, who aimed to establish an original Brazilian art free of European conventions. Di Cavalcanti described

---

[28] "La calma después de la tempestad," in: *La Prensa* (B. A., August 13, 1914), p. 5. José Ugarte, "Por un plato de lentejas ...," in: *El Nacional* (June 19, 1916), p. 3. The Argentine crude oil lobby welcomed these arguments. "La guerra europa y el petróleo," in: *Petróleo* (August 8, 1914), p. 1.

[29] Carvalho, *Brasil, potencia mundial*, pp. 5–8. Morató, *América del Sur*, pp. 62–7. On the role of foreigners, see "El capital extranjero," in: *La Prensa* (B. A., August 5, 1917), p. 4.

[30] "Defesa da produccao nacional," in: *Jornal do Commercio* (September 26, 1914), p. 9. Quesada, "El 'peligro alemán' en Sud América," p. 536. Silva Vildósola, *Le Chili et la guerre*, pp. 56–8.

[31] Katz, *The Secret War*, pp. 498–9.

[32] "Primeiro Congreso de Historia Nacional," in: *Jornal do Commercio* (September 17, 1914), p. 3. "Nuestra cuarta encuesta," in: *Nosotros* 12 (29/1918), pp. 537–9. See also *Revista de Filosofía*, published in Buenos Aires by José Ingenieros Compagnon, *L'adieu à l'Europe*, pp. 302–4. Devés Valdés, *El pensamiento latinoamericano*, Vol. 1, pp. 97–103.

in his autobiography the impact that the war, and especially the Bolshevik October Revolution, had on him and the young artists linked to him like Oswald de Andrade, Mário de Andrade, and Guilherme de Almeida. Four years after the war, these initiatives would culminate in the pioneering Semana da Arte Moderna (Modern Art Week) in São Paulo.[33] Other examples include Mexican muralism or the new poetry of Chilean Vicente Huidobro, who lived in Paris beginning in 1916.[34]

Another part of these currents was young Peruvian Alberto Hidalgo, who published his futurism-influenced *Arenga lírica al Emperador de Alemania* (*Lyrical Address to the Emperor of Germany*) in 1916. In this early work, Hidalgo blatantly opposed the majority opinion, which Senator Cornejo propagated in Peru more than anyone else.[35] His ceremonial address was a potentially scandalous work, for it included praise of the emperor that was, however, full of irony. At one point it is thus suggested that the "bard" wanted to go into "sinful Paris" victoriously, arm in arm with the monarch. In the first instance, though, the address was a typical futuristic praise of war, which destroyed the old and made way for youth to bring about a new beginning.[36]

STRIVING FOR PARTICIPATION

Everyone who participated in the social upheaval in Latin America during the last two years of the war demanded a new beginning or at least radical change. Ultimately, they were concerned with equality and participating in the national polity. The reactions were to the fundamental structural problems of Latin American societies, and yet the connection to the world war cannot be overlooked. Due to the public controversies about how to respond to the warring parties as well as the pros and cons of the war as such, the conflagration entered everyday life and the streets and public places. This was especially the case in Argentina and Brazil, and not just in the big cities such as Buenos Aires, Rio de Janeiro, or São Paulo, but also in the provinces.[37] Even in civil-war-plagued Mexico, the media merged the demand for an immediate end of the war with one for fundamental reforms that would give people equal rights.[38] Argentine

---

[33] Cavalcanti, *Viagem da minha vida*, pp. 83–4. See also Campos, *A construção da identidade nacional*, pp. 83–6. Compagnon, *L'adieu à l'Europe*, pp. 280–2.

[34] Ellis, "Vicente Huidobro y la Primera Guerra Mundial," pp. 334–7.

[35] Sánchez, "Alberto Hidalgo en la literatura peruana," p. 67.

[36] Hidalgo, *Arenga lírica*.

[37] On Argentina, see Tato, "La disputa por la argentinidad," p. 235.

[38] "Historia de la actual guerra en Europa," in: *El Diario del Hogar* (October 7, 1914), p. 2.

psychologist Aníbal Ponce summed up in hindsight the political mobilization that the war had unleashed:

> For us young chaps, who came of age in the midst of the horror of the European tragedy, the war was ... the great "liberator" in the broadest sense. All the things from our lives that lay before it were passive appropriations of childhood, obedient habits of upbringing; everything that followed it could only be the painful conquests of youth, the horror and enthusiasm of the new times. Thanks to the war we were immediately mistrustful of the past.... It lived amongst us – in our streets, our schools, our homes. It destroyed friendships, dissolved fixed bonds, flared tempers. How could anyone in the face of this storm that dragged us along with and forced us to take a stand not be affected?[39]

The students Ponce helped lead in 1918 considered themselves an engine of change. Hope for the engagement of young people, which Colombian Mejía Rodríguez expressed for instance, existed especially in pro-Ally circles.[40] In Argentina, the Comité de la Juventud was a powerful organization that advocated across the country for entering the war and was able to mobilize the masses in rural cities ranging from Rosario to Córdoba and Tucumán. According to Rojas, this was a sign of hope, as the new youth was the strength of the true Argentina, the "Argentinidad."[41] "You are the young workers of the new day," he wrote, "begin it like the young Hercules did when he strangled the snake. Finish it like the Titan, with his hard labor."[42] Socialist Palacios showed he was of a similar mind when he praised justice and morality in a speech to the Committee. These voices all appealed to idealism and moving away from the past, which meant away from imitating European civilization.[43] In his "Credo of the New Generation," Rojas wrote around the end of the war that a grand alliance needed to be formed to tackle social problems and the political chaos of the present. The old elites had shown their incompetence. Their time was up. By contrast, in the spirit of solidarity toward the workers and the poor, the new generation would enforce social reforms, without, however, degenerating into a class struggle.[44]

The Brazilian counterpart to the Argentinean Committee was Bilac's Liga da Defesa Nacional (National Defense League), whose agenda also

---

[39] Ponce, "El año 1918," p. 223. On the image of the call for action, see also Compagnon, *L'adieu à l'Europe*, p. 17.
[40] Mejía Rodríguez, *La France*, p. 21.
[41] Rojas, *La guerra de las naciones*, pp. 15 and 63–5.
[42] Ibid., p. 46.
[43] Palacios, *Prusianismo y democracia*, pp. 5–7. See also Lugones, *La convención patriótica*, p. 9. Deutsch, *Las derechas*, pp. 114–5.
[44] Rojas, *La guerra de las naciones*, pp. 254–311.

gained currency throughout the country. Spokesmen like Bilac were interested, on one hand, in toughening up the youth through military service. To prompt young men, he cited the manliness of the brave young Europeans in the world war. On the other hand, the nation was to be strengthened through the modernization of social structures.[45] The Liga Nacionalista (Nationalist League), established in 1916 in São Paulo by Júlio de Mesquita Filho, cofounder of the leading daily *O Estado*, pursued similar objectives. It, too, was concerned with fortifying the nation through patriotism and the struggle against leftist movements.[46]

The undeniably large mobilization successes of these groups yielded what Ponce called the side effect of politicization and developed a momentum of their own. They culminated in the student movement toward the end of the war that originated in Córdoba. In its initial stage around 1916, this movement centered on the reform of encrusted university structures. It combined the element of youth with the demand for political participation and the casting off of the remaining vestiges of colonialism. The students accordingly claimed the missionary task for themselves to influence and democratize society. Here, the leaders referred to the great catastrophe of the world war, which needed to be avoided in the future, and the October Revolution, which in their view promised a new course for mankind.[47]

The general student strike that began in Córdoba in late March 1918 quickly exploded into a national issue. Well-known intellectuals like Lugones, Ingenieros, Justo, Palacios, and Bunge voiced their solidarity. As Ingenieros, among others, opined, the youth who did not join the movement were old before their time. The manifesto from the movement in Córdoba "to the free people of South America" declared: "Youth is always on the way to heroism."[48] The students' leader, Deodoro Roca, explicitly spoke of a "generation of 1914" that was shaped by the war and whose job it was to fight for the future and the fate of the nation.[49] For his comrade-in-arms, Julio V. González, the Russian Revolution

---

[45] Bilac, *A defesa nacional*, pp. 24–7. Charge d'affaires to Dept. of State (R.d.J., April 5, 1917), NA, RG 59, M 367, Reel 36. For more on the context: Deutsch, *Las derechas*, pp. 146–7. Skidmore, *Black into White*, pp. 156–7.

[46] Deutsch, *Las derechas*, pp. 152–3.

[47] Funes, *Salvar la nación*, pp. 45–8.

[48] "La juventud argentina de Córdoba a los hombres libres de América," in: Cúneo, *La reforma universitaria*, p. 2. Ingenieros, "La reforma," pp. 221–2.

[49] Roca, "La nueva generación americana," pp. 146–9. See also "Orden del día del mitín de solidaridad en Buenos Aires, p. 10.

furthermore represented fertile soil for protest and symbolized a new beginning for all of Latin America.[50]

In Mexico, a student movement had fought since 1916 under the influence of the European war and U.S. imperialism for stronger relations between Latin Americans themselves and the preservation of neutrality. In early 1919, the trend caught on in neighboring countries such as Peru and Chile, soon influencing educated young people throughout the region. A continental consciousness developed against the backdrop of contacts established across Latin America. Figures who would later rise to fame, like Colombian Germán Arciniegas or Peruvians Víctor Raúl Haya de la Torre and Carlos Mariátegui, felt a strong connection to the movement.[51] In retrospect, Haya de la Torre remarked that the lessons of war and the betrayal of the ideals of freedom and equality had finally made the great transnational student movement possible.[52] In the final analysis, the movement had global aspirations. Haya de la Torre confidently wrote that the universities had been responsible for producing the great revolutionaries of his time, such as Lenin and Sun Yat-Sen.[53] Argentine Florentino Sanguinetti also observed in hindsight that the student strike and the workers' strike had complemented each other at a time when the whole world order had collapsed under the weight of the world war.[54] Ponce wrote: "For Latin America, nineteen hundred and eighteen is the birth year of revolutions."[55]

The emphasis on the proximity of the students' and workers' movements was not accidental, as both groups shared in the critique of capitalism, which had made the global catastrophe of war possible in the first place.[56] From its inception in the mid-nineteenth century, the labor movement had experienced rapid growth due to increasing immigration, even though it splintered ideologically into a number of distinct groups. The workers' movement derived its strength from its transnational connections.[57] As evidenced by the social unrest that culminated in 1917/18,

[50] González, "Significado de la reforma universitaria," in: Cuneo, *La reforma universitaria,* pp. 188–96.
[51] Ferrero, *Historia crítica,* pp. 14–17. Arciniegas, "La reforma universitaria," p. 218. See Robinet, "Students facing the Great War in Revolutionary Mexico."
[52] Haya de la Torre, "La reforma universitaria," p. 230.
[53] Ibid., p. 240.
[54] Sanguinetti, "Reforma y contrarreforma," p. 244.
[55] Ponce, "El año 1918," p. 224.
[56] Thus argued Bunge already in 1914: "Nuestra tercera encuesta," in: *Nosotros* 8 (October 1914), p. 144.
[57] Albert, *South America and the First World War,* p. 235. Spalding, *Organized Labour,* pp. 1–47. Alexander, International Labor Organizations, pp. 2–4.

it experienced a veritable "explosion" across Latin America during the war years.[58]

From the perspective of anarchists, the war presented quite a favorable environment. In Mexico, the well-connected Flores Magón brothers wanted to exploit the outbreak of war to ratchet up their propaganda efforts.[59] Unlike Flores Magón, the socialists did not welcome the war as the gateway to worldwide revolution, but instead lamented the countless victims among the workers. At the same time, they, too, recognized the possibility for mobilizing their followers better than ever before. The strikes, therefore, which only gained in strength up until the end of the war, also had political objectives.[60]

These developments were viewed in the United States with some concern. The U.S. government wanted to contain the radical anarchist movements. President Wilson thus welcomed the efforts of the pro-government union American Federation of Labor (AFL) under Samuel Gompers, who had been attempting to promote relations with the leader of the Mexican union Confederación Regional Obrera Mexicana (CROM), Luis Morones, since 1915. Under the heading of Pan-Americanism, Gompers wanted to expand the union's network with Latin American partners. In July 1916, Gompers turned to the workers' organizations of the Americas and urged them to establish a Pan-American Federation of Labor (PAFL) to strengthen the international profile of the working class. In early February 1917, a preliminary committee was founded, which, however, only included delegates from Puerto Rico and Mexico. On November 13, 1918, the inaugural meeting of the PAFL was convened in Laredo, Texas, with delegates from CROM and the AFL. It was not until 1919 that additional countries decided to join.[61]

These attempts toward Pan-American integration were clearly in the interests of U.S. foreign policy and ultimately they remained a peripheral matter. Nonetheless, they were an expression of the increasing transnationalization of the labor movement. This would become increasingly important following the war, as the creation of the International Labor Organization (ILO) in 1919 in the context of the League of Nations

---

[58] Spalding, *Organized Labour*, p. 48.

[59] Yankelevich, *La revolución mexicana en América Latina*, p. 14. Enrique Flores Magón, "Burlemos la ley," in: *Regeneración* (August 8, 1914), p. 3. Ricardo Flores Magón, "Leyendo el porvenir," in: ibid. (August 12, 1916), p. 1.

[60] "La grave situación," in: *La Vanguardia* (August 7, 1914), p. 1. "En homenaje a Jaurès," in: ibid. (August 8, 1914), p. 1. Del Valle, *La cuestión internacional*, p. 27.

[61] *Labor and the War*, p. 152. Andrews, *Shoulder to Shoulder?*, pp. 70–94. See also Alexander, *International Labor Organizations*, pp. 11–21.

shows. That said, the expectations raised by the worker protection pro-visions, which Latin America's governments signed off on, would go unfulfilled for many years.[62]

The labor movement developed a strong commitment to ending the war. As elsewhere, the political left and the church in Latin America were also the most heavily involved in pacifist activities.[63] For example, while the Argentine Catholics organized a pilgrimage to the national shrine in Luján in August 1914 to pray for world peace, *La Vanguardia* criticized that it was in the name of the same religion that Catholics in Europe were killing each other.[64] The socialist movements and parties saw themselves as the true pioneers in the struggle against the war.[65] In early 1917, Senator del Valle still set his hopes on the International to influence the workers in Europe and called for a continental assembly to enforce the principle of the peace-ful settlement of disputes.[66] In Brazil, the Confederação Operária Brasileira took an active antiwar stance and many socialist organizations joined the common peace congresses, culminating in the annual May Day rallies.[67]

But the hope that "the violence would become obsolete as a means of settling international disputes" would not be realized.[68] Not only did many observers in Brazil continue to ridicule the pacifist tendencies, believing that war was a "natural and inevitable fact."[69] The war even exposed the fragility of the movement within its own ranks. For instance, in the socialist organization Vorwärts, composed of German immigrants in Buenos Aires, there were mass resignations of the war-enthusiastic base. By October 1914, the group had only nineteen active members. Soon thereafter, the association's direction announced its loyalty to the German war effort and made its meeting house available for patriotic demonstrations. Subsequently, the association's membership started to rise again.[70] Many came to the conclusion that the struggle against the

---

[62] Rojas, *La guerra de las naciones*, p. 204. Andrews, *Shoulder to Shoulder?*, pp. 75 and 89. Spalding, *Organized Labour*, p. 73.

[63] Tato, "La disputa por la argentinidad," p. 229.

[64] "Por La paz europea," in: *La Vanguardia* (August 24/25, 1914), p. 1. "Religión de amor," in: ibid. (August 3/4, 1914), p. 1. For a critique of religion, see also Melgar, "El espíritu religioso," pp. 370–1. Nin Frías, "El cristianismo y la guerra," pp. 364–5.

[65] "El desastre de una guerra euopea," in: *La Vanguardia* (August 1, 1914), p. 1. "La República Argentina y la guerra," in: *La Nación* (B. A., February 10, 1916), p. 4. Bonow, *A desconfiança*, p. 116.

[66] Del Valle, *La cuestión internacional*, p. 57.

[67] Bandeira/Melo/Andrade, *O ano vermelho*, p. 37.

[68] "Dura lección," in: *La Vanguardia* (B. A., August 6, 1914), p. 1.

[69] "O progresso do pacifismo," in: *Jornal do Commercio* (September 13, 1914), p. 2.

[70] Newton, *German Buenos Aires*, p. 34. Bauer, *La Asociación Vorwärts*, p. 101.

war was ultimately a fool's errand, since the nationalistic fervor had utterly displaced the desire for peace.[71]

Not least, women were involved in the peace movement. This was attested in part by the success of Bertha von Suttner's novel *Lay Down Your Arms!* The Danish film version, released in Latin American cinemas shortly after the outbreak of the war, caused an uproar.[72] Against the backdrop of the war, the media debated the role of women in the nation more fervently than ever. For example, in his classic work of nation literature *Forjando Patria* from 1916, Mexican intellectual Manuel Gamio preferred the "feminine woman," whom he contrasted with the archaic "servile" or "masculinized feminist" woman.[73] Male authors offered clear guidelines for female behavior, especially in countries that had themselves entered the war like Brazil or Cuba. The Brazilian woman was thus to be a model of sacrifice in war and to fight for the ideals of justice and law through her words and righteousness.[74]

There were also practical requirements that women now had to fulfill as mothers of the family. Thrift, hard work, diligence, and a willingness to endure hardship and hunger – the male commentators expected each of these traits from the female half of the population in their contribution to the war.[75] As the war drew to a close, appeals became more frequent for women to marry and retreat into the home in order to contribute to the growth and the morale of the nation by educating as many children as possible.[76]

The women's movement was among the many groups who demanded equality and participation rights in the context of the war. The Chilean women's rights activist Elena Ivens spoke on behalf of many women when, in 1914, she fundamentally criticized the barbaric conflict conducted by men. The fact that a male-dominated judiciary had put suffragettes behind bars before the war because of their violent tendencies seemed absurd. According to Ivens, the inferiority hypothesis directed against women was no longer tenable in the face of the war, which, if anything, proved the moral superiority of women. The struggle for the political and civil rights of women thus appeared more legitimate than ever.[77]

[71] "A hora da guerra," in: *A Careta* (August 8, 1914).

[72] "Abaixo as armas!," in: *Jornal do Commercio* (September 21, 1914), p. 10.

[73] Gamio, *Forjando patria*, p. 129.

[74] Alcibiades Delamare Nogueira da Gama, "O papel da mulher brasileira na guerra," in: *Fon-Fon* (December 1, 1917).

[75] A. Getulio das Neves, "Appello ás mães de familia," in: *Fon-Fon* (January 26, 1918).

[76] Nieto, "La mujer después de la guerra," p. 55.

[77] Ivens, "¿Por qué luchan?"

In fact, the women's movement grew considerably during the war years. In Chile, the bourgeois women's movement launched in 1915 with the establishment of a Círculo de Lectura (Reading Circle) and a Club de Señoras (Women's Club). In Uruguay, in 1916, the Consejo Nacional de Mujeres (National Council of Women) was initiated, while in Argentina, where important women's organizations had existed before 1914, the level of activity clearly intensified during the war years.[78] Women's movements had already been organized before the war among the anarchists and socialists. Authors like Flores Magón, Chilean Emilio Recabarren, and Peruvian Manuel González Prada now stepped up their support. Feminist organizations that were mainly active in the countries of the southern Latin America received new impetus after the war when reforms were carried out to allow women's suffrage in countries like Germany and the United States.[79] The activists and their supporters thought and worked in this time period in transnational dimensions. Both their demands as well as their activities can only be understood against the backdrop of this networking that extended beyond the national framework.

TRANSNATIONAL IDENTITIES

The aspect of transnationalism had particular importance during the war years in the identity debate that Martí and Rodó had kicked off in Latin America around the year 1900. From 1914 onward, Latin American intellectuals scrutinized the European models with new vehemence in an ongoing exchange with each other. As historian Eduardo Devés Valdés has rightly pointed out, the disputed identity models tended to be oriented along cultural lines until 1914. After that, it was primarily social. The war and the Russian Revolution accelerated this change. Now, the center of interest shifted to the indigenous and *campesinos* (peasants) as sources of identity for one's own "race," "*nuestra raza*."[80] Conversely, the tendency to demarcate the "other" became more acute, while the anti-imperialism discourse was especially resonant.

During the war years, the reproach of imperialism was cheap. First, the pro-Ally voices made this criticism to stigmatize Germany and the

---

[78] Lavrin, *Women, Feminism, and Social Change*, pp. 286 and 328.
[79] "De EE.UU.," in: *La Unión* (Valparaíso, September 10, 1918), p. 1. "Nueva era," in: *Nosotros* 12 (115/1918), pp. 365–73. Devés Valdés, *El pensamiento latinoamericano*, Vol. 1, p. 63.
[80] Devés Valdés, *El pensamiento latinoamericano*, Vol. 1, pp. 97–103.

Habsburg Empire's fight against nationalities.[81] By the same token, due to the historical realities in Latin America and the anger at the British sea blockade, it was quickly extended to include the United States and Britain. The best-known voice in the chorus of those who accused the United States of imperialism was Manuel Ugarte. His fame rested on the lecture tours he gave throughout Latin America and in particular his stays in revolutionary Mexico, which the Argentine had undertaken since 1911. Ugarte was also one of the most well-known proponents of Argentina's neutrality, not, however, because he sympathized with the German Reich, but because he feared that the U.S. influence would rise in his country if it entered the war.[82]

Ugarte articulated his viewpoint in his speeches at the Teatro Ideal in Mexico in May 1917: The independence movements at the beginning of the nineteenth century did not result in the continent's economic and cultural autonomy. In this respect, Latin America was in his opinion still a colony. He sharply criticized the hypocritical stance of the United States, which had invaded the Dominican Republic in 1916. The alleged protectors of small nations, Ugarte argued, were in reality the biggest colonialists. Ugarte cited as methods of imperialism the sowing of discord, the encouragement of the accumulation of debt of weak states, and the demoralization and denationalization of countries through the spread of the dominant power's language and culture. By contrast, Ugarte contended that the weak could only find relief through solidarity and joint action.[83]

Many thinkers in the region, such as Peruvian Haya de la Torre, Chilean Gallardo, Argentines Alfredo Colmo and Pedro de Córdoba, Brazilian Fernando de Azevedo, and Venezuelan Rufino Blanco Fombona, concurred with Ugarte and published writings with a similar thrust.[84] In particular, the 1917 pamphlet *Ante los bárbaros* from Colombian writer José María Vargas Vila was widely distributed during these years. The Mexican newspaper *El Demócrata* even gave the pamphlet to its

---

[81] Rojas, *La guerra de las naciones*, p. 17.
[82] Ugarte, *La patria grande*, p. 101. Ugarte's attitude was even reported on in Ecuador, "Ugarte y la neutralidad," in: *La Verdad* (Guayaquil, December 22, 1917), p. 2. See also Díaz Araujo, *Yrigoyen y la Guerra*, p. 207.
[83] Ugarte, *La América Latina*, pp. 23–7.
[84] Hodge Dupré, "La defensa continental," pp. 141–5. Gallardo, "Posición internacional de Chile," p. LXIX. Colmo, *Mi neutralismo*, p. 44. Córdoba, *Nuestra guerra*, p. 3. Azevedo, "Illusão americana," p. 162. On Blanco: Charge d'affaires to Sec. of State (Tegucigalpa, July 16, 1916), NA, RG 59, 710.11/298.

readers as a loyalty bonus.[85] Vargas Vila accused not only the United States, which seemed to have as its motto "Finis Latinorum," but he also attacked the local elites for not resisting Washington's policy of conquest.[86] With the Russian Revolution, the anti-imperialist spirit won additional momentum. Of course, the attacks did not show the same intensity throughout the region, but rather had different gradations. For instance, the voices against U.S. imperialism in Brazil were far less numerous.[87] Nevertheless, there was an underlying fear throughout Latin America of a world-dominating imperialism that was also reflected in abundant cartoons (see Figure 6.2).

If anyone had reason to worry, it was above all the Mexicans, who had suffered two major military interventions on their territory at the hands of the United States in 1914 and 1916. Ugarte, who had traveled to Mexico in 1911, proved a great propagandist of the Mexican Revolution, which, in his opinion, was an unambiguous statement against U.S. imperialism. When Ugarte stopped again in Mexico in 1917 while on his Latin American tour, he explained that, following Europe's collapse, Mexico would necessarily become the new reference point for the Latin Americanist movement.[88] During the Pershing expedition, the Mexican press excelled in making anti-American statements. Thus, *El Demócrata* warned in June 1916 that there could be no real equality with the United States.[89] Journalist Gonzalo de la Parra, for his part, wrote in *El Nacional*: "The United States of the north, a people without a race, without anything autochthonous or distinctly its own, are a ridiculous imperialist country, for they always only suppress weak or small nations."[90]

Besides U.S.-type imperialism, colonialism per se was also under fire in Latin America, since the peace conference at the latest. The belligerent states were colonial powers that recruited large masses of soldiers and auxiliary forces from their colonies for the battle lines in Europe.

---

[85] U.S. military attaché to Military Intelligence Division (Mexico, October 30, 1918), NA, RG 63, Entry 132, Box 3.

[86] Vargas Vila, *Ante los barbaros*.

[87] Compagnon, *L'adieu à l'Europe*, p. 143.

[88] Ugarte, Mi campaña, p. 226. Yankelevich, *La revolución mexicana en América Latina*, pp. 24–43.

[89] "Panamericanismo de duplicidad y Panamericanismo de lealtad," in: *El Demócrata* (June 13, 1916), p. 2.

[90] Gonzalo de la Parra, "Los cerdos que comercian con cerdos han ultrajado a mi patria," in: *El Nacional* (June 19, 1916), p. 1. See also Mario Mata, "Tengamos serenidad ante al in peligro," in: Ibid. (June 20, 1916), p. 3.

UN PLATO SUCULENTO

— Señor, tendrá que aguardar un poco, porque todavía está algo caliente.
— No tengo prisa; esperaré que esté a punto, para que no me haga daño.

FIGURE 6.2 The alarming rise of the United States. Uncle Sam has time to wait until the globe, which Mars, the god of war, serves to him as a feast, has cooled off. *Source*: "Un plato suculento," in: *Caras y Caretas* (December 4, 1915).

Moreover, they fought each other in the colonies themselves, which claimed countless victims from among the civilian population. Latin American observers did not fail to notice this development. In particular, the student movement adopted anticolonialism in its program.[91] Ugarte observed in this context:

> Europe has in Africa and Asia, the United States in Spanish America always been a force of injustice and domination. We have arrived at a point where things need to change. We are witnessing the dawn of a century. Just as we have abolished slavery among human beings, so must we abolish slavery among nations.[92]

However, the few Latin American commentators of the bourgeois press who dealt with the issue did not reject colonial rule in principle, for they remained convinced of the inferiority of the colonized peoples. The primary worry was that this could be extended to the Americas.[93] The U.S. State Department, which was quite worried about the problematic contradiction between its own activities in the Caribbean and the "peoples' right to self-determination," thus found it easy to keep the issues apart.[94]

If imperialism and to some degree colonialism were the "other" from which one disassociated oneself, the question arose as to what defined one's self. A traditional identity model was so-called Hispanicism, which referred to the common Spanish heritage. Since the former mother country maintained neutrality during the war, like many Latin American countries, a proximity was present. Numerous voices, such as that of Argentine Manuel Gálvez in his novel *El Solar de la raza* from 1913, spoke in favor of a close cooperation.[95] The pan-Hispanic movement in Spain itself reciprocated the interest. Madrid wanted to take advantage of the absence of Britain and France to expand its own position. Famous philosopher José Ortega y Gasset thus toured South America in 1916 to cultivate closer ties.[96]

This was particularly evident in the convergence in the area of political symbolism. Since the time of the 400th anniversary of Columbus' voyage in 1892, the Spanish government had celebrated October 12

---

[91] "La juventud argentina de Córdoba a los hombres libres de América," in: Cúneo, *La reforma universitaria*, p. 2. See also Funes, *Salvar la nación*, p. 36.

[92] Ugarte, *Mi campaña*, p. 208. See also Ugarte, *La patria grande*, p. 113.

[93] Huidobro, *La paz europea*, pp. 60–6.

[94] James G. McDonald, Memorandum on Latin America and a possible peace conference (Bloomington, IN, January 19, 1918), NA, RG 256, Roll 8, no. 103, p. 2.

[95] Eduardo A. de Quiñones, "Hispano-Americanismo," in: *El Demócrata* (November 11, 1914), p. 3. Fernández Güel, *Plus Ultra*, p. 249.

[96] Sepúlveda, *El sueño de la Madre Patria*, pp. 111–14 and 199. Compagnon, *L'adieu à l'Europe*, pp. 296–9.

as a national holiday. Its name was officially changed to "Fiesta de la Raza" ("Celebration of the Race") in 1902 to express the closeness of the mother country with the former colonies. The Spanish Unión Iberoamericana (Ibero-American Union) sought to spread this celebration in Latin America. The world war helped to give this movement significant impetus. While some countries had celebrated the date before 1914, many additional states decided to recognize the occasion during the war years. In addition, Spanish cultural policy strove to establish the term "Ibero-America" in contradistinction to "Latin America."[97]

The Latinism the pro-French propaganda repeatedly insisted on, however, was not appreciably weakened. It remained, especially during the war years, an important transnationally valid self-concept. Or, as many commentators did not tire of repeating: it reflected the "essence, according to which our origin and intellectual breeding, is simply Latin."[98] The Latin tendency, however, was not completely unopposed. Shortly after the war, Bomilcar lamented that the pronounced Francophilia of the Brazilians – along the lines of "I will die happy, because I die for France" – had contributed to Brazil's denationalization.[99] Augusto Bunge also did not trust the "pan-Latin chimera," as he put it. He called for having confidence in one's own strength.[100]

A growing number of commentators thought that this could be the indigenist movement. As a result of the condemnation of the colonial past, it was directly opposed to Hispanicism. Devés Valdés dates the rise of the indigenist discussions to the year 1915, when essays, anthropological studies, and political speeches put a spotlight on improving the situation of the "Indios."[101] The indigenous population was transformed from the cause of the nation's sickness, as Bolivian Alcides Arguedas diagnosed it in his 1909 book *Pueblo enfermo*, to the bedrock of its national identity.[102] Arguedas' compatriot Franz Tamayo located the national energy in the country's indigenous population a year later in his *Creación de la nacional pedagogía*. The indigenist sensibility was also stirring in Peru, where Manuel González Prada had published the essay *Nuestros indios*. Here, the Asociación Pro-indígena was founded in 1912. Not least

[97] Sepúlveda, *El sueño de la Madre Patria*, pp. 201–9 and 350–1.
[98] Silva Vildosola, "Le Chili et la guerre européenne," pp. 76–7.
[99] Bomilcar, *A politica no Brasil*, p. 97.
[100] "Nuestra tercera encuesta," in: *Nosotros* 8 (October 1914), p. 144. As Ugarte similarly writes in *Mi campaña*, p. 221.
[101] Devés Valdés, *El pensamiento latinoamericano*, Vol. 1, p. 110. Arroyo, *Nuestros años diez*, pp. 45–76. Sepúlveda, *El sueño de la Madre Patria*, p. 264.
[102] Lorini, *El nacionalismo en Bolivia*, pp. 88–95.

because of the indigenous uprising of the Rumi Maqui in southern Peru in 1915/16 in response to the difficult economic situation of the war years, additional arguments were raised for improving the conditions of this population group. Young, politically active men like Haya de la Torre in Cuzco or Mariátegui in Lima were inspired by this thought. Even Argentine Ugarte already counted the ethnic category in his early work *El Porvenirde América Latina* (1911) as one of the foundations for establishing a separate space in the world distinct from the United States.[103]

In Mexico, on the other hand, the revolution was quite decisive in shaping the indigenist movement.[104] The intellectual vanguard included Manuel Gamio, who called for rediscovering the indigenous heritage. According to Gamio, it was necessary to integrate the *raza de bronce* (bronze race) and to create a homogeneous nation.[105] Ignorance of the indigenous peoples in Latin America had led to their potential being untapped. As the intellectual saw it, the civilization of the indigenous people was not worth any less than the dominant European civilization, which was combatting itself in the name of culture: "Today, one person poisons another with gases, which have been produced by an amazing chemical science in order to snatch away his territory and trade – it's all just a matter of resources."[106] Gamio emphatically appealed for abandoning the "fatal orientation towards foreign countries" in order to learn to appreciate one's own culture.[107]

During the war years, intellectuals throughout Latin America articulated this plea with regional variations and different intensity. In Brazil, however, it was less the indigenous than the Afro-Brazilian population that was discovered as a source of national identity and transnational integration. Here, too, the development started in the years before the war, when, for example, Alberto Torres and Manoel Bomfim expressed criticism about prejudices and racism. In 1911, their compatriot Bomilcar composed an important basic work on the "Revolt of the Lash" ("Revolta da Chibata") in 1910 that was reprinted during the war. Afro-Brazilian sailors rebelled in the incident against corporal punishment in

---

[103] Arroyo, *Nuestros años diez*, pp. 151–90. Merbilháa, "Claves racialistas," pp. 199–210. García, *Indigenismo, izquierda, indio*, pp. 291–2. König, "Nationale Identitätsbildung," p. 316.

[104] Devés Valdés, *El pensamiento latinoamericano*, Vol. 1, pp. 84–5. García, *Indigenismo, izquierda, indio*, pp. 89–90 and 101–6.

[105] Gamio, *Forjando patria*, pp. 5–6 and 10. See also Devés Valdés, *El pensamiento latino-americano*, Vol. 1, pp. 111–2. Funes, *Salvar la nación*, pp. 102–6.

[106] Gamio, *Forjando patria*, p. 105.

[107] Ibid., p. 120.

the navy. In this text, Bomilcar took the view that the assumption that there are inferior races was "absolutely false."[108] According to Bomilcar, the German soldiers were themselves not disciplined by nature, but only acquired their militaristic superiority through proper training. Bomilcar contended that the Russo-Japanese War of 1905 had shown precisely that allegedly inferior races could achieve great things.[109] Not only in Brazil, but in particular in the Caribbean, where (as in Jamaica, Trinidad, and British Honduras) war veterans firmly asserted their demands for equality, antiracist arguments were interwoven with anticolonial arguments at the end of the war.[110] These would gain great importance in the 1920s.

In Latin America, the anticolonial thinking was also fueled not least by a rediscovery of the Orient. While this had begun at the turn of the century, it only intensified in the wake of the First World War. Translations into Spanish facilitated the reception of works "oriental" authors such as, first and foremost, Rabindranath Tagore, whose *Fruit Harvest* (*La Cosecha de la Fruta*) appeared in Buenos Aires in 1917.[111] This was accompanied by a growing interest in oriental philosophy and the new mysticism, and especially Theosophy, which was informed by a suspicion of European rationalism following the horrors of the war. Due to the growing immigration from the Middle and Far East, this thinking also gained a foothold socially in Latin America.[112] Itinerant preachers like Indian Curuppumullage Jinarajadasa in South America or military deserter and Theosophist Linn Gale from the United States, who worked in Mexico from July 1918, caused the theosophical movement to spread throughout the region.[113] They all helped to grow south–south connections, which ultimately arose out of a sense of disappointment over Europe's collapse in the First World War.

A PLACE ON THE GLOBAL STAGE

When the columnists of *La Vanguardia* expressed in April 1917 that the brutal war needed to be followed by a peace that established a fundamentally

---

[108] Bomilcar, *O preconceito de raça no Brazil*, p. 14.
[109] Ibid., pp. 30 and 45. Bomilcar's contemporaries Olavo Bilac (*A defesa nacional*, p. 132) and Basílio de Magalhães argued along similar lines. See Skidmore, *Black into White*, p. 167.
[110] Winegard, *Indigenous Peoples*, p. 227.
[111] Define, "As razões de Tagore," pp. 159–63. González, "Rabindranath Tagore," p. 169.
[112] Gasquet, *El orientalismo argentino*, pp. 1–22. Devés Valdés, *El pensamiento latinoamericano*, Vol. 1, pp. 25–7.
[113] Devés Valdés/Melgar Bao, "Redes teosóficas," pp. 137–43.

new international order, all the sides involved in the war agreed.[114] With the demand that justice should replace violence in the future, the Latin American observers joined the global debate about the postwar order early on.[115] In this system, there was to be a seat at the table for Latin America that corresponded to the continent's growing influence. What ideas informed this expectation and how was it to be realized?

The war showed that weaker states like those in Latin America could not rely on the force of the international law that had been codified before the conflict. Therefore, in the view of many Latin American jurists and diplomats, a new definition of international law was an urgent necessity.[116] In 1916, even the prominent Latin America voices assembled in the volume of French propaganda, *L'Amérique latine et la guerre européenne*, called for a peace that involved the institution of obligatory arbitration or a federation of nations.[117] The peace efforts of U.S. President Wilson seemed in alignment with Latin America's concerns and were therefore wholly supported in public. In this context, Wilson won acceptance as the voice of the Americas, because he made the moral principles long represented by high-ranking Latin American personalities such as Rui Barbosa a part of an overall agenda that found sympathetic listeners beyond the American continent.[118]

From the perspective of the Latin American elites who participated in the debates on the future of the international order, Wilson represented a leading voice among those who fought for the common ideal of the Americas. According to Peruvian Cornejo, this ideal rested on the idea of democracy, whose recognition was the existential basis of Latin America's independence.[119] America, the commentators repeatedly stressed, was different from Europe: "The Americas' industrial peace ensures growing prosperity, (whereas) Europe's armed peace ruins (it)."[120] Americans of the North and South had fought for the right to self-determination

---

[114] "En nuestro lugar," in: *La Vanguardia* (April 24, 1917), p. 1.

[115] Ingenieros, "La religión de la raza."

[116] Barbosa, *Obras completas*, Vol. XLIV, 1917, Part 1, p. 74. Del Valle, *La cuestión internacional*, p. 10. Silva Vildósola, "Le Chili et la guerre européenne," pp. 74–5. Elguero, "La bandera de los pueblos debiles," pp. 83–5.

[117] An example is the former president of Paraguay. Cecilio Báez, "Le Paraguay et la guerre européenne," p. 165.

[118] Rivarola, "América y La paz europea," pp. 319–24. Barbosa, *Obras completas*, Vol. XLIV, 1917, Part 1, p. 112. Cornejo, *La intervención del Perú*, p. 54.

[119] Cornejo, *La intervención del Perú*, p. 10.

[120] Francisco García Calderón, "La ideología de la guerra y América," in: *La Nación* (B. A., August 3, 1914), p. 4.

and popular sovereignty and thereby overcome colonial domination. It was thus possible to identify a community of interests that could rest on the principles of an – albeit multilateral – Monroe Doctrine in conjunction with the Drago Doctrine. Indeed, this applied until 1917 due to the shared neutrality – a condition that could be a strength if the neutrals closed ranks and boycotted the war to foster "the Americas' peaceful isolation."[121]

Wilmart, who further developed this idea in 1914, was moreover certain that the war never would have broken out if Europe had abandoned its secret diplomacy and instead worked together with the American states toward a lasting peace. Due to the close international entanglements, it was necessary, according to Wilmart, to create international bodies for guaranteeing the peace. The Concert of Europe now needed to become a "global concert," with the Americas' full participation.[122] Barbosa provided the following idealistic justification for this view: "America does not just belong to the Americans, America belongs to humanity."[123] The self-understanding was echoed in a speech by Ambassador Naón to the Carnegie Institute in Washington on April 29, 1915. In praising the solidarity of the Americas, he suggested that it could even serve to bring about peace among the Europeans. The shared consciousness, which Naón argued already existed in the Americas, needed to be transferred to the Old World – and indeed to the entire globe – in order to overcome the historical mistakes that had led to war. The ambassador ended his speech with the prognosis that the latent "true Pan-Americanism" that had existed since independence could now be built on.[124] As *El Mercurio* remarked in 1918, this would be helped by the growing interdependencies:

History has taught us a lesson about real rapprochement between the American countries. Two facts have brought the peoples of this hemisphere more closely together: the dissemination of culture and the growth of communication links and their greater rapidity."[125]

Strong supporters of Pan-Americanism as an international organizing force, like Paraguayan politician and jurist Antolín Irala, viewed the United States as the champion of American ideals, which occupied

[121] Wilmart, "El ideal americano," pp. 366–7. See also a publication from the Museo Social Argentino, founded in 1911 on the Parisian model: *El aislamiento pacífico de América*, p. 157.
[122] Wilmart, "La paz europea y América," pp. 393–5.
[123] Barbosa, *Obras completas*, Vol. XLIV, 1917, Part 1, p. 111.
[124] Naón, "Solidaridad americana," p. 215.
[125] "Americanismo," in: *El Mercurio* (September 27, 1918), p. 1.

a special place among the nations because they supplanted imperial-ism.[126] These observers were of the opinion that a subordinate role under U.S. leadership in the service "of a healthy Pan-Americanism," as Ricardo Rojas put it, was in fact advantageous.[127] The image of the utilitarian Caliban, which Rodó had once propagated, had had its day; the United States was now something of "a big brother" to a proud Latin America.[128] There were quite a number of proponents of the spirit of Pan-American cooperation in Brazil, where even the name Monroe had lost its frighten-ing connotation.[129]

One reason the Pan-American idea received so much attention was because of the various conferences and meetings the United States had initiated during the war years. The first step in this direction was the Pan-American Financial Conference in 1915, which, for instance, Costa Rican president González highly welcomed in view of the "terror and disasters" in Europe.[130] The second Pan-American Scientific Congress at the turn of the year in 1915/16, which was also organized in Washington, reached a climax with an Inter-American Declaration of the Rights and Duties of Nations that was inspired by the Chilean Álvarez. The doc-ument attributed to every nation the right to exist, to be independent, to share equality, as well as the right to exclusive jurisdiction over its own territory. Even the Germanophile Quesada took part in this confer-ence, with the prospect of closer intellectual cooperation in the Americas inciting his enthusiasm in particular.[131] Furthermore, Wilson proclaimed in this context the idea of a League of American States, a forerunner of the League of Nations. However, the proposal was not met only with praise.[132]

This showed that while the Latin American representatives certainly sym-pathized with the Pan-American ideal, they were nonetheless wary of sub-ordinating it to the pursuit of global cooperation and solidarity including

---

[126] En favor de los Aliados, pp. 29–32. "Os Estados Unidos e a Grande Guerra," in: *Jornal do Commercio* (July 22, 1915), p. 4.

[127] "La paz americana," in *La Nación* (B. A., January 1, 1916), p. 15. See also "El Presidente Wilson," in: *Caras y Caretas* (June 19, 1915). "Os Estados Unidos na conflagração euro-pea," in: *Jornal do Commercio* (January 31, 1915), p. 3.

[128] Rojas, *La guerra de las naciones*, p. 278.

[129] "Mirando el porvenir," in: *La Prensa* (B. A., December 12, 1915), p. 3.

[130] Alfredo González, "Mensaje del Presidente" (San Jose, May 1, 1916), in: Meléndez Chaverri, *Mensajes presidenciales* Vol. 4, p. 245.

[131] Quesada, "Unión intelectual panamericana," pp. 23–33. See also Quesada, "El 'peligro alemán' en Sud América," p. 535.

[132] Boyle, *Foundations of World Order*, pp. 113–4. Knock, *To End All Wars*, pp. 39–45.

Europe.[133] The discussions over the course of the war clearly indicate that many Latin American decision makers remained quite ambivalent toward Pan-Americanism. Indeed, the experience of U.S. interventionism, especially since Wilson had taken office, proved that suspicion was advisable. Too often, Wilson's idealistic rhetoric had masked purely imperialistic motives and thus seemed particularly hypocritical.[134]

An alternative that gained currency during the war was the idea of continental solidarity without the involvement of the United States. On the diplomatic level, the mediation efforts in the conflict between Mexico and the United States, which led to the ABC Pact, were an important stepping stone for the integration of the three major states in South America (see Figure 6.3). The initiators of this alliance assumed that a hierarchy of states is a "natural condition of international life." The ABC states, accordingly, should pursue their "own Monroismus" and bring about peace and order in South America.[135] Whereas, before the war, Argentina still mainly considered itself and Mexico as "natural" leading powers, the ABC states were the only alternative after the start of the Mexican Revolution. This was because of their "racial superiority," as Argentine diplomat Isidoro Ruiz Moreno explained it.[136] In America, the "continent of peace," even the rivalry between Argentina and Brazil for the leadership role in Latin America should be brought to an end.[137] However, there were significant differences in interpretation even in this context, for the Brazilian government was convinced that the ABC was part of a successful Pan-Americanism with the United States.[138]

This division was even more pronounced after the United States and Brazil entered the war in 1917, and it raised the question of how the rest of America would behave. In his 1917 essay *Nuestra guerra: la coalición contra la Argentina*, Argentine Pedro de Córdoba even stressed the need for a bloc of neutrals to succeed against Brazil and the United States in a likely upcoming war.[139] However far-fetched this may have been, so, too, was the Europeans' misguided belief that all of "Indo-Latin-America"

[133] Del Valle, *La cuestión internacional*, p. 212.

[134] Gallardo, "Posición internacional de Chile," S. LIX.

[135] Quoted in Yankelevich, *La diplomacia imaginaria*, pp. 42–3.

[136] Ibid., pp. 41 and 62.

[137] "A Repercussão da Guerra no Brasil," in: *Jornal do Commercio* (August 9, 1914), p. 4. See also Compagnon, *L'adieu à L'Europe*, pp. 216–17.

[138] "A Era Pan-Americana," in: *Jornal do Commercio* (December 6, 1914), p. 5. Particular attention is paid to the competition in: Compagnon, *L'adieu à l'Europe*, p. 57.

[139] Córdoba, *Nuestra guerra*, p. 75.

EL DESARROLLO DEL A. B. C.

(Dibujo de Sim)

Wilson.—¡Como crecen cada día estos niños! Y pensar que yo tenía presupuestado enviarles juguetes para la Pascua.

FIGURE 6.3 The rapid growth of the "boys" from ABC took President Wilson by surprise.
Source: Sim, "El desarrollo del A. B. C.," in: *Zig-Zag* (December 26, 1914).

would sooner or later understand the necessity for entering the war. Instead, the claims that Latin American unity was necessary to gain respect internationally resounded now louder than ever.[140] Undoubtedly, these voices continued to make themselves heard after the war broke out in 1914. Against the backdrop of the crisis and the encroachments on neutrality, the call for a unified stance won many supporters. Not least for economic reasons did integration seem imperative as a way of offsetting the war-related losses in the area of trade.[141]

The intensity of the demands grew over the course of the war. Rodó reported in December 1916 from Rome that the Europeans perceived the Americas as a single entity, because they were incapable of drawing distinctions. He was convinced that the Americans were indeed coming closer together because of their impressions about the European war and that this had to be the political objective.[142] With the establishment of the South American Football Association in 1916, this type of association was already realized in a very popular and rapidly growing sport.[143] The war thus proved an opportunity for ushering in a new type of regional integration.[144]

The fact that these claims did not remain at the level of political rhetoric was due to the policy of Carranza. He clearly recognized the need for continental solidarity in view of the worrying proximity to the United States. Parallel to his policy toward the German Reich, the Mexican put out feelers to Latin America in 1916. Around the middle of the year, he sent a special envoy, Isidro Fabela, to Argentina, Brazil, and Chile. He also funded numerous propaganda trips, such as of the trade unionists, in order to promote revolutionary Mexico and thereby counteract the bad press the U.S. intelligence services had spread.[145]

In this way, the Mexican government worked on establishing an anti-imperialist and pro-Mexican network. It benefited from a Latin American context, which was influenced not least by the spirit of reform that students had embraced. The Mexican Revolution was considered an alternative nationalist model. It opened up new horizons and intellectuals like Ingenieros and Peruvian writer José Santos Chocano also held it in

---

[140] Cabrera Arroyo, "América y la guerra europea," pp. 245–6.
[141] "Por la fraternidad sudamericana," in: *La Nación* (B. A., October 22, 1914), p. 8. Rodríguez Mendoza, "La Guerra y la América," p. 248.
[142] Rodó, "Al concluir el año," in: *Caras y Caretas* (March 24, 1917).
[143] Rinke, "Globalizing Football," p. 53.
[144] Cornejo, *La intervención del Perú*, pp. 60–1. Gallardo, "Posición internacional de Chile," pp. XXVII–XXIX.
[145] Yankelevich, "Las campañas pro México," pp. 81–9.

high esteem. Ugarte was undoubtedly the most important voice in Latin America who made a plea on behalf of Mexico, while simultaneously calling for the unity of the continent against the United States.[146]

It was on this basis that Carranza was able to clarify his rejection of the U.S. Monroe Doctrine. He set against it his own "Carranza Doctrine," which was designed for Latin America. It contained an explicit rejection of the Monroe Doctrine, citing its one-sidedness, hubris, and damaging consequences for Latin America. Furthermore, Carranza stated the equality of all nations and the dignity of institutions and laws. Citizens and foreigners, moreover, should be equal before the law and the legislatures of all countries needed to adhere to the same principles. Finally, the Mexican demanded that diplomacy in the future be oriented to the interests of civilization and the solidarity of all nations, and not be abused to repress the weak.[147]

With this program, Carranza deliberately opposed Wilson's global claims, while formulating from the perspective of a semi-colonial state like Mexico a postcolonial stance. Carranza's words were especially momentous, because they were uttered in his capacity as head of state in the form of a policy statement, not as an intellectual in an academic forum or in the realm of public opinion. That the Mexican government would seek rapprochement with countries outside the North Atlantic center of power was therefore quite logical. Japan in particular stepped up as a partner. Tokyo wanted to build up its contacts with Latin America due to its interest in natural resources and expanding trade in the Pacific. Argentine Almafuerte responded favorably to Japan's overtures, welcoming "the inimitable sons of the rising sun." The Bolivian government specifically set up a diplomatic mission in Japan, and Ecuador, despite its Foreign Ministry's racist objections, showed a desire for closer trade relations with East Asia.[148] However rudimentary, there were signs here of a trans-Pacific policy that might lead in the future to a new spot on the world stage for several Latin American countries.[149]

As the discussions and measures clearly illustrate, the path to the future was now more open than ever thanks to the world war. The conflict gave rise to emancipatory ambitions – both in economic as well as in cultural

[146] Yankelevich, *La revolución mexicana en América Latina*, pp. 123–6. On Santos Chocano, see: Ibid., pp. 69–72.

[147] Fabela, *La política interior y exterior de Carranza*, pp. 219–22.

[148] Almafuerte, *Almafuerte y la guerra*, p. 11. Schuler, *Secret Wars*, pp. 160–2. MRREE to Embassy in Washington (Quito, February 12, 1918), in: Ecuador, AMRREE, M.1.9.1.

[149] Ingenieros, "Crónicas de Viaje," in: *Obras Campletas*, Vol. 8, p. 173.

terms – that became apparent during or immediately after the hostilities. This does not mean, however, that these processes were triggered only by the war. The First World War, rather, served as catalyst and transformer. The conflict aggravated long-existing sources of potential social conflict everywhere. The problems or the perception of their urgency came to a head during the war and were hotly debated in an increasingly modern press landscape. The transformative element consisted in the fact that the discussions resulted in new social movements with highly distinct orientations. At the same time, they also all had two points in common: First, the movements were transnational. Therefore, they did not remain confined to one or a few countries, but were active in many places and became intertwined with each other. Second, in contrast to old Europe and to some degree the prevailing oligarchies in Latin America, they claimed to represent the youth and thus also to be able to shape the future.

Epilogue

The Global Legacy of the World War

Although the Treaties of Paris formally ended the war, peace remained hard to find on a global scale in 1919. The Latin American eyewitnesses who experienced the transition from a "hot" to a "cold" war watched the developments closely. For instance, Mariátegui remarked six years later in hindsight:

The world war not only shocked and transformed the West's economy and politics, but also its thinking and its spirit. The economic impact is not starker or easier to perceive than the spiritual and psychological consequences. Politicians and statesmen might discover a formula and method to deal with the former, but they will certainly not find a suitable theory or practice to surmount the latter.[1]

In fact, the war propaganda transitioned into a postwar propaganda, especially in Latin America. The German side, above all, tried to refute the claim from the Treaty of Versailles that Germany alone was to blame for the war.[2] The war remained part of the public consciousness to a certain extent because of the Cult of the Fallen, which foreign communities introduced to their countries of immigration shortly after the war.[3] Memoirs, films, and novels, such as Erich Maria Remarque's *All Quiet on the Western Front*, ensured that the topic did not completely fade from memory. In addition, Latin American writers and artists were inspired by the tragedies of world war and created works of enduring value, such as Carlos Gardel with his tango classics "Silencio" or Heitor Villa-Lobos

---

[1] Mariátegui, "La emoción de nuestro tiempo," pp. 4–5.
[2] Rinke, "Der letzte freie Kontinent," pp. 492–3.
[3] For the German side in Buenos Aires, see: Bindernagel, "Migration und Erinnerung," p. 200.

with his symphonies.[4] By the same token, it is not possible to speak of a national culture of remembrance, even in countries like Argentina or Brazil. This is even more the case in other national contexts. Such a processing of the past remained too haphazard.

Nevertheless, the war undoubtedly meant a decisive turning point in the experience of Latin Americans of different nationalities, classes, generations, and genders. The outbreak of the world war initiated a crisis of dramatic proportion. The entire region could only look on helplessly, for the foundation of its economic development broke away along with the collapse of the liberal world economy. The export sector, which was critical to the lifeblood of all countries, went through a period of highly volatile shocks. These trends continued in many places long after the war. Not all countries, though, had the good fortune of being suppliers of war-essential raw materials. The world war gave the Allies a welcome excuse for artificially suppressing the prices of vitally important Latin American commodities (which were key to the war's successful conclusion) and for ruthlessly combating German interests.[5] The Allied economic war and Germany's submarine warfare were thus fundamentally interventions into the sovereignty of Latin American states and flagrant violations of international law.[6] Latin Americans could not help but wonder what gave the Europeans the right to carry out their feud on a global scale.

Even more important than the diplomatic implications of the war were the social effects. Rapidly growing unemployment, unchecked inflation, and the increasingly precarious situation of the working population, especially in the cities, contributed to an incendiary social constellation. This culminated in the wake of the precursors in Mexico and Russia in serious unrest in many parts of Latin America in 1917. The elites were only able to restore order through the application of extreme force. That said, they failed to fix any of the underlying problems. To be sure, the First World War did not create these problems. It nonetheless greatly exacerbated them in Latin America, as in other parts of the world.

---

[4] For a comprehensive discussion of this set of issues, see: Compagnon, *L'adieu à l'Europe*, pp. 179–87.

[5] Albert, *South America and the First World War*, p. 119. Dehne ("How Important was Latin America to the First World War," pp. 157–8) has recently highlighted the often-overlooked dimension of the role of Latin American commodities in the war.

[6] Whether the economic war was "counterproductive" for this reason, as Dehne suggests through the examples of Argentina, Brazil, and Uruguay, is debatable. After all, it inflicted serious harm to many smaller and medium-sized German and ethnic-German companies. Dehne, *On the Far Western Front*, p. 190.

By and large, the public sphere was greatly mobilized and politicized across Latin America. The actors spurring these processes were generally young and came from the new middle class. Some were urban or – to a lesser extent – rural workers recruited from the margins of society. Although the strikers, protesting students, rebellious indigenes, and other forces pushing for social change did not prevail in the years 1917–19, the spirit of the revolution nonetheless remained a decisive factor in twentieth-century Latin American history. Cornejo was right when he admonished his Peruvian senator colleagues in September 1918: "This war, gentlemen, is not a war, it is a revolution – a visible revolution in Russia, an invisible one in the other countries. It is one that, like the light in a mirror, flits about unrecognized, waiting for the event that it reflects."[7] Contrary to the senator's belief, however, it was not the peace conference that would first reveal this revolution. Brazilian politician and journalist Otto Prazeres also recognized the revolutionary character of the upheavals that began in Russia, but which the war had already brought with it in its wake to Latin America:

Besides a loss of illusions, the war will have many additional implications.... The mental revolutions, which result in new ways of thinking and acting, are already perceptible. Many moral, social, and political values will lose the basis upon which they were formed and be fundamentally changed. Lacking the concepts from which they subsisted, the threatened masses will march in search of new principles.[8]

No doubt, the perspective that the Peruvian and Brazilian independently articulated at nearly the same time was elitist. Not everyone in Latin America was affected to the same extent by the war, either directly or indirectly. There were clear differences in the degree of involvement: In the immigrant countries of Argentina, Brazil, Chile, Paraguay, and Uruguay, for instance, the daily confrontations in the public sphere were more vehement than in Central America or the Andean countries of Ecuador, Colombia, and Venezuela. In Mexico, where Europe and the United States carried out their secret war more intensely than anywhere else in the region, the decades-long civil war received greater attention than the First World War. The immediate impact of the war was certainly felt here as well, however. Generally speaking, the Atlantic countries were much more involved in the war's developments than those around the Pacific Rim like Chile or Peru. Considerable differences may also be detected

[7] Cornejo, *La intervención del Perú*, p. 66.
[8] Prazeres, *O Brasil na guerra*, p. 15.

within the individual countries themselves, as certain regions in the hinterlands were impacted far less by the war than the capital and port cities. On the other hand, this did not apply to the export-oriented plantation or mining regions, which had to contend with the war's severe blows. Levels of sympathy and anxiety about the war ran the gamut. Nonetheless, it would be wrong to privilege some Latin American countries over others on the basis of power-political criteria. After all, the need to rationalize one's involvement in world events did not stop at a country's borders. As this study has shown, the urgency of the war in fact cut across all of Latin America.

There were also marked differences in the way the war was perceived. Urban, politically interested, and educated middle and upper classes, which constituted the bulk of newspaper readership, had more immediate access to information about the war. They were thus much more invested in the war of words than the mass of the illiterate lower classes. Nonetheless, their level of interest in the war also far exceeded any previous world event due to the dissemination of images. The national public spheres accordingly grew along with the war, but also because of it. Many people in Latin America and the rapidly modernizing press sensed the First World War to be a genuine sensation. It was especially a godsend for the fledgling tabloid journalism. Yet the marginalized poor, particularly indigenous populations and African Americans, were not integrated into these communication processes. Ingenieros gave the following assessment, albeit with a racist undertone that was typical for the time:

There is no doubt that the people living in the Andes and the *Indios* living at the sources of the Amazon will not feel the impact of the war. They probably don't even know that there has been a European war, assuming, of course, we are to make the unlikely assumption that they actually know that Europe exists. But in all the countries from Alaska to the Magellan Strait that are the products of European colonization, the echo of what happened in Europe will always reverberate, indeed even more so depending on the degree of civilization. It is our inescapable fate, as Sarmiento has already observed, that we "become like Europe."[9]

The quote further shows that the idea of bidding farewell to Europe was not even a question. Among other things, the technical innovations that the war gave rise to elicited a great deal of interest. The Latin American militaries especially wanted to benefit from the experience of the Europeans. They, therefore, brought experts from France, England, and the United States to teach them the new methods of warfare. The concern

---

[9] Ingenieros, "Significación histórica," p. 387.

here was not only with fighting against external foes, but internal ones, which, as the militaries of the region concurred by the end of war, were on the left. Despite the provisions in the Versailles Treaty, German officers were in great demand because of their involvement with the *Freikorps*.[10] This interest in receiving military advice, however, only underlines the change that had taken place in Latin American's relations with Europe. After the war, the Europeans failed to gain anywhere near the degree of the influence that they had had before 1914. The nationalist tendencies in the Americas were now too strong.

Europe remained an important reference point, however, even if it was now also frequently regarded as a counter model to the region's own developmental plans. Indeed, a repositioning took place after the war inasmuch as the old continent even lost its standing as an undisputed archetype where, due to the rise of the United States, this had not yet occurred before 1914. Ingenieros, for instance, was convinced that Latin America would eventually experience problems and successes like those in Europe because of its history. At the same time, however, he remarked that the outcome was uncertain and largely depended on young men, innovators, and the oppressed, who wanted to change society. He forecast that the new societies would settle in somewhere between Wilson's "minimalist" demands for reform and the "maximalist" revolution in Russia, but also anticipated rioting and violence.[11]

Undoubtedly, "anti-Europeanism" developed among many Latin American intellectuals after the First World War. The feeling of disappointment over the "betrayal" of the common civilization ran deep.[12] From their perspective, the long undisputed center of culture, education, and progress was responsible for the most horrific war in human history. Indeed, as Prazeres noted, it was civilizational progress that had finally led to the creation of the most appalling weapons technology.[13] This realization gave rise to new, unsettling thoughts that would preoccupy Latin American thinkers for years to come.

The critical engagement with the self-proclaimed centers of the modern world system and with imperialism in all its forms took on a new character during the war years – in no small measure because its parameters shifted from the reading rooms and the publications of small intellectual circles to the streets. Different actors brought the debate to the

[10] Rinke, *Der letzte freie Kontinent*, pp. 577–656.
[11] Ingenieros, "Significación histórica," pp. 388–9.
[12] Funes, *Salvar la nación*, p. 26.
[13] Prazeres, *O Brasil na guerra*, p. 13.

wider Latin American public sphere, where they fought for their convictions. For Latin Americans, the war was a great decentralizer: it put world orders that had evolved over the centuries into question, while creating a vacuum that allowed new ideas of global, but also of local transformation to take shape.

This did not mean that region's international situation changed in any fundamental way. In the 1920s, Latin America remained a laboratory for informal imperialism and the activities of multinational corporations. The competition for the control of raw materials – especially the new "lubricant of capitalism," crude oil – for exports, and for direct and indirect investments intensified. In all these areas, the United States emerged from the war as the big winner and the Americas' undisputed hegemonial power. Although British interests in Argentina played a special role well into the 1930s, there was also no doubt about the fact that the United States had clearly come out ahead in the war on the Latin American stage. On the diplomatic level, the Latin Americans could do little to stop this development. From the ABC Pact to the neutrality congresses, initiatives to defend the region's common interests failed due to individual nations' attempts to go it alone. With anti-imperialism, however, the experience of the world war helped encourage a powerful transnational discourse beyond the diplomatic sphere that forces of change co-opted for themselves. In the Latin American context, the subject entailed a decidedly anti-American element for some time that gained in importance as the war set in. Once the idea of self-determination and international equality caught on, Latin Americans decided against continuing to play the subordinate role in the repeatedly invoked new world order that the system of states had assigned to them before 1914. This disillusionment was validated after the war, when Latin America effectively became a junior partner to the United States. The "Wilsonian disappointment" of 1918–19 lent credibility to the anti-imperialist discourse. In Latin America, the 1920s would be a decade of anti-imperialist movements. Their breeding ground, no doubt, was the intellectual ferment of the war years.

But was the First World War in fact the primary catalyst of events that had been in the making for many years, as general historians now widely agree? Albert already stated this view in reference to Latin America in 1988. Compagnon recently arrived once again at the same conclusion.[14] This study, however, has shown that the war was not just a catalyst, but

---

[14] Albert, *South America*, p. 5.

a transformer that brought change from the realm of ideas to the social realities of the streets. To be sure, the war years in Latin America did not represent the great "seminal catastrophe of the twentieth century," as they did in Europe. Nonetheless, they were a historic moment that put the focus on the category of social inequality. It would be a legacy of the First World War that people sought answers to the question of the future of the subcontinent in increasingly violent conflict.

The shift in global consciousness shows most clearly the transformative influence of the First World War on the region. Because of the demise of the cultural center in Europe, many commentators in Latin America as early as 1914 confidently viewed their continent to be a model for true peace. The new global postwar civilization, in other words, would need to have its new focal point in the Americas. The meta-narrative about Europe's singular embodiment of civilization and culture was destroyed as a result of the world war. The intrinsically contradictory propaganda of warring parties made it possible to perceive Europe's underbelly. It not only called for countries to take sides, but it also opened up room for them to engage in their own development. The horizon of the world that appeared as a medialized wartime experience in Latin American societies was repeatedly correlated to local experiences. Expectations grew as a result. The hope that Latin America would transform from a hands-off, wide-eyed observer that, despite being affected, only participated in world events reactively into an independent and self-confident actor grew decisively. Due to the global scope of the war, the spatial and temporal distances between the continents diminished; in addition, the experience of being involved in the war was inextricably linked to the experience of the conflict as a unique event in history. As the sirens of *La Prensa* continually announced breaking news from the battlefields in August 1914, an entirely new degree of simultaneity emerged with what Latin Americans had understood as the "world." Today, the concurrence of the world that the media makes possible is taken for granted. One hundred years ago it was revolutionary and held out the promise of a better future. As to what this future would look like and how it should be reached, there were different opinions.

Sources and Literature

Archival Sources

Argentina

Archivo del Ministerio de Relaciones Exteriores (AMRREE-Arg.)
  Series (33) Primera Guerra Mundial
    AH/0001-0004 Alemania
    AH/0005 Austria Hungria
    AH/0006 Bélgica y Francia
    AH/0007-0009 Inglaterra AH/00010 Italia
    AH/00011 Estados Unidos y Japón
    ÁH/00013 Brasil, Bolivia, Cuba, Panama, China, Nicaragua AH/00016-
    00019, 00034, 00037, 00069 sin nombres

Brazil

Arquivo Histórico do Itamaraty, Ministério das Relações Exteriores (AHI)
  Primeira Guerra Mundial
  Directoria Geral dos Negocios Políticos e Diplomáticos Legações en Europa
Fundacão Casa de Rui Barbosa photo collection

Chile

Archivo del Ministerio de Relaciones Exteriores (AMRREE-Chile)
  Vols. 468, 471, 479, 514, 552–4, 562, 603, 604, 613, 669, 743
Archivo Nacional (AN), Archivo del Siglo XX
  Ministerio de Hacienda
    4714 Asociación e Inspección Salitrera de Propaganda, 1914–18

Colombia

Archivo General de la Nación (AGN)
 MRREE
  Cajas 00549, 00556, 00560, 01062, 02039, 02040, 3, 39, 82, 94, 109, 134,
  139, 178, 285

Costa Rica

Archivo Nacional (ANCR)
 Relaciones Exteriores (RREE)
  Cajas 224, 230, 231, 235, 236, 241, 243, 245

Ecuador

Archivo del Ministerio de Relaciones Exteriores (AMRREE), Quito
 B.1.2: Comunicaciones recibidas de la Legación de Alemania, tomo II
 D.1.8: Comunicaciones recibidas del Consulado del Ecuador en Hamburgo,
  tomo VI
 D.1.9: Consulados del Ecuador en Berlín y Hamburgo
 I.1.10.1: Comunicaciones con el Ministerio de Guerra y Marina
 M.1.9.1: Reservadas a la Legación en Washington
 M.1.23.4: Reservadas a las Legaciones en Francia y Gran Bretaña
 U.8: Comunicaciones con las cancillerías

Germany

Politisches Archiv des Auswärtigen Amts (PAAA)
 Weltkrieg
  21899–21906 Weltkrieg, Nr. 24, Stellung des lateinischen Amerika zum
  Weltkrieg, Vols. 1–7.
 Presseabteilung
  121950 Brasilien 2, Presse, Propaganda und Allgemeines, Vol. 1
Bundesarchiv (BA)
 Auswärtiges Amt (AA)
  6683–7 Neutralität, no. 77, Die Haltung der Neutralen im Europäischen
  Krieg, Chile, Vols. 1–6.

Great Britain

The National Archives (TNA)
 Cabinet Papers
 War Trade Intelligence Department
 Blockade Information

Guatemala

Archivo General de Centroamérica (AGC)
Ministerio de Relaciones Exteriores (MRREE)

Mexico

Archivo del Ministerio de Relaciones Exteriores (AMRREE)
Alemania, Actitud de en la Guerra Europea (I y II) 1914–18
39 – 13 – 5
Alemania, Legación [mexicana] en: Reseñas políticas 1918
16 – 23 – 12
Alemania, Situación económica de: 1917 Informes sobre ...
17 – 8 – 126
Inglaterra, Actitud de en la Guerra Europea 1914–18
39 – 13 – 4
Francia, Actitud de en la Guerra Europea 1914–18
39 – 13 – 7

Paraguay

Archivo del Ministerio de Relaciones Exteriores (AMRREE)
Colección Política Internacional (DPI)
Libro 70

Uruguay

Archivo General de la Nación (AGN)
Primera Guerra Mundial (PGM)
Ministerio de Relaciones Exteriores (MREE):
Cajas 724, 735, 737–43, 750, 755–6, 760–2, 774, 783, 787, 797, 800, 806, 810, 821

United States

National Archives (NA)
RG 32: United States Shipping Board
RG 38: Office of the Chief of Naval Operations
Office of Naval Intelligence (ONI)
RG 59: Department of State
RG 63: Committee on Public Information
RG 151: Bureau of Foreign and Domestic Commerce
RG 165: War Department General and Special Staffs Military Intelligence Division (MID)
War College Division (WCD)

RG 182: Records of the War Trade Board
RG 256: Records of the American Commission to Negotiate Peace
  Library of Congress (LC)
Lansing Papers

Published Sources

Magazines and Newspapers

ABC (Quindío, Colombia), 1916
La Actualidad: revista de los Aliados (Mexico), 1915–17
El Abogado Cristiano Ilustrado (Mexico), 1914
Alemania (Berlin), 1915–16
Los Aliados (Santiago de Chile), 1915
Boletín de Información (Havana), 1918
Boletín de la guerra (Mexico), 1918
Boletín de la guerra (Mérida), 1916
Cara-Dura (Buenos Aires), 1915
Caras y Caretas (Buenos Aires), 1914–19
A Careta (Rio de Janeiro), 1914–19
El Comercio (Lima), 1917–19
El Comercio (Quito)1914–19
La Convención Nacional (Guatemala), 1915
Correio da Manhã (Rio de Janeiro), 1914–19
El Correo de Alemania (Berlin), 1914–15
Le Correspondant (Paris), 1914–18
Le Courrier du Mexique (Mexico), 1916–18
La Crónica (Lima), 1914–18
Cuba Contemporánea (Havana), 1914–19
La Cultura Latina (Guatemala), 1915–17
La Defensa (Bogotá), 1916
A Defeza Nacional (Rio de Janeiro), 1914–18
El Demócrata (Mexico), 1914–19
Deutsche La Plata Zeitung (Buenos Aires), 1914–15
El Día (Montevideo), 1914–18
El Diario (Asunción), 1914
El Diario (La Paz), 1917
El Diario de Centro-América (Guatemala), 1914
El Diario del Hogar (Mexico), 1914
El Diario del Plata (Montevideo), 1914–17
El Diario Ilustrado (Santiago de Chile), 1914–19
El Diario Nacional (Bogotá), 1917
El Eco Alemán (Guatemala), 1914–15
Eco de la Guerra (Punta Arenas), 1915–16
El Economista Paraguayo (Asunción), 1914
La Época (Buenos Aires), 1917
A Epoca (Rio de Janeiro), 1914–18

O Estado de São Paulo (São Paulo), 1914–19
Excelsior (Mexico), 1917–19
Fon-Fon (Rio de Janeiro), 1914–19
France-Amérique (Paris), 1914–18
La Gaceta de Chile (Santiago de Chile), 1915–16
A Guerra: revista semanal (Porto Alegre), 1914–15
La Guerra Europea (Mexico), 1916–19
La Guerra Europea (Stuttgart), 1914–18
El Heraldo Conservador (Bogotá), 1916–18
El Heraldo Europeo (Monterrey), 1915
O Imparcial (Rio de Janeiro), 1914–19
El Imparcial (Mexico), 1914
Informaciones Inalámbricas (Mexico), 1918
Jornal do Brasil (Rio de Janeiro), 1914–19
Jornal do Commercio (Rio de Janeiro), 1914–19
El Mercurio (Santiago de Chile), 1914–19
El Mundo Ilustrado (Mexico), 1914
La Nación (Buenos Aires), 1914–19
La Nación (Santiago de Chile), 1917–19
El Nacional (Mexico), 1916–18
The New York Times, 1917–18
Nosotros (Buenos Aires), 1914–19
El País (Mexico), 1914
La Patria de los Aliados (Santiago de Chile), 1918
Petróleo (Mexico), 1914
Por la Verdad (Montevideo), 1918
La Prensa (Buenos Aires), 1914–19
La Prensa (Lima), 1914–19
El Progreso (Cuenca), 1914–18
La Razón (Buenos Aires), 1917
La Razón (Montevideo), 1914–19
A República: Orgão do Partido Republicano Paranaense (Curitiba), 1914–19
El Reflector (Buenos Aires), 1914–15
Regeneración (Los Angeles), 1914–18
Revista Argentina de Ciencias Políticas (Buenos Aires), 1914–19
Revista del Pacífico (Santiago de Chile), 1914–15
Revista do Brasil (São Paulo), 1916–19
El Siglo (Montevideo), 1917
Social (Havanna), 1916–19
The South Pacific Mail (Valparaíso), 1916–18
El Sur (Concepción), 1917–18
Sur América (Bogotá), 1914–18
El Tanque (Valparaíso), 1918
El Tiempo (Bogotá), 1914–18
El Tiempo (La Paz), 1914–19
El Tiempo Nuevo (Santiago de Chile), 1916–18
The Times (London), 1916

Transocean (Bogotá), 1916–18
El Tren (Cuenca), 1914–18
La Unión (Buenos Aires), 1915–19
La Unión (Valparaíso), 1914–19
La Vanguardia (Buenos Aires), 1914–19
Variedades (Lima), 1914–15
La Verdad (Guayaquil), 1917–18
Zig-Zag (Santiago de Chile), 1914–19
El Zorro (Buenos Aires), 1914

Books, Essays, Primary Sources

Abaca, Hilarion, *La guerra europea y la profecía de Leon Tolstoy: con la marcha Francesa*, Rosario de Sta. Fé [ca. 1916].
Ackerman, Carl W., *Mexico's Dilemma*, New York 1918.
Activities of the British Community in Argentina during the Great War, 1914–1919, Buenos Aires 1920.
Adam, Paul, *A los intelectuales de México*, Mexico 1918.
Adám Galareta, Luis L., "Porque estamos en la guerra," *Boletín de Información* 1 (September 1918), pp. 7–8.
El aislamiento pacífico de América: Documentación relativa a la campaña del "Museo Social Argentino" por la neutralización del tráfico maritimo interamericano, Buenos Aires 1916.
Akten zur deutschen auswärtigen Politik, 1918–1945, Serie A, Göttingen 1970–99.
Alberdi, Juan Bautista, *El crimen de la guerra*, Buenos Aires 1915 [1870].
Alemania ante el mundo: la verdad y la guerra, [P. l.] [ca. 1914].
Alfaiano, Donato, *Italia en la guerra: con la verbena "donde vas Alemania,"* Rosario [ca. 1915].
Allande, José María, "Comentarios irreverentes," in: *Caras y Caretas* (February 10, 1917).
Almafuerte [Palacios, Pedro Bonifacio], *Almafuerte y la guerra*, Buenos Aires 1916.
Álvarez, Alejandro, *La Grande Guerre Européenne et la neutralité du Chili*, Paris 1915.
Amarrete, Prudencio, "Los neutrales," in: *Caras y Caretas* (September 12, 1914).
"Las simpatías en la guerra," in: *Caras y Caretas* (October 10, 1914).
"El libro gris," in: *Caras y Caretas* (December 5, 1914).
L'Amérique latine et la guerre europénne, 2 Vols., Paris 1916 and 1920.
Arciniegas, Germán, "La reforma universitaria," in: Dardo Cúneo (ed.), *La reforma universitaria, 1918–1930*, Caracas 1980, pp. 217–19.
Arguello, Santiago, "L'opinion du Nicaragua sur la guerre européenne," in: *L'Amérique latine et la guerre européenne*, Paris 1916, pp. 133–58.
Ariyaga, Vicente/Julio Firtuoso, *La guerra europea: Servia, Japón, Bélgica, Inglaterra Francia y Rusia contra Alemania y Austria; Italia y España en preparación; detalles completos de la situación geográfica de dichas naciones. – número de hombres en pie de guerra*, [Buenos Aires] 1914.

Azevedo, Fernando de, "Illusão americana," in: *Revista do Brasil* 11 (June 1919), pp. 155–62.

Báez, Cecilio, "Le Paraguay et la guerre européenne," in: *L'Amérique latine et la guerre européenne*, Paris 1916, pp. 159–66.

Barbosa, Rui, *Obras completas*, Vol. XLIV, 1917, 2 Parts, Rio de Janeiro 1988.

Barbosa, Ruy/Moacyr, Pedro, *A Revogação da neutralidade do Brazil*, London 1918.

Barés, Manuel A., "Delenda Germaniae," in: *Revista Argentina de Ciencias Políticas* 10 (1915), pp. 226–36 and 495–512 and 11 (1915/16), pp. 38–52.

Barreto, Afonso Henriques de Lima, *Feiras e mafuás: artigos e crônicas*, São Paulo 1955.

Marginália: artigos e crônicas, São Paulo 1956.

Barreto, Plinio, "Eduardo Prado e seus amigos," in: *Revista do Brasil* I (January–April 1916), pp. 173–97.

Barrett, John, "Our Trade Opportunity in Latin America," in: *American Review of Reviews* 50 (1914), pp. 469–74.

Latin America and the War, Washington, DC 1919.

Barroetaveña, Francisco Antonio, *Alemania contra el mundo*, Buenos Aires 1915.

Becú, Carlos A., *El A.B.C. y su concepto político y jurídico*, Buenos Aires 1915.

Benavides Olazábal, F., *En el mundo de la filosofía y de la guerra*, Buenos Aires 1915.

Berenguer, Fernando, *El problema de las subsistencias en Cuba*, Havana 1918.

Bernhardi, Friedrich von, *Alemania y la próxima guerra*, Barcelona 1916.

Bertrán, Luis, "La conflagración europea," in: *Cuba Contemporánia* 6 (8/1914), pp. 86–91.

Bilac, Olavo, *A defesa nacional: discursos*, Rio de Janeiro 1965.

Bomilcar, Alvaro, *O preconceito de raça no Brazil*, Rio de Janeiro 1916.

A política no Brasil ou o nacionalismo radical, Rio de Janeiro 1920.

Bonet, Carmelo M., "Malthus y la guerra," in: *Nosotros* 10 (1916), pp. 49–58.

Borquez Solar, Antonio, "Hexametros a Wilson," in: *Zig-Zag* (December 23, 1916).

Bose, Margarete, *Lo que he visto en Alemania durante y después de la guerra*. Buenos Aires, 1919.

Bott, Ernesto J. J., "Los efectos económicos de la guerra, I, II, III," in: *Nosotros* 12 (18/1918), pp. 476–505, (19/1918), pp. 29–45 and pp. 191–217.

El comercio entre los Estados Unidos y la América Latina durante la Gran Guerra, Buenos Aires 1919.

The Brazilian Green Book: Consisting of Diplomatic Documents Relating to Brazil's Attitude with Regard to the European War, 1914–1917, London 1918.

British Documents on Foreign Affairs [BD], Part II: *From the First to the Second World War*, Series D, *Latin America, 1914–1939*, Vol. 1, *South America, 1914–1922*, Vol. 2, *Central America and Mexico*, London 1989.

Brull, Jaime, "La ansiedad del mundo," in: *Caras y Caretas* (January 2, 1915).

Bueno, Javier, "*Caras y Caretas* en la guerra," in: *Caras y Caretas* (December 26, 1914).

Buero, Juan Antonio, *El Uruguay en la vida internacional: Labor legislativa y periodística (1914–1918)*, Montevideo 1919.

Bunge, Augusto, *El socialismo y los problemas de la paz*, Buenos Aires 1919.

Cabrera Arroyo, J., "América y la guerra europea," in: *Nosotros* 11 (1917), pp. 245–50.

Cámara de Senadores de la República Oriental del Uruguay, *Versión oficial de la sesión extraordinaria celebrada el día 12 de noviembre de 1918*, Montevideo 1918.

Carlès, Manuel, "La République Argentine et la guerre européenne," in: *L'Amérique latine et la guerre européenne*, Paris 1916, pp. 3–22.

Carrasquilla Mallarino, [Eduardo], "Canto de Guerra," in: *Nosotros* 8 (1914), pp. 58–64.

Carvalho, Elysio de, *Brasil, potencia mundial*, Rio de Janeiro 1919.

Castellanos, Julio, "Las consecuencias de la guerra," in: *Caras y Caretas* (October 10, 1914).

Castex, Julián, "La emoción de la guerra," in: *Caras y Caretas* (November 14, 1914).

"Verdades y mentiras," in: *Caras y Caretas* (December 19, 1914).

Castro, Javier, "La guerra en los aires," in: *Caras y Caretas* (August 15, 1914).

Cavalcanti, Amaro, *A neutralidade e as restricções do commercio internacional na presente guerra européa*, Rio de Janeiro 1916.

Cavalcanti, Emiliano di, *Viagem da minha vida: memórias*, Rio de Janeiro 1955.

Cháves, Francisco C., *En favor de los aliados: discursos pronunciados en la ocasión de la gran demonstración en favor de los aliados realizada en Asunción*, London 1917.

Chavez, Ezequiel A., "L'opinion publique mexicaine et la guerre européenne," in: *L'Amérique latine et la guerre européenne*, Paris 1916, pp. 99–131.

Chileno, Un, *Guerra europea de 1914: impresiones recojidas en Berlín*, Santiago de Chile 1915.

Colmo, Alfredo, *Mi neutralismo*, Buenos Aires 1918.

Complete Report of the Chairman of the Committee on Public Information, 1917–1919, Washington, D.C. 1920.

Contreras, Francisco, *Les écrivains hispano-américains et la guerre européenne*, Paris 1917.

Córdoba, Pedro de, *Nuestra guerra: la coalición contra la Argentina*, Buenos Aires 1917.

Cornejo, Mariano H., *La solidaridad americana y la guerra europea*, Lima 1917.

La intervención del Perú en la guerra europea, Lima 1918.

Corredor La Torre, J., "A nos grands frères les français," in: *Voix de l'Amérique latine*, Paris 1916, pp. 36–42.

Correspondencia relacionada con el internamiento de panameños en el campo de concentración de Holzminden, Panama 1917.

Cox Méndez, Ricardo, *A través de la Europa en Guerra*, Santiago 1916.

Creel, George, *How We Advertised America: The First Telling of the Amazing Story of the Committee on Public Information That Carried the Gospel of Americanism to Every Corner of the Globe*, New York 1920.

Cúneo, Dardo (ed.), *La reforma universitaria, 1918–1930*, Caracas 1980.

D'Anthouard, A[lbert], "La politique française au Brésil," in: *Le Correspondant* 272 (July 25, 1918), pp. 193–228.

David, Eduard, *¿Quién es el culpable de la guerra?*, Buenos Aires 1919.

Define, Jacomino, "As razões de Tagore," in: *Revista do Brasil* 7 (February 1918), pp. 159–63.

De la Cova, Rafael, *Venezuela ante el conflicto europeo*, London 1917.

De la Guardía, Ernesto, "La redención a través de los tiempos," in: *Nosotros* 9 (1915), pp. 53–75.

Del Valle Iberlucea, Enrique, *La cuestión internacional y el Partido Socialista*, Buenos Aires 1917.

Di Carlo, Adelia, "La caridad y la guerra," in: *Caras y Caretas* (January 2, 1915).

Díaz Pardo, Horacio, *Cuba ante la guerra*, Havana 1918.

Disposiciones sobre neutralidad (1914–1915), Montevideo 1915.

Documentos relativos a la neutralidad de la República de Colombia respecto de la actual Guerra Européa, Bogotá 1916.

Dohna Schlodien, Nicolás de, *Las hazañas del "Moewe,"* Madrid 1917.

Donoso, Armando, "Nuestra Francia," in: *Zig-Zag* (July 14, 1917).

Donoso, Eduardo, *Impresiones de un chileno, a través de Alemania y Francia durante la guerra*, Santiago de Chile 1917.

Dupuy de Lôme, Emilio, *¡No me hable de la guerra!: monólogo estrenado en el teatro de la Comedia de B. Aires por Rogelio Juárez la noche del 9 de noviembre de 1914*, Buenos Aires 1914.

L'effort politique et charitable de l'Amérique latine, Paris 1918.

Elguero, José, "La bandera de los pueblos débiles," in: *Boletín de Información* 1 (November 1918), pp. 83–5.

Elizalde, R. H., *Circular al Cuerpo Diplomático ... acerca de la neutralidad del Ecuador*, Quito 1915.

Elliott, L. E., "South America and German Commerce," in: *Pan-American Magazine* 27 (5/1918), pp. 247–53.

Empleo, contrario al Derecho internacional de tropas de color en el teatro de la guerra europeo, Berlin 1915.

En favor de los aliados: discursos pronunciados en la ocasión de la gran demonstración en favor de los aliados realizada en Asunción (Paraguay) el 11 de julio de 1917, London 1917.

El Estado General de la Nación durante los gobiernos liberales, Vol. 1, *Archivo del liberalismo*, Asuncion 1987.

Fabela, Isidro (ed.), *La política interior y exterior de Carranza*, Mexico 1979.

Falcó, Angel, *Troquel de fuego: bocetos en rojo sobre la tragedia, 1915–1916*, Buenos Aires 1917.

Fernández Güel, Rogelio, *Plus Ultra: La raza hispana ante el conflicto europeo*, Madrid 1917.

Ferrara, Orestes, "América Latina y la Gran Guerra," in: *Nosotros* 12 (1918), pp. 6–13.

Foppa, Tito Livio, *Mambrú se fue a la guerra*, Buenos Aires 1919.

Fóscolo, Vitelio, *Alemania ante la Guerra: estudio psíco-sociológico*, Buenos Aires 1914.

Freire, V. da Silva, "Guerra e alimentação nacional," in: *Revista do Brasil* 3 (1918), pp. 259–85.

Gaillard, Gaston, *Amérique latine et Europe occidentale: L'Amérique latine et la guerre*, Paris 1918.

Gallardo Nieto, Galvarino, *Neutralidad de Chile ante la guerra europea*, Santiago 1917.

"Posición internacional de Chile ante la guerra europea," ibid., pp. VII–CXIII.

Panamericanismo, Santiago de Chile 1941.

Gamio, Manuel, *Forjando patria*, Mexico 1960 [1916].

Garcia, Eugênio Vargas (ed.), *Diplomacia brasileira e política externa: documentos históricos, 1493–2008*, Rio de Janeiro 2008.

García Calderón, Francisco, *Ideologías*, Paris 1918.

García Calderón, Ventura, "Pourquoi nous sommes francophiles," in: *Voix de l'Amérique latine*, Paris 1916, pp. 61–7.

García Godoy, Federico, "La France et Saint-Domingue," in: *L'Amérique latine et la guerre européenne*, Paris 1916, pp. 87–98.

Gedult von Jungenfeld, Ernesto, *Aus den Urwäldern Paraguays zur Fahne*, Berlin 1916.

Gerlich, Fritz, "La política norte-americana y la doctrina de Monroe," in: *La Revista Latino-América* 1 (1/1917), pp. 35–45.

Gil, Pío, *Diario íntimo*. Vol. 2. *La guerra de 1914 y otros temas*, Caracas 1999.

Gómez Carrillo, Enrique, "Préface: le péril allemand dans l'Amérique du Sud," in: *Voix de l'Amérique latine*, Paris 1916, pp. 5–13.

González, Joaquín V., "Rabindranath Tagore," in: *Revista de Filosofía* 7 (1917), pp. 169–79.

"La paz internacional y el derecho de las naciones," in: *Revista de Filosofía* 9 (1919), pp. 279–303.

González, Julio V., "Significado de la reforma universitaria," in: Dardo Cúneo (ed.), *La reforma universitaria, 1918–1930*, Caracas 1980, pp. 187–206.

González Cadavid, Eligio, *El héroe*, Buenos Aires 1918.

La Guerra Mundial de 1914: traducciones de relatos verídicos y de artículos de fondo de las mejores publicaciones alemanas, Guayaquil 1915.

Guerrero, Jenaro, *Alemania en la lucha*, Bogotá 1915.

Gutiérrez y Sánchez, Gustavo, *La neutralidad y la beligerancia de la República de Cuba durante la guerra actual*, Havana 1917.

Hale, William B., "Our Moral Empire in America," in: *The World's Work* 28 (1914), pp. 52–8.

Haya de la Torre, Víctor Raúl, "La reforma universitaria y la gran lección de la guerra," in: Dardo Cúneo (ed.), *La reforma universitaria, 1918–1930*, Caracas 1980, pp. 230–1.

"La reforma universitaria," in: Dardo Cúneo (ed.), *La reforma universitaria, 1918–1930*, Caracas 1980, pp. 232–40.

Hidalgo, Alberto, *Arenga lírica al Emperador de Alemania: otros poemas*, Arequipa 1916.

Hintze, Otto, *Alemania y la guerra europea*, Vol. 1, *Alemania: su política y sus instituciones*, Barcelona 1916.

Holder, Arthur L. (ed.), *Activities of the British Community in Argentina during the Great War 1914–1919*, Buenos Aires 1920.

Homet, Juan B., *Diario de un argentino: soldado en la guerra actual*, Buenos Aires 1918.

Los horrores de la guerra, Rosario de Santa Fe [ca. 1914].

Huidobro, Emilio, *La paz europea*, Lima 1918.

Huneeus Gana, Roberto, *Por amor a Chile y por gratitud a Alemania*, Santiago de Chile 1917.

Iaroschewsky, M., "La revolución en Rusia," in: *Nosotros* 11 (1917), pp. 289–94.

Ibarguren, Carlos, *La literatura y la gran guerra*, Buenos Aires 1920.

La historia que he vivido, Buenos Aires 1999 [1955].

Los ideales de México y la guerra europea, Mexico 1918.

"Informes diplomáticos de los representantes del Imperio Alemán en el Uruguay, 1912–1915," in: *Revista Histórica* 69 (Montevideo, 1975), pp. 117–202.

Informe del Ministerio de Relaciones Exteriores al Congreso, Bogotá 1915–19.

Ingenieros, José, "La religión de la raza," in: *Caras y Caretas* (October 31, 1914).

"Patria y cultura," in: *Caras y Caretas* (November 7, 1914).

"El nuevo nacionalismo argentino," in: *Caras y Caretas* (November 14, 1914).

"La formación de una raza argentina,"in: *Revistade Filosofía* 5 (1915), pp. 464–83.

"Significación histórica del maximalismo," in: *Nosotros* 12 (1918), pp. 374–9.

Los tiempos nuevos, Buenos Aires 1947.

Obras Campletas, 8 Vols., Buenos Aires 1961–2.

"La reforma en América Latina," in: Dardo Cúneo (ed.), *La reforma universitaria, 1918–1930*, Caracas 1980, pp. 221–2.

Las intenciones de Alemania contra la América Central y la América del Sur, Washington, no date given [1917].

Ivens, Elena, "¿Por qué luchan?," in: *Zig-Zag* (October 24, 1914).

Kaulen, Julio, *Las verdaderas causas de la guerra según artículos de reputados autores franceses escritos años antes de estallar el conflicto*, Santiago de Chile 1918.

Kinkelin, Emilio, *Los estragos del hambre en Alemania*, Buenos Aires 1919.

Mis correspondencias a La Nación durante la guerra europea, 2 Vols., Buenos Aires 1921.

Kirkpatrick, F. A., *South America and the War*, Cambridge 1918.

Kuempel, Juan, *La guerra*, Valparaíso 1915.

Labor and the War: American Federation of Labor and the Labor Movement of Europe and Latin America, Washington, DC, 1918.

Lavaerd, H., "Después de la guerra," in: *Revista Argentina de Ciencias Políticas* 9 (1914/15), pp. 445–52.

Lavalle, Juan Bautista de, *El Perú y la gran guerra*, Lima 1919.

Las negociaciones de Berlín y la ruptura con el gobierno alemán, Lausanne 1920.

León Sánchez, Manuel, *La guerra mundial vista desde México*, Mexico 1917.

Si el ejército alemán llegase a México, Mexico 1918.

Noticias falsas: las atrocidades alemanas y la propaganda yanqui-aliada; conferencia sustentada el jueves 15 de agosto de 1918, en la Academia Metropolitana de México, Mexico 1918.

Los submarinos y las listas negras: conferencia sustentada el 3 de septiembre de 1918, en la Academia Metropolitana de México, Mexico 1918.

Lima, Manoel de Oliveira, *Na Argentina: impressões 1918–1919*, São Paulo 1920.

Lima, Henrique da Rocha, "Delenda est Germania," in: *A Guerra: revista semanal* 6 (December 1914), pp. 7–15.

Lobato, José Bento Monteiro, *Críticas e outras notas*, São Paulo 1965.

López, Nicolás F., "The Attitude of Ecuador," in: *South American Opinions on the War*, Washington, DC 1917, pp. 20–7.

Lugones, Leopoldo et al., *La convención patriótica del Comité Nacional de la Juventud y la proclama de los intelectuales argentinos sobre el gobierno imperial alemán y la guerra internacional*, Buenos Aires 1917.

Mi beligerancia, Buenos Aires 1917.

Mackenna, Alberto, *Le Triomphe du Droit*, Santiago de Chile 1916.

Mann, Wilhelm, *Kampf um den Kultureinfluss in Chile sowie dem übrigen Lateinamerika*, Valparaíso 1918.

Mariátegui, José Carlos, "La emoción de nuestro tiempo," in: *Amauta* 31 (1930) [1925], pp. 4–5.

Marthur, Eduardo, "Los buitres," in: *Caras y Caretas* (October 31, 1914).

Martínez, José A., "La entrada de Cuba en la guerra universal," in: *Cuba Contemporánea* 14 (May 1917), pp. 5–11.

Más y Pi, Juan, "Con los nuestros: un comentario al margen de la Guerra Grande," in: *Nosotros* 8 (1914), pp. 228–32.

Materialien, betreffend die Friedensverhandlungen, Teil 10, *Sachverzeichnis zum Friedensvertrage: Autorisierte Ausgabe im Auftrage des Auswärtigen Amtes*, Charlottenburg 1919.

Matiz, Reinaldo, *Amistad Colombo Germana*, Bogotá 1918.

Medeiros e Albuquerque, José, "Le Brésil et la guerre," in: *L'Amérique latine et la guerre européenne*, Paris 1916, pp. 35–47.

Melgar, Ramón, "El espíritu religioso y la guerra," in: *Revista de Filosofía* 8 (1918), pp. 363–75.

Memoria de relaciones exteriores y culto presentada al honorable congreso nacional, Buenos Aires 1913–21.

Mejía Rodríguez, Alfonso, *La France, notre mère intellectuelle, conférences et articles*, n.p. 1918.

Meléndez, Carlos, *Las relaciones entre los Estados Unidos de América y El Salvador*, Washington, DC 1918.

Meléndez Chaverri, Carlos (ed.), *Mensajes presidenciales.* Vol. 4, *1906–1916*. Vol. 5, *1918–1928*, San José 1983–5.

Melgar, Ramón, *La bancarrota de una civilización: guerra europea de 1914*, Dolores 1914.

Mesquita, Julio, *A guerra, 1914–1918*, Vol. 1–4, São Paulo 2002.

Ministerio das Relações Exteriores, *Guerra da Europa: Documentos Diplomáticos*, Vol. 1, *Attitude do Brasil, 1914–1917*, Vol. 2, *Attitude do Brasil, 1918*, Rio de Janeiro 1917 and 1918.

Mintz, Steven (ed.), *Mexican American Voices: A Documentary Reader*, Chichester ²2009.

Montesa, Gil, "La guerra más grande de los siglos," in: *Caras y Caretas* (August 22, 1914).

Montoro, José Enrique, "Las causas de la guerra," in: *Cuba Contemporánea* 6 (9/1914), pp. 138–50.

"Alemania y la Guerra Europa," in: *Cuba Contemporánea* 6 (10/1914), pp. 378–401.

Morató, Octavio, *América del Sur y la futura paz europea*, Montevideo 1918.

Moura, João Dunshee de Abranches, *Porque devemos ser amigos da Alemanha*, Rio de Janeiro 1914.

Brazil and the Monroe Doctrine, Rio de Janeiro 1915.

A illusão brazileira, Rio de Janeiro ³1917.

A Allemanha e a paz: appello ao Presidente da Camara dos Deputados ao Congresso Nacional do Brasil, São Paulo 1917.

Naón, Rómulo S., "Solidaridad americana ante la guerra europea," *Revista Argentina de Ciencias Políticas* 10 (1915), pp. 215–22.

Neves, Abdias, *O Brasil e as espheras de influencia na Conferencia da Paz*, Rio de Janeiro 1919.

Niemann, August, *Der Weltkrieg: Deutsche Träume*, Berlin 1904.

Niessen-Deiters, Leonore, *Krieg, Auslanddeutschtum und Presse*, Stuttgart 1915.

Nieto de Herrera, Carmela, "La mujer después de la guerra," in: *Social* (March 1919), p. 55.

Nin Frías, Alberto, "El cristianismo y la guerra," in: *Nosotros* 10 (1916), pp. 364–73.

Nogales, Rafael de, *Cuatro años bajo la media luna*, Caracas 1991 [1924].

La nueva interpretación de la Doctrina de Monroe, Washington, DC, no date given [1917].

Palacios, Alfredo L., *Prusianismo y democracia*, Buenos Aires 1917.

The Papers of Woodrow Wilson, ed. Arthur S. Link, Princeton, 67 Vols., 1966–92.

Papers Relating to the Foreign Relations of the United States [FRUS], 1917–19 Washington, DC 1931–3.

Pardo Suárez, Vicente, *Ladrones de tierras*, Havana 1918.

Payró, Roberto, *Corresponsal de guerra: cartas, diario, relatos (1907–1922)*, Buenos Aires 2009.

Peixoto, Afrânio, *Minha terra e minha gente*, Rio de Janeiro 1916.

Pérez Triana, Santiago, *Some Aspects of the War*, London 1915.

The Neutrality of Latin America, Cambridge 1916.

Perón, Juan, *Guerra Mundial 1914*, Buenos Aires 1931.

Piccione, Enrico, *La guerra ante la historia y la ciencia*, Santiago de Chile 1918.

Pinheiro, Nuno, *Problemas da guerra e da paz: legislação de guerra do Brasil*, Rio de Janeiro 1919.

Ponce, Aníbal, "El año 1918 y América Latina," in: Dardo Cúneo (ed.), *La reforma universitaria, 1918–1930*, Caracas 1980, pp. 223–5.

Prazeres, Otto, *O Brasil na guerra: algumas notas para a historia*, Rio de Janeiro 1918. *Proceedings of the First Pan-American Financial Conference, May 24 to 29, 1915*, Washington, DC 1915.

Quesada, Ernesto, "El 'peligro alemán' en Sud América," in: *Revista Argentina de Ciencias Políticas* 9 (1914/15), pp. 387–407.

La actual civilización germánica y la presente guerra, Buenos Aires, ²1914.

"Unión intelectual panamericana," in: *Revista de Filosofía* 7 (1917), pp. 23–33.

Ramos, Juan P., "Alemania ante la guerra," in: *Revista Argentina de Ciencias Políticas* 9 (1914/15), pp. 427–44.

Alemania ante la guerra, Buenos Aires 1915.

Die Bedeutung Deutschlands im europäischen Krieg, Stuttgart 1917.

Rebolledo, Miguel, *México y Estados Unidos*, Mexico 1917.

Requisición de los vapores alemanes refugiados al puerto de Montevideo por el gobierno del Uruguay en 1917, Montevideo 1918.

Ribas, Federico, "Desde Paris: un aviador argentino en la guerra," in: *Caras y Caretas* (January 8, 1916).

Rinke, Stefan/Fischer, Georg/Schulze, Frederik (eds.), *Geschichte Lateinamerikas vom 19. bis zum 21. Jahrhundert: Quellenband*, Stuttgart 2009.

Rivarola, Rodolfo, "América y la paz europea," *Revista Argentina de Ciencias Políticas* 13 (1917), pp. 319–24.

Rivero, Nicolás/Gil del Real, J., *El conflicto europeo: actualidades y diario de la guerra*, Havana 1916.

Robertson, William S., "Argentina's Attitude to the War," in: *The Nation* (March 1, 1917), pp. 234–5.

Roca, Deodoro, "La nueva generación americana," in: Dardo Cúneo (ed.), *La reforma universitaria, 1918–1930*, Caracas 1980, pp. 145–9.

Rocuant, Enrique, *La neutralité du Chili: les raisons qui l'ont conseillée et qui la justifient*, Santiago de Chile 1919.

Rodó, José Enrique, "La solidarité des peuples latines," in: *Voix de l'Amérique latine*, Paris 1916, pp. 71–2.

Rodríguez Mendoza, E., "La Guerra y la América," in: *Revista chilena* 28 (1919), pp. 225–49.

Rojas, Ricardo, *La Argentinidad*, Buenos Aires 1916.

Rojas, Ricardo, *La guerra de las naciones*, Buenos Aires 1924.

Roldán, Belisario, *Una madre, en Francia: novela inédita original*, Buenos Aires 1917.

Ruptura de relaciones diplomáticas con el gobierno imperial de Alemania, Lima 1918.

Salomon, El Sargento, *La guerra europea: relación en versos – con la marcha "Italia neutral,"* Rosario Sta. Fé [ca. 1915].

Sanguinetti, Florentino V., "Reforma y contrarreforma en Buenos Aires," in: Dardo Cúneo (ed.), *La reforma universitaria, 1918–1930*, Caracas 1980, pp. 241–54.

Sayé, Pedro, *Crema de menta*, Asunción 1916.

Scholz, Alfred, *Brasilien im Weltkriege*, Siemerode ²1933.

Schönberg, Karl von, *Vom Auslandsdienst in Mexiko zur Seeschlacht von Coronel: Kapitän zur See Karl von Schönberg, Reisetagebuch 1913–1914*, ed. Gerhard Wiechmann, Bochum 2004.

Silva Vildósola, Carlos, "Le Chili et la guerre européenne," in: *L'Amérique latine et la guerre européenne*, Paris 1916, pp. 49–77.

Le Chili et la guerre, Paris 1917.

Soignie, Fernando de, *Crónicas de sangre*, Havana, no date given [1919].

Solveira de Báez, Beatriz Rosario (eds.), *Argentina y la Primera Guerra Mundial según documentos del Archivo del Ministerio de Relaciones Exteriores y Culto*, 2 Vols., Córdoba 1979/94.

South American Opinions on the War, Washington, DC 1917.

Spiegel von und zu Peckelsheim, Edgar, *El submarino U 202: diario de la guerra*, Madrid 1917.

Storni, Julio S., *Mi opinión sobre la neutralidad*, Corrientes 1917.

Sux, Alejandro, *Las voluntarios de la libertad: contribución de los latino-americanos a la causa de los Aliados*, Paris 1918.

Taborda, Saúl, *Escritos políticos 1918–1934*, Córdoba 2009.

Troeltsch, Ernst, *El espíritu de la cultura alemana*, Buenos Aires [um 1916].

Turcios R., Salvador, *Al margen del imperialismo yanquí*, San Salvador 1915.

Ugarte, Manuel, *La América Latina ante la Guerra europea*, Mexico 1917.

Mi campaña hispanoamericana, Barcelona 1922.

La patria grande, Buenos Aires 2010 [1924].

Uriburu, José Félix, *La guerra actual: apuntes y enseñanzas*, Buenos Aires 1915.

U.S. War Trade Board (ed.), *Trading with the Enemy: Enemy Trading List*, Washington, DC 1917.

Valle Iberlucea, Enrique del, *La guerra europea y la política internacional*, Buenos Aires 1914.

Vargas Vila, José María, *Ante los bárbaros*, Bogotá 1985 [1917].

Vergara Biedma, Ernesto, *Guerra de mentiras: el discurso de Wilson y el peligro yanqui*, Buenos Aires 1917.

Vial Solar, Javier, *Conversaciones sobre la guerra*, Santiago de Chile 1917.

Vicuña Mackenna, Benjamín, *Páginas de mi diario durante tres años de viaje, 1853–1854–1855*, Santiago de Chile 1936.

Vieytes, Lerón, *Después de la guerra: diálogo dramático en verso de palpitante actualidad*, Buenos Aires 1917.

Villanueva, Carlos A., "Le Vénézuela et la guerre européenne," in: *L'Amérique latine et la guerre européenne*, Paris 1916, pp. 187–202.

Voix de l'Amérique latine, Paris 1916.

Wilmart, Raymond, "I. El ideal americano. II. Peligros," in: *Revista Argentina de Ciencias Políticas* 9 (1914/15), pp. 363–86.

"La guerra," in: *Revista Argentina de Ciencias Políticas* 10 (1915), pp. 513–6.

"La paz europea y América," in: *Revista Argentina de Ciencias Políticas* 12 (1916), pp. 393–8.

Wilson, Woodrow, "El programa de la paz," in: *Caras y Caretas* (December 21, 1918).

Yañez, G. F., "La Guerra Europea," in: *Estudios* 7 (1914), pp. 441–8.

Zarraga, Miguel de, "El amor y la guerra," in: *Social* (November 11, 1916), p. 8.

Secondary Literature

Aguilar Bulgarelli, Oscar, *Federico Tinoco Granados en la historia*, San José 2008.

Aillón Soria, Esther, "La política cultural de Francia en la génesis y difusión del concepto l'Amérique Latine, 1860–1930," in: Aimer Granados/Carlos Marichal (eds.), *Construcción de las identidades latinoamericanas: ensayos de historia intelectual, siglos XIX y XX*, Mexico 2004, pp. 71–106.

Albert, Bill, *South America and the World Economy*, London 1983.

South America and the First World War, Cambridge 1988.

Albes, Jens, *Worte wie Waffen: Die deutsche Propaganda in Spanien während des Ersten Weltkriegs*, Essen 1996.

Alexander, Robert J., *International Labor Organizations and Organized Labor in Latin America and the Caribbean: A History*, Santa Barbara 2009.

Andrews, Gregg, *Shoulder to Shoulder? The American Federation of Labor, the United States, and the Mexican Revolution, 1910–1924*, Berkeley 1991.

Appelbaum, Nancy, "Racial Nations," in: idem et al. (eds.), *Race and Nation in Modern Latin America*, Chapel Hill 2003, pp. 1–31.

Arroyo Reyes, Carlos, *Nuestros años diez: la Asociación Pro-Indígena, el levantamiento de Rumi Maqui y el incaísmo modernista*, n.p. 2005.

Ayala Mora, Enrique et al. (eds.), *Historia General de América Latina*, Vol. 7, *Los proyectos nacionales latinoamericanos: sus instrumentos y articulación, 1870–1930*, Madrid 2008.

Baecker, Thomas, "The Arms of the Ypiranga: The German Side," in: *The Americas* 30 (1/1973), pp. 1–17.

Bagú, Sergio, *Argentina en el mundo*, Buenos Aires 1961.

Bailey, Thomas A., *The Policy of the United States Toward the Neutrals, 1917–1918*, New York 1979 [1942].

Bakewell, Peter, *A History of Latin America*, Malden ²2004.

Bandeira, Moniz/Melo, Clovis/Andrade, A. T., *O ano vermelho: a revolução russa e seus reflexos no Brasil*, Rio de Janeiro 1967.

Bauer, Alfredo, *La Asociación Vorwärts y la lucha democrática en la Argentina*, Buenos Aires 2008.

Bayly, Christopher A., *The Birth of the Modern World, 1780–1914*, Malden 2004.

Bernecker, Walther L., *Die Handelskonquistadoren: Europäische Interessen und mexikanischer Staat im 19. Jahrhundert*, Stuttgart 1988.

Bertolli Filho, Cláudio, *A gripe espanhola em São Paulo, 1918: epidemia e sociedade*, São Paulo 2003.

Bertucci, Liane Maria, *Influenza, a medicina enferma: ciência e práticas de cura na época da gripe espanhola em São Paulo*, Campinas 2004.

Bieber, León E., "La política militar alemana en Bolivia, 1900–1935," in: *Latin American Research Review* 29 (1/1994), pp. 85–106.

Bilsky, Edgardo, *La Semana trágica*, Buenos Aires 2011.

Bindernagel, Franka, "Migration und Erinnerung: Öffentliche Erinnerungskultur deutschsprachiger Migrant/innen in Buenos Aires, 1910–1932," Diss. phil., Freie Universität Berlin 2014.

Biondi, Luigi, *Classe e nação: trabalhadores e socialistas italianos em São Paulo, 1890–1920*, Campinas 2009.

Blancpain, Jean-Pierre, *Migrations et mémoire germaniques en Amérique Latine à l'époque contemporaine: contribution à l'étude de l'expansion allemande outre-mer*, Strasbourg 1994.

Bley, Helmut/Kremers, Anorthe (eds.), *The World during the First World War*, Essen 2014.

Bösch, Frank/Hoeres, Peter (eds.), *Außenpolitik im Medienzeitalter: Vom späten 19. Jahrhundert bis zur Gegenwart*, Göttingen 2013.

"Im Bann der Öffentlichkeit? Der Wandel der Außenpolitik im Medienzeitalter," in: idem (eds.), *Außenpolitik im Medienzeitalter: Vom späten 19. Jahrhundert bis zur Gegenwart*, Göttingen 2013, pp. 7–35.

Boghardt, Thomas, *The Zimmermann Telegram: Intelligence, Diplomacy, and America's Entry into World War I*, Annapolis 2012.

Bonilla, Heraclio/Rabanal, Alejandro, "La Hacienda San Nicolás (Supe) y la Primera Guerra Mundial," in: *Economía* (Lima) 2 (3/1979), pp. 3–47.

Bonow, Stefan Chamorro, *A desconfiança sobre os indivíduos de origem germânica em Porto Alegre durante a Primeira Guerra Mundial: cidadãos leais ou retovados?* Diss. phil., Porto Alegre 2011.

Bouret, Daniela/Remedi, Gustavo, *Escenas de la vida cotidiana: El nacimiento de la sociedad de masas, 1910–1930*, Montevideo 2009.

Boyle, Francis Anthony, *Foundations of World Order: The Legalist Approach to International Relations, 1898–1922*, Durham 1999.

Bra, Gerardo, *La doctrina Drago*, Buenos Aires 1990.

Bravo Valdivieso, Germán, *La Primera Guerra Mundial en la costa de Chile: una neutralidad que no fue tal*, Viña del Mar 2005.

Brown, Matthew (ed.), *Informal Empire in Latin America: Culture, Commerce and Capital*, Oxford 2008.

Buchenau, Jürgen, *In the Shadow of the Giant: The Making of Mexico's Central America Policy 1876–1930*, Tuscaloosa 1996.

Bugiato, Caio Martins, "O Impacto da Revolução Russa e a fundação do Partido Comunista no Brasil," in: *História social* 14–15 (Campinas, 2008), pp. 141–57.

Bulmer-Thomas, Victor, *The Economic History of Latin America since Independence*, Cambridge 1994.

Burkholder, Mark A./Johnson, Lyman L., *Colonial Latin America*, Oxford ⁴2001.

Burns, Bradford, *The Poverty of Progress: Latin America in the Nineteenth Century*, Berkeley 1980.

Campos, Maria Inês Batista, *A construção da identidade nacional nas crônicas da Revista do Brasil*, São Paulo 2011.

Cardim, Carlos Henrique, *A raiz das coisas – Rui Barbosa: O Brasil no mundo*, Rio de Janeiro 2007.

Caruso, Laura Gabriela, "La huelga general marítima del Puerto de Buenos Aires, diciembre 1916," in: *Revista de Estudios Marítimos y Sociales* 1 (1/2008), pp. 1–17.

Cavalcanti, Pedro, *A presidência de Wenceslau Braz 1914–1918*, Brasília 1983.

Cavieres, Eduardo, *Comercio chileno y comerciantes ingleses, 1820–1880*, Santiago 1988.

Centenário da imigração japonesa no Brasil: 1908–2008, São Paulo 2008.

Chevalier, François, *América Latina de la independencia a nuestros días*, Barcelona 1983.

Chicote, Gloria B., "La cultura de los márgenes devenida en objeto de la ciencia: Robert Lehmann-Nitsche en la Argentina," in: *Iberoamericana* 9 (33/2009), pp. 103–20.

Compagnon, Olivier, "1914–18: The Death Throes of Civilization: The Elites of Latin America Face the Great War," in: Macleod, Jenny/Purseigle, Pierre (eds.), *Uncovered Fields: Perspectives in First World War Studies*, Leiden 2004, pp. 279–95.

"'Si loin, si proche … ': La Premiere Guerre mondiale dans la presse argentine et bresilienne," in: Jean Lamarre /Magali Deleuze (eds.), *L'envers de la médaille: guerres, témoignages et representations*, Laval 2007, pp. 78–91.

"Entrer en guerre? Neutralité et engagement de l'Amérique latine entre 1914 et 1918," in: *Relations internationales* 137 (2009), pp. 31–43.

L'adieu à l'Europe: L'Amérique latine et la Grande Guerre (Argentine et Brésil, 1914–1939), Paris 2013.

Conniff, Michael L., *Panama and the United States: The Forced Alliance*, Athens 1992.

Conrad, Sebastian/Sachsenmaier, Dominic, "Introduction," in: Idem (eds.), *Competing Visions of World Order: Global Moments and Movements 1880s–1930s*, New York 2007, pp. 1–28.

Competing Visions of World Order: Global Moments and Movements 1880s–1930s, New York 2007.

Contreras, Manuel E., "La minería estañifera boliviana en la Primera Guerra Mundial," in: *Minería y economía en Bolivia*, La Paz 1984, pp. 15–38.

Corbière, Emilio J., *Orígenes del comunismo argentino: el Partido Socialista Internacional*, Buenos Aires 1984.

Couyoumdjian, Juan Ricardo, "En torno a la neutralidad de Chile durante la Primera Guerra Mundial," in: Walter Sánchez/Teresa Pereira (eds.), *Cientocinquenta años de política exterior chilena*, Santiago de Chile 1977, pp. 180–205.

Chile y Gran Bretaña durante la Primera Guerra Mundial y la postguerra, Santiago 1986.

Couyoumdjian, Juan Ricardo/Muñoz, María Angélica, "Chilenos en Europa durante la Primera Guerra Mundial, 1914–1918," in: *Historia* 35 (Santiago de Chile, 2002), pp. 35–62.

Cuenca, Álvaro, *La colonia británica de Montevideo y la gran guerra*, Montevideo 2006.

Cuenya Mateos, Miguel Ángel, "Reflexiones en torno a la pandemia de influenza de 1918: el caso de la ciudad de Puebla," in: *Desacatos* 32 (January–April 2010), pp. 145–58.

Cunningham, Michele, *Mexico and the Foreign Policy of Napoleon III*, Basingstoke 2001.

Davis, William C., *The Last Conquistadores: The Spanish Intervention in Peru and Chile, 1863–66*, Athens 1950.

Dawson, Frank G., *The First Latin American Debt Crisis:The City of London and the 1822–1825 Loan Bubble*, New Haven 1990.

Dehne, Phillip A., *On the Far Western Front: Britain's First World War in South America*, Manchester 2009.

"Britain's Global War and Argentine Neutrality," in: Johan Den Hertog/Samuel Kruizinga (eds.), *Caught in the Middle: Neutrals, Neutrality and the First World War*, Amsterdam 2011, pp. 67–84.

"How Important Was Latin America to the First World War?," in: *Iberoamericana* 14 (2014), pp. 151–64.

Deutsch, Sandra McGee, *Las derechas: la extrema derecha en la Argentina, el Brasil y Chile, 1890–1939*, Buenos Aires 2005.

Devés Valdés, Eduardo, *El pensamiento latinoamericano en el siglo XX: entre la modernización y la identidad*, Vol. 1, *Del Ariel de Rodó a la CEPAL, 1900–1950*, Santiago de Chile 2001.

Devés Valdés, Eduardo/Melgar Bao, Ricardo "Redes teosóficas y pensadores (políticos) latinoamericanos 1910–1930," in: *Cuardenos Americanos* 78 (1999), pp. 137–52.

Devoto, Fernando J., *Historia de los italianos en la Argentina*, Buenos Aires 2006.

Díaz Araujo, Enrique, *Yrigoyen y la guerra*, Mendoza 1987.

Doron, Rafael, *Legionarios de Argentina: Voluntarios de la Legión Judía en la Primera Guerra Mundial*, Buenos Aires 2010.

Doß, Kurt, *Das deutsche Auswärtige Amt im Übergang vom Kaiserreich zur Weimarer Republik: Die Schülersche Reform*, Düsseldorf 1977.

Drews, José Pablo, "Estampas desde las trincheras: José Enrique Rodó y su lectura de la Gran Guerra," in: *Thémata: Revista de Filosofía* 48 (2013), pp. 135–42.

Durán, Esperanza, *Guerra y revolución: las grandes potencias y México, 1914–1918*, Mexico 1985.

Earle, Rebecca, *The Return of the Native: Indians and Myth-Making in Spanish America, 1810–1930*, Durham 2007.

Ellis, Keith, "Vicente Huidobro y la Primera Guerra Mundial," in: *Hispanic Review* 67 (3/1999), pp. 333–46.

Enders, Arnelle/Compagnon, Olivier "L'Amérique Latine et la guerre," in: Stéphane Audoin-Rouzeau/Jean-Jacques Becker (eds.), *Encyclopédie de la Grande Guerre 1914–1918*, Paris 2004, pp. 889–902.

Fausto, Boris, *Trabalho urbano e conflito social 1890–1920*, São Paulo 1976.

Fermandois, Joaquín, *Mundo y fin de mundo: Chile en la política mundial 1900–2004*, Santiago de Chile 2004.

Ferrero, Roberto Aquiles, *Historia crítica del movimiento estudiantil de Córdoba*, Vol. 1:*1918–1943*, Córdoba 1999.

Fiebig-von Hase, Ragnhild, "Der Anfang vom Ende des Krieges: Deutschland, die USA und die Hintergründe des amerikanischen Kriegseintritts am 6. April 1917," in: Wolfgang Michalka (ed.), *Der Erste Weltkrieg: Wirkung, Wahrnehmung, Analyse*, Munich 1994, pp. 125–58.

Fischer, Steven Roger, *Island at the End of the World: The Turbulent History of Easter Island*, London 2005.

Fischer, Thomas, *Die Souveränität der Schwachen: Lateinamerika und der Völkerbund, 1920–1936*, Stuttgart 2012.

Flynn, Dennis O./Giráldez, Arturo "Globalization Began in 1571," in: Barry K. Gills/William R. Thomson (eds.), *Globalization and Global History*, London 2004, pp. 208–22.

"Born Again: Globalization's Sixteenth Century Origins," *Pacific Economic Review* 13 (2008), pp. 359–87.

Fogarty, Richard S., *Race and War in France: Colonial Subjects in the French Army, 1914–1918*, Baltimore 2008.

Foote, Nicola/Goebel, Michael (eds.), *Immigration and National Identities in Latin America*, Gainesville 2014.

Frank, Andre Gunder, *Latin America: Underdevelopment or Revolution*, New York 1969.

Franzina, Emilio, "La guerra lontana: il primo conflitto mondiale e gli Italianid' Argentina," in: *Estudios migratorios latinoamericanos* 44 (2000), pp. 66–73.

Frey, Marc, "The Neutrals and World War One," in: *Defense Studies* 3 (2000), pp. 3–39.

Freytag, Nils, "Neuerscheinungen zum 1. Weltkrieg. Einführung," in: *sehepunkte* 14 (2014), No. 7/8 [07.15.2014], URL: www.sehepunkte.de/2014/07/ forum/ neuerscheinungen-zum-1-weltkrieg-178/.

Fuentes Codera, Maximiliano, *España en la Primera Guerra Mundial: Una movilización cultural*, Madrid 2014.

Funes, Patricia, *Salvar la nación: intelectuales, cultura y política en los años veinte latinoamericanos*, Buenos Aires 2006.

Garambone, Sidney, *A primeira Guerra Mundial e a imprensa brasileira*, Rio de Janeiro 2003.

Garay, Narciso, *Panamá y las guerras de los Estados Unidos*, Panamá 1930.

Garcia, Eugênio Vargas, *O Brasil e a Liga das Nações (1919–1926): vencer ou não perder*, Porto Alegre 2000.

García, Manuel Andrés, *Indigenismo, izquierda, indio: Perú, 1900–1930*, Sevilla 2010.

Gasquet, Axel, *El orientalismo argentino 1900–1940: de la revista Nosotros al grupo Sur*, College Park 2008.

Gazmuri, Cristián, *El "48" chileno*, Santiago de Chile 1998.

Geli, Patricio, "Representations of the Great War in the South American Left: The Socialist Party of Argentina," in: Helmut Bley/Anorthe Kremers (eds.), *The World during the First World War*, Essen 2014, pp. 201–14.

Gerhardt, Ray C., "Inglaterra y el petróleo mexicano durante la primera guerra mundial," in: *Historia Mexicana* 25 (1975), pp. 114–42.

Gilderhus, Mark, *Pan American Visions: Woodrow Wilson in the Western Hemisphere, 1913–1921*, Tucson 1986.

Gills, Barry K./Thomson, William R. (eds.), *Globalization and Global History*, London 2004.

Goebel, Michael, "Una biografía entre espacios: M. N. Roy – del nacionalismo indio al comunismo mexicano," in: *Historia Mexicana* 62 (2013), pp. 1459–95.

Goñi Demarchi, Carlos A./Scala, José N./Berraondo, Germán W., *Yrigoyen y la Gran Guerra*, Buenos Aires 1998.

Gonzalo, Marisol de, "Relaciones entre Estados Unidos y América Latina a comienzos de la primera guerra mundial: formulación de una política comercial," in: *Boletín histórico* 47 (Caracas, 1978), pp. 181–241.

Gosine, Mahin, "Sojourner to Settlers: An Introduction," in: idem/Narine Dhanpaul (eds.), *Sojourners to Settlers: Indian Migrants in the Caribbean and the Americas*, Hamburg, PA, 1999, pp. 3–21.

Goulart, Adriana da Costa, "Revisiting the Spanish Flu: The Influenza Pandemic in Rio de Janeiro," in: *Historia, Ciência, Saúde. Manguinhos* 12 (1/2005), pp. 101–42.

Graham, Richard (ed.), *The Idea of Race in Latin America*, Austin 1990.

Gravil, Roger, "The Anglo-Argentine Connection and the War of 1914–1918," in: *Journal of Latin American Studies* 9 (1977), pp. 59–89.

The Anglo-Argentine Connection, 1900–1939, Boulder 1985.

Gruzinski, Serge, *Les quatre parties du monde: Histoire d'une mondialisation*, Paris 2004.

Guerrero Yoacham, Cristián, *Las conferencias del Niagara Falls*, Santiago de Chile, 1966.

Guthunz, Ute, "La construcción de imágenes de amigo-enemigo y los cambios de alianza: Cuba y la guerra hispano-cubano-americana," in: *Iberoamericana* 22 (3/4, 1998), pp. 6–21.

Haber, Stephen/Klein, Herbert S., "The Economic Consequences of Brazilian Independence," in: Stephen Haber (ed.), *How Latin America Fell Behind: Essays on the Economic Histories of Brazil and Mexico, 1800–1914*, Stanford 1997, pp. 243–59.

Halperin, Tulio, "¿Para qué la inmigración? Ideología y política inmigratoria y aceleración del proceso modernizador: El caso argentino, 1810–1914," in: *Jahrbuch für Geschichte ... Lateinamerikas* 13 (1976), pp. 437–89.

Geschichte Lateinamerikas, Frankfurt am Main 1994.

Hardach, Gerd, *Der Erste Weltkrieg, 1914–1918*, Munich 1973.

Harris III, Charles H./Sadler, Louis R, *The Archaeologist Was a Spy: Sylvanus G. Morley and the Office of Naval Intelligence*, Albuquerque 2003.

Hawkins, Nigel, *The Starvation Blockades: Naval Blockades of World War I*, Barnsley 2002.

Hertog, Johan den/Kruizinga, Samuël, "Introduction," in: Idem (eds.): *Caught in the Middle: Neutrals, Neutrality and the First World War*, Amsterdam 2011, pp. 1–14.

Hilton, Sylvia-Lyn/Ickringill, Steve J. S. (eds.), *European Perceptions of the Spanish-American War of 1898*, Bern 1999.

Hodge Dupré, Eduardo, "La defensa continental de América Latina en el pensamiento de Manuel Ugarte y Víctor R. Haya de la Torre (1900–1945)," in: *Latinoamérica* 52 (Mexico, 1/2011), pp. 139–64.

Hölscher, Lucian, "The First World War as a 'Rupture' in the European History of the Twentieth Century: A Contribution to the Hermeneutics of Not-Understanding," in: *German Historical Institute London Bulletin* 35 (2/Nov. 2013), pp. 73–87.

Hoffmann, Katrin, "¿Construyendo una 'comunidad'? Theodor Alemann y Hermann Tjarks como voceros de la prensa germanoparlante en Buenos Aires, 1914–1918," in: *Iberoamericana* 9 (2009), pp. 121–37.

Horne, John/Alan Kramer, *German Atrocities, 1914: A History of Denial*, New Haven 2001.

Howe, Glenford D., "West Indian Blacks and the Struggle for Participation in the First World War," in: *Journal of Caribbean History* 28 (1/1994), pp. 27–62.

Race, War and Nationalism: A Social History of West Indians in the First World War, Kingston 2002.

Jaksic, Iván/Posada Carbó, Eduardo (eds.), *Liberalismo y poder: Latinoamérica en el siglo XIX*, Santiago de Chile 2011.

Janz, Oliver, *14: Der große Krieg*, Frankfurt am Main 2013.

"Einführung: Der Erste Weltkrieg in globaler Perspektive," in: *Geschichte und Gesellschaft* 40 (2014), pp. 147–59.

Jeismann, Michael, Propaganda, in: Hirschfeld, Gerhard/Krumeich, Gerd/Renz, Irina (eds.), *Enzyklopädie Erster Weltkrieg*, Paderborn 2003, pp. 198–209.

Jenkins, Jennifer, "Fritz Fischer's 'Programme for Revolution': Implications for a Global History of Germany in the First World War," in: *Journal of Contemporary History* 48 (2013), pp. 397–417.

Johnson, Benjamin H., *Revolution in Texas: How a Forgotten Rebellion and Its Bloody Suppression Turned Mexicans into Americans*, New Haven 2003.

Kaplan, Edward S., *U. S. Imperialism in Latin America: Bryan's Challenges and Contributions, 1900–1920*, Westport 1998.

Katz, Friedrich, *The Secret War in Mexico: Europe, the United States and the Mexican Revolution*, Chicago 1981.

Kersffeld, Daniel, *Rusos y rojos: judíos comunistas en los tiempos de la Comintern*. Buenos Aires 2012.

"El activismo judío en el comunismo de entreguerras: Cinco casos latinoamericanos," in: *Nueva Sociedad* 247 (September–October 2013), pp. 152–64.

Kloosterhuis, Jürgen, *"Friedliche Imperialisten": Deutsche Auslandsvereine und auswärtige Kulturpolitik, 1906–1918*, Frankfurt am Main 1994.

Knock, Thomas J., *To End All Wars: Woodrow Wilson and the Quest for a New World Order*, Princeton 1992.

Kocka, Jürgen, "Der Große Europäische Krieg – 90 Jahre danach," in: Helmut Bleiber/Wolfgang Küttler (eds.), *Revolution und Reform in Deutschland im 19. und 20. Jahrhundert*, Half-Vol. 2, *Ideen und Reflexionen*, Berlin 2005, pp. 179–90.

König, Hans-Joachim, "Europa in der Sicht Lateinamerikas," in: Andreas Michler/ Waltraud Schreiber (eds.), *Blicke auf Europa: Kontinuität im Wandel*, Neuried 2003, pp. 331–84.

"Nationale Identitätsbildung und sozialistische Projekte bei Mariátegui," in: idem, *Von Kolumbus bis Castro: Aufsätze zur Geschichte Lateinamerikas*, Stuttgart 2006, pp. 303–21.

König, Marcus/Neitzel, Sönke, "Propaganda, Zensur und Medien im Ersten Weltkrieg," in: Frank Bösch/Peter Hoeres (eds.), *Außenpolitik im Medienzeitalter: Vom späten 19. Jahrhundert bis zur Gegenwart*, Göttingen 2013, pp. 125–45.

Kramer, Alan, *Dynamic of Destruction: Culture and Mass Killing in the First World War*, Oxford 2007.

Krumeich, Gerd, "Ernest Lavisse und die Kritik an der deutschen 'Kultur' 1914–1918," in: Wolfgang J. Mommsen (ed.), *Kultur und Krieg: Die Rolle der Intellektuellen, Künstler und Schriftsteller im Ersten Weltkrieg*, Munich 1996, pp. 143–54.

Kuntz Ficker, Sandra, "El impacto de la Primera Guerra Mundial sobre el comercio exterior de México," in: *Iberoamericana* 14 (2014), pp. 117–37.

Lai, Walton Look, "The Chinese Indenture System in the British West Indies and Its Aftermath," in: Andrew R. Wilson (ed.), *The Chinese in the Caribbean*, Princeton 2004, pp. 3–24.

Lamarre, Jean/Magali Deleuze (eds.), *L'envers de la médaille: guerres, temoignages et representations*, Laval 2007.

Langewiesche, Dieter, "Das Jahrhundert Europas: Eine Annäherung in globalhistorischer Perspektive," in: *HZ* 296 (2013), pp. 29–48.

Langley, Lester D., *The Banana Wars: United States Intervention in the Caribbean, 1898–1934*, Wilmington 2002.

Lascano, Diego M., *Graf von Spee: de China a Malvinas – la Primera Guerra Mundial en aguas de Chile y Argentina*, Santiago de Chile 2002.

Lavrin, Ascuncíon, *Women, Feminism, and Social Change in Argentina, Chile, and Uruguay 1890–1940*, Lincoln 1995.

Leipold, Andreas, *Die deutsche Seekriegsführung im Pazifik in den Jahren 1914 und 1915*, Wiesbaden 2012.

León Rivera, Francisco, "La presencia de la Gran Guerra en la vanguardia latinoamericana: Los casos de Alberto Hidalgo y Vicente Huidobro," in: *Hallali* 4 (2010). www.revistahallali.com/2010/04/19/la-presencia-de-la-gran-guerra-en-la-vanguardia-latinoamericana-los-casos-de-alberto-hidalgo-y-vicente-huidobro/ (January 30, 2014)

Leonhard, Jörn, *Die Büchse der Pandora: Geschichte des Ersten Weltkriegs*, Munich 2014.

Lida, Clara Eugenia, *España y el Imperio de Maximiliano: finanzas, diplomacia, cultura e inmigración*, Mexico 1999.

Liebau, Heike et al. (eds.), *The World in World Wars: Experiences, Perceptions and Perspectives from Africa and Asia*, Leiden 2010.

"Introduction," in: idem (ed.), *The World in World Wars: Experiences, Perceptions and Perspectives from Africa and Asia*, Leiden 2010, pp. 1–28.

Liehr, Reinhard (ed.), *América Latina en la época de Simón Bolívar: la formación de las economías nacionales y los intereses económicos europeos, 1800–1850*, Berlin 1989.

Lomnitz, Claudio, *The Return of Comrade Ricardo Flores Magón*, New York 2014.

Lopreato, Christina da Silva Roquette, *A semana trágica: a greve geral anarquista de 1917*, São Paulo 1997.

Lorenz, Federico, "La gran guerra vista por un argentino," in: *Todo es Historia* 352 (1996), pp. 48–65.

Lorini, Irma, *El nacionalismo en Bolivia de le pre y posguerra del Chaco (1910–1945)*, La Paz 2006.

Luebke, Frederick C., *Germans in Brazil: A Comparative History of Cultural Conflict during World War I*, Baton Rouge 1987.

Macleod, Jenny/Purseigle, Pierre (eds.), *Uncovered Fields: Perspectives in First World War Studies*, Leiden 2004.

Madueño, Víctor A., "La primera guerra mundial y el desarrollo industrial del Perú," in: *Estudios Andinos* 9 (17–18/1981), pp. 41–54.

Manela, Erez, *The Wilsonian Moment: Self-Determination and the International Origins of Anticolonial Nationalism*, Oxford 2007.

Marichal, Carlos, *A Century of Debt Crises in Latin America: From Independence to the Great Depression, 1820–1930*, Princeton 1989.

Martin, Percy A., *Latin America and the War*, Gloucester 1967 [1925].

Matsuda, Matt K., *Pacific Worlds: A History of Seas, Peoples, and Cultures*, Cambridge 2012.

Matute, Álvaro (ed.), *Estudios de historia moderna y contemporánea de México*, Mexico 1986.

McCaa, Robert, "Missing Millions: The Demographic Costs of the Mexican Revolution," in: *Mexican Studies* 19 (2003), pp. 367–400.

McCreery, David, "La pandemia de influenza en la ciudad de Guatemala," in: *Anales de la academia de geografía e historia de Guatemala* 71 (1995), pp. 111–32.

Meagher, Arnold J., *The Coolie Trade: The Traffic in Chinese Laborers to Latin America 1847–1874*, Bloomington 2008.

Meißner, Jochen/Mücke, Ulrich/Weber, Klaus, *Schwarzes Amerika: Eine Geschichte der Sklaverei*, Bonn 2008.

Merbilháa, Margarita, "Claves racialistas y reformistas en la invención de un nacionalismo continental: *El porvenir de la América latina* (1911), de Manuel Ugarte," in: *Anuario de Estudios Americanos* 68 (1/2011), pp. 191–221.

Meyer, Lorenzo, *Su majestad británica contra la Revolución Mexicana, 1900–1950: El fin de un imperio informal*, Mexico 1991.

México y el mundo: historia de sus relaciones exteriores, Vol. 6, *La marca del nacionalismo*, Mexico 2010.

Michalka, Wolfgang (ed.), *Der Erste Weltkrieg: Wirkung, Wahrnehmung, Analyse*, Munich 1994.

Michel, Paul-Henri, *L'Hispanisme dans les républiques espagnoles d'Amérique pendant la guerre de 1914–1918*, Paris 1931.

Miller, Nicola, *Reinventing Modernity in Latin America: Intellectuals Imagine the Future, 1900–1930*, New York 2008.

Mock, James R., "The Creel Committee in Latin America," *Hispanic American Historical Review* 22 (1942), pp. 262–79.

Molina Jiménez, Iván, "Mercancias culturales," in: Michael Zeuske/Ulrike Schmieder (eds.), *Regiones europeas y Latinoamérica, siglos XVIII–XIX*, Frankfurt a.M. 1999, pp. 271–82.

Monteón, Michael, *Chile in the Nitrate Era: The Evolution of Economic Dependence, 1880–1930*, Madison 1982.

Morgner, Christian, *Weltereignisse und Massenmedien: Zur Theorie des Weltmedienereignisses*, Bielefeld 2009.

Mörner, Magnus/Sims, David, *Adventurers and Proletarians: The Story of Migrants in Latin America*, Pittsburgh 1985.

Moya Pons, Frank, *The Dominican Republic: A National History*, Princeton 2010.

Mulligan, William, *The Origins of the First World War*, Cambridge 2010.

Murillo Jiménez, Hugo, *Tinoco y los Estados Unidos: génesis y caída de un régimen*, San José 1981.

Nassua, Martin, *"Gemeinsame Kriegführung, gemeinsamer Friedensschluß": Das Zimmermann-Telegramm vom 13. Januar 1917*, Frankfurt am Main 1992.

Neff, Stephen C., *The Rights and Duties of Neutrals: A General History*, Manchester 2000.

Neiberg, Michael S., *Fighting the Great War: A Global History*, Cambridge 2005.

Newton, Ronald C., *German Buenos Aires, 1900–1933: Social Change and Cultural Crisis*, Austin 1977.

Notten, Frank, *La influencia de la Primera Guerra Mundial sobre las economías centroamericanas 1900–1929: un enfoque desde el comercio exterior*, San José 2012.

Olinto, B. Anselmo, "'Uma epidemia sem importância': A influenza espanhola e o colpaso do sistema de saúde no sul do Brasil," in: *Quipu* 10 (1993), pp. 285–303.

Orlove, Benjamin, "Giving Importance to Imports," in: idem (ed.), *The Allure of the Foreign: Imported Goods in Postcolonial Latin America*, Ann Arbor 1997, pp. 1–30.

Ortega, Willmen, "Las listas negras y el comercio entre Venezuela y Alemania durante la Primera Guerra Mundial," in: *Mañongo* (Carabobo) 23 (No. 43/2014), pp. 113–36.

Otero, Hernán, *La guerra en la sangre: los franco-argentinos ante la Primera Guerra Mundial*, Buenos Aires 2009.

Palacio, Juan Manuel, "La antesala de lo peor: la economía argentina entre 1914 y 1930," in: Ricardo Falcón (ed.), *Nueva historia argentina*, Vol. 6, *Democracias, conflicto social y renovación de ideas, 1916–1930*, Buenos Aires 2000, pp. 101–50.

Parra, Yolanda de la, "La Primera Guerra Mundial y la prensa mexicana," in: Álvaro Matute (ed.), *Estudios de historia moderna y contemporánea de México*, Mexico 1986, pp. 155–76.

Paul, Gerhard, *Bilder des Krieges – Krieg der Bilder: Die Visualisierung des modernen Krieges*, Paderborn 2004.

Pereira Castañares, Juan Carlos, "Las relaciones diplomáticas entre España e Hispanoamérica en el siglo XIX," in: Juan Bosco Amores (ed.): *Iberoamérica en el siglo XIX: Nacionalismo y dependencia*, Pamplona 1995, pp. 107–54.

Perez, Jr., Louis A., *Intervention, Revolution, and Politics in Cuba, 1913–1921*, Pittsburgh 1979.

Pike, Frederick B., *Hispanismo, 1898–1936: Spanish Conservatives and Liberals and Their relations with Spanish America*, Notre Dame 1971.

Pinto Vallejos, Julio, "Crisis salitrera y subversión social: los trabajadores pampinos en la pos-primera guerra mundial (1917–1921)," in: *Boletin del Instituto de Historia Argentina y Americana "Dr. Emilio Ravignani"* 14 (2/1996), pp. 61–92.

Prados, Leandro, "Lost Decades? Economic Performance in Post-independence Latin America," in: *Journal of Latin American Studies* 41 (2009), pp. 279–307.

Py, Pierre, *Francia y la Revolución Mexicana, 1910–1920: o la desaparición de una potencia mediana*, Mexico 1991.

Rama, Carlos, *Historia de las relaciones culturales entre España y América Latina, siglo XIX*, Mexico 1982.

Randall, Stephen/Graeme Mount, *The Caribbean Basin: An International History*, London 1998.

Rausch, Jane M., "Colombia's Neutrality during 1914–1918: An Overlooked Dimension of World War I," in: *Iberoamericana* 14 (2014), pp. 103–15.

Renda, Mary A., *Taking Haiti: Military Occupation and the Culture of U.S. Imperialism, 1915–1940*, Chapel Hill 2001.

Rey de Guido, Clara (ed.), *Cancionero rioplatense (1880–1925)*, Caracas 1989.

Rinke, Stefan, *"Der letzte freie Kontinent": Deutsche Lateinamerikapolitik im Zeichen transnationaler Beziehungen, 1918–1933*, Stuttgart 1996.

"Nach Norden oder Süden? Deutsche Auswanderer in den Amerikas im langen 19. Jahrhundert," in: Josef Raab/Jan Wirrer (eds.), *Die deutsche Präsenz in den USA/The German Presence in the U. S. A.*, Münster 2008, pp. 25–56.

Las revoluciones en América Latina: las vías a la independencia 1760–1830, México 2011.

Historia de Latinoamérica: desde las primeras culturas hasta el presente, México 2016.

América Latina y Estados Unidos: Una historia entre espacios desde la época colonial hasta hoy, Madrid/México 2015.

"The Reconstruction of National Identity: German Minorities in Latin America during the First World War," in: Nicola Foote/Michael Goebel (eds.), *Immigration and National Identities in Latin America*, Gainesville 2014, pp. 160–81.

"Globalizing Football in Times of Crisis: The First World Cup in Uruguay 1930," in: idem/Kay Schiller (eds.), *The FIFA World Cup, 1930–2010: Politics, Commerce, Spectacle and Identities*, Göttingen 2014, pp. 49–65.

"'Ein Drama der gesamten Menschheit': Lateinamerikanische Perspektiven auf den Ersten Weltkrieg," in: *Geschichte und Gesellschaft* 40 (2014), pp. 287–307.

"Thunderstorm and Lightning: A First Look at Latin America and the First World War," in: Helmut Bley/Anorthe Kremers (eds.), *The World during the First World War*, Essen 2014, pp. 79–88.

"'Ein monströses Attentat gegen die menschliche Kultur': Der Kriegsausbruch 1914 in Lateinamerika," in: Jürgen Angelow/Johannes Großmann (eds.), *Wandel, Umbruch, Absturz: Perspektiven auf das Jahr 1914*, Stuttgart 2014, pp. 29–41.

Rivarola, Milda, *Obreros, utopías y revoluciones: formación de las clases trabajadoras en el Paraguay liberal, 1870–1931*, Asunción 2010.

Rizo Patrón Boylan, Paul, "Las emigraciones de los súbditos realistas del Perú hacia España durante la crisis de la Independencia," in: O'Phelan Godoy,

Scarlett (ed.), *La independencia en el Perú: de los Borbones a Bolívar*, Lima 2001, pp. 407–28.

Robinet, Romain, "Students Facing the Great War in Revolutionary Mexico: The Intellectual Youth and the Quest for a New Order (1914–1921)," in: Olivier Compagnon/Maria Inés Tato (eds.), *Toward a History of the First World War in Latin America*, Frankfurt, forthcoming.

Romero, Robert Chao, *The Chinese in Mexico: 1882–1940*, Tucson 2010.

Roopnarine, Lomarsh, *Indo-Caribbean Indenture: Resistance and Accommodation; 1838–1920*, Kingston 2007.

Rosenberg, Emily S., *World War I and the Growth of United States Preponderance in Latin America*, PhD Diss., New York 1973.

Rumeu de Armas, Antonio, *El tratado de Tordesillas*, Madrid 1992.

Salewski, Michael, *Der Erste Weltkrieg*, Paderborn 2004.

Salvatore, Ricardo D., "Imperial Mechanics: South America's Hemispheric Integration in the Machine Age," in: *American Quarterly* 58 (2006), pp. 662–91.

San Martín, José Narciso, *El petróleo y la petroquímica en la Argentina, 1914–1983*, Buenos Aires 2006.

Sánchez, Luis Alberto, "Alberto Hidalgo en la literatura peruana," in: Álvaro Sarco (ed.), *Alberto Hidalgo: el genio del desprecio*, Lima 2006, pp. 67–72.

Schmidt, Hans, *The United States Occupation of Haiti: 1915–1934*, New Brunswick 1995.

Schoonover, Thomas, *Germany in Central America: Competitive Imperialism, 1821–1929*, Tuscaloosa 1998.

Schuler, Friedrich E., *Secret Wars and Secret Policies in the Americas, 1842–1929*, Albuquerque 2010.

Segesser, Daniel Marc, *Der Erste Weltkrieg in globaler Perspektive*, Wiesbaden 2010.

Sepúlveda, Isidro, *El sueño de la Madre Patria: Hispanoamericanismo y nacionalismo*, Madrid 2005.

Siepe, Raimundo, *Yrigoyen, la Primera Guerra Mundial y las relaciones económicas*, Buenos Aires 1992.

Skidmore, Thomas E., *Black into White: Race and Nationality in Brazilian Thought*, Durham [2]1993.

Small, Michael, *The Forgotten Peace: Mediation at Niagara Falls, 1914*, Ottawa 2009.

Smith, Richard, *Jamaican Volunteers in the First World War: Race, Masculinity and the Development of National Consciousness*, Manchester 2004.

Solveira de Báez, Beatriz Rosario, *La Argentina, el ABC y el conflicto entre México y Estados Unidos 1913–1916*, Córdoba 1994.

Sondhaus, Lawrence, *World War One: The Global Revolution*, Cambridge 2011.

Souza, Christiane Maria Cruz de, *A gripe espanhola na Bahia: saúde, política e medicinaem tempos de epidemia*, Rio de Janeiro 2009.

Spalding, Jr., Hobart A., *Organized Labor in Latin America: Historical Case Studies of Workers in Dependent Societies*, New York 1977.

Spenser, Daniela, *Los primero tropiezos de la Internacional Comunista en México*, Mexico 2009.

Stichweh, Rudolf, "Zur Soziologie des Weltereignisses," in: Stefan Nacke et al. (eds.), *Weltereignisse: Theoretische und empirische Perspektiven*, Wiesbaden 2008, pp. 17–40.

Stolley, Karen, "Writing Back to Empire: Juan Pablo Viscardo y Guzmán's 'Letter to the Spanish Americans,'" in: David S. Shields/Mariselle Meléndez (eds.), *Liberty! Egalité! ¡Independencia!: Print Culture, Enlightenment, and Revolution in the Americas, 1776–1838*, Worcester 2007, pp. 117–31.

Storey, William K., *The First World War: A Concise Global History*, Lanham 2009.

Strachan, Hew, *The First World War*, Vol. 1: *To Arms*, Oxford 2001.

The First World War: A New Illustrated History, London 2003.

"The First World War as a Global War," in: *First World War Studies* 1 (2010), pp. 3–14.

Streckert, Jens, *Die Hauptstadt Lateinamerikas: eine Geschichte der Lateinamerikaner im Paris der Dritten Republik*, Cologne 2013.

Streeter, Michael, *Epitácio Pessoa: Brazil*, London 2010.

South America and the Treaty of Versailles, London 2010.

Central America and the Treaty of Versailles, London 2010.

Suter, Jan, Prosperität und Krise in einer Kaffeerepublik: Modernisierung, sozialer Wandel und politischer Umbruch in El Salvador, 1910-1945, Frankfurt a.M. 1996

Tato, María Inés, "La disputa por la argentinidad: rupturistas y neutralistas durante la Primera Guerra Mundial," in: *Temas de historia argentina y americana* 13 (July–December 2008), pp. 227–50.

"La contienda europea en las calles porteñas: manfiestaciones cívicas y pasiones nacionales en torno de la Primera Guerra Mundial," in: idem/ Martín O. Castro (eds.), *Del centenario al peronismo: dimensiones de la vida política argentina*, Buenos Aires 2010, pp. 33–64.

Tato, María Inés,/Castro, Martín O. (eds.), *Del centenario al peronismo: dimensiones de la vida política argentina*, Buenos Aires 2010.

/Castro, Martín O. "El llamado de la patria: británicos e italianos residentes en la Argentina frente a la Primera Guerra Mundial," in: *Estudios Migratorios Latinoamericanos* 25 (2011), pp. 273–92.

/Castro, Martín O. "Contra la corriente: los intelectuales germanófilos argentinos frente a la Primera Guerra Mundial," in: *Jahrbuch für Geschichte Lateinamerikas* 49 (2012), pp. 205–23.

/Castro, Martín O. "La Gran Guerra en la historiografía argentina: balance y perspectivas de investigación," in: *Iberoamericana* 14 (2014), pp. 91–102.

/Castro, Martín O. "Luring Neutrals: Allied and German Propaganda in Argentina during the First World War," in: Troy R. E. Paddock (ed.), *World War I and Propaganda*, Leiden 2014, pp. 322–44.

Thomson, Guy (ed.), *The European Revolutions of 1848 and the Americas*, London 2002.

Thorndike, Guillermo, *Los imperios del sol: una historia de los japoneses en el Perú*, Lima 1996.

Tooze, Adam/Fertik, Ted, "The World Economy and the Great War," in: *Geschichte und Gesellschaft* 40 (2014), pp. 214–38.

Ulloa, Berta, *México y el mundo: historia de sus relaciones exteriores*, Vol. 5, *La lucha revolucionaria*, Mexico 2010.

Vázquez, Josefina Zoraida, "Una dificíl inserción en el concierto de las naciones," in: Antonio Annino/François-Xavier Guerra, (eds.), *Inventando la nación: Iberoamérica Siglo XIX*, Mexico 2003, pp. 253–86.

Vega Jiménez, Patricia, "Primicias de la Primera Guerra Mundial en la prensa costarricense (1914)," in: *inter.c.a.mbio* 4 (5/2007), pp. 271–308.

Velásquez, Ramón J., "Venezuela y la primera guerra mundial (1914–1918)," in: *Boletín de la Academia Nacional de la Historia* 88 (2005), pp. 28–67.

Veliz, Claudio, *The Centralist Tradition of Latin America*, Princeton 1980.

Vigevani, Tulio, "Interesse nacional e fundamentos da politica exterior do Brasil: Ruy Barbosa e sua ação a favor da participação na Grande Guerra," in: *História* (São Paulo) 15 (1996), pp. 13–26.

Vinhosa, Francisco Luiz Teixeira, *O Brasil e a Primeira Guerra Mundial: A diplomacia brasileira e as grandes potências*, Rio de Janeiro 1990.

Vivas Gallardo, Freddy, "Venezuela y la Primera Guerra Mundial: de la neutralidad al compromiso Octubre/1914-Marzo/1919," in: *Revista de la Facultad de Ciencias Jurídicas y Políticas* (Caracas) 61 (1981), pp. 113–33.

Weinmann, Ricardo, *Argentina en la Primera Guerra Mundial: neutralidad, transición política y continuismo económico*, Buenos Aires 1994.

Winegard, Timothy C., *Indigenous Peoples of the British Dominions and the First World War*, Cambridge 2011.

Winseck, Dwayne R./Pike, Robert M., *Communication and Empire: Media, Markets, and Globalization, 1860–1930*, Durham 2007.

Woodard, James P., *A Place in Politics; São Paulo, Brazil, from Seigneurial Republicanism to Regionalist Revolt*, Durham 2009.

Yankelevich, Pablo, *La diplomacia imaginaria: Argentina y la Revolución Mexicana 1910–1916*, Mexico 1994.

"Las campañas pro México: estrategias publicitarias mexicanas en América latina (1916–1922)," in: *Cuadernos americanos* 9 (Mexico, 49/1995), pp. 79–95.

La revolución mexicana en América Latina: intereses políticos e itinerarios intelectuales, Mexico 2003.

Chronology

1914

April	U.S. invasion of Veracruz, Mexico (April 21)
May–June	Peace Conference (ABC) in Niagara Falls (May 18–June 30)
August	Outbreak of the First World War
	Latin American governments declare neutrality
	Opening of the Panama Canal (August 15)
October	First issue of *La Unión* appears (October 31)
November	Battle of Coronel (November 1)
December	Battle of the Malvinas/Falkland Islands (December 8)

1915

January	Plan of San Diego, Texas (January 16)
February	Unrestricted German submarine warfare in war zone around the British Isles (February 4)
	Reform of the Brazilian army (February 23)
March	Intensification of blockade of Germany
	Sinking of the *Dresden* at Juan Fernández (March 14)
	Founding of the Liga pelos Aliados in Brazil (March 17)
May	Sinking of the *Lusitania* (May 7)
	Restriction of German submarine warfare (May 13)
	Italy's entry into the war (May 23)
	Demonstrations of support for Italy in the La Plata area
	First Pan-American financial conference (May 24–9)

	ABC Pact (May 25)
July	U.S. Marines invade Haiti (July 28)
November	*Presidente Mitre* incident (November 28)
December	Second Pan-American Scientific Congress in Washington, DC (December 27, 1915–January 8, 1916)
	Intensification of the Trading with the Enemy Act (December 23)

1916

January	Inter-American Declaration of the Rights and Duties of Nations (January 6)
February	Argentine protest against blacklists
	Intensification of German submarine warfare
March	Pancho Villa's troops attack Columbus, NM (March 9)
	Germany declares war on Portugal (March 9)
	U.S. punitive expedition under General John J. Pershing against Pancho Villa (March 14, 1916–February 7, 1917)
	First British "Blacklist" for South America
May	Sinking of the *Rio Branco* (May 2)
	U.S. intervention in the Dominican Republic (May 13)
June	Ratification of the Bryan-Chamorro Treaty (June 19)
	Battle of El Carrizal (June 21)
September	Founding of the Liga da Defesa Nacional (September 7)
December	Wilson's peace initiative
	German Empire refuses mediation of the United States
	Allies reject the peace initiative
	Second Pan-American Scientific Congress (December 27, 1916–January 8, 1917)

1917

January	Wilson proclaims a Pan-American Pact (January 6)
February	Germany resumes its unrestricted submarine warfare (February 1)
	United States ruptures relations with Germany (February 3)
	Sinking of the Peruvian cargo ship *Lorton* (February 4)
	Constitution of Revolutionary Mexico (February 5)
	Mexican appeal to the neutrals (February 12)

March	Publication of the Zimmermann telegram (March 1)
April	Sinking of the *Monte Protegido* (April 4)
	Sinking of the *Paraná* (April 5)
	United States' declaration of war (April 6)
	Brazil severs relations with Germany (April 11)
	Anti-German mass protests in Brazil and Argentina with attacks on German institutions (April 14–15)
	Counterdemonstrations in Buenos Aires (April 22 and 24)
May	Resignation of Brazilian Foreign Minister Müller (April 3)
	Sinking of Brazilian *Tijuca* and *Lapa* (April 20 and 22)
June	Brazil annuls neutrality decree (June 1)
	Seizure of German ships in Brazil (June 2)
	Sinking of Argentine *Oriana* (June 6)
	U.S. Atlantic squadron in South America; sinking of Argentine *Toro* (June 22)
	Pro-Ally rally in Buenos Aires (June 22)
July	Formal Argentine protest (July 3)
September	Beginning of Luxburg Affair (September 7)
	Mass protests in Argentina (September 12 and 22)
	Uruguay seizes German ships (September 14)
	Argentinean Comité Nacional de la Juventud founded (September 15)
	Argentine Congress votes to rupture relations with the German Reich (September 22)
October	First blacklist of the United States (October 6)
	Uruguay breaks off relations with Germany (October 7)
	First official celebration of Día de la Raza in Buenos Aires
	Sinking of the Brazilian *Macau* (October 18)
	Brazilian declaration of war (October 26)
November	October Revolution in Russia (November 7)
	Martial law declared in Brazil with regard to German property (November 16)
	Inter-Ally conference with participation of Brazil and Cuba (November 29–December 3)
December	Brazil charters German ships to France (December 3)

1918

January	Wilson's "Fourteen Points" speech (January 8)
	Argentine sales of wheat to the Allies (January 14)

February	Neutrality conference in Buenos Aires
March	Expropriation of Santa-Catarina railroad (March 6)
	General strike of Córdoba students (March 31)
May	May Day in Rio de Janeiro with declarations of solidarity for the Russian Revolution (May 1)
	Bunsen mission in Latin America
	Uruguay leases German ships to the United States (May 24)
August	Brazilian naval units deployed (August 1)
	Introduction of universal conscription in Cuba (August 3)
September	Carranza Doctrine (September 1)
	Peru seizes German ships (September 5)
October	Prohibition of German banks in Brazil (October 11)
November	Brazilian naval units reach Gibraltar (November 10)
	Armistice (November 11)
	Founding of the Pan-American Federation of Labor in Laredo, Texas (November 13)
	Mass protests against soaring food prices in Santiago de Chile (November 22)
	Demonstration of "maximalists" in Buenos Aires (November 24)
	Founding of the Liga Patriótica Militar in Chile (November 30)

1919

January	"Tragic Week" in Argentina (January 7–14)
	Beginning of the general strike in Lima (January 13)
	Beginning of the Paris Peace Conference (January 18)
	Founding of the Liga Patriótica Argentina (January 19)
April	Abolition of blacklists
May	Suppression of strike in Lima (May 27)
June	Signing of the Treaty of Versailles (June 28)

Index

The references to tables may be denoted by t, to figures by f, and to footnotes by n with no comma following page number